The Domestication of Competition

Competition is deeply built into the structures of modern life. It can improve policies, products and services, but is also seen as a divisive burden that pits people against one another. This book seeks to go beyond such caricatures by advancing a new thesis about how competition came to shape our society. Jonathan Hearn argues that competition was 'domesticated', harnessed and institutionalised across a range of institutional spheres in the late eighteenth and early nineteenth centuries. Responding to crises in traditional forms of authority (hereditary, religious), the formalisation of competition in the economy, politics, and diverse new forms of knowledge creation provided a new mode for legitimating distributions of power in the emerging liberal societies. This insightful study aims to improve our ability to think critically about competition, by better understanding its integral role, for good and ill, in how liberal forms of society work.

JONATHAN HEARN is Professor of Political and Historical Sociology at the University of Edinburgh and President of the Association for the Study of Ethnicity and Nationalism. His published writings explore themes of social power, nationalism and identity, Scotland and its Enlightenment, liberal and civil society, and competition.

The Domestication of Competition

Social Evolution and Liberal Society

JONATHAN HEARN
University of Edinburgh

CAMBRIDGE
UNIVERSITY PRESS

CAMBRIDGE
UNIVERSITY PRESS

Shaftesbury Road, Cambridge CB2 8EA, United Kingdom

One Liberty Plaza, 20th Floor, New York, NY 10006, USA

477 Williamstown Road, Port Melbourne, VIC 3207, Australia

314–321, 3rd Floor, Plot 3, Splendor Forum, Jasola District Centre, New Delhi – 110025, India

103 Penang Road, #05–06/07, Visioncrest Commercial, Singapore 238467

Cambridge University Press is part of Cambridge University Press & Assessment, a department of the University of Cambridge.

We share the University's mission to contribute to society through the pursuit of education, learning and research at the highest international levels of excellence.

www.cambridge.org
Information on this title: www.cambridge.org/9781009199155

DOI: 10.1017/9781009199131

First published 2023

Printed in the United Kingdom by TJ Books Limited, Padstow Cornwall

A catalogue record for this publication is available from the British Library.

A Cataloging-in-Publication data record for this book is available from the Library of Congress
Names: Hearn, Jonathan, author.
Title: The domestication of competition : social evolution and liberal society / Jonathan Hearn, University of Edinburgh.
Description: Cambridge, United Kingdom ; New York, NY: Cambridge University Press, 2023. | Includes bibliographical references and index.
Identifiers: LCCN 2022045889 (print) | LCCN 2022045890 (ebook) | ISBN 9781009199155 (hardback) | ISBN 9781009199148 (paperback) | ISBN 9781009199131 (epub)
Subjects: LCSH: Competition–Social aspects. | Competition (Psychology)–Social aspects.
Classification: LCC HB238 .H43 2023 (print) | LCC HB238 (ebook) | DDC 338.6/048–dc23/eng/20221005
LC record available at https://lccn.loc.gov/2022045889
LC ebook record available at https://lccn.loc.gov/2022045890

ISBN 978-1-009-19915-5 Hardback

Contents

Figures and Tables

Figures

Tables

Acknowledgements

This book was a while in coming. It has its origins in a midcareer fellowship from the Independent Social Research Foundation in 2013–2014 (Grant RA2401), which started me thinking about this topic in depth and realising its scope. Along the way, a book I was previously committed to write and a four-year period of departmental headship gave me further reasons to take my time. But at last, a period of sabbatical granted by the Subject Area of Sociology and the School of Social and Political Science at the University of Edinburgh, along with the strictures of a pandemic, gave me the chance to write it.

Academic work is always heavily indebted to a wider community of scholars who test one's ideas through criticism and feedback. I am grateful for the opportunities to present ideas from various parts of this book in conferences and workshops at the University of Chicago Center of Beijing at Renmin University, Zhejiang University, Institute for the Study of Christianity and Culture at International Christian University in Tokyo, University College Dublin, the University of Warwick, Girton College at Cambridge University, and the University of Edinburgh. In these events and other contexts, I have particularly benefitted from comments from Arianna Andreangeli, Julie Brownlie, Raul Carstocea, Phil Cerny, Simon Clarke, Graham Crow, Will Davies, John A. Hall, Iain Hardie, Geoffrey Hodgson, Poul F. Kjaer, John Levi Martin, James McAlister, David McCrone, Lindsay Patterson, John Scott, Liz Stanley, Yanfei Sun, Tobias Werron, Andreas Wimmer, Naoki Yajima, and Dingxin Zhao. I am grateful to these people and the anonymous reviewers of articles and book proposals for their critical feedback. For the book itself, I have benefitted especially from the careful reading of a draft by Graham Crow, which improved my writing and gave me further things to think about, and from the intellectual support and encouragement of John A. Hall, who also read a draft and whose criticisms prodded me to state more fully in the Conclusion my worries about the state of domesticated competition in the present. I'd also like to thank the CUP editorial team, John Haslam, Toby Ginsberg, Shaheer Husanne, and Emma Lockley, for their guidance and support. As usual, despite all these contributions, only I am accountable for the book's contents and arguments.

Finally, the steady patience and love of my family, Lovel, Iskra, and Gale, have helped me keep the world in perspective despite its twists and turns, and despite immersing myself in the writing of another book. I come up for air because of you.

Introduction

To check the pulse of current attitudes towards competition, try entering the word into a Google Images search. You will be immediately met with a host of images designed for easy insertion into presentations. The default context is the world of business. Cartoon and photographic figures lunge towards finish lines and scrabble towards mountain peaks. Sometimes they do this while wearing suits and grasping briefcases and laptops. Sometimes they team up in tugs of war, or box in the ring, or more gruesomely, a plasticine figure stands with a raised fist on top of a pile of plasticine bodies.

Search 'competition quotes' and the messages become more explicit. For example:

> 'No competition. No progress.'
> 'When you're really good, no one is competition, no one.'
> 'You can't always be the most talented in the room, but you can be the most competitive.'
> 'Look in the mirror ... that's your competition.'

But there are also notes of dissent:

> 'A flower does not think of competing with the flower next to it, it just blooms.'
> 'I am in competition with no one. I run my own race. I have no desire to play the game of being better than anyone.'

And ambivalence:

> 'Competition brings out the best in products, and the worst in people.'
> 'If you continuously compete with others, you become bitter, but if you continuously compete with yourself, you become better.'

These examples of folk wisdom provide a small window into the pervasive mood of our times in regard to competition.

A combination of enthused commitment, hard-bitten realism, resistance, and resignation. It is one we will recognise from public discourse more generally found in journalism and electronic and social media. There are also folk explanations for why we live in an environment of pervasive competition. Some think it is a direct expression of our biological nature, as creatures driven by a Darwinian struggle for existence. Some think it is an effect of capitalism, bearing down even harder on our lives in an age of neoliberalism. Some think it is a peculiar trait of 'Western' culture.

In this book I will be offering reasons to doubt the adequacy of any of these explanations, although we will find partial truths in each one. Here at the outset, after making the case for why this matters, I will provide a working definition of competition, and an elaboration of the concept, that will frame and guide the investigation. Then I will present the core thesis that gives the book its title: the domestication of competition, followed by an overview of the book's chapters and argument.

Why Does It Matter?

Part of what this book argues is that competition is a natural part of life, one that we must learn to live with. But more substantially it argues that competition is basic to how modern liberal forms of society work. So, understanding it well is an essential part of understanding where many of us live – having a handle on our situation. Competition has its 'upsides' and 'downsides'. For example, it gives the economy much of its dynamism, and capacity to change and evolve, but it also causes unemployment, social instability, and overdriven consumerism. And the benefits and penalties of competition tend to fall on people unevenly. Competition is also basic to democracy, which rests on the possibility of open, civil contestation for political leadership. Broad based competition is a requirement for a healthy democracy. However, monopolies on access to the political process undermine democracy and its capacity to legitimate the system. Thirdly, open competition among ideas is essential to liberal society. Whether it's in relation to public opinion and policy, scientific claims, or cultural values, our ideas and beliefs need to be tested, and this cannot be done without competition among diverse viewpoints. The downside, however, can be an ‘overproduction’ of contestation, as public discourse is so cheap to produce, and the number of points to divide over potentially infinite.

This book tries to understand how a form of society emerged in which these are the recurring benefits and liabilities. The main focus is on how competition becomes institutionalised in the modern nation state, particularly in its liberal, democratic, and capitalist form. Other forms of state-society, and the international arena of competition among states and other transnational bodies, lie mostly beyond this book’s remit. Nonetheless, understanding competition at the national level, among those societies that have most actively incorporated it as an organising principle, may provide a firmer foundation for understanding it at an international level. Global peace and the ability to solve or at least address global problems depends on cultivating international co-operation and holding zero-sum forms of inter-state competition in check. We need to compete to solve collective problems (and create incentive structures for doing so), rather than competing to control diminishing global resources.

I claim in this book that we need to understand what competition is, why it has evolved the way it has, if we are to be able to intervene in its dynamics. More philosophically, we need to overcome simplistic ‘for’ and ‘against’ attitudes, that obscure the phenomenon itself. Competition has both good and ill effects, and tendencies to praise or demonise it wholesale simply obscure this fact. To be critical is not just to condemn, but to offer judgements about the better and worse forms of some phenomenon, and criteria for those judgements. We get into trouble when we begin moralising about it as a whole, instead of treating the concept as a tool of social description and analysis. We may want to evaluate particular instances of competition as cruel and brutal, but others may be benign and even beneficial. In my view, forcing desperate workers to compete for inadequate wages just to survive is wrong, but requiring scientists to compete with each other over their truth claims benefits social knowledge, and is right. Only if we treat competition in general as a morally neutral concept can we make such evaluative distinctions, and talk about competition in a way that is both critical and productive, rather than just condemnatory or laudatory.

This book tries to help us understand why competition is so basic to the formation of liberal society, as a necessary foundation for any critical inquiry into it. As will become apparent, this book is written in sympathy with a certain kind of liberalism. But its primary aim is to understand how more liberal forms of society, that could engender ideologies of liberalism, came about in the first place, how they crystallised out of conditions that no one controlled or fully intended.

Defining Competition

It is always good to begin by defining terms, and doing so here will preview aspects of the general argument, and alert readers to ways in which I treat the concept of competition that may be unfamiliar. Competition is a situation in which rivals seek to outdo each other in obtaining some scarce end. It is *rivalry over some limited good*. As David Hume observed, if we lived in a world of absolute plenty there would be no need for 'justice' because we would all have everything we need and desire (Hume 1975: 183–4). The same goes for competition – without scarcity it has no purpose. But the world isn't like this, the things we need and want are scarce and we do come into competition with one another. However, some things are naturally limited (e.g. land) and others are artificially limited (e.g. presidencies). The significance of this will become more apparent as we go along.

Let me elaborate by first identifying some common errors in thinking about competition, before going on to unpack its effects and dynamics. Although I will at points draw on the way competition is understood in evolutionary biology, it is often understood through a rather crude biological or genetic reductionism, which I reject. While some biologically based aspects of behaviour, such as a male propensity for aggression (Batrinos 2012), may obviously feed into competitive behaviour, competition itself is such a complex, and as I have defined it, 'situational' behaviour, that there is unlikely to be anything like 'a gene for competition'. In the animal kingdom one does find supposedly genetically based stereotyped behaviours, such as 'ritual' performances among males to attract a mate, that address competitive situations. But these are basic parts of the life cycle that every male must face, and thus relatively 'hardwired' into the species. With humans, the situations in which we find ourselves competing, or even deliberately manufacturing competitions, are so variable, contingent, and incidental that they could not possibly be derived directly from specific genes. Loose talk of 'competitive instincts' driving human behaviour and explaining a competitive social world is precisely that – loose talk, which sheds little light on the matter.

Closely related to this biological reductionism is the problem of psychologising competition. By this I mean defining competition most basically as a psychological drive or disposition. This may be derived from biological assumptions, but it may also be given sociological sources, such as learned behaviour and culture. It is true that people will become psychologically adapted to the social environments they must survive in, and if an environment is full of competitive situations they must confront, they will likely develop a personal psychology prepared to compete, and perhaps even to seek out competition. But in keeping with my definition, I see competition grounded in the objective situation itself, not the psychological adaptation to it. Too often we talk as though competitiveness is the cause of competition, rather than the other way around. As though, if we could just change people's psychology, we could do away with unwanted competition. In etymological research on the development of the word 'competition' in English, as represented by historical dictionaries and encyclopaedias, it is evident that while the definition of competition as a situation of rivalry is quite old, going back at least to the seventeenth century, the concept of being 'competitive', as represented by the word, does not clearly appear until the nineteenth century (Hearn 2021). We should not put the cart before the horse.

Another area of confusion, that arises particularly among those who have a completely or primarily negative view of competition, is what I might call 'distancing' or 'denaturalising'. Here, competition is seen as a harmful effect of some contingent historical and social process, an episode that we might get beyond. It may be seen as a peculiar trait of 'Western', 'European', or perhaps 'Enlightenment' culture. But the most usual culprit is capitalism. There can be no denying that capitalism cultivates competition in the economy and beyond. People, firms, and states are pitted against each other in struggles over limited goods such as jobs, markets, profits, and natural resources. And competition in the economy narrowly defined spills over into politics, culture, and so on. But this does not warrant the view that capitalism is the root of competition. Any careful survey of the non-Western and/or pre-capitalist world will reveal lots of competition. Conspicuous here is military competition between states and dynastic rivalry over territory and resources, and religious rivalry over belief systems and claims to divine authority. Where there are elites, there is rivalry. Having said that, pre-capitalist economies also generate competition and conflict among everyday people at the bottom of the social hierarchy, over limited goods such as arable and hunting land. Anthropologists and archaeologists have long noted the pattern of competitive feasting and feuding led by community leaders ('Big Men', chiefs) in pursuit of the prestige that enables them to lead (Keesing 1983, Sahlins 1963). There was no pre-competition Eden that we have lost our way from, we just compete over different things and in different ways today.

My aim is that this book will reinforce these various claims about misunderstandings of competition, through its account of what competition actually is. For the rest of this section I want to expand on my minimal definition of competition offered above. While I will leave a fuller discussion of the relevance of evolutionary biology to my treatment of the idea of social evolution in regard to competition in Chapter 2, here I will highlight some of the analogical parallels with the concept of competition in evolutionary biology, because I think it aids a sharper conceptualisation.

It is readily apparent that there is a close association between the concept of competition and theories of evolution, from Darwin on. While it is necessary to make a clear distinction between biological and social evolution, at the conceptual level there are continuities in how the mechanisms of competition function in both contexts. It is notable that while the word 'competition' occurs frequently in Darwin's *Origin of Species*, and often in critical statements of the basic theory (e.g. Darwin 2003: 585–599), in current work on biological evolution the word is not very prominent most of the time. This is partly because it has been replaced by a more precise technical language of 'fitness', 'adaptation', and 'selection' that subsumes processes that can be analysed in terms of competition. I strongly suspect however, that this is sometimes also due to a desire by evolutionary biologists to avoid confusions generated by the fact that our popular concept of competition is heavily freighted with associations lifted from forms of social competition that rest on non-biological social conventions such as markets. The problem (for them) is not so much economics borrowing its notion of competition from biology, but biology appearing to borrow its notion from economics, or some other non-biological domain. Nonetheless, in my view the widespread use of the term does not indicate confusion, but rather a recognition of the underlying formal similarities, that mean that the concept is applicable to both biological and social domains, and maintains a core meaning across those, without implying any subterranean causal connections.

Given the basic definition, of rivalry over limited resources, the next questions are about the characteristic effects of competition. Usually, the first thing people think of here is the elimination of rivals through competition – there are winners and losers. In biological evolution the 'competitive exclusion principle' (Futuyma 2013: 531, Hardin 1960) holds that when two or more species require the same resources or ecological niche to survive, one will inevitably force out the other, due to some adaptive advantage, no matter how minor. Social competition sometimes also has this form. Two states with exclusive conceptions of sovereignty cannot both claim the exact same territory. Some firms will squeeze other firms out of certain markets. But our tendency to think of this 'eliminationist' form first probably has something to do with the fact that myriad artificial forms of social competition are contrived to decisively allocate scarce resources (school places, jobs, houses, awards, positions, etc.). In the natural world however, elimination due to direct competition is relatively rare. Moreover, species can become inadequately adaptive and extinct for a host of reasons that have little to do with such direct competition.

Another core dynamic of competition found in biological evolution has borrowed its name from a process of social evolution: 'arms races' (Dawkins and Krebs 1979, Vermeij 1987). These can be 'symmetrical', that is, within a species, or similar species, as when selection favours maximal height for trees competing to rise above the forest canopy and obtain light. Or they can be 'asymmetrical', between rather different species, as in predator-prey relationships, such as the refinement of a hawk's distance eyesight and the camouflage and capacity for stillness of field mice, or flowers with deep cups and insects with long proboscis to access well-hidden nectar. As the terminological borrowing implies, we can find many parallel examples in social evolution. Most obviously there is the competitive dynamics of military technologies, in which states seek to outdo potential opponents in both offensive and defensive capacities. Current struggles around hacking and internet security come to mind. But formal convergence among social forms competing in the same environments – firms, universities, political parties – are also examples of 'symmetrical' arms races, where the same traits, such as organisational designs and practices, generalise within a population, rather than different but reciprocal traits developing in opposition to each other.

However, all this focus on direct competitions and their outcomes obscures a much more fundamental effect of competition – differentiation and diversification. In biological evolution this is sometimes called 'ecological character displacement' or 'adaptive radiation' (Futuyma 2013: 183–185; 532, Schluter 2000). The variety of finches all descended from a common ancestor that Darwin catalogued on the Galapagos Islands, each adapted to a slightly different niche, is a classic example. Frequently the effect of ecological competition is to magnify minor variations in a population, causing morphological divergence ('radiation') as different groups exploit slightly different resources. In effect, they 'get out of each other's way'. In the social world, this is also an effect of competition. Fundamentally similar commodities are diversified to capture different market niches, strains of social theory diverge into competing schools and research programmes, religious sects multiply and diverge in search of 'true believers'. Competition doesn't just eliminate the unsuccessful, or lock agents into permanent contention, it also elaborates social complexity and diversity, expanding the division of labour in ways that can be highly beneficial to society.

Finally, the idea of competition is often counterposed to that of co-operation. But this is misleading, because competition is one of the major stimulants to co-operation (Bowles and Gintis 2011: 4, Tomasello 2016: 9–10). In biological evolution 'mutualism' (Boucher 1985, Futuyma 2013: 529–531) refers to the interdependencies that develop among species as their interactions enhance each other's probability to survive and reproduce ('fitness'). Within social species, communities can form complex divisions of labour and patterns of co-operation that enable their survival (Bourke 2011). In both inter- and intra-species cases co-operation is conditioned by a wider context of competition, or what Darwin called more generically the 'struggle for existence'. In the social world this relationship is even more apparent. Co-operation within a group makes it both more able to achieve shared aims, and more able to see off contenders. The efficacy of sports teams depends on close co-operation in seeing off their rivals. Social co-operation within nation states has often been stimulated by war with external enemies. Similar things could be said about successful economic firms, platoons, social movement organisations, and so on.

Dissension in the team is a classic recipe for failure against one's competitors. Having said this, co-operation can take this 'tight' form, within clearly bounded units in competition with other such units, but it can also take much 'looser' forms, as in sets of mutually supportive energy exchanges within a local ecology, or a functionally diversified set of firms constituting a mutually reinforcing industry. Not all co-operation is driven by competition, it can be the result of more general pressures for survival, or strategies to excel. But competition often provokes co-operation.

The Domestication of Competition

As outlined above, competition is a basic structural condition affecting the trajectory of change in various ways (elimination, 'arms races', differentiation, co-operation), in both the biological and social worlds. Let me now present the idea of the 'domestication of competition', as a way of understanding how the role of competition in human social life has changed in recent centuries. The phrase is deliberately discordant, seeming to splice together separate fields of inquiry. I do this to lodge the basic idea in the mind. This thesis summarises the book's argument, and is what the book seeks to justify, through its application to historical materials.[1]

Human history was fundamentally redirected by the domestication of plants and animals. First wild dogs developed a mutualistic relationship with hunting and gathering peoples 12,000 or more years ago. And there are some indications that the domestication of animals as food, may have emerged around the same time out of hunting practices that involved corralling and selectively killing large prey such as elk, in ways that preserved the viability of the prey population in question. But the most extreme shift developed between about 12,000 and

[1] After writing most of this book I became aware of Joseph Henrich's book *The Weirdest People in the World* (2021), which combines anthropology and social and evolutionary psychology to try to understand the distinctive psychological makeup of Western, Educated, Industrialised, Rich, Democratic (i.e. WEIRD) populations. Henrich also articulates a concept of 'domesticated competition' (see Chapter 10) which is congruent with my own approach. His ultimate focus is more on the emergence of a package of psychological traits – individualism, impersonal morality, analytic thought – whereas I am more concerned with the evolution of a package of liberal institutions based on competition, but our approaches have much in common.

10,000 years ago with the domestication of cereals (wheat, barley) in the 'fertile crescent' (today: Iraq, Syria, Lebanon, Palestine, Israel, Jordan, northern Egypt, and south-eastern Turkey). This shift happened again, independently, in other parts of the world (e.g. the Indus Valley, Mesoamerica). Most archaeologists believe the profound change in food-getting was the unintentional effect of a series of small efforts to preserve and intensify naturally occurring food sources, that by degrees triggered the emergence of agricultural society. The point is that while we think of extensive domestication today as an arena of human intention, scientific intervention, and so on, in its origins the role of intention, and foresight, was probably very limited. Small behaviours and practices that were proto-domesticating probably took a long time before they reached the tipping point that transformed the energy producing capacity, scale, and structure of foraging societies (Price and Bar-Yosef 2011, Wenke and Olszewski 2007).

By analogy, we can think of 'competition' as something that has become 'domesticated'. Here I concern myself only with competition as a human social practice, leaving aside the biological processes we have used as examples above. The distinction is between (undomesticated, 'wild') competition as a sheer fact of social interaction, such as conflicts between different groups over limited food sources, territory, shelter, and other resources, versus a deliberate, intentional way of organising social practices within the group. The former tends to ultimately be resolved by force or the threat of superior force, while the latter, 'domesticated competition', involves participants willingly submitting themselves to an organised contest to resolve disputing claims over scarce goods. We might also talk about 'natural' versus 'artificial' competition, bearing in mind that both kinds of interaction are 'social'. These are ideal types, often blurred in reality, but it is an important distinction nonetheless. The modern world, particularly that of the liberal, democratic, capitalist nation states, is one where domesticated competition proliferates and displaces, or holds in check 'wild' competition. As we will see in greater detail as the narrative unfolds, the eighteenth and nineteenth centuries saw a leap in the domestication of competition across the whole array of institutional spheres: military, economic, political, and ideological/cultural.

Just as the domestication of plants and animals was foreshadowed and present in nascent forms for a long time before agriculture took off, the same is true with the domestication of human competitive behaviour. Board games of strategy developed in early agrarian societies: senet (Egypt), liubo (China), mancala (north Africa). On a much larger scale, the Olympic games of ancient Greece (Fisher and van Wees 2010), the 'ballgames' (*Ollamaliztli*) of various Mesoamerican people from the Maya to the Aztecs (Scarborough and Wilcox 1993), and the medieval European circuit of tournaments (Crouch 2005), all channelled social, martial, and political competition into more stylised forms. Notable with these last three examples is that these 'games' all echo forms of combat, and seem to have served both to keep relevant populations in combat-readiness, and to sometimes provide an alternate context for resolving conflicts more normally prosecuted in battle. Moreover, these were heavily laden with religious symbolisms, and were also seen as ways of divining the favour of Gods. These contests were not self-justifying, but rather operated under divine sanction, and provided access to divine judgement. My point here is that these forms of domesticated competition nonetheless, evolved and operated in the premodern shadow of martially organised societies bound together by shared supernatural beliefs. As we will see, it is precisely a crisis in this kind of society that opens up the space for domesticated competition to develop much further. Of course, one can also find premodern versions of the kinds of economic and political competition that are still part of everyday life today, such as vendors competing to sell their wares in urban markets, and election to political office in ancient Greece, Rome, and the Renaissance Italian city-states. But these are notable for their rarity, limited extent, and instability as practices before the modern era. They foreshadow later competitive institutions, but do not characterise the overarching form of the societies in which they occur.

In one respect evolution, whether biological or social, is just an accumulation of results from contingent circumstances of advantage and disadvantage. This is history as 'one damn thing after another'. But within that randomness there is a pattern. Over given periods, traits and features that confer advantages tend to consolidate and spread. Just as plant and animal domesticators expanded and marginalised foragers, in our modern period, those societies that have institutionalised competition, incorporating it across social structures and becoming systematically competitive societies, have tended to become dominant. Specifically, this has taken the form of the liberal, democratic, and capitalist nation state. But here I must immediately qualify the argument, because in both processes, it is not simply specific societies that displaced others, but also sets of institutions and practices that have spread across from one society to another, through borrowing and diffusion. Many foragers became cultivators, and in our time, many states-societies have gravitated towards the liberal, democratic, capitalist model, or what I have just called 'systematically competitive society'. Social practices, ways of organising behaviour, unlike genes, can travel across the boundaries between units with relative ease, given the right conditions.

The crux of the conceptual argument presented here is that by 'domesticating competition' humans have intervened in the social evolutionary process itself in a fundamental way. The domestication of plants and animals increasingly intervened in the process of biological evolution, altering species in ways that would not have happened otherwise, in a manner that far exceeds the normal influence of species on each other's evolutionary development, in terms of rapidity and direction of change. In a similar manner, as humans have increasingly internalised the processes of competition into the very workings of their societies, including their various effects (elimination, differentiation, co-operation), they have seized a fundamental driver of social change and intensified it. Around 12,000 years ago we crossed a threshold in terms of our intervention into the biological evolution of other species, with profound implications for our own long-term social evolution, and around 300 years ago we crossed another threshold in terms of our intervention into social evolutionary processes themselves. Modern society, particularly in its liberal, democratic, capitalist form, tries to harness the fundamental forces of social evolution through the domestication of competition. However, these processes are too complex to ever fully be under human control.

Overview

The rest of this book will flesh out this argument. It is divided into three major parts. Part I provides a general overview of relevant literature, and the theoretical underpinnings of the argument. Part II, the largest part, provides the long-term historical narrative of the domestication of competition. And Part III offers a cultural and critical analysis of competitive liberal society as a type of society. Some readers may prefer to concentrate on the parts – theory, history, social analysis – that most interest them.

Part I addresses the research contexts and debates in which the question of the origins, nature, and role of competition arises, and the theoretical framing of the study.

Chapter 1 examines three main historical processes that have framed and provoked my interest in questions of competition. First, the classic problem that has come to be known as 'the rise of the West' (Daly 2015). What caused the rise to global power of Western Europe and its settler societies in the last few centuries? I suggest the domestication of competition must be part of the answer. Second, as I have already suggested, the domestication of competition is associated with the rise of a particular kind of nation state, what we might call the currently dominant model of capitalist liberal democracy. Why is this? And third, does what has come to be known as 'neoliberalism' have a special role to play in explaining the current state of competition? One often encounters this idea in critical discussions of neoliberalism, but my argument suggests that the pervasive role of competition in modern society has historically deeper roots, whatever its current transformations.

If Chapter 1 is about the questions that provoke this study, Chapter 2 presents the theoretical approach that informs the argument and its analysis. I view the generation and distribution of power in society, and how and why that evolves over time, as the fundamental context for social inquiry. I see theories of social power, and of social evolution, as inherently linked (Hearn 2014a). The chapter defines what we mean by social power, and closely related concepts of domination, authority, and legitimacy, arguing that power needs to be understood as something distributed among agents. Thus the definition of social actors is also central, and especially the fact that in the modern period these are increasingly collective, corporate entities, based on modes of association other than kinship (Coleman 1993). The sharpening and proliferation of such corporate actors, and the domestication of competition, are reciprocal processes. Competition and competitors are mutually defining. Drawing on the tradition of cultural ecology, I will also clarify what I mean by 'social evolution', emphasising a shift in focus from 'societies' to forms of social organisation as the key units of analysis.

Part II of the book substantiates its thesis through a closer analytic historical narrative about the transformation of European society in the modern period, primarily the eighteenth and nineteenth centuries.

Its chapters are organised in terms of Michael Mann's (1986) distinction between military, economic, political, and ideological forms of power, which I address in the introduction to Part II.

Chapter 3 provides the key historical antecedents for Chapters 4–7, focusing on changes in the domains of kinship, religion, and law. It examines the decline of traditional authority in medieval Europe, specifically the weakening of inherited monarchical and aristocratic rule, and of the Church and associated belief in supernatural beings. At the same time, the power of state-based law was consolidating and expanding, developing new ideas of 'legal persons', as 'fictions of law', that would become crucial to the creation of new corporate actors and the domestication of competition. This shift combined with intensifying trans-Atlantic competition among European empires, and novel experiments in republican and democratic government in America and France, created a new context for the development of law and competition.

Chapter 4 looks specifically at the reorganisation of military power in this period, which is closely related to the declining power of aristocracies. The rise of the modern state and its monopoly of legitimate force made militaries and law enforcement bureaucratic functions of the state, rather than localised privileges of divided nobilities. The pacification of the nobilities, the subduing of their traditions of martial competition to the modern state, opens up scope for more civil forms of competition. The 'wild' can now be replaced by the 'domesticated'.

Chapter 5 turns to the economic sphere, with special attention to the emergence of the modern economic corporation, as a competitor *par excellence*. I examine its origins in medieval antecedents, how post-revolutionary US was the ideal environment for its initial cultivation and elaboration, and its subsequent development in Europe and beyond. The economic firm is in many ways the 'ideal type' of the modern corporate actor, but I am concerned to show in the next two chapters that new corporate actors in the political and ideological/cultural spheres are also crucial to the general domestication of competition in liberal societies.

Chapter 6 considers the transformation of competition in the political sphere and the functions of the state. While prefigured in British politics of the seventeenth and eighteenth centuries, like the modern company the modern political party and party systems first emerged in the young US, largely in the same period. Despite early condemnation of parties and factions by political leaders (Washington, Adams, Jefferson), within a few decades the modern party system had taken shape, emerging out of more rough-and-tumble, quasi-militarised factionalism, before spreading to Europe as democracy supplanted aristocracy across the nineteenth century. The chapter also briefly examines the rise of adversarial law, and the replacement of patronage by competitive examinations for government appointment, as two further examples of the state's institutionalisation of conflict through formalised competition.

Chapter 7 tackles what is by far the most diffuse and difficult arena in which to describe our theme of the social transformation of competition. Here the focus is on contestation in the arena of knowledge, ideas, beliefs, and truth claims. My narrative concentrates on the gradual emergence of the modern university out of its medieval forebearers, the disruptive impact of the Enlightenment, and the broader emergence of associational life in civil society. Here the range of corporate actors is more complex and varied, and interacts closely with those in the economic and political spheres. But competition is different here, because while economics and politics involve competition over more clearly limited resources (capital, market share, political office, administrative structures), truth claims can be, and are, produced cheaply and in abundance. The peculiarly pungent atmosphere of current social media-driven public debates is just the latest expression of this.

Part III steps back from the previous historical narrative to take a more analytic view of the systematically competitive society we now find ourselves in, viewing it as a kind of culture and set of values, and as an object of critique. The introduction to Part III sets the stage for this by summing up the narrative and main themes of Part II.

Chapter 8 articulates a conception of culture, and examines competition as a system of beliefs and practices legitimating the social order. I emphasise the prominent role of science, games, and sports in formalising and naturalising competition in daily life, thereby legitimating distributions of social power. I push this argument about legitimation further by exploring competition as a form of ritual. While we often think of the modern period as one in which the role of ritual has weakened in social life, domesticated competition in its myriad forms exhibits many of the core features of ritual, such as liturgical form, specialist practitioners, and dramatisation of the social order.

Understood this way, the systematisation of competition in modern liberal societies suggests a society still legitimated by ritual, albeit of a secular form.

Chapter 9 asks how we can critically evaluate competition in this kind of society, particularly from within its own terms of reference – that is, as an 'immanent critique'. The premise that domesticated competition is a work of human artifice implies that it is something we have some control over and can shape. I argue that the pervasive image of the rule-governed game, and ideas such as 'the level playing field', encode the basic cultural resources from which any criticism must be constructed. Moreover, competition works best within certain bounded spheres of practice – e.g. business, democracy, science – and its worst distortions are often a result of competition transgressing these boundaries, as when money interferes with politics. I argue that maintaining such separation and balances of power among distinct institutional spheres, arenas of competition, is critical for liberal society.

In a short Conclusion, I provide a final review of the book's argument. Although much of the book is concerned with making the case for certain forms of competition, at the end I reflect with some trepidation on the current fraught state of domesticated competition and liberal society, and their possible futures.

A final point about my perspective before I proceed. The approach I take is shamelessly generalist. Much of my work, such as that on nationalism and national identity in Scotland, and bodies of theory on nationalism and social power, is relatively specialised. But I have always had very broad interests in the sciences, social sciences, and humanities. This is part of what first attracted me to the American four-field approach to anthropology in which I was trained, that combines culture, linguistics, archaeology, and biology. My academic career has moved from anthropology to sociology, with liaisons with politics. In this book, developed primarily through extensive critical reading, I move across a wide range of historical and other literatures, seeking to develop a broad and synthetic account of my subject. It is an argument that runs across many centuries, large parts of the world, and several disciplines. I rely heavily on the work of others, seeking a broad understanding. Whatever the hazards of such a generalist approach, I think it is necessary, to get our minds around the big questions that confront us.

PART I

The Ideas

If 'domesticated competition' is the answer, what is the question? All research develops in dialogue with existing areas of enquiry, debate, and theorisation. In the next two chapters I situate this study within relevant areas of research, and present the conceptual and theoretical apparatus that guides the study. Often this is done in a single chapter, that reviews one or two relatively unified literatures on a specific area of research and its theoretical debates, plumping for some theoretical position. But because the thesis pursued here is so broad, provoked by many different areas of research and theorisation, I have treated these separately. My aim is to produce an argument that brings together various lines of inquiry into 'the rise of the West', the emergence of the nation state, and the current period of neoliberalism, while also synthesising theoretical problems around how we understand social power, the social actor, and social evolution. My argument about competition arises out of this integrating perspective.

Before proceeding, it might be helpful if I clarify how I understand the relationship between 'conceptualisation' and 'theory', distinct issues which nonetheless run through the next two chapters. It is common to use 'theory' as a covering term for all the intellectual abstractions we generate in the process of trying to generalise about substantive research, and to treat it as the 'highest level' of generalisation and abstraction. The entire enterprise is divided into: theory, methods, data. This way of talking tends to confound processes of theorisation and conceptualisation that I think should be distinguished. I think of theory as any kind of explanatory hypothesis, however particular or general. One can have a theory of a specific event, e.g. 'what caused the financial crisis of 2008?', or process, e.g. 'how did the Inuit maintain demographic balance with the carrying capacity of their environment?'. One can also theorise at a more general level – 'what are the usual causes of political revolutions?', or 'what accounts for the formation and spread of modern capitalism?'. Theorising on this scale is more challenging, but necessary. But to be a theory it needs to be an account of why and how things happen in the real world, however particular or general. However, theories are not constructed only out of direct empirical observations. They themselves rest on and are built up out of 'concepts', which again can be more particular or general, more concrete or abstract. Concepts of 'chairs' and 'roads' rarely cause much controversy, but what we mean by 'moral obligation' and 'capitalism' can be more contentious. Before we can build up a theory of, say, 'what causes revolutions', we need a concept of 'revolution', and a host of other supporting concepts. And this starts to reveal the difficulties, because while we can and should scrutinise our concepts, compared to, say, the STEM sciences, in the social sciences and humanities concepts are normally much more embedded in everyday thought, more inherited and taken for granted than theories, which are more explicitly formulated. Theories can be called into question by contrary evidence, identifying flaws in argumentation, as well as interrogating the suitability and coherence of their very concepts. Concepts themselves however, have a certain irreducibility, and are tested more by their utility, both in terms of how they support theories and make them workable, and a *prima facie* plausibility in how they bundle together areas of experience. In the work of abstraction, some of the time we are 'building theories', but some of the time we are testing and revising our basic building blocks of concepts. A classic example is the concept of 'race', which across the twentieth century went from being primarily an idea of biological types, to being one of symbolic and ideological categories. This happened as the concept's utility was tested both in the science of human biology and genetics, and in social science research into race relations as a form of social stratification. This underlying conceptual shift reflected both the impact of science and changing social norms and values, and had profound consequences for how, and in what fields, explanations of racial inequality were theorised.

My key point is that while theorising may reshape concepts, ultimately conceptualisation comes before theorisation, and is the point at which the boundary between 'science' and 'common sense' is most blurred. Scholars can never lift themselves entirely out of the world of common sense, and can only craft and customise some of their concepts, which inevitably swim in a sea of everyday ideas. This is both a blessing and a curse: a blessing because it obliges 'theorists' and scholars more generally to attend to the connections between their ideas and common experience, and to put their arguments about the world in terms that can be understood beyond a narrow range of specialists or initiates to a theoretical school; a curse because conceptualisation, especially in the social sciences and humanities, is inevitably enmeshed in common sense assumptions that evade careful scrutiny, and bring with them biases, lacunae, and so on (Brubaker and Cooper 2006: 31–33). This is not defeatism, but a plea for realism, and a certain circumspection in terms of what we think can be achieved either through concepts or theories, especially as they become highly refined.

To return to my opening point, contemporary social theory is often more a compendium of novel concepts ('structuration', 'biopower', 'habitus', 'assemblages', etc.) formulated to bring certain issues into focus, than a body of theories in the stricter sense proposed above. While these concepts may be elaborated into theories, that is not what they are in the first instance. I say all this because the discussion in the next two chapters needs to be understood as being as much about problems of conceptualisation as about theory. By convention, these are the 'theory chapters'. But their main function is to lay the conceptual foundations of a theory of modern, 'domesticated' competition, and that theory is demonstrated by the whole book, not just these chapters.

1 *The Context of the Question*

Bodies of research around three main historical processes have provoked and framed my interest in the question of competition. First, the classic problem that has come to be known as 'the rise of the West', regarding what caused the rise to global power of Western Europe and its settler societies in the last few centuries, a position that now appears to be yielding to rising powers elsewhere in the globe, especially China. I think the transformation of competition is an important element in understanding this history. Second, this is also the historical and geographical context for the original development of the modern nation state. Moreover, the domestication of competition is especially associated with the rise of a particular kind of nation state, namely the highly influential model of capitalist liberal democracy. What does this tell us about how that and other types of nation states took shape? And third, does what has come to be known in recent decades as 'neoliberalism' have a special role to play in explaining the current state of competition? One often encounters this idea in critical discussions of neoliberalism, but my argument suggests that, whatever its current transformations, the pervasive role of competition in modern society begins much earlier, and for other reasons, hence the importance of the previous two contexts. This chapter aims to lay out these research contexts that have helped form this study.

The Rise of the West

I regard the domestication of competition as a process first taking place in the North Atlantic cultural sphere generated by the global expansion of European powers from the sixteenth century (Hearn 2009), with specific emphasis on the anglophone sphere of the US, Britain, and its empire in the eighteenth and nineteenth centuries. This inevitably locates my argument within what has often been called 'the rise of the West' (Daly 2015, McNeill 1998). A host of arguments have been put forward to explain the rise to power of this set of European states and their North American colonies that eventually became independent states. At the more materialist end, and more strictly in terms of the European subcontinent, some have emphasised geographic advantages (Diamond 1997, Jones 1988) such as the effects of multiple waterways of rivers and seas as a means of moving goods and stimulating commerce (Cosandey 1997) and the physical accessibility of coal when new technologies became able to exploit it (Pomeranz 2000). Science and associated improved technologies of ocean travel, military force (Cipolla 1980, McNeill 1982), and industrial production have all been credited with giving the 'West' an edge (Goldstone 2009, Mokyr 1990). Many others have placed greater emphasis on institutions and associated ideas – for instance, grounding the growth of modern science in the role of the medieval Christian church in fomenting a spirit of restless, integrating inquiry that would yield humanism and the Enlightenment (Dawson 1958). The specific emergence of sharper notions of private property and the rule of law out of medieval institutions is also often regarded as critical to European advances (North and Thomas 1973, Pipes 1999, Rosenberg and Birdzell 1986). Such explanations shade into those that put more stress purely on values. Greater levels of individualism and voluntary co-operation, particularly in England due to less binding kinship structures, have been credited (Macfarlane 1978, 1987) as has been the unleashing of bourgeois virtues and an entrepreneurial ethos by the growth of a commercial economy (McClosky 2006). I cannot adequately survey this entire literature here, but this is a taste, and below I will focus on a couple of themes particularly relevant to this study: rationalisation and an arena of multiple competing polities. But first it is helpful to abstract two key dimensions that shape all proposed explanatory theories – temporal and spatial – and situate this study in those contexts.

Arguments about the causes of the rise of the West can be placed along a temporal continuum, from those that emphasise the historical depth of the process to those that stress the more recent and contingent nature of a process that becomes, indeed, more of an event and less a process. Either it was 'a long time coming' or an 'unexpected turn'. An example of the former is Alan Macfarlane's (1978) claim that a distinctive pattern of individualism in England, reflected in the processes of property and land inheritance and already apparent in the Middle Ages, ultimately stemmed from Germanic customs brought over with

Anglo-Saxon settlers. This unique individualism in due course fed into the rise of capitalism and European dominance. Another example is found in the work of the historian of ideas Christopher Dawson (1958), who argued that the innovations of humanist and Enlightenment thought, which he believed explained 'the rise', were themselves explained by the peculiar early separation of religious and worldly powers after the collapse of the Roman empire, in institutions of church and monarchy, which created a uniquely tense social dynamic that generated intellectual innovation. Examples of more 'contingent' readings can be found in recent arguments of what has come to be known as 'The California School' (Goldstone 2000), which has been one of the more influential approaches in recent years. Kenneth Pomeranz (2000) has sought to explain the divergence of the developmental fates of Europe and China, which he sees as largely having the same potential for economic development up to about 1750. But by that point the European colonial accumulation of new resources from overseas, combined with the fortuitous conjunction of new machine technologies and readily accessible coal reserves, gave Europe a new advantage, allowing it to pull ahead. With a similar emphasis on late and contingent conjuncture, Jack Goldstone (2009) specifies a set of circumstances beginning in late seventeenth-century England. This includes a settled balance of power between the Anglican Church and various dissenting sects, and between the Crown and Parliament in the Bill of Rights of 1689, which opened up an ideological space for the practical adoption and spread of Newtonian science and led to the transformational invention of steam-powered water pump (for mining).

Of course, many arguments fall in between these extremes and combine both long-term processes and relatively punctuated but crucial events. Temporally, the present thesis about competition hinges on a relatively late shift, around the eighteenth century. The change emerges out of an historically specific set of conditions having to do with the decline of traditional religious and monarchical authority structures, especially in Northern Europe, and the responsive adaptation of newer, more legal-constitutional forms of authority to the power vacuum that had emerged. This unfolds over these two phases – the unravelling and then reconstituting – of power in European society. This argument is presented more fully in Chapter 3. However, any historical shift such as this can itself be explained by antecedents, which in turn have antecedents to the point of infinite regress. I limit my argument to what I think changed and why in this critical period, but so far remain agnostic on the question of how much that change was already ordained by previous conditions.

The other key dimension is spatial – to what degree are the explanations contained within the usual geographic boundaries of Europe versus couched in terms of Europe's relationship with what lies beyond, especially in its imperial and colonial relationships. There is a long history of doing European history as if it were in isolation from the rest of the world, subject entirely to endogenous processes (Wolf 1982: 3–7). Thankfully this prejudice began to be left behind a long time ago. William McNeill's seminal 1963 book, *The Rise of the West: A History of Human Community*, covered 5,000 years of Eurasian history, capped off by the rise of Europe to global power. McNeill emphasised how much Europe had inherited from other civilisations, how much its rise was built on the platform of that inheritance. Indeed, for him, strategic 'borrowing' becomes a kind of prime mover of long-term historical change. More recently, Janet Abu-Lughod (1989) argued that it was the interlinking of European trade with a series of regional Eurasian trade networks reaching all the way to China, especially in the decades around 1300, that lifted Europe's relatively underdeveloped civilisation. When Central Asian systems went into decline for historically contingent reasons, Europe was then poised to pull ahead. And E. L. Jones (1981) has emphasised, among other factors, the next historical boon, when developments in seafaring allowed Europeans to reach the Americas, opening up vast new exchanges of goods and commerce.

But, of course, this story has a dark side – unequal exchange and exploitation. Many of those broadly working in the area of world systems theory (Chirot and Hall 1982) have stressed the rapaciousness of these external relations (e.g. Blaut 1993, Frank 1969, Hobson 2004). Wallerstein's (1974, 2007) world systems model focuses on relationships of unequal and exploitative exchange between regions not encompassed by an overarching imperial system, but rather linked by interdependencies of commerce between separate polities. The first world system in his analysis was internal to Europe, featuring the underdevelopment of Poland as a 'bread basket' relying on cheap serf labour, supplying the rapidly industrialising trading states of Northern Europe, especially England. The next historical step was the expansion of this system to the wider world, in which Europe and later the US became the 'cores' of the world system, leaching value out of peripheralised societies in Africa, Latin America, and the rest of the world. In this view, the 'rise of the West' is largely due to Europe's predation on other societies, including not just unequal exchanges between agrarian economies supplying cheap peasant labour and raw products and industrial economies turning these into value-added goods but also the 'primitive accumulations' of land acquisition by force and slavery. I cannot go into the numerous debates about the viability of explanations that emphasise Europe's exploitative relations with the rest of the world. The point here is simply to recognise that this is one very important strand of 'exogenous', as opposed to 'endogenous', explanations.

As I have already suggested, the spatial scope of the present account is both smaller and larger than 'Europe'. I view the anglophone world of Britain and its American colonies, especially those that became the US, as the epicentre of the process I am describing, which then radiates out into wider Europe before spreading to much of the rest of the world. Thus, as to 'where' the rise of the West happened, like many 'Atlanticist' historians (Greene and Morgan 2009), I emphasise a circum-North Atlantic world defined especially by the conquest of the British and French empires of American territories and peoples and problems of overstretch and crisis, which led to two critical revolutions – the secession of the British North American colonies and the toppling of the *ancien regime* in France. The rise of the West took shape across the North Atlantic, not narrowly in geographical Europe.

Many of the key themes explored in debates about the rise of the West can be brought under the wider heading of what Max Weber called 'rationalisation' (Kaesler 2017, Kalberg 2005: 27–30, Weber 2005: 53–67). While developments in religion, science, capitalism, and law have each received special emphasis and been prioritised in analyses, all of these can be viewed as effects of, or fundamentally affected by, a wider process of rationalisation. Weber's contribution to the question of the rise of the West is usually pigeonholed in his better-known thesis of the 'Protestant ethic and the spirit of capitalism' (2002), where he argued that traditional capitalism became highly dynamic and transformative 'modern' capitalism because of a reorientation in religious values, especially in Calvinism. Chronic uncertainty about the urgent matter of personal salvation in the new Protestant sects caused believers to throw themselves into their work and the pursuit of wealth and its reinvestment in search of confirmation that they were leading worthwhile lives. For Weber, this was an historical moment in which new ideas and values critically redirected behaviour in consequential ways, kick-starting modern capitalism. But once 'up and running', capitalism develops and spreads under its own commercial and bureaucratic dynamic, no longer reliant on this religious work ethic.

However, this was specifically a study of a critical moment in the European rise of capitalism and modernity and an attempt to demonstrate that ideas can matter as much as material conditions. More broadly, Weber thought that, while all civilisations display rationality, which is especially encoded in major religious traditions and institutions, it took on a peculiar and accelerating dynamic in 'the occident'. Rationalisation, for Weber, meant the systematic ordering of thought and practice, rendering the world, and our pursuit of ends within it, more calculable (cf. Swidler 1973: 36–38). Bureaucracy is often held up as the prime example and outcome of rationalisation, with its ordered hierarchy of offices distinguished from persons, specialised training, habits of record-keeping, and so on (Weber 1978: 956–958). The two key bureaucracies of modern society are those of the state and the capitalist corporation. Rationalisation was central to his understanding of modern capitalism, as relying on a stable legal infrastructure of property and contract, as rendered more calculable by the separation of work and household and the rise of 'free labour', and by the formalisation of accountancy and the bureaucratic organisation of the factory itself (Weber 2005: 130–136). However, rationalisation was a process that Weber saw happening across society – for instance, in the systematisation of theology and in the formalisation of style and techniques in the arts.

The present study's focus on the formalisation of competition, rendering it more peaceful, rule-bound, and defining more clearly the actors who can compete in any given sphere of activity, resonates closely with Weber's notion of rationalisation. In rejecting notions of capitalism that portray it as, at root, the expression of sheer greed, Weber argued:

> On the contrary, capitalism *can* be identical with the *taming* of this irrational motivation, or at least with its rational tempering. Nonetheless, capitalism is

distinguished by the striving for *profit*, indeed, profit is pursued in a rational, continuous manner in companies and firms, and then pursued *again and again*, as is *profitability*. There are no choices. If the entire economy is organised according to the rules of the open market, any company that fails to orient its activities toward the chance of attaining profit is condemned to bankruptcy. (2005: 56, original emphasis)

That this vision of rationalised capitalism entails also the institutionalisation of competition is obvious. In a tantalisingly brief passage elsewhere, Weber defined competition as 'peaceful conflict', which can be 'regulated' and 'oriented to an order' (1978: 38). Less obvious from the longer quote is that Weber saw the rationalisation of capitalism as simultaneously bound up with the wider rationalisation of society, and especially law (Weber 2005: 65–67). This research was not devised as either a verification or application of Weber's concept of rationalisation, but I recognise the compatibility and correspondences. My aim is to illuminate a very specific process, one that can be couched in these terms.

Another highly relevant theme that recurs in the 'rise of the West' literature concerns the effects of political fragmentation and competition between polities. This is an idea that goes back a long way. In an essay of 1742, David Hume speculated:

*That nothing is more favourable to the rise of politeness and learning, than a number of neighbouring and independent states, connected together by commerce and policy.*The emulation, which naturally arises among those neighbouring states, is an obvious source of improvement: But what I would chiefly insist on is the stop, which such limited territories give both to *power* and to *authority*. (1985: 119, original emphasis)

Hume was thinking of European states of his day and the classic Greek city-states. Reading Hume, Adam Smith, and others, the historian of political thought Istvan Hont (2005) argued that Enlightenment discourses on political competition became newly fused with those on economic competition, in a way that permanently shaped the formation of the nation state, from that time to the present. He saw 'jealousy of trade' as an important engine of history.

The theme of inter-polity competition has been central to the analyses of several comparative historical sociologists. Charles Tilly (1992: 67–95, *passim*) argued that war was basic to the formation of states in Europe over the long term. From about 1500, as the technological means and international and imperial stakes of warfare grew, a set of more sharply defined states emerged in an international system. Internally, these states developed ways to mobilise capital in support of warfare, mobilised more people for battle, and disarmed their populations and taxed them more heavily, thereby strengthening demands for political representation from below in return and intensifying the relationship between states and their evolving citizenries. Externally, territorial boundaries sharpened, as rivalry between relatively equal contenders to power intensified, both within Europe and in colonised lands (cf. Parker 1996). Eventually, these emerging sovereign states, with their greater organisational capacities, outcompeted other early modern political and economic forms in Europe such as city-states and urban leagues (Spruyt 1994).

While recognising the importance of this refinement of warfare, Michael Mann and John A. Hall offer a more general take on the role of competition, which in a way echoes Christopher Dawson's emphasis on the importance of Christendom. Surveying the European *longue dureé* from ancient Mesopotamia to eighteenth-century Europe, Mann (1986) defines two major political types: extensive 'empires of domination' and intensive 'multi-power-actor' civilisations. After the attempt to create a European empire on the basis of Christendom failed for Charlemagne and his successors (c. 800–888), Europe became a patchwork of rival polities of various sizes, but all nonetheless bound together by an overarching Christian identity and belief system, which provided normative support for commercial and diplomatic interactions despite constant conflict. According to Mann, 'It was essentially a competitive civilisation – competition flourished within state boundaries, between states, and right across state boundaries – but competition was normatively regulated' (1986: 504).

Hall (1986) similarly emphasises the unifying effects of Christianity that ranged over the various autonomous powers of dynasties, states, and civil societies. Comparing 'the West' with the religious civilisations of Islam, India, and China, he contrasts the tendency of states in those systems to monopolise power and block the development of relatively autonomous powers, with the peculiar European path in which the 'liberties' of states and other actors were enabled to develop, generating new levels of collective power. Along similar lines, Walter Scheidel (2019) has recently argued that the greatest contribution of the Roman Empire to the rise of Europe was that empire's collapse. The fractious arena of competing and co-operating polities and institutions that arose in its wake – protected from Eurasian conquest by mountains and loosely held together by evolving Roman religious and legal institutions – was the true seedbed of modernity, beginning on its divergent path from this early point.

These themes of Weberian rationalisation and political and military competition have recently been brought together in Dingxin Zhao's monumental study *The Confucian-Legalist State: A New Theory of Chinese History* (2015). Because he explicitly addresses the nature and role of competition and ultimately contrasts the path of China with the 'rise of the West', he provides a good way of capping the present discussion. Zhao adapts Mann's historical-analytic model, dividing the sources of social power into four major institutional spheres: ideological, military, economic, and political. I do the same in this book, and I introduce Mann's model more fully in the introduction to Part II. Mann treats these four spheres as relatively autonomous but highly interactive, with none taking simple priority over the others in the overall composition of social power. Zhao argues that instrumental, means–end rationality operates most effectively in the military and economic arenas of power, where the material success or failure of social action is more readily apparent. In the ideological and political realms, the outcomes of social action are more situational and ambiguous and less cumulative. Military and economic competition are more historically dynamic as drivers of social change and development. Zhao also distinguishes between the focus of economic instrumental competition on 'private goods' (personal wealth) versus the military focus on 'public goods' (survival of the polity). In short, Zhao sees Chinese history as profoundly shaped by the early crystallisation, due to endemic inter-polity warfare, of a vast bureaucratic-legal state ('Confucian-legalist') controlling extensive military capacities. The rationality of war made China. This model consolidated in the Western Han Empire and endured to the end of the Qing empire (c. 206 BCE–1911 CE). In contrast, Zhao argues that in Europe, due to expanding trade opportunities, it was the rationality of economic competition abetted by an increasingly scientific mindset that drove the rise of the West. Unlike the 'California School', he does not think economic modernisation could have just as easily broken through in China but for a few factors of timing. The Confucian-legalist state was an obstacle to this. Although my focus is on only the last 500 years on the other side of the world, and I conceptualise competition rather differently, I share Zhao's conviction that competition is central to paths of historical development and operates differently in the military, economic, political, and ideological spheres.

These various strains of explanation for the 'rise of the West' are not necessarily mutually exclusive; it is a question of prioritising causal importance (Carr 1961: 115–116). The argument presented in this book does not flatly contradict any of these. Instead, it offers a different prioritisation and a different core narrative of social change in which competition is central. The argument is not that there is some abstract force called 'competition' that enters into this history at a certain point, but rather that competition is basic and a constant part of human social life, and thus, fundamental changes in how it is organised and performed are diagnostic of, and consequential for, social development. Focusing on competition helps reveal some of the key formal properties and effects of the 'rise of the West', but the causes of that process are multiple, complex, and contingent and involve many of the processes long articulated in the literature: population growth, increasing productivity, heightened geopolitical conflict, technological innovation, and associated shifts in institutions, ideas, and values. What I am providing here is not a total explanation of the rise of the West, but a missing thread that changes our perspective on the question.

Nationalism

Scholars have long debated how to understand the origins and historical depth of the phenomenon of nationalism (Smith and Gellner 1995). My approach falls squarely within what has been called the 'modernist' camp (Hearn 2006). Whatever the contributing antecedents of ethnicity, identity, and culture from medieval Europe and beyond (Grosby 2001, Hutchinson 2000, Smith 1986), my interest is in nationalism as a structure of belief and identity that emerges in conjunction with the formation of the modern nation state (Breuilly 1993, Gellner 1983, Hobsbawm 1992, Malesevic 2019). It develops with the hardening of territorial claims and boundaries and associated spheres of state jurisdiction. It is made possible by expanding the spheres of literacy and communication (Anderson 1991, Mann 1992). It is fundamentally bound up with the distinctively modern claim to 'rule by the people' and that those in power ultimately get their legitimacy from those below (Bendix 1978, Canovan 2005). This new relationship between rulers and ruled triggers new problems of social identity, and what holds together both the vertical and horizontal relationships of the new members of more tightly defined and legally integrated states.

This topic returns us to the point above about when and where, time and place. It is conventional to talk about nation states originating in Europe, evolving out of longstanding dynastic states that had developed larger bureaucratic superstructures under absolutism. Several recent commentators have made us more sensitive to the fact that an age of nation states doesn't simply succeed an age of empires, as Ernest Gellner (1983) sometimes seemed to suggest, but that in many of the key cases (Britain, France, Spain), nation states initially form and incubate within empires, in complex hybrid ways (Kumar 2010). The modern world of the nation state system emerged by degrees out of an age of imperialism. This somewhat complicates the 'when' question. As to the 'where' question, answers move in at least two directions. Some have claimed that England around the sixteenth century was the precocious first case, translating the Bible into English, fusing Protestant and national identities, and extending new opportunities for nobility down the social scale, eroding the traditional boundary between aristocrats and ordinary people (Greenfeld 1992, Hastings 1997). However, Benedict Anderson (1991) early on offered an intriguing alternative to the standard account of nationalism beginning in Europe and spreading out from there. He claimed that it first emerged out of the status contradictions of the populations he called 'creole pioneers', European peoples born and raised in the colonies of New Spain. According to Anderson, caught between their high new-world status ruling over subjugated indigenous populations and their lower 'colonial' status in the eyes of the metropoles they came from, with paths of career advancement frustrated beyond their colonial settings, these people increasingly came to identify as the peoples of new, 'New World' nations. Anderson locates this process specifically in the Spanish colonies in the early nineteenth century, largely ignoring the new regimes brought about by the American and French revolutions in the late eighteenth century. I find this unsatisfactory.

To recapitulate, my argument locates the emergence of the paradigmatic and highly influential first cases of modern nation states (embedded within empires) in these two revolutions, the one enabling a set of colonies to secede from their homeland and set up independent, constitutional government, the other toppling a traditional elite *in situ*, to replace it with a new, highly ideologically charged and campaigning vision, and experiment in self-government (Finer 1997, Hearn 2009). These pivotal events arose out of the multi-polity competition discussed above, but here more specifically between three empires – Spanish, British, and French – contending for control over American lands. We will look at the events more closely in Chapter 3. The basic point here is that the where and when of the emergence of the modern nation state, and of the 'rise of the West' more generally, are intimately bound up with each other, and both need to be 'decentred' from a strictly European frame, to a circum-North Atlantic frame.

Inherent in the claim just made about the centrality of the American and French Revolutions for understanding the emergence of nationalism and nation states, are typological assumptions. If these are the defining cases, what are we to make of the other forms that modern states have taken, the other paths along which they have evolved? There are various ways of categorising different forms of nationalism. Some are more concerned with the basic territorial structuring of relations and conflicts between states, and national or ethnic groups. Michael Hechter (2000) has focussed on the territorial agendas of nationalisms: cores incorporating outlying peripheries, separate polities being unified into a single polity, irredentist claims on co-ethnics in neighbouring states, and secessions by territorially concentrated ethnic minorities. Considering Central and Eastern Europe, especially post-1989, Rogers Brubaker (1996) sets up a tripartite interactive model of nationalist claims: 'nationalising nationalisms' where an ethnic majority imposes its identity on other ethnic minorities within a state territory; 'homeland nationalisms' where movements lay claim to their embattled co-ethnics in other countries (irredentism again); and the 'minority nationalisms' of regionalised ethnic populations caught between these two other kinds of claims.

Other typologies are more concerned with the entire historical process of nationalism. A classic example is John A. Hall's (1993) division into types based on the basic problematics of politics, and specificities of historical and geographic circumstance. Hall begins with the transatlantic conflict between Britain and France in the eighteenth century, and ways that the intensifications of warfare and commerce forced rulers to legitimate the demands they were making on subjects by incorporating them into national projects, and for those subjects to reimagine themselves as national peoples. Subsequently from the late eighteenth century, partly to keep up, reforming absolutist monarchs such as Frederick the Great sought to transform and modernise their domains in a more top down, bureaucratic fashion, eventually creating Germany out of the fragmented principalities of the Holy Roman Empire. Meanwhile, in the early nineteenth century, across the ocean in Latin America, Anderson's creole pioneer dynamic was at work, leading to a set of quasi-liberal independence movements, breaking away from the declining Iberian empires of Spain and Portugal. Back in Europe, the process migrated east, as urban commerce and education spread, and various 'small nations' (Hroch 2000) such as the Czechs began to identify as such, and pushed for recognition and opportunity against the carapace of the Habsburg Empire. Finally, 'integral nationalism', the paradigm being Germany's Third Reich, viewed the emerging world of nation states as one of a 'Darwinian' struggle for territory and dominance. That Germany can be seen as exemplifying two different kinds of nationalism at different points in its longer trajectory, indicates the historical and conditional nature of Hall's typology. Hall notes subsequent waves of new national independence movements, including the decolonial nationalisms of Africa and Asia, and the wave of Eastern European nation states emerging from the collapse of the USSR. But these would seem to fit the established model of populations seeking national statehood, the new normal, given the opportunity of imperial decline. In this way Hall attempts to chart an unfolding history in which previous nationalisms provide precedents for later nationalisms, and yet also, in which there are typical responses elicited by certain types of situations, especially imperial overstretch and decline, and general pressures to 'keep up' in an evolving world of nation states.

Two ideas run through Hall's account. One is the principle of 'asocial society' (1993: 5–7) which he borrows from Immanuel Kant, who said: 'The means which nature employs to bring about the development of innate capacities is that of antagonism within society, in so far as this antagonism becomes in the long run the cause of a law-governed social order' (1991: 44, orig. 1784). Kant goes on to offer the image of a tree that grows in isolation, low and misshapen, in contrast to trees that grow together in a forest, straight and tall, in their competitive pursuit of limited sunlight (Ibid.: 46). Hall invokes a similar image of evolving nation states locked into parallel paths, as they both compete with and adjust to each other. The other closely related idea is, as he puts it, that 'openness increases cohesion' (1993: 17). Hall's claim is that authoritarian regimes invite nationalism as resistance, but more liberal regimes are able to harness social conflict towards national ends.

This points us towards the most enduring though debated typology of all, the simple binary of nationalisms into 'ethnic' and 'civic' varieties, between those based on particularising cultural and sometimes racial forms of identity, and those based on citizenship and universal notions of rights (Mann 2004: ch 3). This has been used to contrast historical nationalisms in Europe, between 'east' and 'west', that is, the nationalisms of the dynastic states of the Atlantic seaboard, especially Britain and France, and perhaps the Netherlands, versus those of the formerly fragmented Holy Roman Empire, now Germany and Italy, and the Habsburg imperial patchwork of people further east (Brubaker 1992, Kohn 1967, Plamenatz 1976). This dichotomy has been criticised for failing to recognise that all civic traditions are culturally grounded, that liberalism has only really developed within national communities (Kymlicka 1999, Yack 1999). However, as with all ideal types, the fact that we cannot expect to find 'pure' examples in reality, even that these are not possible, does not eliminate their analytic value. It is still meaningful to say, as I think Hall would, that liberal and authoritarian regimes can have a profound and differentiating effect on how national identities are formed. And for the present thesis, the argument is that there is a close connection between the domestication of competition and the liberal or civic type. Understanding what we mean by 'liberal nationalism' (Miller 1995, Tamir 1993, Taylor 1999) entails going beyond the presence of valued liberal principles of equal rights, rule of law, tolerance, and so on, and grappling with Kant's cultivated antagonism. I argue that modern nationalism arose especially out of the historical transatlantic conflicts between imperial Britain and France, generating the American and French Revolutions, and new forms of state and society in the US, France, and to a degree Britain. And despite key differences in their liberalisms, France being more state-centric, and Britain and the US being more individual-centric (Hall 1995), together, this bundle took the lead in developing liberal forms of society. It is a form of society in which the people rule, by means of mutual contestation, and in which the traditional authority of aristocracies and churches has been greatly reduced.

Let me bring this discussion of typologies up to date by schematically comparing the characteristic political regime types of the twentieth and twenty-first centuries, underscoring the central importance of liberal democracies, the bearers of liberal forms of nationalism. Liberalism and democracy are not the same thing, the former being a matter of the rule of law and equal rights, the latter of openly contested election to office. They are realised to varying degrees in different cases, and research aiming to track historical changes often collapse criteria of liberalism into the general category of democracy, and/or deal with the variation with graded typologies from autocracy to democracy (Desilver 2019, Mukand and Rodick 2020). Nonetheless, the number of democracies in the world has steadily grown, despite setbacks in the 1930s and 1940s, with democracies overtaking autocracies and mixed or 'anocratic' regimes since the end of the Cold War. Today over half the world's population lives in democracies, and four in five of those who live in autocracies, live in China (Roser 2020). So there is good reason to argue with caution that, so far, despite the ups and downs, liberal and democratic solutions to the problem of regime legitimacy have enjoyed success. I would argue this is because liberal democracy harnesses the social dynamism of competition, while also using competition to control and mediate social conflict over limited goods. This gives it flexibility and adaptability. But it is just one answer to modern problems of power and its legitimation. The major alternative regime types of this era can be significantly differentiated from liberal democracy by how they deal with competition:

- *Liberal Democracy* – is premised on the controlled cultivation of competition. Ideologically, open competition is routinely extolled in economics, in politics, and in public discourse. In reality it is also routinely subverted through various kinds of cartels, monopolies, and patterns of social conformity. And yet there are also lively discourses critiquing these failures, even if with limited success, and these criticisms are necessary, precisely because competition is so integral to the ideological justification of the social order.
- *Communism* – tends to see competition as one of the pathologies of capitalism. Ideally communism promises a just and egalitarian distribution of relatively abundant goods according to need, thus obviating the need for competition. But in reality, the system has to suppress competition, especially in the political and ideological

spheres. Nonetheless, particularly in the realm of politics, competition is always present and inevitable, and has to go on 'behind the scenes', in terms of power games and palace intrigues within the single party. Power in complex society is by definition organisational and hierarchical, with increasingly limited places as one moves up the hierarchy. These places are always foci of rivalry, whether this process is officially sanctioned or not.

- *Fascism* – violently suppresses political and ideological competition, while at the same time being ideologically premised on the glorification of fierce competition between states, nations, and 'races'. Understood here as a specific historically bounded type represented by the Third Reich, Mussolini's Italy, and Spain under Franco, fascism's idealised notions of harmony within the society are counterposed against the idea of the true people in zero-sum struggles against their enemies. Hitler was known to cultivate rivalry for his favour among his close staff, pitting them against one another, fomenting disorganisation, despite the bureaucratisation of the regime. (Speer 1971)
- *Other authoritarian regimes* – limit political competition in various ways, for instance, Saudi Arabia functions as a system of extensive patronage networks based on royal and aristocratic kinship, again, encompassing major dimensions of political competition within those networks.

Clearly the liberal democratic path of cultivating competition is only one strategy for organising social power developing over the last two centuries, and there are no guarantees of its longevity. But the success and spread, however imperfectly, of the liberal democratic model of the nation state, suggests its efficacy in generating and legitimating power. Other types of regimes become particularly reliant either on intense ideological commitment, which is difficult to sustain over long periods, or on 'performance legitimacy' (Zhao 2009) to counterbalance the absence of more direct access to power for their peoples. In the latter case, the depoliticised power of the consumer substitutes for the more active power of the citizen, able to compete more fully in various spheres, and most crucially to invest in the competition among contending political representatives.

Viewing different regime types as strategies for legitimating power raises the classic topic of 'nation building'. As Andreas Wimmer (2018) has observed, the first generation of theorists who worked on this (e.g. Bendix 1964, Deutsch 1953, Geertz 1963) thought analogically about the relationships between the original formation of modern nation states in Europe, and the newly forming postcolonial states in Asia and Africa (2018: 3). Precisely because of its initial formulation in the context of 'new states', nation building has strong instrumentalist connotations, of searching for the design to produce well-functioning nation states. But reality doesn't work like this. Nation states are partly 'built' through conscious, deliberate action, but also partly formed out of given circumstances, which are unpredictable and uncontrollable. This is especially true in regard to whatever we consider to be the 'first cases'. Later cases have pre-existing models to live up to, or consciously avoid, but the first cases are much more improvised, whatever the goals and intentions. There is an unavoidable tension between intentional efforts at 'nation building', and larger historical processes of 'nation formation', that escape the ambit of human intention.

The idea of nation building has also been discredited in recent years by efforts, particularly in the Second Gulf War in Iraq, to democratise by force. However, Wimmer argues that this isn't the only paradigm available, stressing the need for nation building to develop indigenously, and over the long-term, through the negotiation between diverse interests over shared social goods. For the present argument, the point is that it concerns that initial phase of nation building, as the first nation states were coming into being. Competition, when regulated, turns out to be one of the key forces and processes of nation building. To the broad repertoire of factors involved in nation building – shared ideas, values, identities, and institutions, sustained by networks of communication and exchange – we need to add competition, which of course is itself both an idea and an institution. It is a key mechanism for bending conflicts of interest towards common causes. One might say that the shift from more 'wild' to more 'domesticated' competition is definitional of what a nation state is, at least in its liberal democratic form.

Before leaving this topic let me reiterate that my approach is 'modernist' and my argument belongs in the Gellnerian tradition of explaining nationalism in terms of long-term structural trends. Gellner focused on the functional demands of industrial society, on its need for 'modular' individuals bound together by common culture, rather than rigid stratification by symbolically reinforced caste hierarchies. Modern society for Gellner was legitimated by its productivity, and the opportunity to participate in its benefits. My argument about competition is not intended as a total explanation of the rise of the nation state (or of the 'West'), instead it focuses in on a key mechanism through which productivity was stimulated, and legitimacy achieved, not just in the economy, but across society: it avoids Gellner's econocentrism. Like almost any argument about historical structural change, it includes an element of functionalism, in the sense of various institutions, ideas, and organisations adapting to one another amid change. But as it is not about a theoretical system in abstraction from historical change, 'function' is not viciously circular. It is about ongoing mutual adjustment within evolving sets of real relations. Domesticated competition helps knit together the modern liberal nation state, driving its dynamism, and legitimating the social order.

Neoliberalism

In recent years discussions about the nature of competition and its apparent prominence in contemporary social life, especially within capitalist liberal democracies, have been framed by the idea of 'neoliberalism' (Centeno and Cohen 2012, Davies 2014, Gane 2019, Jones 2012). This idea is now routinely invoked in both academic and more popular discourse, in attempts to account for a widespread sense of an oppressive ratchetting up of competition, not just in the economy, but across all institutional spheres. Without denying this intensification of competition, roughly since the 1970s, the present argument seeks to locate a deeper history of modern competition, which I claim helps us understand it better. Thus, somewhat against the trend, I do not focus on neoliberalism in this book, but let me elaborate here on how my thesis relates to these discussions. I distinguish between two basic strains of analysis, the one with more debts to Marx, Weber, and more materialist accounts of capitalism, the other with a special debt to Foucault, and a conception of neoliberalism more rooted in a history of ideas, and notions of discourse and rationality. I then explore some relevant permutations – the idea of the 'competition state', and recent critiques of 'meritocracy'. I wind up this discussion by considering the case of 'ordoliberalism', the economic philosophy that developed in 1930s Germany, becoming an important influence on neoliberal thought, and on current economic policy in Germany and the

European Union. My approach to competition can seem especially sympathetic to ordoliberalism, a point that is somewhat accidental, but nonetheless worth examining.

The term neoliberalism is often used too loosely to add much clarity to matters, and has an overabundance of referents. It can be used to label an historical period, a global process, an ideology, a policy agenda, but often, in more casual use, seems to suggest a mysterious omnipresent force dominating our lives – a 'zeitgeist'. Nonetheless, the basic parameters of neoliberalism are widely agreed in the academic literature. Some definitions place more emphasis on a political or economic philosophy, for instance, as: 'the free market ideology based on individual liberty and limited government that connected human freedom to the actions of the rational, self-interested actor in the competitive marketplace' (Jones 2012: 2). While others place more emphasis on a set of policies pursued by states: 'Neoliberalism urges freeing up commodity markets and international capital flows, deregulating labor markets, balancing state budgets, and generally reducing state intervention in the economy' (Mann 2013: 130). Either way the upshot is an intensification of competition between states, regions, cities, firms, and individuals, as state economic controls on capital investment and the conditions of labour have been loosened, and the balance of power between capital and labour has shifted in capital's favour. And there is broad agreement about the historical moment that led to its rise. Exacerbated by the 'oil shock' of the 1970s, a crisis of accumulation hit countries with expanding middle classes and welfare states, and stagnating industrial economies, resulting in what was often called 'stagflation' – slowing growth with rising prices. This created an intellectual crisis among politicians and economists seeking ways to respond, leading to the supplanting of the previous neo-Keynesian orthodoxy in economics and government policy with what became known as neoliberalism (although this is rarely a term of self-ascription). The new theory had been incubating in intellectual networks and associations (most famously the Mont Pelerin Society, see Mirowski and Plehwe 2009), think tanks, and university economics departments, before capturing political parties of the right and then the left, and spreading through the media into a wider public common sense. This transformation operated on two fronts: within the domestic economies of the core capitalist states, especially the US and the UK, and as an agenda spread internationally through structural adjustment policies as terms of lending imposed by the IMF and World Bank on various governments in Latin America and East Asia when these faced national debt crises. Neoliberalism is one of the latest of many globalising processes (Centeno and Cohen 2012).

This is the brief sketch. In almost all accounts, the diagnostic features of neoliberalism are largely the same: easing the search for cheaper labour by loosening capital controls; privatisation of industries and collective assets that were formerly publicly owned; the transformation of public institutions and even states to operate more closely according to market principles, like corporations; and a characteristic contradiction between advocating the shrinkage of the state, and relying on an increasingly powerful state as an aggressive prosecutor of these changes. A fundamental effect has been the normalisation and, indeed, glorification and elaboration of competition across institutions, daily practices, and popular culture.

The strain that owes more to Marx and Weber has tended to treat neoliberalism as a pragmatic project for the rejuvenation of capitalism. David Harvey (2005, 2007) diagnoses neoliberalism as an ideology and strategy to restore capitalist class domination in the face of social democratic advances during the decades of economic growth in the US and Europe after World War Two. It is the latest chapter in the long history of class struggles within capitalism, now operating more fully at a global and not just a national scale. In *The Strange Non-Death of Neoliberalism* (2011) Colin Crouch has emphasised the way large corporations in particular have captured the policy agenda, so that despite their role in the financial crisis of 2008, they have on the whole fared well. They enjoy what he calls 'privatised Keynesianism', that is, where the state prioritises supporting and subsidising private corporate interests rather than the provision of public goods. In what I think is one of the best short but comprehensive analyses, Michael Mann (2013: ch 6) develops three points. First, that claims for the increased efficiencies of a neoliberal regime, to enhance humanity's collective productivity and thus overall power, have not been realised. Instead, its power-effects have been distributive, concentrating wealth and power in the hands of particular classes and states. Second, that the global penetration of neoliberalism has been more uneven than many globalist accounts suggest – these tend to be 'anglophone-centric' (contra Harvey 2005). And third, it is a mixed bag. Analytically we need to distinguish between: 'principled neoliberalism elevating markets and individualism, the interests of capitalists, the interests of political elites, and a conservatism that uses the state to enforce morality, law and order, nationalism, and militarism' (2013: 131), in ways that are often poorly aligned with the basic principles of neoliberal ideology. In the arguments of Harvey, Crouch, and Mann, neoliberalism is a distinctive historical episode, but also a revived and intensified version of the existing logic of capitalism.

Another strain of thinking has been heavily influenced by Michel Foucault. Foucault was prescient in the late 1970s in recognising the significance of the emergence of this new economic paradigm, which he explored in a series of lectures delivered in 1978–1979 (2008), a few years before his premature death. Foucault was more inclined to emphasise the difference of neoliberalism with what had gone before, and seemed to be at once ambivalent towards and attracted to the ideas of neoliberalism, and their promise of an escape from normalising state power (Brown 2015: 55, Zamora and Behrent 2016). Foucault's treatment of neoliberalism is of a piece with his wider account of liberalism and what he called 'governmentality' that he was developing at the same time. Foucault argued that there was a shift around the eighteenth century to a new form of governing, in which the direct rule of a sovereign over subjects was replaced by a new political economic conception of society as a distinct reality, made up of things and people, that needed to be governed more indirectly. The emerging liberal order recognised people as relatively autonomous actors, but sought to establish the discursive and practical parameters within which action takes place. Government became a matter of 'an action upon an action', and this more indirect mode is what is captured by the idea of 'governmentality' (Foucault 2000: 201–222, 340). Regarding neoliberalism, Foucault saw this as a specific set of ideas, emerging out of the Freiburg school of ordoliberalism (discussed further below) and Chicago School economics, that contrasted significantly with classical liberal economic theory. For Foucault the latter was organised according to principles of free exchange among equals (however idealised), and epitomised by the economics of Adam Smith. Neoliberalism by contrast emphasises not exchange but competition as its core principle, thereby yielding legitimated inequalities. Foucault's diagnosis centres on a revised image of 'homo economicus' as no longer the exchanger, but rather a competitive entrepreneur, viewing this as the ever more dominant image of the modern person, and part of a rationality of government. In a sense, driving the 'action upon action' even deeper into the self. In Foucault's analysis, neoliberal thought is associated with material and institutional changes, however, in keeping with his general focus on discourse and knowledge, Foucault's approach suggests that an analysis of economic theory can serve as a key to the analysis of social change as a whole.

Many analysts of neoliberalism have taken their cue, not uncritically, from this Foucauldian mode of thinking, in which neoliberalism is not so much an effect of economic powers and interests on the rest of society, but a more 'global' transformation of society and its institutions, from the state down to the self (Gane 2014). Wendy Brown (2015) regards neoliberalism as a process in which 'homo economicus' displaces 'homo politicus', thus undermining the basic conditions for democracy. As the economic theory captures the state and shapes social policy, the imperative to artificially reproduce dynamics of market competition throughout society's institutions is realised. Brown objects that Foucault lacks an idea of the demos, of the people as a unified political body, seeing people only as the subjects of states, but not as citizens (2015: 73–74). What Brown may not appreciate is the degree to which competition was already basic to the emergence of democracy itself. Will Davies (2017), while less directly engaged with Foucault than Brown, similarly defines neoliberalism as 'the pursuit of the disenchantment of politics by economics' (2017: 6). Davies sees neoliberalism not so much as the marketisation of society, as the dissemination of a principle and ethos of competition through critically placed 'expertise'; competition as a kind of rationality of measurement and evaluation that tends to dissolve social bonds. Again, institutionalised competition is cast here as an intrusion on a prior political logic, before neoliberalism, but I will be arguing that the institutionalisation of competition defines the original formation of the modern liberal state.

Another line of argument, somewhat influenced by Foucault's ideas, is the thesis of the 'competition state' (Cerny 2010, Genschel and Seelkopf 2015, Jessop 2002). Here the main focus is on the state as an actor in a global arena, and the underlying image is one of states becoming more like firms, strategising within a field of economic competition. As Phil Cerny puts it:

> the state still has a major national role to play, but that role is increasingly to expose the domestic to the transnational, to prise open the nation-state to a

globalising world, in the interest of ensuring that citizens keep up with the multiple pressures and demands of that increasingly integrated and interdependent political, economical and social ecosystem. The foreign or external is no longer external or 'outside'. (2010: 6)

While notions of 'national competitiveness' are hardly new (Porter 1990, cf. Krugman 1994), the idea of a thoroughgoing internal and external transformation of states, as they collectively adapt to a global environment girdled by international markets and laws conducive to shared terms of competition, is. Cerny describes this as a shift from '*raison d'Etat*', where the rationality of the state is primarily turned inwards to managing its own populations and territories, to a '*raison du Monde*', in which 'maintaining and promoting competitiveness in a world marketplace and multi-level political system' (2010: 6) provides the key reasons of state. While this approach may tend to overstate the coherence of the global arena, the redirection of attention to the effects of international politics on competition is salutary.

Turning back from the state to the self, there has been a recent spate of critical studies of 'meritocracy' (Littler 2018, Markovits 2019, Sandel 2020), which examine the insidious ways that competition becomes valorised, and itself validates processes that lead to inequalities. The original critique of meritocracy was Michael Young's sociological novel *The Rise of the Meritocracy, 1870–2033* (1958), in which Young projected a near future in UK society where extensive intelligence testing has replaced heritable status based on class, but the inevitable social ranking far from achieving a legitimate order, has merely generated new alienations and stimulated new demands for a more egalitarian order. However, Young's disparaging use of the term was soon eclipsed by more vernacular and positive use as a name for a fair society where people are justly rewarded for their talents and efforts. Jo Littler (2018) explicitly places her argument 'against meritocracy' in the context of neoliberalism, seeing meritocracy as a cultural means for its legitimation. Ideologically, it appears to contradict plutocratic tendencies towards the concentration of inherited wealth and opportunity (cf. Piketty 2013), suggesting talent and effort are consistently rewarded. It individualises human improvement, essentialises notions of ability, and leaves the given order of what is valued unquestioned. Although Littler does not focus systematically on competition, being more concerned with the cultural performances and framing of skill and talent that validate 'success', competition is a steady background condition for her argument. Daniel Markovits (2019) is more concerned with how meritocratic principles operate through institutions, especially education, to reinforce growing economic inequality, with a focus on the US case. Markovits argues that as society has polarised into a super-rich elite and stagnating or declining wealth in the middle ranks and below, both wealth and work itself have become maldistributed. Meritocratic competition, for instance, to get into the leading Law Schools, requires such an intense investment in the human capital of the aspiring student, that only extreme wealth can acquire this opportunity. And success condemns elite workers to gruelling hours and commitments that corrode lives and relationships, meanwhile workers further down the scale are often undersupplied with any opportunity for work, their lives under resourced, and undervalued. Markovits calls this pathological dysfunction the 'meritocracy trap', which ensnares both 'winners' and 'losers'. With a similar analysis, the philosopher Michael Sandel (2020) has argued that we need to temper our meritocratic hubris with a greater appreciation of the role of luck in our fates, and our need for humility and dignity to achieve societies based on some notion of the common good.

I think these authors are right to identify meritocracy as an ideology that often legitimates inequality, and glorifies competition in the process. But as Adrian Wooldridge (2021) has argued, meritocracy is also, still, a critique of the monopoly of access to opportunities by certain social groups simply on the basis of status. It is difficult to imagine a world that values talent, skill, and competence, and does not to some degree sort people according to those values. My main reservation about these critiques is that I don't think the idea of meritocracy adequately encompasses the reasons why we compete, or the purposes competition can serve. Competition is more than a psychological disposition or a cultural convention, it is, as I have said, a situation. Because I have suggested that competition can have a positive value, and that it has a special relationship to liberal forms of the nation state, I conclude this section with a brief consideration of ordoliberalism, a strain of economic theory that sought especially to promote the value of competition in the economy, and argued it should be actively created and safeguarded by the state.

Ordoliberalism (Cerny 2016, Gane 2019, Gerber 2001: 232–265) derives its name from the journal *Ordo*, founded in 1948 by Franz

Böhm and Walter Eucken, which was a venue for the development of this body of theory. In the 1930s Böhm and Eucken and other key figures had begun to share ideas at the University of Freiburg, concerned that the weakness of the liberal state and its legal system had led to the collapse of Weimar and the rise of the Nazis. Ordoliberalism, like neoliberalism, is rooted in neoclassical liberal economics, but whereas neoliberalism, more associated with the US and the UK, tends to emphasise the naturalness of competitive markets in conflict with the 'unnatural' interventions of the state, the ordoliberals had a keen sense of the necessary role of the state in creating the legal conditions for markets and competition. Ordoliberals saw a liberal market economy as a system of constitutive rules and regulations that make robust competition possible, and hold its usual enemies (cartels, monopolies) in check. Thus, ordoliberalism and neoliberalism tend to approach the question of competition from opposite ends: as artificial versus natural. Moreover, some ordoliberals such as Wilhelm Röpke also saw the need for moral and social structures to ground society and set limits on competition, not just the state and its laws (Gane 2019: 48–50). In the recent 'neoliberal period' since the 1970s, the ordoliberal strain has had a strong influence on economic policy in Germany and the European Union. Hence the European Union is one of the major growth areas for competition law (Gerber 2001: 257–264). In this book I too claim that competition properly delimited can provide benefits to society. However, I stress the formation of institutionalised competition from the early formation of the liberal state, and treat it not as a market specific factor, but as something built into the legitimation of power throughout society, however much it may reach its apogee in the economy.

Conclusion

A historically particular thread of competition runs through these discussions. From the European cultural zone of Christendom, containing numerous contending polities of various kinds, emerges the modern nation state system. From the clash of transatlantic empires emerges two new polities, based on written constitutions and evolving notions of democracy. From those same imperial contests emerge two successive global hegemons, Britain and the US, bound together by a degree of common culture despite their differences. Their hegemony is intimately bound up with the rise of capitalism and the evolving model of liberal democracy, with the UK and US eventually becoming the seedbed of neoliberalism and its global spread, which we associate with the revival of capitalist competition. This rough narrative suggests a peculiarly close relationship between this genealogy of liberal forms of society, and the institutionalisation of competition. The second part of this book will flesh out that narrative.

None of this indicates that the domestication of competition could not have happened elsewhere, that argument, however, would require a broader comparative framework, and have to grapple with the imponderables that arise whenever we try to explain why something didn't happen, as opposed to why it did. The 'where' of the matter in this argument is the North Atlantic world of interactions created by European imperialist expansion, and the 'when' pivots on the revolutions that generated new experiments in society and government, with new problems of how to organise and legitimate power. Neoliberalism is a late chapter in a story that began with these revolutions. As to which way the story goes from here – now that the West has risen and Asia appears to be rising – that is beyond my remit. I do not claim that the story ends here.

2 *The Theoretical Approach*

I should start by distinguishing between my theoretical apparatus developed below, my approach to competition, and the general 'field' of theoretical writing specifically about competition. Why am I not grounding my argument in the latter? One answer is that while there are recent sociological attempts to theorise competition, these are just too diffuse (see: Arora-Jonsson, Brunsson and Hasse 2020, Colagouri 2012, Duina 2011, Hartmann and Kjaer 2015, Stark 2020, Werron 2015, Zhao 2015). Although they provide interesting ideas which I may invoke here or there, Hartmann and Kjaer are right that 'competition is not a major topic within sociology' (2015: 141), and a unified theoretical literature has not developed around it so far. Another answer is that theorising is often based on economic theory in particular, in ways that import some of the biases and preoccupations of that discipline, such as the 'rational economic actor' (e.g. Brenner 1987, Hunt 2000). I want to avoid this. Nonetheless, there was an early interest in a more general concept of competition for sociology evident in the writings of Max Weber, Georg Simmel, and Karl Mannheim, which I will briefly explore at the end of this introduction.

This chapter doesn't just develop a concept of competition – minimally: rivalry over some limited good – which has already been presented and elaborated in the Introduction. Instead, it provides more fundamental assumptions about society, history, and social change, that explain how I conceptualise and theorise competition. Most basic here are three premises: (1) that the human need for power is the most basic thing shaping human society; (2) that power in human society is distributed among social actors, so we must conceptualise these with care; and (3) that the pursuit of power by social actors is a major driver of social change, and that this implies a theory of social evolution. So, the body of the chapter is organised under the themes: Power, Actors, Evolution. These sections lay out a general theoretical position in regard to each theme, and build towards a general understanding of competition. This broad approach is necessary because competition is not a bounded area of study, but something that cuts across all aspects of social life; doing this provides the most thorough explanation of what competition is, and why, in the context of human society, it has developed the way it has.

Let me set the stage for what follows with a brief consideration of an earlier period of sociological reflections on competition. It would seem that there was some potential for a general 'sociology of competition' to develop in the early twentieth century, but this was marginalised by other theoretical and research agendas, and 'competition' was perhaps surrendered to the economists for a period. What is noticeable about the early forays of Weber, Simmel, and Mannheim, is their interest in competition, not as a target of critique, or ultimate principle of society, but as a basic category of social interaction encountered across various social domains, not just the economy, and, each in his own way saw the concept as integral to understanding liberal forms of society. There is a sense in which this study returns to that same attitude.

As already mentioned in the previous chapter, Weber gave a tantalizingly brief treatment of the concept of competition, even though it runs through all his studies. In the passage in question (1978: 38–40) he was primarily concerned to clarify his terminology with regard to 'conflict', 'competition', and 'selection', particularly the last, given the impact of Darwin on social scientific language. Weber distinguishes between 'conflict' as simply the direct opposition of wills, and as previously noted, 'competition' as 'peaceful conflict', which is 'regulated' and 'oriented to an order'. A few pages later Weber notes that association through the market is particularly conducive to competition in this sense (1978: 43). While conflict and competition may lead to 'selection' – the increase or decrease in frequency of certain social traits, institutions, and practices – selection can also happen without such confrontation. Weber stresses that selection is 'fortuitous', and implies only fitness in relation to a given environment, not any intrinsic superiority.

In an essay originally published in 1908, Georg Simmel (1964: 57–85) addressed the concept of competition with a characteristic concern for the formal analysis of social relationships. Simmel's key point is that competition is never simply a zero-sum conflict between two actors, but is always carried out in regard to a 'third' party, be that an individual, a group, a whole society, or possibly all at once. Competition, more than mere conflict, serves some higher good that benefits others beyond the competitors, be it material productivity, advances in knowledge, or some other end. 'Modern competition is described as the fight of all against all, but at the same time it is the fight of all *for* all' (Simmel 1964: 62, original emphasis). Moreover, competition does not just allocate rewards, but compares the efforts of competitors before an audience of the public (cf. Werron 2015). Simmel treats competition as something particularly characteristic of modern liberal society, in which people feel themselves to be individuals clearly distinguished from an objective social world, more anonymous, and less bound by intimate social ties. Competition is a creature of modern law and morality, which sanction this rule-bound mode of interaction, as long as it is not abused. Fair competition, among abstracted individuals before the court of 'third parties', becomes constitutive of a modern notion of justice.

Karl Mannheim wrote 'Competition as a Cultural Phenomenon' in 1928 (1993: 399–437). In keeping with his 'sociology of knowledge', Mannheim seeks to relate processes of competition specifically to 'public interpretations of reality' as these appear in the 'existentially determined thought' of various social groups. Mannheim posits four ideal patterns of how knowledge and truth are generated and maintained, in a rough historical chronology of Europe. The first is the common sense 'consensus' of relatively stable, traditional, homogeneous, and small-scale communities, where scope for disagreement is constrained. The second is the 'monopoly' claimed by authorities, often in regard to sacred texts, epitomised by the medieval Roman Catholic Church. Mannheim notes that these two patterns can co-exist. Competition enters with the third pattern, associated with the decline of the Church's monopoly of religious authority and the rise of rival institutional centres of authority in science and universities, but also a multiplication of competing patterns of ideas associated with emerging social strata and class fractions. This happens as the economic, political, and social world becomes more complex in the Enlightenment period, loosely defined – I will return to these ideas in Chapter 7. Mannheim then posits a fourth pattern, associated with the rise of modern ideologies such as liberalism, conservatism, and socialism, arguing that after the 'atomised competition' among ideas that characterised the third stage, in the fourth, the pattern was one of 'concentration', of aggregation and synthesis as ideological tendencies pulled together factions, and borrowed from their opponents. Mannheim explicitly discusses the development of thought on the model of evolutionary selection, driven by the rivalries of social actors (cf. Hull 1990): 'In actual life, it is always some volitional centre which sets thought going; competition, victory, and the selection based upon it, largely determine the movement of thought' (1993: 420). The essay ends tentatively, suggesting that in the modern world all epistemological claims will ultimately rest on pragmatic competitive success: there is no ultimate 'ground' of knowledge left to be found.

These three thinkers share a certain early twentieth century German intellectual milieu shaped by commitments to an embattled liberalism, confronted by conservative, socialist, and, for Mannheim, fascist ideologies. It is the same general milieu that fostered ordoliberal answers to Germany's economic and political instability, discussed in the previous chapter. What is striking to me is the way they lift the question of competition out of its usual economic context and explore it as a more general principle social life, especially modern social life in liberal forms of society. In some respects, I am picking up where they left off.

Power

I define human power as the capacity of some agents, broadly defined, to achieve intended and foreseen effects on other agents, and the world more generally (Hearn 2012: 16, a modification of Wrong 2002: 2). I will unpack this definition as I go along, but first let me address the normative question. If one is unsettled by my claim above that 'the human need for power is the most basic thing shaping human society', it is likely because one has a basically negative view of power, a view very different from the one I take. The first step is for me to illuminate this difference. For me power is a morally neutral concept, specific instances of power can be normatively evaluated positively or negatively, but power itself is just a fundamental condition of our existence. In its most minimal sense, power is the capacity to do things, to cause change – fire can burn wood to ashes, the sun can warm the earth, or the impact of a large meteorite can redirect the course of evolution. However, as humans we are especially concerned with a more specific sense. Most definitions in the social sciences further emphasise the effects of some people on others (see Lukes 2005, Morriss 2002, Wrong 2002). The first thing to point out is that the effects we can have on each other, the instances of power, can be either brutal or benevolent, cruel or kind. There is a tendency to assimilate the concept of power to that of domination, understood as some people controlling others, either against their will, or at least against their own best interest (Lukes 2005: ch 3). But a moment's reflection tells us that power can be quite the opposite, for instance, the power of a state to remedy poverty, of a doctor to cure a patient, of an adult to protect a child: harm is not an intrinsic feature of power.

However, causation is, and in human affairs we are particularly interested in power as causal relations between people: how some do things to others, or get those others to do things. This points to one of the most important conceptual distinctions in the study of power, that between 'power to' and 'power over' (Ball 1993, Morriss 2002: 32–35, Pansardi 2011). 'Power to' is the more basic power conception: the capacity *to* have effects, whether on humans, or some other aspect of the world. We rarely object to having the power to do things, although our capacities, such as to deeply damage the planet, can become frightening. Rather, we routinely talk positively about empowering people, giving them the power to achieve things. Power *over*, however, is a different matter; this is normally understood as the power of some people *over* others. In some societies with sharp, symbolically elaborated social hierarchies, this situation might be understood as normal and proper. But for those from more modern, theoretically egalitarian forms of society, that prize individual autonomy and self-determination, it is more likely to seem like a moral problem. But of course, such forms of society are replete with power over, in households, workplaces, bureaucracies, and patterns of economic stratification. While there is a degree of ideological rejection of power over, the reality of large scale, complex, global society is that power over is raised to an extreme level. This creates an inherent contradiction, periodically expressed in moments of rejection and delegitimation of authority structures, in calls to 'take back control'. Formalised competition has a peculiar albeit imperfect capacity to mediate this contradiction. We are generally happy to have the power to succeed in a competition, and to enjoy the power over others this may deliver, even while we may also feel discomfort at the sense that it is the institutions of competition that have power over us. But here is the rub: powers 'to' and 'over' are not two contrary options between which we can simply choose – they are conjoined (Mann 1986: 6–7). Our capacities to do things are conditioned by the degree to which we coordinate our efforts into ever more complex forms of action. At a smaller social scale there can be a degree of coordination among equals, an attractive middle path that some have called 'power with' (Allen 1998). But once the activity in question reaches a certain size and complexity of coordination, hierarchy enters in. There is a need for leadership, command-obedience relationships, and functional divisions of labour – many capacities we value can only be achieved in this way. Again, power over increases power to, and whether the power achieved is for good or ill, is a separate normative question. I will return to this point when we discuss social evolution, because it turns out to be a key to the dynamics of social change.

Now let me return to the question of 'agency', and its nemesis 'structure'. I have slid back and forth between attributing power to 'people' and to 'agents', and will try to make it clearer why the latter term is important. I have defined power as the capacity of an agent to achieve intended and foreseen effects, and this encodes a definition of agency. Contrary to some arguments (e.g. Foucault 1980: 97, Latour 1986), agency is not simply any action or effect. The aforementioned meteorite's impact on the Earth, or a speed bump's role in slowing down traffic, does not make them agents, they are causes, or elements in a causal nexus, but not agents. Most of us define agency more narrowly, and with good reason, because this narrower definition allows us to identify an important category of phenomena. Agency involves will and intention. If you involuntarily knock over a glass, that is not agency, but if you offer one to your guest, that is. However difficult it may be to pin down intention as an event in the mind, the brain, or even in the body caught up in a complex train of action, we gain nothing by imputing its presence where there is no evidence that it exists, nor by denying that, in the universe of causation, some causal processes are distinguished by the presence of this element. There are too many causal processes we want to assess where the presence or absence of will and intention is critical to a causal account. The capacity of human beings to take in information, respond to situations, and alter courses of action, often quite profoundly, is difficult to describe let alone analyse without any conception of will and intention, and it is this insistence on the aspect of intention that obliges us to add 'foreseen' to our definition. One may buy a lottery ticket with the 'will to win', but winning is a matter of luck, only minimally related to intention. The money may bring some power, but the success is not an effect of the gambler's power. This question of agency raises another issue I will take up more closely in the next section on Actors. While the human individual is the paradigm of the agent, it is not the only kind of agent; the combination of power to and power over involves mechanisms for gearing up agency from individuals to larger collectivities organised for directive action – this point will become crucial to the book's argument.

There are sometimes debates over whether power is located in agents or social structures (Elder-Vass 2008, Sewell 1992). Individuals often seem dwarfed in their powers by the social structures that encompass them and shape their choices, and seem to have power over them. But if we are true to the claim I have made, that human power is the expression of agency as intention, then social structures cannot themselves be powerful, because they have no intentions, as much as they may be partially the product of intentions. They may distribute possibilities and probabilities. A system of social stratification will tend to limit the options of those at the bottom, and enhance the options of those at the top, but it is not exercising power. Some structures might be said to have power in the primary sense, as brute causal forces like the sun or the meteorite. A bureaucracy may unleash a causal process by some institutional logic beyond any specific human intention, although this is more likely to be some very complex hybrid of intended and unintended processes. A bureaucracy after all needs people with wills and goals to animate it, no matter how deranged its ends might become. And this example points us back to the idea that human will and intention are often magnified by being collectivised, even when they spin out of control. The bottom line is that agency works not so much against structures as through them.

Having said that, we often bundle rather different things under the heading of 'structure'. A bureaucracy is actually a very large form of organisation, and people's lives in modern society are generally structured by a manifold of large and small organisations. Organisations are also agents, entities that aggregate individual human powers into complex forms of action. But we also use 'structure' in other senses that do not identify organisations or agents. Our lives are structured by all sorts of patterns of distributions – demographic, economic, ideological – even language itself is structuring. In the first instance I recommend thinking of both 'structure' and 'agency' not as causal forces, but as modes of description. In some accounts it is useful to describe and highlight structural patterns, in others we want to describe patterns of social action, and we can be interested in both. However, if we are interested in power, agency, as a locus of causation, becomes a primary concern, and structure becomes a context shaping agency, but also shaped by agency. Structures do not have power, but they shape what agents who do have power can do, and in the intermediate form of organisations, can become macro agents, crucial in amplifying power.

Some conceptions of power place considerable emphasis on its elusive, ephemeral, centreless nature. Foucault (1980: 92–108) argued against the idea of power as something centred in a 'king' or 'the state', with the power to control through punishment and forbidding, and instead preferred images of power as something endlessly circulating through the social body, uniformly dispersed throughout the system. This quickly becomes a fairly meaningless and useless conception of power. The important point about power is not that it has *a* centre, Foucault was right about that, but that it has many centres, a point he doesn't seem to have fully appreciated. Foucault sometimes spoke of a play of forces, of strategic games (1990: 81–102), which implies this point, but he seemed more interested in the game in the abstract, than the players. Power *is* distributed, concentrated in some places, and not in others, and more specifically, in some actors more than others. The study of power always becomes the study of shifting balances of power, whether between persons, organisations, states, or whatever; we cannot conceptualise this usefully if our notion of power becomes too ephemeral and shifting.

Finally, our thoughts on power, especially when we insist on its connection to agency, are wedded to questions of morality (Morriss 2002: 38–42). The descriptive question of who had the power to do what, does not require, but at least serves the normative question of what they ought and ought not to have done. We can choose not to go there in our inquiries, but to the extent that one prosecutes moral questions, these stand on the question of power and agency, and their distribution. Responsibility lies with those who have or had the power to make a difference; those without sufficient power are absolved of responsibility. Thus, the arrangement of power in any social setting, vast or small, always invites questions of authority and legitimacy, that is, who or what institutions are invested with recognised and accepted power, and the moral accountability that such power entails. A central claim of this book is that competition is formalised and elaborated not simply as a means of accumulating power in some hands, although it does that, but more crucially as a new means of justifying distributions of power, once older forms of authority and its legitimation have weakened.

Altogether, I have argued that for a concept of power concerning human affairs to be useful, we need to distinguish between, and yet appreciate the complex interdependence of, power as the capacity *to* have effects, and as the control of some *over* others. Moreover, while social structures may shape the disposition and possibilities of powers, it is power as agency, that is, located, willed, and intended action, that ultimately interests us. The study of power is primarily the study of the changing balance of forces between various agents. While we may evaluate the utility of social systems and structures, and whether they achieve what we want them to, with agency comes accountability and culpability, and agentic powers are subject to moral validation and critique. This is both an objective fact about how society works, and the basis of any normative argument we might choose to make (which I will return to in Chapter 9).

Actors

The preceding conceptualisation of power implies the central importance of agents. I will tend to use the term 'actors' rather than agents, acknowledging that 'agent' in some contexts, especially economic and legal theory, can have a more specific meaning of one who carries out the will of another ('the principal'), and I am for the most part interested in cases where will and action are largely contained within the same 'body' (cf. Coleman 1990: 17, footnote 14; Shapiro 2005). If 'agency' is being used in the narrower 'principal/agent' sense, I will specify that. My main concern here is to clarify, and historicise, what counts as an actor. We think of the individual human being as epitomising the social actor, and with good reason, but crucial to the argument of this book is the extension of actor-hood to collective bodies, especially in the last two or three centuries. I will explore the importance of social actors through the ideas of Max Weber, James Coleman, and Pierre Bourdieu.

It is worth noting at the outset some of the varied ends, conditions, and constraints that shape human agency. Typically, we imagine actors in relatively stable and legible environments, planning a path to their objectives. But action sometimes responds to exigent circumstances, formulating immediate ends under extreme pressure and constraint, and actors may be obliged to act in contexts of obscurity and unpredictability, whether immediate or long-term, with little ability to anticipate the effects of their actions. Some have argued that this is the context in which ideological innovation is most likely to happen, precisely because of the loss of more material control of events (Hall 1986: 20–21). Of course, actors routinely come up against the opposition of other social actors, and are frustrated or redirected by that fact. To make matters more confusing, actors can realise ends through inaction, or may address circumstantial constraints through deliberately indirect ends meant to obscure ultimate ones. And as suggested above, the one who 'wills' (principal) and the one who 'acts' (agent) may be separate. This is not an exhaustive treatment, but is offered to sensitise us to the extreme variability of circumstances in which actors define and pursue their ends (cf. Emirbayer and Mische 1998), which is to say, realise power.

Weber built his sociology particularly around the concept of 'social action', that is, actions that can be understood as meaningful to other social actors (1978: 22–26). Social action can be prompted by emotions or affectual responses, or be habitual, unreflective, and 'traditional', but Weber's interest in rationalisation meant that he took a particular interest in two, interacting ideal types of social action. On the one hand actors can be oriented to ultimate values that define the ends of their actions, but on the other they can be instrumentally oriented to the means for achieving those ends. Ultimate values may imply ultimate sacrifices – such as death to maintain honour – but they may also become the ever-receding end point behind more immediate goals, eventually fading from view, leaving only the routine of those proximate goals of action. Weber worried that this was the main tendency of bureaucracy and capitalism – there is a built-in tension between these two orientations, which are both, in Weber's sense, 'rational', the one organising behaviour around a central orienting purpose or value, the other directing behaviour towards the most effective means for pursuing ends.

Weber is also known for his argument for 'methodological individualism'. Without going into the entire history of debates around this term (see: Hodgson 2007, Jepperson and Meyer 2011, Lukes 2006: 5–9, 94–101, Udehn 2002), I want to offer a reading of what it meant for Weber, and of how it relates to his exposition of 'basic sociological terms' in *Economy and Society* (1978: ch 1).[1] Steven Lukes quotes Weber in a letter written shortly before his death:

> ... if I have become a sociologist ... it is mainly in order to exercise the spectre of collective conceptions which still lingers among us. In other words, sociology itself can only proceed from the actions of one or more individuals and must therefore adopt strictly individualistic methods. (Quoted in Lukes 2006: 96)

Puzzlingly, as many have noted (e.g. Lukes 2006: 100, footnote 3), despite his assertion Weber's actual substantive studies rarely seem to observe his own stricture, often offering more meso-level analyses of the interactions of social groups, organisations, institutions, and belief systems, with few individuals in sight. When we turn to the chapter in question, we find Weber grappling particularly with the relationship between individuals and collective actors (see esp. 1978: 13–18). Weber stresses that an individualistic method does not imply individualistic values, nor does associated attention to rationality assume that rational calculation is the predominant human motive; he argues that the human individual, with consciousness, cognitive capacities, and orientation to the meanings of others, is a unique level of analysis. Biology may reveal neurological processes with explanatory significance for behaviour, but the human mind, the ground of social action, is an emergent phenomenon not reducible to these processes. And analyses of society as a whole can usefully draw on organic metaphors, to address functionalist questions about the relationship of parts to wholes, leaving aside individuals, even though there are dangers of reification of the organic metaphor involved here. However, for some purposes it is 'convenient or even indispensable to treat social collectivities, such as states, associations, business corporations, foundations, as if they were individual persons,' although 'these collectivities must be treated as solely the resultants and modes of organisation of the

[1] I use the standard English edition of Weber's *Economy and Society* edited by Roth and Wittich for this discussion. However, Keith Tribe's excellent new translation of the first four chapters (the last written and most complete of the drafts of Weber's unfinished work), along with Tribe's commentary, tends to further support the reading of Weber I am offering here (see: Weber 2019).

particular acts of individual persons, since these alone can be treated as agents in a course of subjectively understandable action' (1978: 13). Nonetheless, collective entities are a crucial focus because:

> These concepts of collective entities which are found in both common sense and in juristic and other technical forms of thought, have a meaning in the minds of individual persons, partly as of something actually existing, partly as something with normative authority. ... Actors in part orient their actions to them, and in this role such ideas have a powerful, often a decisive, causal influence on the course of action of real individuals. (1978:14)

Actors realise their actions through these collective entities much of the time. Despite this, Weber is adamant that 'there is no such thing as a collective personality which acts' (1978:14). Weber wants at once to strike a blow against the prevalent tendency (not only in his time) to treat larger collectivities, especially classes, nations, ethnic groups, and races, as unified actors endowed with shared consciousness; while at the same time he knows he must provide an alternative account of why people invest their individual agency in these things, these larger agents, or their proximate organisational representatives. Weber's methodological individualism offers an alternative basis for explaining the aggregation of human behaviour, and a check on 'the spectre of collective conceptions'.

Attention to this argument helps explain why the rest of Weber's chapter, which can seem like a compendium of concepts that show up in his work, is laid out the way it is. It serves to analyse the key factors and relationships that link individuals to these critical collective entities, working through a series of conceptual definitions, roughly in the order of: social action and its main types, social relationships and their tendencies towards openness and closure, what makes social order legitimate, communal versus associative types of social groupings, organisations and their powers (especially churches and states), and the nature of power and domination. In other words, it builds up, from the concepts we need to understand the individual social actor, to those we need to understand collective behaviour, and how individuals get organised into legitimated orders of power and domination. This is why domination, authority, and legitimacy were so central to his work – because they illuminate how individuals become subordinated to collectivities (Hearn 2012: ch 2).

Like Weber, James S. Coleman was a kind of methodological individualist. His *Foundations of Social Theory* (1990) offered a comprehensive treatise supporting his often highly mathematicised rational choice theory (see Marsden 2005). I do not follow Coleman's approach in this regard, and find several points of disagreement. Coleman argued that viable theory must always trace a causal path from macro-level structural process, to micro-level individualist processes, and back up again to the structural level. It is impressive when (if) we can do this, but I think this is too rigorous a criterion for adequate theory. I would not rule out, on principle, arguments that make causal claims entirely at the macro-structural level, or achieve only one leg of the macro to micro or micro to macro journeys. Even if they are incomplete, such arguments can still be illuminating and contribute to theory building. I am less ambitious or perfectionist than Coleman in what I think theory can achieve. Most fundamentally I don't accept Coleman's claim that only purposive action is really susceptible to systematic theorising. Coleman accepted that human behaviour is frequently non-rational, but claimed that this aspect was in effect unanalysable, and outside the bounds of theorising. We should therefore build up theory from a utilitarian image of individual actors as driven by interests in, and control over, resources and events. For Coleman, to explain human behaviour is to reveal underlying rational purposes, and relate these to larger structural processes, through simplifying assumptions of utility maximisation (1990: 13–19). I am more heterodox or eclectic in my view of social theory; I recognise Coleman's claim that much of the time we are interested in purposive action, and this sometimes provides the clearest way into analysing social interactions. But I don't think Coleman adequately appreciates the implications of Weber's distinction between value-based and instrumental forms of rationality, and the ways rationality is embedded in affect, convention, and socialisation, which shape its purposiveness (cf. Adams 2010). I also think there are benefits to bracketing off questions about rational choice sometimes, so that patterns in social life can be revealed that would be less apparent if one were looking only for purposive action.

However, Coleman had a key insight into the historical changes that made modernity, one that my own research confirms and elaborates. Coleman called this 'the emergence of new persons' (1974: 13–31), that is the florescence of 'corporate actors' in the modern period. Developed at length in *Foundations* (1990), the idea is more succinctly summed up in other places (1974, 1993), and is congruent with

Weber's concern I have emphasised, to build up collective actors out of individual ones. Coleman recognised the momentous importance of changes in law in the 'West', that allowed the 'natural person' in law to be supplemented and in many respects superseded by 'juristic persons', that is, various kinds of legally constituted corporate actors – it is a shift that corresponds to industrialisation and urban growth. For Coleman, this shift occupies the same conceptual space as various other classic transition narratives in the social sciences, such as Tönnies' *Gemeinschaft* to *Gesellschaft* (Coleman 1993: 2, 5). The shift is from the primordial social organisation of the family, to modern, deliberately and legally constructed organisations, as the defining feature of society (cf. Perrow 1991). I will return to this historical process in the next chapter, but as an historical watershed event, it runs throughout the book's argument.

For Coleman this shift implies profound changes in the nature of social control (1993: 8–10). It means that people's lives move from being primarily regulated by norms, status, and moral forces embedded in face-to-face and familial relations, to being regulated by rules, laws, and incentives attached to particular positions in formal structures. He recognised that this depersonalisation could be alienating. To some degree he thought organisational design could compensate, both through its incentivisation structures, and by reproducing elements of small-scale social ties within the organisation. Like many others, Coleman saw sociology itself as a response to this accelerating historical shift, struggling to keep pace with irreversible change, and to realise its role to advise society on how to adapt. Coleman emphasised purposive action in his theory of society, and correspondingly saw society as increasingly dominated by purposively constructed organisations. The social sciences in Coleman's view need to take an active role in redesigning society's organisations. My purposes are not this programmatic, but I think Coleman's insight into the historical transformation of actor-hood is crucial, and supports my argument about how competition was domesticated, as a new population of 'artificial persons' became the key competitors in society.

Pierre Bourdieu's ideas help us bring these various social actors into relatively stable patterned relationships. Long ago Alexander Lesser (1961) advocated an emerging concept of 'social fields' as a way of conceptualising patterns of social interaction that cut across, and could not be adequately captured by, relatively static and bounded notions of 'society'. Bourdieu took this idea and heavily elaborated it into his key social analytic concepts of 'fields' and 'capitals' (e.g. 1991: ch 8, 2005). Put simply, Bourdieu defines the various values and strategic resources that people struggle over as forms of 'capital', so that capital is not just economic wealth, but can also be prestige, social connections, culturally valued knowledge, and so on. A field is an arena in which people compete over some form of capital, for instance in business, politics, education, and the arts. In regard to the present discussion, competitors in Bourdieu's model can be either individuals, or collective entities (firms, theoretical schools, etc.). Moreover, struggles within fields happen at two levels. First, just to obtain and monopolise the capital relevant to the field in question, but more deeply at a symbolic level, to define capitals themselves, to determine the very values people struggle over.[2] The various fields also aggregate into a kind of 'field of fields', the 'field of power' (Bourdieu 1996, Swartz 2013: 61–64). While not precisely defined, this ends up being the arena of the national state (France in Bourdieu's work), although conceptualised in less bounded terms than the word 'state' often implies. So one might argue that struggles over whether a given state-society is to be defined by theocracy, free market capitalism, socialism, and so on, are struggles over the basic values (or capitals) in the field of power – which capital will dominate the others. In a fairly standard modernist narrative, for Bourdieu the number and distinctness of fields increases and becomes more elaborated as societies grow in scale and become more complex.

As my reference to Lesser suggests, in my view Bourdieu's approach, while having merit, is a bit more common sensical, and less original, than its distinctive terminology might suggest (Jenkins 2002: 89). I too will be looking at various institutional arenas in which people and organisations compete (militaries, companies, political parties, etc.), but I won't be invoking Bourdieu's terminology. I'm acknowledging a conceptual correspondence because Bourdieu has been so influential in recent years, and is often seen as a prime example of a sociologist who focuses on competition. However, in Bourdieu's work the concept

[2] An example of the wider influence of Bourdieu's thinking can be found in the theory of 'strategic action fields' (Fligstein and McAdam 2011), which attempts to bridge the studies of social movements (often weakly centred and bounded) and of organisations (often highly centred and bounded) into a more unified model of social action. Again, the focus is the struggle for power among actors.

of competition itself does not get much close attention, and is usually just assumed in his studies of fields. He pays more attention to the varieties of capitals than to the nature of competition. Nonetheless, I minimally share with Bourdieu the view that social actors, the bearers of power, need to be studied in the context of relatively stable fields of often competitive interaction, such as universities.

Evolution

I have examined questions of power and social actors in preparation for this final section on evolution as a frame for understanding social change and the domestication of competition. I need to take some care here in clarifying my position. I begin by addressing some common confusions about what the idea of social evolution entails, before laying out the pared down conception of it that informs this study. I will then look more closely at the importance of the power to/over dynamic, and the significance of how we conceptualise social actors, for this conception of social evolution. I then relate this to the domestication of competition thesis.

Despite an established and extensive field of research premised on the idea of social and/or cultural evolution,[3] there is still a lot of distrust, misunderstanding, and debate about it (see e.g. Fracchia and Lewontin 2005, Gough et al 2008, Henrich, Boyd and Richerson 2008, Runciman 2005). So I will start by clarifying my position on three key questions. First, while the human capacity for sociality obviously has some basis in biology, apart from that starting point, I am not concerned with the impact of biology and genetics on social evolution in this study (see Freese et al. 2003). There are valid and interesting lines of research into 'coevolution', the interactions of genetics and culture, as in lactose tolerance developing among cattle herders (Durham 1990, Richerson and Boyd 2005), and also into 'evolutionary psychology', which attributes human behaviours and cognitive biases to genetically encoded environmental adaptations

[3] I will not distinguish between 'social' and 'cultural' for the purposes of the present discussion, and will generally treat 'social' as the broader terms that includes 'cultural'. However, I note that in the literature 'cultural' often denotes a focus on knowledge, ideas, and more broadly 'information' as that which is 'inherited', and that inheritance as the process that needs to be explained.

(Buss 1999, Tooby and Cosmides 1992). But these inquiries are far from my concerns: 'social' implies 'non-biological' for my purposes.[4]

Second, in the nineteenth and early twentieth century much social evolutionary thinking was decidedly teleological, endowing evolution with a unidirectional progressive logic, whether that end was Hebert Spencer's peaceful commercial society in which individualism was maximised and the state minimised, or Karl Marx's communist utopia in which property and the state would wither away (Runciman 2009: 16–20). This mistake still gets attributed to evolutionary thinking, despite the fact that its core point in both biology and the study of society, is that order and pattern can emerge 'spontaneously' in the absence of any divine, cosmological, or historical telos, given certain constant processes and mechanisms. It is in fact one of the least teleological modes of explanation available – and that is part of its attraction. A further confusion arises here, which accepts the non-teleological nature of biological evolution, and the order it generates, but argues that humans *are* purposive and goal-directed, which places human society outside of the process of evolution. This would work as a rebuttal only if humans 'thought as one'. But their capacity to formulate ends is just one of many evolved abilities, one distributed across individuals and groups. Precisely because our capacity for telos is divided, working at cross-purposes (indeed, competing), and pregnant with unintended consequences, it becomes just one more evolved capacity contributing to the emergence of a general evolved order that cannot itself be construed as the simple outcome of human intent.

Third, social evolution is often treated as in an either/or relationship with history – explanation must take one or the other strategy. In its most polarised formulation, history deals in sequences of particulars and their causal connections, but with no underlying developmental logic, while social evolution sees all human history as the expression of underlying laws of change and development (whether teleological or

[4] Conventionally in the social sciences, 'social evolution' designates human non-biological evolution. However, while it is beyond my scope here, it is interesting to note that in the science of evolutionary biology, 'social evolution' is a term for varied sociality among all kinds of species, from termites to chimps. Moreover, as multicellular lifeforms evolved from the aggregation of unicelled organisms, there are complex historical-evolutionary questions about the distinctions and boundaries between individual organisms and 'societies' (see: Birch 2017, Bourke 2011, Rubenstein and Abbot 2017). I will return to this point in the Conclusion.

not). I would argue that whenever we identify processes of social change driven by adaptation as social entities struggle to survive, we are dealing with social evolution, but that this need not be an exhaustive account of human history. History is the basic subject matter of research into social change; evolution is a certain way of thinking about processes that affect that history, without exhaustively accounting for it. Theories of biological evolution give a certain explanatory interpretation of the natural history of life, but that history is subject to other forces besides evolution. Most comparative historical sociology distinguishes itself from history plain and simple, by searching for generalisable patterns in social change and development, and mechanisms that might account for them. By my reckoning social evolutionism is one way of doing this, one way of explaining human history (Mann 2016, cf. Runciman 2009: 192–212).

The University of Edinburgh, where I work, is known for its 'strong programme' in the sociology of scientific knowledge, which treats all scientific knowledge as socially constructed, even that which is regarded as factual and 'true' (Bloor 1976). Somewhat tongue-in-cheek, if I were to define my own approach to social evolution, it would have to be a 'weak programme'. As just suggested, I see my use of evolutionary ideas as a way of bringing systematicity to historical sociological questions, and as compatible with many other non-evolutionary comparative historical approaches. That said, my approach arises out of serious considerations of various problems in social evolutionary theory, and I will try to outline the position that emerges here. To begin with, for my purposes I would define evolution as a process of morphological change in the units of a population, due to adaptation and selection, in order to survive in specific environments. As with Darwin's investigations into the contemporary and historical diversity of life forms, I begin from a curiosity about the diversity of forms of social organisation, why these are so varied, and why and how they have changed over time. Even without a theory of genetics, Darwin was able to gain remarkable explanatory power by focusing on the question of how interactions between organisms, and sometimes whole species, and their environments, led to the 'natural selection' of better adapted over less well adapted organisms and species. As already suggested, in social evolution the telos of social actors enters into the process of adaptation, affecting morphological change. But the same imperative, to survive in a given environment, holds across biological and sociological domains.

A moment ago, I alluded to the fact that the human capacity for purely social evolution nevertheless has a basis in the biological nature of the species. It is worth anchoring the rest of this discussion in a baseline conception of human nature. I have been particularly influenced here by the work of Michael Tomasello and colleagues, using comparative studies of the cognitive and moral abilities of great apes (especially chimpanzees and bonobos) and those of human children, in order to reconstruct the key divergences of the human species from its closest primate relatives (Tomasello 1999, 2014, 2016). What distinguishes humans is a unique ability for 'joint attention', for the individual to focus on co-operative tasks with another in a way that assumes the presence of a 'mind' in the other, that needs to be understood, in order to achieve the joint task. This expanded our capacities for food-getting and predation avoidance, and was a basic prod to the development of language. Though other primates will engage in joint activities (e.g. hunting) in response to immediate stimuli, this does not seem to involve the presumption of other thinking beings with which one works and strategises. However, human children develop this ability at a very early age. In Tomasello's evolutionary hypothesis this capacity and orientation to co-operative tasks between actors first leads to feelings of mutual obligation between co-operators, and eventually this is generalised to the morality of the social group, bound by notions of collective commitment ('we-ness'), and of right and wrong that regulate behaviour within the group. This is a species-specific solution to the general pressures of competition, with other species and other members of one's own species, and the need for co-operation. With these cognitive and moral developments, humans are enabled to co-operate, and thus also to compete, at more complex and extended levels (see also Bowles and Gintis 2011). In light of our previous discussion of 'methodological individualism', a key implication here is that far from being in a zero-sum relationship, individuality and sociality are highly developed and interdependent human traits that evolve together. Human co-operation and prosocial interests, serve both individual and group survival, and whatever its roots in primate egoism, it is a defining feature of the species, and of human nature, which has made us the most powerful species on the planet, for now at least.

Let me unpack one more aspect of my 'morphological approach' – it is 'agent-centred' *not* 'information-centred'. I am interested in how social forms, especially collective actors, are changed by adaptation to their environments. I am not particularly concerned with how traits, understood as bundles of information, are inherited. A lot of social evolutionary theory has proceeded on the assumption that it must supply an analogue to genetics for society and culture, identifying the forms in which information is 'passed down' (Lewins 2015: ch 3). Most famously Richard Dawkins' concept of the 'meme' has served this purpose (Dawkins 1989, Dennett 1995, Runciman 2009). Others have found this idea too literal to be workable, and have preferred to talk more generally about social learning and the transmission of knowledge, scripts, routines, practices, and so forth (Hodgson and Knudsen 2010, Mesoudi 2011). But in both cases the basic image is of some discrete mental unit being passed from person to person, and generation to generation. There is no doubt that this happens some of the time, but much of human social and cultural reproduction simply cannot be placed into this particulate generational inheritance paradigm (Hull 2001: 110–113). Cultural stuff persists and disappears, but much of the time there is no clear, single moment of transmission. This is especially true of things like institutions (money, marriage) and organisations. Is the United Nations a single persisting thing, or has it been 'reproduced', and if so, how many times? This is probably not a meaningful question. This is not to say that nothing is transmitted through time, but simply that this may happen in many different ways, and have little resemblance to genetic transmission. At best the jury is still out on the utility of genetic analogies for understanding social and cultural transmission.

But this is not a counsel of despair, because just like Darwin, we don't need a genetic theory to make progress. Attending to patterns of morphological change, especially in major forms of institutions and organisations, with the assumption that these change, increase, decrease, persist, or disappear, because of their success or failure in adapting to environments, is sufficient to formulate an explanatory model. The philosopher of science David Hull (2001) made a conceptual distinction between 'replicators' and 'interactors', for instance, an organism has both a function of reproducing itself, and of interacting with its environment to survive. In Hull's terms I am focussing on processes of interaction, and leaving aside processes of replication.

This brings us back to the question of actors, and what I am calling an 'agent-centred' perspective. A basic question for social evolution is:

what is the unit of analysis that evolves? To invoke an analogy for limited illustrative purposes, we can say that a trait evolves (e.g. the eye), that a species evolves (badgers, eagles, etc.), or that a system evolves (e.g. a local ecology of many species and other natural forces). But the trait evolves only if it serves the survival of the organisms that make up the species, and the ecology, while subject to nonbiological forces, is significantly the outcome of the efforts of its various species to survive. I see the process of the struggle for existence among species as primary for evolution, and the transformation of traits and development of ecosystems as secondary processes, driven by that primary 'struggle for existence', as Darwin put it. In the domain of social evolution, it is forms of social organisation, collective actors, 'juristic persons', that play this same primary role. Correspondingly, various organisational 'traits' (technologies, routines, practices, rules, roles, conventions, etc.), which may be either invented or borrowed, survive, or not, because of how they serve the survival of the organisation. Similarly, changes in the wider 'ecology' of organisations (e.g. industries, or Bourdieu's 'fields') are not driven by a logic at the systemic level, but by the rough and tumble of competition among organisations as agents.

My interest in social evolution began as I studied anthropology and became familiar with what is commonly called 'cultural ecology' (Cohen 1971, Johnson and Earle 2000, Nolan and Lenski 2006, Steward 1972). Particularly in the hands of Julian Steward, this fruitful paradigm was especially good at identifying how core sets of cultural institutions helped particular societies adapt to particular ecological environments. Societies, or cultures, were seen as evolving along multiple possible paths, determined by specific society-environment relationships. But by the time I was studying many of those who had been trained in this tradition (e.g. Eric R. Wolf, Sidney Mintz) were turning to more Marxian modes of analysis and what came to be called 'political economy' (Roseberry 1988). This was largely because anthropological research was increasingly in the context of sub-groups of societies, such as peasants, deeply embedded in wider social connections of capitalism and states, and a growing awareness that these relationships had existed for a long time and often been ignored by anthropologists seeking more pristine, self-contained cultures (Wolf 1984). The cultural ecology approach worked better for more historical and archaeological cases, but as societies become more densely interactive and enmeshed in complex political and economic interdependencies, the whole society-environment relationship is overwhelmed and goes out of focus. This has bearing on my agent-centred approach. In human prehistory, before the rise of states, the primary form of social organisation was the small society that reproduced its livelihood in relation to some environment. There was a general congruence between 'society' and 'social organisation', as a collective actor. This pattern persists in some places for a long time. However, as populations grow, economic exchange relations extend, and political power centralises and becomes more stratified, various forms of organisation, economic, religious, kin-based, and so on, associated with sub-groups (social strata, lineages, locality-based) proliferate, and the cohesion of whole societies as actors loosens. So, there is a problem with trying to maintain the idea of social evolution as 'the evolution of societies', because 'societies' have lost 'actor-hood', becoming less and less the organisations that struggle to survive. Instead, this struggle falls on the myriad of forms of organisation that make up society, competing in various fields, and on the overarching organisational form, the state. It is these that have the capacity to be agents, and therefore the objects of social evolution, not societies.

The entire history of human social evolution is one of expansion of 'power to': to harness energy from the natural world, to transform the material world, to achieve ever more complex ends (agriculture, pyramids, the internet). That expansion has entailed the increase in 'power over', as hierarchies of command and obedience to achieve ends have grown and multiplied, sustained by often massive networks and organisations, political, economic, military, and ideological (Mann 1986). While the sheer performative efficacy of 'power to' in 'delivering the goods' – food, income, housing, education, healthcare – can be self-legitimating, satisfying those on the receiving end, the 'power over' necessary to achieve these ends is steadily in need of justification. Organisations need a degree of solidarity and authority in order to work – authority that must achieve legitimacy in the eyes of those subject to it. For much of human history the dual development of power to and power over was primarily embedded in forms of social organisation based on kinship and locality, though major religions have long provided an alternative organisation of power. But in the modern period, Coleman's proliferation of 'juristic persons', purpose made and legally constituted organisations, the most extreme case being the constitutional state, have provided a new context for the development of power to and over, and raised new problems for the legitimation of power and authority.

Conclusion

Let me sum up the model of competition and evolution that emerges from this discussion. Competition amongst organisations is a central factor in social evolution; it is a spur to organisations' innovations and borrowings of features such as technologies and practices, that is, 'traits', in search of advantage. Meanwhile, whole fields of organisational interaction are systemically altered by the effects of competition, as organisations imitate, differentiate, conglomerate, and so on. Certainly, social evolution is impinged upon by non-human and contingent factors – climate changes, plagues, exhaustion of resources – that don't stem immediately from competition, although they may intensify or even slacken it. Organisational competition isn't the whole story, but it is a continuous causal dynamic we can investigate.

In the modern period, by harnessing and 'domesticating' competition around the late eighteenth and early nineteenth centuries, through the florescence of organisational forms, humans in effect harnessed a basic evolutionary process, as they had done previously with the domestication of plants and animals, but this time it was social not biological evolution they were intervening in. As new populations of artificial beings were created and placed in competition with one another, dynamics of adaptation and innovation were intensified, accelerating both material and ideational productivity. Organisations, these artificial agents, are endowed by their makers with purposes and ends, with telos, but the interference pattern of aligning and contrary purposes that results is not under any higher control. The result is an unplanned and changing order, complete with unintended consequences.

Competition is not just a generative process; to the degree that it is humanly instituted, it provides an alternative mode for legitimating power distributions. In place of traditions that legitimate authority in terms of superior force, divine rule, charisma, or inherited status, the domestication of competition turns competition itself into the legitimating factor. Those who are entitled to hold and wield power are those who have succeeded in a rule governed contest of ability – a democratic election, a market, the scientific struggle among ideas. The need for supernatural or merely traditional authority is obviated. True, if rules regulating competition are broken, legitimacy can weaken (Beetham 1991: 16), and some forms of governing may become unbearable to the ruled, even if it is the result of a competitive process. Moreover, those older forms of authority are still available and functioning. No order of authority and legitimacy is pure, perfect, or guaranteed, but the relative strength of this new, formalised competition-based authority lies in its exceptional flexibility and adaptability, as it selects from a field of contenders, lowering those who have 'underperformed', and raising those who perform better. It appears to have a certain 'antifragility' (Taleb 2012) compared to more rigid authoritarian systems. The global spread of institutions of democratic politics, capitalist markets, science, liberal freedoms, while uneven and irregular, is evidence of the adaptive advantages these competition-based institutions bestow on societies.

All significant social evolutionary shifts start somewhere and then radiate if successful. In this case I have located the rise of competition's domestication, allied with the expansion of modern organisations, in the transatlantic world created by European conquest, and pivotally, the history of Britain and the US. This is a contingent historical process and does not bestow any moral worth or shame on the places and societies where it emerges. No more than the origins of agriculture in the fertile crescent, the Indus Valley, and central Mesoamerica, bestows any particular moral judgement on those place and societies. That's just the way it happened. This is a causal explanation, not an evaluation of moral worth.

PART II

The Analytic Narrative

After the next chapter (3), the following four chapters are structured around Michael Mann's well-known 'IEMP model', in which he divides the major sources of social power in human history into four main categories: ideological, economic, military, and political. Mann's approach to analysing social power is probably best known for this quadripartite division. It provides both a major frame for doing global comparative sociohistorical research, in the Weberian tradition, and an alternative to approaches (e.g. Parsons 1951) that mistakenly construct a tightly integrated notion of 'society' as the object of research. Mann's 'sources' are complexes of social networks, organisations, and institutions, each oriented to a particular mode of power as an end. These interact and combine in reality in many ways, but are analytically distinct, and are more basic than 'society', a concept Mann treats with caution, arguing that 'Human beings are social, not societal' (1986: 14), that is, requiring social relationships, but not necessarily tightly bounded community.

Mann's fourfold model is a heuristic device for purposes of comparative thinking, but it doesn't in itself capture his understanding of power, which I would describe as organisational and Weberian (1986: ch 1). I share his understanding of human beings as having a fundamental need for power, and caught in a tension between power as a collective capacity to do things versus something unevenly distributed involving patterns of domination. He also emphasises that power can be organised in ways that are either narrow or broad in their scope or 'reach', and either through explicit authority or conventionalised behaviour. Mann claims that innovations in power organisation often happen at the margins of greater power networks, 'outflanking' established practices, and spreading accordingly. It is these basic organisational dynamics, as much as the division into ideological, economic, military, and political forms, that define his approach in my view (Hearn 2012: 126–130).

Having said this, I also diverge from Mann in key ways, and don't see myself as simply 'applying' his model. My particular concern, laid out in Chapter 2, with power as agency, and the problem of creating social actors, is not that important in Mann's work. For me this problem is central to the organisational nature of human power. For another thing, I have explicitly styled my approach as a kind of 'weak evolutionism', and Mann is generally sceptical about the value of evolutionary approaches (see 1986 ch 2; 2016), believing that the multicausality of social change undermines the coherence of evolutionary theories. I on the other hand see the long-term trend towards the concentration of social power, and associated changes in the morphology of social organisation, as a manifestation of the central tendency of human social evolution, that is, adaptation in the competitive pursuit of power. Mann might regard my evolutionism as so 'weak' that it doesn't qualify as such, and I might regard his entire model as tending towards evolutionism, despite his rejection of that paradigm. Examining this disagreement with care would take us too far afield, although I think I address some issues in the previous chapter.

There are also differences that are not so much matters of disagreement as of presentation of the narrative argument. My interest here is in a specific historical transition, what I have called the domestication of competition, centred on the late eighteenth century. I am not using the four sources as a rubric that enables comparison across separate and distant historical cases. My diagnostic purposes are more holistic, seeking precisely to understand how innovations in the institutionalisation of competition, and the proliferation of corporate actors, spread across these four domains at roughly the same time, in specific countries, creating a distinctively new pattern. I identify this pattern with the emergence of liberal forms of society, and liberal democratic states, although like Mann I don't want to reify the notion of society, preferring to see this as the emergence of organisational forms that have spread, variably, around the globe.

Because I am focused on a particular process of developmental change, a time and a place, I approach the four 'sources' in a particular order: military, economic, political, and ideological ('MEPI'). These chapters trace a broad shift in the transatlantic European world of the eighteenth and nineteenth centuries, especially the anglophone part of it, from agrarian regimes ruled primarily on the principle of aristocracy, to increasingly commercial and capitalist regimes ruled on the principle of democracy. Within this frame, sequentially in chapters 4–7, I examine: (1) changes in military organisation and the rise of modern, unified, state-based militaries; (2) changes in economic organisation and the crystallisation of the modern company form; (3) changes in political organisation, and especially the unintended emergence of competitive party systems in emerging democratic regimes; and (4) the emergence of a new field of organisations engaged in competitions over beliefs and ideas, involving the weakening authority of established religions, the rising authority of science, innovation and spread in communications media, the rise of the modern university, and elaboration of civil society. In each of the four 'spheres' the opportunities for, and therefore processes of, changes in the key corporate actors are different. In the military sphere the move, in conjunction with the rise of the modern state, is away from a plurality of locally controlled militias, towards single state-linked military system. Violent competition among actors is brought under one roof and controlled. This consolidation is a precondition for, and moves in the opposite direction to, change in the other spheres. In the expanding economic sphere, a relatively small number of private and state sponsored economic 'firms' are overtaken by a proliferation of easily registered companies. In the political sphere, because positions of authority in democratic hierarchies that are competed over are by definition limited, there is some elaboration of factions and interest groups into political parties, but the number of these that any system can bear is limited. However, in the ideological sphere, the main things actors compete over are truth claims, what counts as legitimate belief and knowledge. There is no limit to the number of truth claims that can be made, leading to a hyper-proliferation of all manner of actors in civil society making such claims. Each sphere has its own dynamic of competition and actor formation, conditioned by its specific field and objects of competition. But together all share in the expansion of corporate actors and their rivalries, and influence and interact with each other (see Table II.1).

Before I follow these four chronologically overlapping histories of change in different institutional and organisational spheres, I provide a more general frame for this process in Chapter 3; there I look at the whole idea of a pivotal historical shift around the eighteenth century, and its relevant antecedent history and geopolitical context. I focus especially on problems confronted by traditional forms of authority in

Table II.1 *The directions of change across the four spheres of power processes*

From		To	
Sphere or 'source'	Aristocratic/Agrarian Regime	Democratic/Capitalist Regime	Effects on Corporate Actors
Military	Local militias →	State militaries	Consolidation
Economic	Family and elite operations →	Modern companies	Proliferation
Political	Factions →	Political parties	Limited elaboration
Ideological	Churches →	Universities/civil society	Hyper-proliferation

this period, and the 'prehistory' of the new corporate forms to be followed in the subsequent chapters. I am trying to define the historical conditions and context that triggered this evolutionary change, this shift towards modernity. Rather than the four spheres (or 'sources'), I organise this overarching discussion in terms of key changes in worldly aristocratic power structured by kinship, the social imagining of power by intellectuals in the context of religion, and the role of law in negotiating power, and creating corporate actors.

3 The Decline of Traditional Authority and the Rise of Corporate Actors

This chapter provides an overarching frame, setting up the following four chapters. It is a frame defined not so much by clear temporal limits at either end, as by a pivot point, in the late eighteenth century, around the key transatlantic revolutions of America and France. This chapter works up to this pivot point, while subsequent chapters will do the same, but also move beyond it. Broadly we are talking about what is conventionally known as the 'early modern' to 'modern' period, but I am more concerned with process than periodisation. As will become clear, the reason for a geographic focus in which Britain and the emerging US are central, is because they embody specific legal traditions and approaches to colonisation that were especially conducive to the emergence of modern corporate actors that are basic to my story – they were in the vanguard of the process I am discussing.

Let me summarise the theoretical model developed in Chapter 2. Human beings are fundamentally concerned with acquiring and sustaining power over their lives. They do this collectively, and this stimulates the development of forms of social organisation to achieve various ends. As it grows more complex, social organisation entails hierarchy: to achieve more power to do things, humans must submit themselves, or be subordinated, to forms of power over, to command-obedience relationships within organisations. Power is a matter of action, achieving ends, and this entails not just individual actors, but collective, corporate actors, or 'organisations'. As these adapt to environments and come into competition with each other, they evolve. The modern period is defined by a crucial juncture, in which the piecemeal adaptation of inherited organisational forms is increasingly overtaken by a more deliberate, 'constructivist' approach to social organisation. Human social actors take the matter in hand, adapting more by organisational design, creating the corporate actors, from firms to states, through which they pursue their ends: these proliferate and reconfigure the social world, accelerating social change. However, the entire competitive organisational process this brings about is too complex, too dispersed in its conflicting ends, to create a social world under general human control. Instead, it increases the organisational power available to humankind, as the domestication of plants and animals increased available energy, but the evolutionary process remains, as ever, contingent, open ended, and uncontrolled.

There is a further issue. Societies perennially face a basic power problem: if increasing 'power to' entails increasing 'power over', there is a constant difficulty of how to legitimate the 'power over', and how it distributes 'power to'. Therefore, this chapter is particularly concerned with the problem of authority and its legitimation. It is concerned with how power arrangements are validated, and how in this period traditional European modes of legitimating authority were weakening, working less effectively, and being openly questioned in intellectual circles. The Reformation, wars of religion and empire, market expansion, population growth, and absolutising monarchies all added strains to what has sometimes been styled 'the general crisis of the seventeenth century' (Rabb 1975). While the eighteenth century, of 'Enlightenment', especially in Britain, was in some ways a return to stability in Europe, it was also the calm before the storm that broke out in revolutions by the century's end. I tend to think that 'crisis' is too strong and narrow a term for this large period, which contained many crises and recoveries; rather, it was a peak period in a long systemic shift between one set of ways of legitimating power, to another.

The next four chapters analyse this process in terms of Mann's four sources of social power, as a way of comprehending the whole. This chapter focuses on three more specific but critical threads, three lines of institutional and organisational stress and change. First, it looks at changes in the actual worldly structures of power, in which kinship and its political elaborations in aristocracy and monarchy, give way to new states, bureaucracies, and patterns of patronage. This culminates in the Revolutions of 1776 and 1789. Second, it examines how power is imagined in intellectual discourse, with religion increasingly displaced by humanist naturalism and science – this comes into its own with the Enlightenment. Third, it looks at changes in European legal systems, that eventually enabled the rise of a world of corporate actors. Here we come up to the cusp of this shift, following its development in the various following chapters. Together these threads trace the emergence of a world in which competition moves from being a circumstance power must deal with, to being a strategy for managing and legitimating power – a naturalised form of authority.

Kinship and Worldly Power

Let us begin with the actual structures that regulate the distributions of social power. The historical shift away from kinship to other institutions as basic organising principles for modern society is a familiar refrain, but it is also profoundly true. Underpinning Henry Maine's 'status to contract' (1986[1861]), Ferdinand Tönnies' '*Gemeinschaft* to *Gesellschaft*' (2001[1887]), and Emile Durkheim's 'mechanical to organic solidarity' (1964[1893]), is the idea of the weakening and displacement of the kinship principle in social organisation. For much of human history, across all human society, kinship, in diverse ways, has provided the original organising principle, and the idiom through which power is distributed. Drawing on Marx, Eric Wolf called this the 'kin-ordered mode of production' (Wolf 1982: 88–100), where consanguineal and affinal relatedness provide an ideological structure for locating people within the group, and the ligaments along which social labour is mobilised to meet communal needs. Moral claims, on persons and resources, are made in terms of kin relatedness. As these kin-ordered systems become more extensive there are tendencies towards the centralisation of power and authority within certain privileged lineages, a pattern that anthropologists and archaeologists call 'chiefdom' (Earle 1987, Wolf 1982: 96–99). At the extreme, chiefdoms are incipient states, with a core household commanding communal resources, administering customary law, and having some quasi-military group able to enforce rules and judgements. Usually in this arrangement there has also developed a distinct class of religious specialists. The distinction between this and a simple kingdom, is mainly semantic. When one chiefdom/kingdom becomes powerful enough to conquer or otherwise subordinate others in its vicinity, one increasingly gets patterns of tribute-taking, in which resources are transferred from the subordinated to the centre in the form of tribute or rent, no longer on the basis of kinship obligations: such tribute extraction can sit atop more kin-based systems. This encapsulates the path by which the Celtic and Germanic tribes of northern Europe developed before the arrival of the Romans, and how they reconstituted power relationships after the fall of the

Roman Empire and the decline of the urban commercial life it had built up.

When considering European medieval history it is easy to forget that its complex history of monarchic, aristocratic, and feudal systems, is a particular version of this kin-ordered mode overlain by tribute-taking proto-states (Adams 1994a, Haldén 2020, Sharma 2015). But kinship seems to have suffered a peculiar fate in Europe. As Marc Bloch observed (1961: 134–142), the extensive, society-wide kinship systems of the pre-Roman period seem to have become very attenuated, except in some hinterlands such as the clan system of the Scottish Highlands. The feudal society of the Middle Ages by contrast was based on contracts of vassalage and fealty, not kin ties in the first instance. Various processes from the Roman period onwards probably helped sever the stronger ties between kinship and rulership, including waves of dynastic conquest, such as the Norman conquest of England in 1066, population migrations, the return to growth of city life detaching people from their rural communities, and ecclesiastical laws designed to limit the growth of kindred-based power and siphon off heritable wealth (Goody 1983). At any rate, by the thirteenth century, at the zenith of feudalism, something more akin to the multigenerational nuclear family, tracing its lineage bilaterally, was the widespread pattern (Macfarlane 1987: 150–151). But the catch is, as Peter Haldén (2020) powerfully argues, while integrated kinship systems encompassing all members of society from top to bottom had disintegrated, kinship remained the idiom of power and its legitimation. Kings and nobles inherited the right to rule, and claimed exclusive rights in relation to commoners on the basis of descent and 'blood'. High politics remained a matter of strategic marriages, successful biological reproduction, and the intergenerational transfer of wealth and status in aristocratic families. The history of power in Europe is the history of the slow unravelling of the hereditary principle, with the historical trend tipping decisively against it during the late eighteenth century political revolutions.

For the rest of this section I will trace the decline of this kinship-based idiom of rule, first in regard to monarchy, and then in regard to nobility, although these are of course aspects of the same system. I will leave aside the few early cases of republicanism, such as Florence and Venice, the Old Swiss Confederacy, and the Dutch Republic; these largely urban experiments in non-monarchical rule, nonetheless, were oligarchic alliances of great families, often in fierce competition with one another, not fully modern republics based on equal citizenship (Adams 1994a, 1994b, Finer 1997a: 950–1023, Spruyt 1994). Kinship was still quite central to the organisation of power. After that I will consider the strains put on the entire system by transatlantic imperial expansion and competition.

European feudalism was an effect of limited monarchical power. Kings, and sometimes queens, had to strike bargains of vassalage with other great noble families, to ensure their own rule and ability to engage in inter-dynastic war. The result was a tenuous system often riven by its own internal power struggles and competing claims to kingship. The decline of 'high' feudalism from the fourteenth to the fifteenth century enabled the growth of the absolutist monarchical states in Europe in the sixteenth century. In varying ways and to varying degrees, monarchs increasingly centralised power in their courts and in their persons. They made greater claims to tax the resources of their vassals and subjects, attempted to institutionalise effective and uniform administration of justice within their territories, sought to build larger and better technologically equipped armies and navies, and expanded their territories and resource bases through imperialism, colonialism, and support for commercial exploration and profit-seeking. Absolutist states made the monarch's will the ultimate source of law, and were characterised by the abolition in the late sixteenth and early seventeenth centuries of traditional assemblies of nobles/estates that had had a legal right to consultation in decisions. The courts of absolutist monarchs expanded into more professionalised bureaucracies, managing the exigencies of war and military development. This centralisation was a symptom of intensifying military competition between European states, and a corresponding struggle of monarchs to control powers within their domains, especially large magnates, and extract more resources from vassals and trade to support war. In some cases, especially England, this centralisation stimulated, through the resistance of nobles and commoners, the emergence of more 'mixed' forms of government in which despotic royal power was counterbalanced by what Mann would call 'infrastructural powers' (1993: 59–61), allowing the centralising state to penetrate society more indirectly through secondary institutions. In others, especially France, this centralisation tended to become intensified, resulting in a kind of power stand-off (cf. Hall 1986: 23) between monarch and nobles, leading to stagnation, and crisis. If feudal society was a complex of quasi-contracts between a hierarchic array of 'private' aristocratic families, the absolutist state was formed by raising one of these 'private' powers, the monarch, unquestionably above all others. But in so doing, the monarchy became a kind of proto-public entity in regard to its subjects, in particular, the elaboration and extension of uniform systems of law within the sovereign's territory tended to have this effect. The eventual emergence of constitutionalism was about the fuller realisation of legal distinctions between the public and the private, and identifying the state specifically with public power (Bobbio 1989: 1–21, Weintraub 1997). For the present narrative and period however, the key point here is that this growth in monarchical authority was also a symptom of disarray in the other loci of authority in early modern European society. One of these was the Church, which I deal with in the next section, the other was the aristocracy.

Regarding this period there have been debates about a supposed 'crisis of the aristocracy' (Stone 1965) around the seventeenth century, as incomes in kind declined in value and the costs of elite consumption inflated. More recent scholarship (Asch 2003, Brown 2011, Dewald 1996) has emphasised that rather than being a 'crisis' it is more a matter of transformation of the role of nobilities over several centuries, which nonetheless maintained position in many quarters, and did not really lose power until the wider establishment of the liberal constitutional state from the nineteenth century. Changes in the social functions and roles of the European nobilities are diagnostic. The roots of these nobilities were in systems of rewards for feudal military service, which generated a fractious field of local powers, monopolising force and law in their domains, and in almost constant jealous competition with one another, and for royal favour. Numbers varied across dynasties, from around one per cent to at most ten per cent of the population. There were rich and poor nobles with their own internal hierarchies of patronage, and mobility into and out of the noble class steadily confounded myths of ancestral entitlement and inherited abilities. But as the art of warfare in particular was transformed in the 'military revolution' (Roberts 1967, Rodgers 1995) of the fifteenth and sixteenth centuries, relying more on professionalised armies, navies, and gunpowder armaments, the relationship of these nobilities to military service changed (Storrs and Scott 1996). Some drifted away from the past military roles of their families, but a large proportion moved into a new professionalised caste of military leaders, trained at new academies, and appointed within the expanding bureaucracies of military office (navies, not part of the feudal inheritance of noble custom and practice, were more demotic in their recruitment). This strong association of the 'aristocracy' with military leadership in Europe persists up to World War One. Meanwhile, other nobles secured their futures by moving into the new administrative offices associated with bureaucratic and legal expansion ('*noblesse de robe*'), which was also a new route into noble status for aspiring non-nobles. At the same time the growing importance of court as a focus of royal patronage stimulated a movement of the richer nobles into the towns, and the acquisition of more urbane behaviours and values, mixing with new literati and merchant classes, and generally shedding a more martial habitus for one more 'civilised' (Elias 1994).

So, while on the one hand, with absolutist centralisation nobilities were losing their old powers and claims to participation in politics, they were also retooling themselves, finding new ways to win royal favour and perform valued social functions. At the same time there was a winnowing of the noble class, the richer being more able to secure positions, the poorer declining into obscurity. This was a process of adaptation and subordination to a larger and differently stratified political system, one in which their traditional distinctive claims to power and authority – local monopolies of violence, dependence of monarchs on their supply of order, enforcement, and military service, mixed with ideologies of a naturally and divinely stratified social order – was being undermined. It is clear that their roles and claims to inherited status were being called into question and satirised in the sixteenth century by figures such as Erasmus, Thomas More, and Machiavelli (Dewald 1996: 33–36). As Dewald observes, the German poet Nicodemus Frischlin:

> Described the nobles as impious blasphemers, and complained that 'the most ignorant and crudest little nobles … puffed up with incomprehensible madness about their ancestry', wanted to be given preference over the learned and competent. (Dewald 1996: 34)

This sceptical trend accelerated in the seventeenth and eighteenth centuries, as egalitarian Christian sects and Enlightenment values further eroded beliefs in this stratum's inherited right to rule.

The present story is of course often told in terms of the rise of the modern bourgeoisie displacing the power of the noble elites. While there is some truth to this, it needs to be qualified. Commercial and proto-industrial forms of capitalism were growing. The rising class of merchants, traders, and adventurers increasingly became an alternative source of revenue for the crown, in some cases inter-married with urbanising and civilising nobilities, and generally vied with the nobilities for social and political influence. This contributed to the erosion of noble power, and introduced a new line of dependency for the monarch. The effects on widespread social understandings of authority are more equivocal however. Kings and nobles were traditional holders of recognised, legitimated authority, and as their powers came into question, so did their authority. The rising merchant class enjoyed no such traditional recognition, and so their increasing powers were more anomalous within the traditional power system, a disruptive element, but not an immediate and direct challenger for recognised authority. Ideological efforts to validate this emerging class's status, such as Bernard Mandeville's famous *Fable of the Bees* (1989), which celebrated their industriousness and productivity, did not so much anoint them as naturalise them. However, we might view Weber's *The Protestant Ethic and the Spirit of Capitalism* (2002) as an argument not just for the role of religious ideas in shaping economic behaviour, but also at least implicitly as one about a search for personal and public legitimation of this anomalous power position by this emerging class (Poggi 1983). Like the nobles before them, the merchants were doing the Lord's work, now with an emphasis on industry rather than warfare, and entitled to their position because of this sacred purpose. Broadly, the linked rise of the merchant class and stringent Protestant religion, signalled weaknesses in the inherited system of power, authority, and its legitimation.

There was a broader North Atlantic and imperial context to these changes regarding who holds power, and how (Hearn 2009). It was not just that the *ancien régime* was entering decline in Europe, it was being put under strain and at some points torn apart because of the way its major players, Spain (as part of the Habsburg Empire), France, and Britain, had, through their rivalries, globally extended the field of contest. Clashing empires sought to capture territories and extract wealth to support wars both at home and abroad, and they did this in different ways, with different colonising strategies derived from their European 'constitutions' (in the sense of the overall composition of social power, before constitutions were written down). To put it in schematic and exaggerated terms: Spain's New World dominions resembled feudal spoils of war, an attempt to transplant the European manorial social order; France's empire was an agrarian-extractive bureaucracy, with relatively few personnel at the top; while Britain's North American colonies took the form of an alliance of small, commercially based polities: the significance of this difference will be developed below. In their struggles for imperial dominion Britain eventually pulled ahead, defeating France in the Seven Years War (1756–1763) and driving both the British and French imperial economies into debt. Imperial overstretch 'snapped' in the two defining revolutions of the late eighteenth century, which set on course the formation of modern nation states. The British Americans, through war, seceded from the British Empire, creating a novel and fractious political experiment in the US. The French overhauled their stagnating polity through violent revolution, instituting a new constitution and social order, albeit one that preserved many aspects of what had gone before (Tocqueville 2011). Both revolutions drew on the pool of new and radical ideas (republicanism, democracy, popular sovereignty, liberty) that had been accumulating over the long weakening of the European power system, putting these into action in hitherto impossible ways (Palmer 1959). In particular, the US and France created the modern constitutional state. Much was contingent and accidental in these major events; there is no whiggish argument of political destiny here. The point is that it was the imperial arena of competition in this period that pushed the old regimes to the point of fragmentation and collapse, thereby creating new niches in which new social and political forms could develop.

This section has been about how the real world organisation of power relied on the kinship principle to define groups of actors in families and lineages, and their associated clients, as the key carriers of social power. These dynastic/clientelistic nodes operated across an institutional range, organising warfare, administering domains and justice, attempting to control and exploit production and trade, and enforcing ideological coherence through support of religion. But as these last two indicate, these areas were somewhat less under their control, being more in the hands of separate specialised actors, merchants and traders on the one hand, and the clergy and the Church on the other. The former tended to develop within its own non-aristocratic family lines, creating a shadow kin-network of power.

The latter, while it had become interdigitated with aristocratic family networks, nonetheless had its own separate, non-kin-based principles of service and promotion, ensconced in the institutions of the church. It was a separate kind of organisation, with more of the features we associate with modern bureaucracy. With the great extension of the system under conditions of imperial competition and colonialism, which included the bureaucratic expansion of absolutising states, the kinship and inheritance principle of rulership, monarchy, and aristocracy, became ever more a set of elite kin-based nodes within an expanding network of new nobilities, appointees, clients, self-governing colonists, and mercenaries. Expanding educated middle classes, either from outside or the lower marginal reaches of the aristocratic systems, supplied further personnel. The elite familial nodes were diminishing in ratio to the wider personnel of the rival imperial systems, which were getting too big for narrow kin-based rule to provide adequate authority and legitimacy.

To close the circle of this part of the argument, with the revolutionary emergence of anti-aristocratic constitutional states, the kinship principle was finally broken. The comprehensively kin-ordered society had been long gone, but kinship had endured as an increasingly dubious principle of power and hereditary rulership. The new constitutional states, soon to be imitated across the globe (Armitage 2007), abandoned the idea of a heritable right to rule. True, stable property regimes in increasingly capitalist economies afforded new ways to pass on power across generations, without the burden of formal rulership. And while espousing human equality and the right of the people to govern themselves, emerging elites often saw themselves as having demonstrated a natural right and talent for leadership, and saw much human inequality, between men and women, slaveholders and slaves, as naturally based. Despite their founding constitutional moments, new institutions of democracy that could replace traditional systems of aristocratic rule and manage the distribution and transfer of political power would take shape gradually and experimentally, as we will see in Chapter 6.

Religion and Imaginary Power

This section takes up another angle of how power worked and was changing in this European system. Power works not only according to its actual distribution among organised, flesh and blood actors, as important as that is. It also operates according to how people imagine it works, what they think power is, its ultimate ground. In the medieval world the Christian religion was central to these questions, explaining and endorsing the system of social stratification according to God's plan. I would go further and make the general claim, that all religions, understood as belief in supernatural forces and beings operative in the natural world, are ultimately discourses on power (Asad 1983, Hearn 2012: ch 8). This works in various ways. Responding to normal human anxieties and uncertainties about the limits of our natural powers, religions provide techniques to harness supernatural forces through magic, and the means to appeal for the intervention of supernatural agents. Religion provides comprehensive explanations of human fates and fortunes, tracing these back to the highest powers that be. It also provides supernatural justification for given social orders, endorsing distributions of human power by locating them in a larger cosmic order. When societies are larger and more complex, one often encounters a distinct division of labour between specialists in religious knowledge and practice, and specialists in political leadership, with the former having a clear role in validating the latter, but at the same time maintaining a clear distinction between the other-worldly and this-worldly powers of the two groups. Because religion is so concerned with power, it inevitably becomes an institutional arena through which social power is contested and struggled over. Contending appeals are made to supernatural actors, and contending claims made to understand the right relationship between persons, society, and the supernatural order.

Medieval Christianity was one variant of this general pattern. The church spanned a vast array of kingdoms and principalities, providing an overarching normative order (Mann 1986: ch 10), bolstering and sometimes challenging monarchical authority. Popes and kings ruled over separate but coinciding domains, commanding distinct organisational hierarchies, each with its own traditions of law (see next section). Christianity, syncretised with traditional folk religion, provided a supernatural and cosmological account of the powers that lay behind and validated, or challenged, the worldly powers of kings, nobles, and other people in positions of superiority. It supplied a cast of supernatural agents, the ultimate one being God, but served by angels and interceding saints, and perverted by demons and witches, with an unofficial supporting cast of sprites, fairies, ghosts, and poltergeists, and supernatural forces, curses, second-sight, and so on. This system, with its various internal tensions, evolved along with feudalism from the fall of the Western Roman Empire up to the early modern period.

Given that the actual structures of worldly power and its transmission were coming under severe strain, as discussed above, it is not surprising that traditional and authorised ways of imagining power and its supernatural actors were as well. From about the sixteenth century European Christianity entered into a series of religious crises. The entire centre of power in Europe was shifting northward in this period, as the flow of trade across the Atlantic increasingly overtook that flowing through the Mediterranean. Dissenting religious tendencies eventually broke forth in the Reformation, which took hold especially in Northern Europe, where commercial cities and their growing merchant classes were becoming more powerful, and a counterweight to church and crown. Protestantism appealed especially to these groups, and spread through social networks of commerce and literacy. This dovetailed with the growing geopolitical power of northern states, with imperial projects and sharpening visions of national sovereignty, abetted by rather contingent events such as Henry VIII's break with Rome (1534), which opened up further possibility for the growth of national churches. The Protestant-Catholic conflict and its relations to sovereignty was central to a series of wars in the sixteenth and seventeenth century. A series of rebellions and wars around these issues erupted across Europe in the early sixteenth century across the Holy Roman Empire, the British Isles, Scandinavia and the Baltics, the Low Countries, and France. The most lengthy and lethal of these, running into the seventeenth century, were: the French Wars of Religion (1562–1598); the Eighty Years' War in the Low Countries and the Holy Roman Empire (1568–1648); the Thirty Years' War in the German lands of the Holy Roman Empire (1618–1648); and the War of the Three Kingdoms (England, Scotland, Ireland), including the 'English Civil War' (1639–1651). The last was preceded by the Tudor conquest of Ireland, violently imposing Protestant rule on that Catholic country. The Peace of Augsburg (1555) first articulated the principle *cuius regi*, *eius religio*, that the ruler chooses the religion that subjects or citizens must follow, and that this must be respected by external powers. This principle was further codified by the Peace of

Westphalia (1648) at the end of the Thirty Years War, which further endorsed state sovereignty over territories, borders, and domestic affairs. The key point for this discussion is that by the end of this period of international conflict, principles of religious toleration and state sovereignty were much more established, and the population of religious and political actors, churches and states variously competing with each other, had permanently expanded.

In the late seventeenth and early eighteenth centuries the intensity of religious wars subsided. Britain saw a period of political stabilisation stimulated especially by the new settlement of powers between King and Parliament, limiting the former and empowering the latter, agreed in the Glorious Revolution (1688–1689). It was the age of what came to be known as the 'Enlightenment', when science and reason supposedly confronted religion and irrationality, but the process was more mixed than this suggests. Some historians have emphasised the transitional nature of this period, how despite our retrospective search for a great confrontation between 'religion' and 'science', many key figures of the emerging scientific view, such as Newton, Boyle, and Bacon, argued compatibility, and sought to resolve the conflicts between these two worldviews (Henry 2008, Wootton 2016). For them the careful study of the natural world was a window into the divine order. This is true, but it shouldn't obscure the fact that there were deep tensions, raging debates, and associated factions around this shift. The entire Christian religious view of the world was facing sceptical challenges. The Enlightenment has also often been misrepresented as a unified 'project', a dogmatic programme of rationalisation and domination that incubated in Europe and then spread out across the globe (for critiques of this idea see: Robertson 2020: 769–780, Schmidt 2000, Wokler 1998). As Vincenzo Ferrone (2015) has shown, confusion results when we view a complex historical process through a philosophical lens, retrospectively finding coherence and purpose that was not there originally. The Enlightenment was a field of debates and positions, pulling in many directions. It was an emergent openness to the exploration of conflicting and contending ideas, aided by conditions of peace, prosperity, civility, literacy, information flow, and increased curiosity about the natural world – not a 'project'. In regard to how this process interacted with traditions of religious thought, there is a 'high' story of theological dispute, and a 'low' story of popular belief in magic. I take the low story first.

This is a period also known for the 'decline of magic' (Thomas 1971). As Michael Hunter (2020) observes, lively debates flourished between the time of the Restoration (1660) of the monarchy in Britain and about 1750, by which point the case against beliefs in magic and witchcraft had largely been won, at least in educated, literate society. From this point the fascination with magic and the supernatural receded to the domain of arts, populating poetry, and novels with ghosts and spirits, rather than real life (despite occasional revivals of supernatural beliefs among the literati ever since). Much of this transformation involved subjecting famous cases to scrutiny in disputing publications, such as John Wagstaffe's *The Question of Witchcraft Debated* (1671), which systematically challenged the veracity of witchcraft beliefs. On the sceptical side were urban 'freethinkers', deists, and denizens of coffee houses, labelled 'scoffers' by their opponents, including a considerable number of medical doctors who sought more naturalistic and psychological explanations for people's claims to supernatural experiences. The sceptics were inclined to seek evidence, and alternative explanations. Among the believers defending such supernaturalism there were, not surprisingly, a large number of clergy, but also other 'philosophers'. What Hunter shows is that on this side, it was not so much a gullible desire to believe in the uncanny that drove apologies for magical beliefs, but a strong sense that the more fundamental ideological infrastructure of Christian beliefs would also be challenged. Hunter summarises the dramatic shift in dominant views over the period in question with two quotes:

> On the one hand, we have John Edward's 1695 condemnation of 'the denial of *Dæmons* and *Witches*', on the grounds that 'besides that this is an open defiance to unquestionable History, Experience and matter of Fact, and so introduces the worst sort of Scepticism (which is the high-way to Atheism) it is evident that this supplants the belief of *Spiritual Beings* or *Substances*'. On the other, we have Conyers Middleton's confident view in 1749 that 'the belief of witches is now utterly extinct, and quietly buried without involving history in its ruin, or leaving the least disgrace or censure upon it'. (Hunter 2020: 168)

Evident in Edward's complaint is that the belief in '*Dæmons* and *Witches*' is of a piece with the essential beliefs in '*Spiritual Beings* or *Substances*', and that tearing at the one thread will threaten the entire fabric. This points us towards the 'high' story, the more philosophical dispute that was at stake here. The entire Christian belief system was seen as being under threat from a new brand of philosophical scepticism and naturalism, that tended towards atheism, embodied in figures such as Thomas Hobbes, Baruch Spinoza, and latterly David Hume.

Here again we have to challenge the cliché of scientific rationality opposing religious irrationality. Church authorised Christianity had always sought rational coherence, especially since the infusion of Aristotelean philosophy into theology by St Thomas Aquinas (1225–1274). What was being challenged by the sceptics was not just a jumble of supernatural beliefs, but an integrated mode of explanation, in which any belief in causation required an ultimate source, an ultimate cause, in the will of God, and correspondingly, the human capacity for freewill, for choice, was grounded in that same ultimate source of will. This was seen as providing an account of the world that encompassed the new materialist theories of 'matter and motion' as the key to causation, associated with figures like Newton and Bacon, and the more dangerous Hobbes, while preserving the divine as the final animating source, and endowing humans with will and purpose, rather than leaving them as mere machines. The Christian study of this encompassing, compatibilist system, was called 'natural religion', and was taught as such in universities. It was not really science, empiricism, and the investigation of nature that was threatening, as long as these were resolved with some version of Christian doctrine. But there was in the new trend a refusal to take this further step, which brought about charges of 'atheism' against those who claimed to be believers in God of some sort. Hobbes disdained theological disputation as a dangerous waste of time, but did not deny God. Spinoza's abstract and pantheistic philosophy attempted to resolve God and nature, but in a rather unchristian way. Even the great 'atheist' and sceptic David Hume allowed for the possibility of God, although he registered his indifference to that possibility.

The case of Hume is instructive. Hume first published his *Treatise of Human Nature*, 'an attempt to introduce the experimental method of reasoning into moral subjects' (subtitle) in 1739, and wrote it while these controversies were very much in the air. Paul Russell (2008) has argued very persuasively that assessments of Hume have lost sight of this context over the years, and failed to appreciate the degree to which the *Treatise* was explicitly conceived as a project of 'irreligion', that is, as a direct challenge to then prevalent rational proofs of God, the soul, and associated supernatural ideas. To the idea of God as the ultimate and necessary cause of all causes, Hume replied we have no experience of causation itself, only the habit of expecting new sequences of events to resemble those we have experienced in the past (1978: 69–179). To the idea of the 'immateriality of the soul', that is, some sense of being and personal identity that exists before birth and persists after physical death, Hume suggested (never quite to his own satisfaction) that all we have is a string of experiences, with no evidence of a subject watching over these experiences (1978: 232–252, 1985: 590–598). To the idea of miracles, Hume argued that the testimony of our senses must always outweigh the word-of-mouth testimony of authorities (1975: 109–131). Later philosophers have read Hume's arguments as sceptical analyses of concepts of causation, identity, and evidence, failing to grasp that these were angles of attack on core ideas of natural religion.

There were multiple forms and varying degrees of religious belief among those who engaged in the Enlightenment's arguments. Some were Christian apologists seeking compatibility with the new scientific naturalism, some were deists preferring a distant God who sets the world in motion and stands back, but still providing some moral ground, and others, like Voltaire, were iconoclastic atheists. But the effect of these debates in this context was that attempts to explain not just the workings of nature, but society and human behaviour, increasingly dispensed with the supernatural, finding human agency, treated as yet another natural force, as sufficient unto itself. Society might be established by a 'social compact' among individuals seeking a solution to the dangers of anarchy and ways to meet shared needs (Hobbes). Moral order might be the result of myriad self-interested actors coordinating with each other, each to meet their own ends (Mandeville). Or it might be an effect of our natural sympathy and susceptibility to the judgements of others, as we seek their approval, and avoid their disapproval (Smith). But there is no necessary role here for God or other spirits; they can be invited to watch from the stands, in deistic fashion, but the explanation works fine on its own, needing only natural human beings to animate it. Which brings us back to our key theme of crises: the rivalries of supernatural beings for our faith and our souls had been, not eliminated (not to this day), but displaced, marginalised, rendered non-essential. Instead, the competitions among human actors, over earthly power and ideas, increasingly took centre stage.

Law and Constructed Power

From kinship and religion, we turn to law, as a third dimension of power and its legitimation. This section differs from the previous two. Those were concerned with showing how previous systems and practices were unravelling, becoming less able to provide legitimation for the given distributions of power, with law it is more a question of how this field grew, in ad hoc ways, to supply new terms of legitimation, including new conceptions of the social actor. As modern law gets assembled out of various sources, it develops an institutionally autonomous identity grounded in the practice of lawyers and judges trained to address social conflict over rights and duties, as a practical matter. The change monarchy undergoes in the modern period is substantially a shift from the 'rule of persons' (mostly men) to the 'rule of law', and thus to a degree, the rule of those who make law. Lawyers and judges increasingly shape the terms of social order, and parliaments eventually emerge as true legislatures, not just mediators between monarchs, nobles, wider populations, and resources. Law and the state transform together, and kinship and religion increasingly become marginalised and privatised together. In what follows I first sketch the general foundations of European law, and then look more specifically at the emergence of 'juristic personality', as a key factor of the emergence of the modern corporate actor. The idea of juristic personality became a particular focus of attention and debate among some legal scholars, historians, and political theorists from about 1890 to 1920, and I look at this discourse to bring the underlying issues more fully in focus. The most basic framing point to make here, which the following aims to substantiate, is that a world which values the autonomy and integrity of individuals; a civil social sphere in which people are free to self-organise as they see fit; and a form of state which is limited in its powers and aims to secure both individuality and relatively autonomous forms of social organisation, will be one in which the idea of the person expands to serve multiple duties, linking the three levels of individuals, groups, and states. And such a world is one primed to proliferate competition between these various kinds of 'persons'.

Asking 'what is law?', Brian Tamanaha suggests there are three main answers: (1) an evolving body of inherited rules and customs, studied through 'historical-sociological jurisprudence'; (2) decisions and commands emanating from the state, studied through 'legal-positivism';

and (3) the embodiment of universal morality and justice, associated with theories of 'natural law' (2017: 38–39). Legal theorists have variously sided with these approaches for centuries. For our purposes we are more concerned with the first two, as a product of both tradition and the state, leaving the ultimate grounding of law in moral theory to one side. I agree with Tamanaha that the study of law requires a realism grounded in the various social sciences, that treats law as evolving ways of actually managing social relations, not as a set of justified abstractions about how people ought to behave. For the present discussion I am viewing law as an outcome of various actors' efforts to stabilise their power relations, often in regard to property claims, and wider communal efforts to manage inevitable social conflict. Whatever its claims to antiquity, law is continually being constructed through these processes. All societies, no matter how small, have at least loose and flexible shared rules about how people should conduct themselves in regard to one another, enforced by informal social sanctions. However, as societies become larger and more complex, the question of who decides and who enforces the application of the rules arises, and oral custom increasingly becomes written law, and is more closely associated with the power of political rulers, and bodies of legal specialists. Moreover, at least until a more secular age, law tends to be somewhat caught in a rivalry between religious and political authority, and their respective claims to legitimacy.

The history of European law presents a very complicated overlay of factors shaping law over the long-term.[1] First, various local Celtic traditions of customary law were overlain by Roman law as the empire expanded northwards. Roman dominion brought with it procedures of judge-led investigation of cases, professionalised jurists, and central legislation from Rome. Roman law was particular to urban based communities (*civitas*), and Roman citizens had recourse to the *ius civile* (civil law) of Rome through their urban governments. But with the scope of the empire, it became necessary to develop a second body of law that applied to foreigners and non-citizens, and their interactions with citizens, across the empire, the *ius gentium* (law of peoples). This created a more 'universal' field of law, planting the idea of a 'natural' basis for law, and a new space of legal innovation. Meanwhile,

[1] The next couple of paragraphs draw on Grossi (2010), and especially Herzog (2018).

Christianity became a permitted religion in Rome in 312 CE, and by 383 was the official religion of the empire. From an intermittent persecutor of the Christians, the empire became a persecutor of pagans, and a promoter of the Church. As with Judaism, Christianity regarded God as the ultimate source of law, not citizens and their emperors. Over the fourth and fifth centuries these religious and civil principles converged, and the Church Christianised the empire, and the empire Romanised the Church, not least in endowing it with a territorial administrative structure that mirrored the political administration, and with Latin and the capacity to cultivate its own body of 'canon' law. The Church was 'legally constructed as a corporation (*universitas*), a status that in Roman law was held by the state and other public bodies, allowing them to own property, receive gifts, and make contracts' (Herzog 2018: 41). After the dissolution of the Western Roman Empire (c. 395–476 CE), with the aid of new monastic orders and missionaries, Christianity gradually spread throughout most of Europe, both preserving and bringing the legal and organisational traces of Rome with it. With the empire gone, the canon law of the Church continued to evolve in a dispersed and piecemeal way, despite attempts at greater codification under Charlemagne's reign (768–814 CE). It enjoyed a legal-religious monopoly that ranged over the limited local spheres of customary law commanded by kingdoms and other communities. The decline of Rome was also associated with the spread of Germanic peoples out of the areas of the Rhine and the Danube, to the north, west and south, bringing with them their own traditions of unwritten, customary, kin-based law: these may have merged to some degree with local law-customs that predated the Roman invasion. Tamar Herzog sums up the legal world of Europe around 1000 CE: 'Made of fragments of Roman, Germanic, local, or canon law, the legal universe that contemporaries inhabited was highly segmented, multivalent, and compound and reflected a great variety of norms that originated in multiple orders' (2018: 57).

From the twelfth century, with feudalism at its limit and monarchies becoming more powerful, Europe saw a revival of scholarship and growth in universities, driven partly by the rediscovery or revival of Roman texts, especially the *Corpus Juris Civilis* of Justinian. This led to the development of 'Scholastic' hermeneutic methods that sought the 'correct' reading of historical Latin legal documents, and to a systematisation and codification of the patchwork of Roman,

Germanic, local, feudal, and canon law. This process has often been portrayed as a recovery of the systematic law of Rome, but the outcome was more synthetic than that suggests. The result was the *ius commune*, or 'common law', providing the basis for what has come to be known as the continental 'civil law' tradition, in which the emphasis is on comprehensive, rationally consistent codification of laws, their applications, and designated punishments. Judges investigate cases and reach decisions, largely through the application of the relevant laws. But of course, there is also the English 'common law' tradition, not to be confused with the *ius commune*, which was also passed on to Britain's various colonies. Its origins are from about the same period as that of the *ius commune*, but their paths diverge. In a bid to consolidate their power over their Norman vassals, the Plantagenets, from the initial reign of Henry II (1154–1189 CE), imposed a unified system of royal courts across all feudal jurisdictions (i.e. a 'common law'). Gradually, and increasingly, this overarching legal venue and process brought appeals to kings from plaintiffs unhappy with local decisions, and 'writs' of decisions issued by the monarch or an agent began to establish precedents and a new core body of law. In the seventeenth century, with the consolidation of Protestantism and increasing subordination of the monarch to parliament, other legal systems (e.g. canon, customary) in England became subsidiary to the evolving common law, which sought consistency through the comparison of present cases to legal precedents, rather than through systematic codification of the whole body of law. Today these 'civil law' and 'common law' traditions, along with Islamic and customary legal traditions, provide the main broad types of law in the world.

Much more can be said about the expansion and consolidation of these two legal traditions with the growth of the modern state, however, from this point I am more concerned with the slow emergence of 'juristic personality', that is, the idea of the artificial person in law.[2] But before I re-enter history, let me emphasise the continuing relevance of

[2] I mainly use the term 'juristic personality' because this is the term used by Weber as translated in Roth and Wittich's edition of *Economy and Society* (1978), and Weber is central to my theoretical framework. This is a common translation of the German term. However, there are multiple terms in English which mean the same thing: 'juridical', 'jural', 'legal', combined with 'personality' or 'personhood'. The French say '*personne morale*'. This variability can make searching the relevant literature a challenge.

this idea up to the present time of writing this book. Corporations today are constituted as juristic persons subject to specific rights and duties. In the US, in various major cases brought against them, corporations are known to invoke, as legal persons, various Amendments to the US Constitution, such as the Fourth Amendment against unlawful seizure of property, or the First Amendment which guarantees 'freedom of speech'. In 2010 a US Supreme Court decision found in favour of the conservative non-profit corporation Citizens United and against the Federal Election Commission (FEC), upholding the former's claim that in restricting its right to spend its money on a partisan election advertisement, the FEC was interfering with Citizens United's First Amendment right to free speech. The case, which struck down previous contrary decisions, rested on and endorsed the premise that Citizens United was a person in law, with the same rights to free speech, here expressed as money spent supporting a political campaign, as any other 'natural' person. Defenders see it as protecting constitutionally enshrined rights of citizens, however organised into larger bodies, whereas critics see it as abusing the idea of juristic personality in order to ensure the power of wealthy corporations to distort the democratic political process.[3] For the moment my point is simply that the idea of juristic personality has turned out to be of continuing consequence for the workings of money and politics in one major liberal democracy, thus justifying what might seem a somewhat arcane series of historical threads in what follows.

But before picking up the historical thread, I outline some of the main conceptual issues. Juristic personality is a legal property of incorporated organisations, most familiar here is the company, but trusts and incorporated charities (charitable companies) also have legal personality. Unincorporated associations, whether charitable or not, lack juristic personality. Juristic personality is often summed up as the capacity to 'sue and be sued', and is associated with 'limited liability' and 'entity shielding', that is, the protection of the members' private assets from actions against the corporation (as a legal person), and the protection of the corporation's assets from actions against the member as a private person. Together, these features enable incorporated organisations to be coherent social actors, with rights and duties, in

[3] I cannot go into the complexities of this case here. See: Bowie (2019), Brown (2015: 151–173), Gerken (2014), Padfield (2014, 2015), Winkler (2018).

their given fields of action. As we will see, the idea of juristic personality converges from multiple strands in European law, and only eventually becomes especially associated with the modern economic corporation. The medieval world generated forms of juristic personality for its own needs, which then became available for new purposes, particularly as commerce expanded and the corporation developed. The modern corporation isn't simply the outgrowth of earlier organised economic enterprises, but a coalescence of these with the principle of juristic personality. Broadly, its rise corresponds to a shift from land and other 'immovables' (churches, towns) as the key form of property and power, to other forms of property such as investable capital, ships, trade goods, and so on. But the earliest forms of juristic personality developed for other purposes, such as asserting ecclesiastical control of church properties against landed patrons, enabling nobles to transfer lands to inheritors without suffering heavy royal taxations at the point of transfer, clarifying the rights and statuses of burghs and guilds, and to deal conceptually with the growing distinction between the individual person of the monarch, and the 'office' of the monarch as sovereign. We can abstract three main forms that juristic personality takes, and purposes it serves, to help guide us through the historical narrative that follows. First, and most familiarly, it unifies communities of individual real persons into corporate actors, with legal standing to hold property, trade, govern, and so on. Second, by creating the 'fiction' of a legal person, the distinction between an 'office' and the succession of actual persons that occupy it, could be better conceptualised, and rights and duties could be attached to the office itself, as a 'person'. Third, allowing groups ('trusts') to act as caretakers that can hold and transmit property over time, on behalf of another. These three problems/functions overlap: the organisation needs to not only coordinate the actions and resources of its members, but also have legal continuity over time, beyond the individual lives of its members. The 'owners', between which something is transferred in trust, form a kind of collective being over time. Although historically, the legal precedents for addressing these problems are distinct and situation-specific, they converge on the basic logical problems of juristic personality: collective action and continuity over time. There isn't one genealogy of the modern corporation, it coalesces out of a variety of factors.

As already suggested, Roman law provided a couple of key concepts in this evolution, that helped secure the legal status of 'corporations', in the broadest sense.[4] The idea of *persona ficta*, the granting, by the Roman state, of a fictional legal identity to allow groups/organisations a continuing identity beyond the lives of their members, was picked up by the medieval canon law, as was the closely connected idea of *universitas*, of state-constituted corporate bodies (such as the church). These legal ideas were especially reinvigorated under Pope Innocent IV (1185–1254), in the general revival of Roman legal ideas in the formation of the *ius commune*. This was a period of strong assertion of papal power and authority against the secular powers of monarchs. These two ideas were distinctive for emphasising the 'artificial' nature of *persona ficta* and *universitas*, and their dependence on a 'concession' from the law maker, whether pope or king: they were the gifts of church and state.

England, again, took a somewhat different path. The legal records around the reign of Henry III (1216–1272), including the writings of the jurist Bracton (1210–1268), show no clear concept of the 'corporation', but show that many kinds of chartered communities (*communitas*) have been long established. Originally these special grants of rights and privileges to monasteries, universities, colleges, burghs, guilds, learned and professional societies, and companies, did not entail any notion of juristic personhood. Such charters had been variously granted by monarchs, lords, and the church, without much reference to overarching law. The idea of *universitas* was present, but this was applied only to major church institutions of learning, such as Oxford and Cambridge, and sometimes large cities, such as London. The practice of royal chartering in particular grew in the thirteenth century. By the reign of Edward IV (1442–1483), the concept of the corporation now clearly exists, and is applied to various bodies, especially municipal ones, although the distinction between incorporated and unincorporated entities is still somewhat hazy. In the 1400s we find lawyers puzzling over where accountabilities lie in the relationships between 'corporations aggregate' (i.e. incorporated groups as a whole), corporate heads (Mayors, Deans, etc.), and individuals who are also members of such bodies. It is here that the idea that corporations must be made through 'concessions', the grants of monarchs or

[4] The following draws on Coleman (1990: 531–542), Gierke (1900), Harris (2018: 91–94), Maitland (1900, 2003), Seidentop (2014), Weber (1978: 705–752), and especially Pollock and Maitland (1899).

parliaments, arises more distinctly. The process of chartering had long been in existence, creating such bodies in an ad hoc way, but the legal status of such bodies was becoming a more explicit issue, as power became increasingly concentrated in the monarchy. Legal personhood gradually articulated with various chartered entities, and is in some sense a legal response to the proliferation of such bodies.

Two particular legal processes worthy of note were also happening over this same period. First, there had been growing struggles between landed lords as patrons establishing the churches on their lands, which they thus owned, and the Church, or its Bishop, over the control of those local churches and the appointment of its priest or other officer. The Church wanted to retain control at the transfer of occupancy, and through any period of non-occupancy. At this point the Church was rather ahead in its legal sophistication, and went through various devices, such as locating ownership in the 'four walls' of the individual church, or in its patron saint. But eventually they arrived at the idea of the 'corporation sole', that is, a corporation with only one member, the local priest, but one that extends over time to successive occupants of the office. This is a key moment in the articulation of the modern idea of office. It also came to be used as a way of understanding kingship, as a continuous office that transcends the individual king (as the saying has it: 'the king is dead, long live the king' (Runciman and Ryan 2003: xvi)), and this conception helps support a notion of sovereignty, whether monarchical or not, that exists as an abstract principal, and not just a practical reality. Thus, it became common to distinguish between 'corporations sole' and 'corporations aggregate', in the more conventional sense of an incorporated group actor.

The other process was the rise of the particularly English idea of the 'trust'. Here the context was secular power struggles between landed nobles and the monarch who had powers to tax and otherwise interfere at the point of transmission of lands and property from the lord to his heir (normally according to the rule of primogeniture). Additional risk of loss of control was at stake if the lord died while the eldest inheriting son was still a minor. Here the novel incorporated body of the 'trust' came to the aid of the noble in this struggle. The lord 'gave' his holdings to the trust, a body which could change its personnel over time, and which 'gave' the properties back to the heir when of age. So here, in the 'corporation sole' and the 'trust', we see two very specific law made variants of the corporation idea, connected to problems of continuity between persons, but quite distinct from the problems corporations face as economic firms.

In the age of European imperial/colonial expansion, after c.1500, royal and parliamentary chartering is extended in two new ways. First, colonies are established in conquered lands, and the British North American colonies were particularly corporate in form (Kaufman 2008). Some (Massachusetts, Connecticut, Rhode Island, New Hampshire, Maryland, Pennsylvania) were established as refuges for religious dissenters, but others (Virginia, North and South Carolina) were, from the start, conceived as economic ventures seeking revenue and commodities, gold and silver at first, but later furs, tobacco, and other commodities of growing popularity in Europe. Over time this distinction between religious and commercial bases of colonies tended to blur. Like the chartered towns of the homeland, they had economic rationales and powers of self-government, augmented by their relative distance from Great Britain. This tendency towards economic corporate enterprise tended to distinguish the British from the more top-down Spanish, Portuguese, and French colonial projects. Moreover, they brought the chartering traditions with them, appropriating those powers as needed, to establish their own townships and institutions, such as Harvard College. The other major corporate innovation in this period was the formation of the chartered long-distance trading companies such as the Dutch East India Company, the English East India Company, and the Hudson's Bay Company. Phillips and Sharman (2020) have recently dubbed these 'company-states' because of the way their powers combined those of economic firms and territorial states, with capacities for military force and territorial governance: we will come back to these issues in Chapter 5.

These developments point to a key fact, that the chartered corporation increasingly took on properties of sovereignty in practice, no matter how delegated in origin. The reciprocal point is that the emerging modern sovereign states, post-Westphalia, with the church more marginalised from struggles over sovereignty, were themselves increasingly obliged to define themselves as moral subjects with juristic personality, operating within a 'law of nations' grounded in notions of natural law. As Emer de Vattel said in 1758, at the start of his influential treatise *The Law of Nations*:

> Nations or states are bodies politic, societies of men united together for the purpose of promoting their mutual safety and advantage by the joint efforts of their combined strength.

> Such a society has her affairs and her interests, she deliberates and takes resolutions in common; thus becoming a moral person,[5] who possesses an understanding and a will peculiar to herself, and is susceptible to obligations and rights. (Vattel 2008: 67)

The modern state becomes the ultimate corporate actor, a quasi-juristic person in international law, above which any co-operative aggregations are relatively provisional and fissile, and within which the basic terms of legal corporateness have to be sought. The very notion of sovereignty now attaches to the corporate body of citizens and their state, not to monarchs transferring rule through dynastic families. My main point here is the structural parallelism between developments within state-societies and between states in the international community (cf. Meyer 2000, Meyer et al 1997). Both require a clearer understanding of the legitimate actor in law, even if the law is weak and often vaguely defined between states, and sometimes oppressively powerful within states.

By the beginning of the nineteenth century, the idea of juristic personality in regard to corporate actors, and the protection of their relative autonomy, was increasingly well established in law. An early critical case confirming this was the 1819 US Supreme Court decision in the case of *Trustees of Dartmouth College v. Woodward*.[6] Dartmouth, chartered by King George III in 1769, was reincorporated by the state of New Hampshire after the Revolution. To protect its interests in the elite educational corporation it subsidised, the state legislature sought to appoint Trustees to the College's board. With the help of lawyer and alumnus Daniel Webster, the College resisted in the courts, arguing that New Hampshire was trespassing on the Federal Government's constitutional authority over contractual obligations. The Supreme Court decision written by Chief Justice John Marshall stated:

> A corporation is an artificial being, invisible, intangible, and existing only in contemplation of law. Being the mere creature of law, it possesses only those properties which the charter of its creation confers upon it, either expressly or as incidental to its very existence. These are such as are supposed best calculated to effect the object for which it was created. Among the most

[5] Note that in French, the language in which Vattel wrote, '*personne morale*' was the cognate of juristic person.

[6] *Trustees of Dartmouth College v. Woodward, 17 U.S.* 518, 636 (1819).

important are immortality, and, if the expression may be allowed, individuality; properties, by which a perpetual succession of many persons are considered as the same, and may act as a single individual. (quoted in Vinogradoff 1924: 601–602)

Here we have a classic mature statement of the idea of corporations as juristic persons. The next major phase in the story of incorporation is the rapid multiplication of corporations after the American Revolution, in which the economic enterprise became increasingly important. We pick this up in Chapter 5, where we will start by looking at the general history of the modern company.

Before concluding, as a way of summing up this section, let me turn to the heightened scholarly attention that was paid to the idea of juristic personality at the end of the nineteenth and the beginning of the twentieth century, because the previous question of the nature of the state and its relationship to the idea of juristic personality was a key focus of that attention.[7] By this stage the principle of juristic personhood was well established, to the point where scholars were asking themselves how it came to be this way, and what was the significance. The seminal figure here is Otto von Gierke (1851–1921), the German jurist and intellectual historian whose *Das Deutsche Gennosenschaftsrecht* (*The German Fellowship Law*), published in four volumes, 1868–1913, became influential in Britain and to a degree in the US. Following German unification in 1871, work began on the construction of a unified Civil Code (*Bürgerliches Gesetzbuch*) for the new state, between 1881 and 1900. This process led to debates between 'Romanists', influenced by the jurist and historian Friedrich Carl von Savigny (1779–1861), and 'Germanists', among which Gierke was prominent. Romanists sought to place the new German legal system in the continental tradition of codified civil law, descending from Rome, while Germanists sought a more indigenous tradition, in tune with other trends towards the preservation and celebration of German culture. For Gierke the idea of 'fellowship' (*Gennosenschaft*), that is, how law deals with social bonds, was central. Gierke took a stand for what has been labelled 'reality theory', that saw various kinds of social groups as having an inherent quality of personality, expressed in collective will and actor-hood: this conception applied up to the level of the state itself. For Gierke the legal notion of juristic personality was

[7] This section draws especially on Harris (2006) and Runciman (1997).

necessitated by this underlying reality. He was highly critical of two approaches to juristic personality that were well established in the 'Roman' tradition of legal thought. Gierke rejected the 'fiction' and 'concession' theories, the entwined ideas that legal personhood was entirely an artificial legal creation, and that it is created (and revoked) entirely at the pleasure of the state/sovereign. Gierke thought that this approach failed to grasp the social realities that pre-exist the legal order. His belief in the reality of group personality might be regarded as somewhat mystical, involving the very reification of social groups that Weber later warned against (see Chapter 2). Socially and politically, Gierke was critical of increasing individualism driven by markets and liberalism, and tended towards conservatism over his lifetime.

The English legal historian F. W. Maitland (1850–1906) took a deep interest in Gierke's work, and in effect imported the terms of the Romanist/Germanist debate into Britain and anglophone scholarship. Maitland and Frederick Pollock drew on Gierke's ideas in their influential book *The History of English Law before the Time of Edward I* (1898, second edition), and Maitland translated and wrote an introduction to parts of Gierke's third volume of *Genossenschaftsrecht* in 1900. Maitland also addressed various issues of legal personhood in other lectures and papers (see Maitland 2003). Although Maitland was not given to strong programmatic argument, he clearly sympathised with a more organic account of law, that saw it evolving ad hoc in response to underlying social realities. Maitland regarded the idea of the 'corporation sole' as a nonsense that created two persons in the same body, who could not 'sue' each other in any meaningful way; but he regarded the legal institution of the 'trust' as an example of English legal resourcefulness in the face of a concrete problem. It is perhaps not surprising that for an English historian, in a powerful state with no written constitution, and a common law tradition based on the case-by-case evolution of law, the idea of a more organic approach to group personality might appeal.

Maitland and Gierke's ideas in turn influenced a group of scholars and political theorists known as the 'pluralists', prominently: J. N. Figgis (1866–1919), Ernst Barker (1874–1960), Harold Laski (1893–1950), and G. D. H. Cole (1899–1959) (see Runciman 1997). With the exception of Barker, they tended towards a kind of 'guild socialism', with strong support for trade unions and a distrust of an overly powerful state, promoting a vision of society with multiple centres of power, holding each other in check. It was in this sense that they picked up on the 'reality theory', again wanting to assert the principal of self-constitution of social groups and their interests from below. This paradigm, while not entirely absent, transferred weakly to the US, Harold Laski being the only member of the British group who spent any time there during his career. By the 1920s we find commentary in the American law journals about the idea of juristic personality, looking back on these theoretical debates with a degree of bemusement, wondering what exactly was at stake (see: Dewey 1926, Smith 1928, Vinogradoff 1924).

By the time of these debates, juristic personality in companies and other incorporated bodies had become well established and widespread. These particular debates reflect their overlapping times and places. They were part of how the forming German state was defining its constitutional and cultural identity, with and against its neighbours. And across Europe and the US, they reflected the various tensions between the growing power of industrial corporations, the counterpower being asserted by the labour movement and socialism, and the expanding power of the bureaucratic state. The point here is not to resolve an old dispute between 'reality' versus 'fiction/concession' theories of juristic personality, but rather to recognise its unresolvability. It is the dispute itself that is most indicative, and still with us in cases such as *Citizens United v. FEC*. Today, critics on the left of the overweening power of economic corporations are inclined towards a revival of 'concession theory', in the sense of 'what the state gives, the state can take away', and thus powerful corporations should be on notice not to abuse their rights as 'persons' (see Kayiklik 2019, Padfield 2014). The debate is a manifestation in the domain of professional law and social science scholarship of one of the most fundamental questions: to what degree is society a 'reality' that must be accepted on its own terms, versus to what degree is it something 'designed' and 'constructed'. It is both. The political question is how do these different conceptions affect distributions of power, and serve contestations over those distributions. In the modern world, especially liberal democracies, instead of inherited rights to rule through kinship, or supernaturally sanctioned orders of power, we have legally constituted terms of contestation that provide legitimation, with a nagging underlying uncertainty as to its ultimate moral ground.

Conclusion

This chapter has sought to trace changes in the way power is distributed among social actors, and the way 'power' and 'social actors' are understood and constituted, across three analytic themes: kinship, religion, and law. The main argument is that the distribution of power among competing kinship networks, which generated monarchical and aristocratic socio-political structures, was gradually supplanted by the constitution of major social actors, corporations, and modern states, as power-holders, through law. This process of change became acute in the imperial overstretch of Britain and France, and the two revolutions that ensued, in some ways opening the door for the fuller development of the law-based rather than kin-based way of managing power. This new context was propitious for the elaboration of the idea of the juristic person, long gestating in medieval Europe. At the same time, the supernatural terms of medieval Christianity, for making sense of the order of power in the world, was also coming under pressure. A world of belief, in which the sanctioning and challenging of real-world distributions of power were couched in terms of divine will, but also populated by an intervening array of lesser supernatural beings and forces, increasingly confronted science and scepticism. This religious tradition didn't end, but it fragmented, and its relationship to the legitimation of the order of power became looser and more indirect. Increasingly that role was relinquished to law and the modern state.

Let me review our three themes. The kinship principle grows and expands, from the organisation of small tribal societies, to monarchies based on aristocracies, until it reaches its limits in vast trans-oceanic empires. At this point the ability of the principle to justify the hereditary power of some over others weakens, no matter how much imperial 'power to' the system is delivering to some of its subjects. The principle is challenged and unravelled in a series of revolutions, most spectacularly in the British North American Colonies and France. From this point on, the state, no longer defined by a hierarchy of kinship and heredity, but rather by notions of citizenship, develops, gradually supplanting the imperial model, or at least subordinating it to the nation state form and stripping it of its kinship rationale. Empires often have pretentions to dominate as much of the world as they can. Nation states on the other hand, however hegemonic, are conceived as territorially bounded members of an international community of putative equals, but still competitors.

Religion, specifically European Christianity, does not decline in the same way as kinship. Religion is in fact rejuvenated in Protestantism, in its many varieties, although these also tend to disassociate from the old regime of monarchy and the hereditary principle of rule, emphasising communities of shared belief, rather than chains of descent. And while revivified, Christianity is also fragmented, becoming an arena of competing denominational claims to truth and the path to salvation. But with the Enlightenment there is also a redistribution of entitlement to make authoritative truth claims. Science and scepticism corral Christianity into a distinct sphere of responsibility for morality, and existential needs for meaning, increasingly excluding it from any special authority over interpreting the natural world. In the process the natural world becomes depopulated of supernatural beings and forces, and God retires from active duty, leaving only mortal human actors, alone or in concert, to intervene in the course of history and the workings of society.

Law, on the other hand, slowly consolidates and grows in authority, along with secularisation and the emergence of the nation state. The church gradually yields its legal powers to the state, and the state's power over the people is increasingly legitimated as a domain of rational shared law, not as an inherited right or divine appointment. The status of the juristic person moves from being a special grant of the monarch, to a routine provision of the law, available to all kinds of self-organised bodies. It becomes a means of managing and cultivating self-organisation in society, of fostering a private sphere of competitive activities beyond the public purview of the state. Indeed, law itself is a mode of domesticating society, so it is not surprising that it should be central to the domestication of competition, partly through the institution of juristic personality. It is not that every organised body takes this form, many are too small, ephemeral, and modest in their aims and risks (clubs, associations, minor charities) for it to be worth it. But the larger players, with some aim towards permanence and power are almost always organised this way, and this sets the dominant contours and dynamics of social power within which unincorporated bodies must operate. Juristic personality also addresses one of the puzzles of social evolutionary theory raised in the previous chapter. How do social entities persist over time, if they do not reproduce over generations, as species do? As we've seen, juristic personality allows social entities to persist, despite changes in personnel, organisation, and practices. These social actors are potentially immortal, sustained by law, with no need to reproduce (unlike dynasties).

Just as the decline of the dinosaurs created space for mammals to expand and thrive, the weakening of kinship and religion as organising principles created space for corporate-legal form to develop and elaborate. To say that these changes illustrate the principle of social evolution is not to say that they represent any moral improvement, or inevitable developmental logic. It is to say that the given circumstances were favourable to the growth of the modern, constitutional, law-governed state as an actor on the world stage, and to the proliferation of legally constituted corporate actors within states. This tended to displace kinship and religion, in many ways relegating them to a more 'private' sphere. The argument is that this new model was more adaptive, more able to take advantage of opportunities, more able to cultivate concentrations of social power, and therefore survived and came to dominate large parts of the globe.

4 From Militias to Militaries

The next three chapters are concerned with new forms of competition and corporate actors emerging primarily within the nation state as it consolidates: they are about the expansion and elaboration of competition. The narrative of this chapter moves in a somewhat contrary direction, in that it is about the placing of limits on martial competition, and the unification of military actors within the nation state, even as states themselves are becoming more coherent and distinct military actors. This military process is, in fact, something of a precondition for the others that follow.

I pursue the topic in three main parts. First, I look at the *status quo ante* of 'feudal' militarism in Europe, and how this was highly fractious and often destabilising, and yet had 'proto-domesticated' aspects to its social organisation of competition among elites. Second, I examine three ideas central to the sociological and historical literatures on militarism and the rise of the modern state: the 'bellicist thesis' that war is central to modern state formation, the more specific idea of the 'fiscal-military state' as a new way of financing and prosecuting war, and the associated idea of a 'military revolution' in technologies and organisations of warfare. These form a closely related package of ideas. I also explore various criticisms that have been made of them. Thirdly, I look at some ideas that have been central in the sociology of modern militaries, especially in liberal democracies, as they have stood after these transitions, namely the professionalisation and bureaucratisation of armed forces, and 'civil-military relations' which supposedly keep modern militaries subordinate to civil government. At the end I relate this long narrative to the social evolution of power and the modern state as a corporate actor.

Feudal Militarism[1]

The broad and varied form of society that emerged in Europe around 950–1350 CE, after the 'Dark Ages', is normally called feudalism. In this social pattern power was vested in the ownership of manorial lands, and command over peasant labour, combined with advanced means and skills of violence. Society was organised into interdigitating hierarchies of kings and vassals (nobles), in other words great lords and lesser lords, by degrees, under them. The feudal manor was normally a reward for military service, and while these were often theoretically retained by the monarch, they became, in practice, the heritable domains of noble lineages. Knighthood was the status that came with this military service, a status that becomes more dignified and elaborated into multiple ranked levels of nobility (e.g. dukes, barons, counts) as the system developed. Knights, or lesser lords, built up around themselves and their households, families and networks of retainers and clients who could also be turned out for military service, mostly as pike-wielding infantry, and later on as archers. Central to the knight's role was the war machine of the Middle Ages, the horse controlled by iron stirrups, and steel weaponry and armour that evolved to become more lethal and protective over the centuries. Part of the original purpose of the manor grant was to provide an economic base for the military vassal to maintain this expensive equipment and retinue.[2] Over time wooden motte and bailey fortifications were replaced by stone castles, and swords and pikes were joined by long-bows, crossbows, and catapults, and the military value of the mounted knight reached its limits as better armed infantry and gunpowder technologies became increasingly important for warfare.

What did they fight over? Kings mobilised vassals and their followers in the thousands to defend or expand their lands and overlordship in battles of dynastic consequence. Some of these were at the 'marches' of kingdoms seeking to expand against pagans in the east and the

[1] This section is generally informed by Bloch 1961, esp. pp. 123–162, Finer 1997a: 876–883, Mann 1986: 390–393.

[2] This outline is necessarily schematic. At times in the Middle Ages monarchs employed mercenaries from abroad, and those owing military service could often pay 'scutage', to hire another in lieu of service. Nonetheless, the lord-vassal relationship and its military duties provides the basic skeleton of this kind of society.

Islamic Caliphate in the south. However, 'A great deal of the warfare during this period consisted of fairly small-scale campaigns to reduce defiant vassals' (Finer 1997a: 880), and noble houses were continually involved in jealous feuding with each other over material advantage such as claims to land, and over prickly points of honour. Personal feuds often became blood-feuds or vendettas involving whole houses and clans, sometimes enduring over generations. Low-level 'private warfare' percolated steadily through noble society. Kings and bishops often struggled to control this behaviour among the nobles, seeing it as a general threat to peace and order, but this was difficult to achieve in a society dominated by men, many of them young, trained to display valour and take offence easily.

The European nobilities were part of a trans-societal elite culture, which valued military valour and expertise. This was exemplified by the system of tournaments that flourished between 1100–1300, where mock battles allowed young aristocrats on the rise to display their skills and courage, in bids to enhance their prestige (Crouch 2005). Originating in northern France sometime before 1100, the tournament spread more widely, despite periodic efforts of monarchs and the church to clamp down on a practice that often broke out into uncontrolled violence, and underscored the unruly nature of nobilities. It served the need of maintaining battle-readiness among the warrior class during periods of relative peace, as well as providing an arena for status competition (quite literally a 'field' in Bourdieu's terms) among a martial elite when war itself was not available. Tournaments were normally sponsored by a local lord as patron, and could go on for days, attracting audiences of travelling nobles and generating local commerce around supporting activities. The standard form of the event involved dividing the various companies in attendance into two relatively equal teams, and began with opportunities for one-on-one jousting between newer knights seeking to prove their skills and courage. The main event, the 'grand tournament', began with two long lines of knights charging at each other with lances. After the first great clash the lines would turn (from which the event supposedly gets its name) and do it again. This would eventually break down into smaller melees, and sometime into chases well off the field. The aim was to knock others off their horses and force them to surrender. The higher the status of the captive the higher the prize, and as in real medieval warfare, arranging the ransom of the captive was a key goal. The entire enterprise led to many injuries, and often deaths. At the end great sponsoring magnates often awarded prizes for the best performance of the day, and hosted lavish dinners for those they favoured. In the tournament, the real social function of nobilities, as providers of force, whether for local social order or inter-dynastic conflicts, was symbolised and romanticised. It embodied and performed the idea of 'chivalry'. This entire ethos and elite way of life achieved a kind of adventurist 'overspill' in the Crusades (1095–1291) to 'reclaim' the holy lands, as popes sought to redirect the wasteful practice to the glory of Christendom. As this system created an oversupply of nobles and knights out to prove themselves, the Crusades acted as something of a release valve for this politically dangerous abundance of violent energy.

As we see in the next section, in time the complex of knightly warfare was replaced by more effective means of war, and the noble culture of honour was increasingly curtailed by law. One form of ritualised elite violence exemplifies this transition – the duel.

> In fact while the late sixteenth century – at least in western and central Europe – saw a clear decline of the conventional feud and related 'crimes' such as hiring of paid assassins to get rid of enemies, a form of resolving problems quite popular in Italy, for example, other forms of interpersonal violence among noblemen were on the increase. The duel as an ideally strictly regulated combat between two noblemen, sometimes supported by seconds, became increasingly popular in this period. In France and temporarily in England, the popularity of the duel assumed endemic proportions at the beginning of the seventeenth century. (Asch 2003: 73)

As military roles became more regulated, litigation became a more conventional form of seeking redress among the nobility, and absolutising monarchs clamped down more effectively on aristocratic violence and feuding, duelling became an alternative for the performance of honour through a caste-based right to violence. Originally recognised as a form of legal redress, at least in France in the mid-sixteenth century (Dewald 1996: 116–117), the practice was increasingly discouraged by monarchs and the church, and tended to go underground. It also went 'down market' as it escaped the confines of noble culture and became a convention for resolving conflicts of honour among mere gentlemen in the eighteenth and nineteenth centuries. Duelling represents a 'last gasp' of the feudal culture of aristocratic honour (Asch 2003: 73–76, Brown 2011: 159, 219, Dewald 1996: 116–117).

The violence and militarism of feudal to early modern society, culturally displayed in the tournament and duelling, was especially distributed among aristocratic families and households, creating chronic problems of order within these monarchic (and also republican) states. Kinship provided a primary infrastructure for violent modes of competition, that could spread across a reticulated social structure with little regard for national boundaries, and with corrosive effects on social solidarity: it was a brake on modern state formation. The organisation of martial capacity was constantly being assembled out of pools of knights, retainers, and sometimes mercenaries, lacking any clear, enduring corporate form – that would change in the next period.

Military Change and the Rise of the Modern State

Feudal warfare based on the warrior class of mounted knights was eventually overtaken by advances in technological, organisational, and financial means in the conduct of war, that made them obsolete. I have already raised (in Chapter 1) the thesis that warfare and escalating military competition was central to the formation of modern nation states in Europe (Contamine 2000, Hoffman 2017, Kennedy 1987). Happening between about 1400 and 1800, the key dimensions of this process can be summarised as territorial, fiscal, and technological, and for analytic reasons I will pull these apart a bit. But the reality is of course that they are densely interconnected, and converge in their effects on the expanding administrative powers of the state. The most general theoretical claims in this direction, with special emphasis on territorial outcomes, have been made by Charles Tilly (1975, 1992). Tilly has summarised the evolution of warfare in Europe since about 1000 in terms of four periods and processes:

1. *Patrimonialism* (up to the fifteenth century), in other words the feudal system we have just been discussing.
2. *Brokerage* (c. 1400–1700) involving rulers' frequent reliance on contractors to hire mercenary forces with monies borrowed from independent 'capitalists' and bankers.

3. *Nationalisation* (c. 1700–1850), when states create mass armies and navies out of their own populations, and these forces are administratively integrated into the state.
4. *Specialisation* (from the mid-1800s) in which armed forces (including police) increasingly differentiated and diversified, becoming a more distinct division of the modern state and its expanding fiscal and regulatory capacities. (based on Tilly 1992: 29)

This can serve as a loose frame for the rest of the chapter. However, let me focus here on Tilly's broad claim about the role of military competition in the consolidation of territorial states in Europe across these periods. Critical of relatively teleological theories of economic and political development, that saw Europe as laying down a developmental path for other states to follow, Tilly drew more on a 'realist' international relations paradigm, in which state formation was the outcome of relatively open-ended processes of political competition (1975). In Tilly's analytical model, states that want to survive and grow must engage in four activities. They must: bring under control any challengers within their territory ('statemaking'); do war with external rival states ('warmaking'); come to the defence of allies, both internal and external to the state ('protection'); and to fund all these activities states must derive resources (that cannot be found elsewhere) from their populations ('extraction') (1992: 96, *passim*). From the basic dynamic set up by these interdependent processes we get a hardening of law and order and policing, the refinement of military capacities, clearer institutions of diplomacy between states, and the institutionalisation of taxation across a wider tax base. In short, states become bigger and stronger. The conspicuous historical effect in western Europe is the transformation of the feudal patchwork of around 500, interdigitating kingdoms, principalities, city-states, and other polities, into around twenty-five sovereign national states (1975: 15).[3] A further effect of this shift is that 'wars became more lethal and less frequent' (1992: 72), with many more battle deaths resulting from fewer

[3] Recently Philip T. Hoffman has presented this argument in terms of economic game theory, in which European rulers were locked into cycles of competitive warfare that encouraged constant investment in military technology and progressively eliminated competitors (states), because the gains were potentially very high, and the costs were relatively low (2017: 29–34).

states fighting shorter wars. Following this process forward, Tilly observes:

> During the last five hundred years, then, three striking things have occurred. First, almost all of Europe has formed into national states with well-defined boundaries and mutual relations. Second, the European system has spread to virtually the entire world. Third, other states, acting in concert, have exerted a growing influence over the organisation and territory of new states. The three changes link closely, since Europe's leading states actively spread the system by colonization, conquest, and penetration of non-European states. The creation first of a League of Nations, and then of a United Nations, simply ratified and rationalized the organization of all the earth's peoples into a single state system. (1992: 181)

Hendrik Spruyt (1994) has objected that Tilly rather overplays the role of war, arguing instead that the coherence of sovereign territorial states as international actors, operating in an arena of similar actors across a range of military, political, and economic interests, made this political form superior and caused it to displace other forms (e.g. city states, commercial leagues). In another intriguing challenge to Tilly's thesis, one which resonates with my emphasis on the centrality of kinship for elite social organisation in the previous chapter, Vivek S. Sharma (2015, 2017) has argued that the logic of the consolidation of European states had less to do with warfare, and more to do with the principles of dynastic politics. Sharma argues that strategic dynastic marriages, including possibilities for female inheritance, and the principle of primogeniture, helped to consolidate territories into more complex dynastic hierarchies, through norms of kinship, property, and public authority shared though large parts of Europe. In effect Sharma accuses Tilly of reading the dynamics of modern nation state militarised competition over territory back into the medieval and early modern past, failing to appreciate the role of monarchy itself, as a system of rule, in European political and territorial consolidation. I don't think this overturns Tilly's thesis, but it does qualify it in an interesting way (cf. Haldén 2020).

Another important part of the European process is the development of what has been called the 'fiscal-military state' (Brewer 1989, Mann 1988). I will focus on the idea as formulated by Michael Mann (in ways very continuous with Tilly) in the context of comparative historical sociology, but acknowledge that there is also a distinctive strain of work by historians that has taken up this term.[4] The British state in the eighteenth century provides the premier case of the fiscal-military state, but its historical roots go back further, and its form is part of the general transformation of western European states. What Mann shows, especially in regard to the case of England, is that the major expenses of the medieval state were military, and that as the opportunity and ability to borrow funds increased, and could be spread over time in repayments, the capacity to invest in the costs of war (numbers of soldiers, new weaponry, large navies, etc.) also increased: the scale of warfare expanded accordingly. Mann relates this process to the wider expansion of state power from the twelfth to the eighteenth century. As states became more obliged to secure the property interests of an evolving capitalist class which provided necessary funds and industry supporting war, these states had to develop more extensive and systematic means of taxation, and larger bureaucracies to manage matters of both finance and warfare. The state became larger, more sharply territorially defined, with a clearer and growing domain of activities which it governed. In Mann's terms the 'infrastructural powers' of the modern state – in which rulers and ruled co-operated in the business of rule – were driven forward by this process. The various corporate and incorporate bodies of medieval society, noble lineages, churches, towns, and guilds, were transformed into a more diverse civil society, invested in the success of the increasingly national states that housed them (see Mann 1984, 1986: ch 13).

These changes in the military and fiscal dimensions of the state were also driven by what historians have called 'the military revolution', a term that should be understood as an analogy to the 'industrial revolution' rather than political revolution, despite having political effects (McNeill 1982, Parker 1996, Roberts 1967, Rodgers 1995).[5] This area of research is full of debates too complex to cover here, but we can roughly divide its themes between matters of technology and those of organisation, bearing in mind that deliberate innovations in human organisation are 'techniques' for achieving ends. On the more

[4] E.g. Brewer (1989), Harling and Mandler (1993), O'Brien and Hunt (1993), Storrs (2008).

[5] More recently the term 'military revolution' has been extended by the term 'revolutions in military affairs' (RMAs), focused on changes to warfare since the mid-twentieth century, and defining the concept in more encompassing social, economic, and political terms. See: Murray and Knox (2001), Sabaté (2016).

technological side, western Europeans famously took the gunpowder technology of the Chinese and developed it into a new range of weaponry, both muskets used in field combat, and cannon used in assaults on fortification, as well as in the field. At the same time crucial advances in shipbuilding, beginning with the Portuguese caravel design, led not just to colonial expansion, but also to the growth of navies and ships armed with cannons as floating fortresses. In a classic example of an arms race, new gunpowder cannonry became able to demolish traditional castle walls and turrets, making established siege warfare on such structures obsolete. This led to new innovations in fortifications, leading to the 'bastion' or 'star' fort design, often known as the *trace italienne* because of its Italian origins. These larger fortifications were flatter, roughly circular, with triangular bastions protruding on all sides to provide covering lines of fire on any assault. Broad surrounding ditches and angled brick walls were better at deflecting and absorbing the impact of cannon fire. And here the technological change connects directly to organisational change, because to defend and attack such large structures, armies had to become bigger. Horses became less important while an armed and drilled infantry became more important. Strategy and tactics (including supply lines to provision much larger forces fighting longer wars) became more important, and command structures and administrative support grew, with military leaders increasingly formally trained at specialised academies. And whereas great medieval battles were normally decided in a single event, modern warfare was increasingly fought on several fronts: field battalions operating in multiple locations, naval forces at sea, and siege warfare of fortifications. Central to the idea of the 'military revolution' is the fact that these changes, which ramified through society, in many ways preceded the 'industrial revolution' we associate with the expansion of civilian production and consumption in the eighteenth and nineteenth centuries. The expansion of the means of warfare had its own previous impact on technological innovation, the organisation of work, demands for resources, and so on (Cipolla 1965). As discussed above, this massification of warfare had implications for wider social mobilisation, as states built up standing armies and navies, taxed subjects/citizens, extended their scopes of administration, and called on people to identify in more national terms.

The military revolution thesis has operated at two levels. At one level, most germane to this book's argument, it provides an explanation for the changes in the territorial shape and administrative capacity of states in Europe – the great winnowing and sharpening of polities mentioned above. But it has also been used to explain the entire rise to global dominance of the European powers of the 'West', arguing that it was the superiority in the means of violence and warfare, developed in this ramping up of European warfare, that enabled European colonisers to then conquer and subordinate peoples in other lands (Parker 1996). The economic historian Philip T. Hoffman (2017) has offered one of the most recent versions of this argument. In his view, although the effects of disease on indigenous populations of the Americas was a factor, in cases such as the Spanish conquest of the Aztecs and the Inca, it was gunpowder technology that enabled very small and outnumbered forces to take control of these lands. And in Eurasia, where disease was less of a factor due to long-term contacts, it was the advantage in this military technology that was decisive. Despite sharing in the general knowledge and practice of gunpowder technology, for various reasons, states in China, Japan, India, Russia, and the Ottoman Empire, did not see the same level of steady escalating warfare among relative equals. So again, when European colonialism spread across the globe, militarily they were relatively vulnerable to European superiority. Taking issue with globalist versions of the military revolution theses found in Parker and Hoffman, Sharman (2017) has argued that the complex of large armies, fortifications, and superior firepower were less important to European expansion than the ability to make and bring on side local allies, exploiting local rivalries, and indigenous rulers' own interests in developing trade relations with Europeans to increase their own power. Similarly but more strenuously, taking it as primarily a thesis about European expansion, Jacob and Visoni-Alonzo (2016) have argued that the entire idea of a 'military revolution' needs to be discarded; they claim that military change across global history has been instead 'evolutionary', and the European case unexceptional, especially in relation to Eurasia. For Jacob and Visoni-Alonzo Europe's period of hegemony is more a matter of global political economy, and not military superiority *per se*.

It is fairly clear how the steady pressures of warfare led to escalating innovations in military technology, and in the means to finance war, and how this would have intensified the administrative powers of the forming modern state. The changing organisational form of militaries themselves, and how they were composed and provided with personnel, soldiers, and generals, is a further question. In the temporal dimension, this is a question of how the medieval feudal hosts of lords, knights, and their retainers, sometimes combined with paid mercenary forces, turned out for relatively short campaigns, were transformed into mass armed forces, either volunteer or conscripted, grounded in ideas of national identity, citizenship, and democracy. This shift involves a gradual replacement of dynastic monarchies by nation states, and the rise of republicanism as a political principle. It also involves the long-term professionalisation of armed forces (Brooks 2020, Huntington 1957, Nuciari 2018). In a sense, the knightly class were professionals, as a hereditary caste monopolising specialised skills, but so were mercenaries and their brokers, who trained for and pursued warfare as a career, at least for parts of their lives. As the military revolution led to drilled standing armies with specialised skill sets, the role of the soldier as a citizen service was further professionalised. As we will see in the next section, this trend entered a new phase in recent decades, something closer to our modern sense of the term 'professional', with a shift towards smaller, all-volunteer standing armies, with clearer career paths for individual soldiers, as well as for its highly educated military leadership.

The historical transition towards standing national armies employed by the state, replacing armies led and recruited by aristocrats, is not a smooth one. By the mid-eighteenth century, wars such as the Seven Years' War (1756–1763) were still being fought by a combination of aristocrat-led forces, mercenaries, and militias mobilised for the duration of the war. The American and French Revolutions led to the mobilisation of much wider, popular armies. The French *levée en masse* (mass conscription during the Revolution) laid the ground for the mass conscripted Napoleonic armies that would follow. Prussia established and maintained a mass army from 1814 to 1870, but other European countries returned to the aristocratic model for much of the nineteenth century, abandoning standing armies once the French threat was over. In the US mass armies, volunteer at first, later conscripted, were raised for the Civil War, but dissolved once the war was over. World War One was the next great episode of mass national army mobilisation, the one in which the connection between aristocracy and military leadership reached its limit and then declined. From then on national armies were much more fully established as divisions of government led by trained professionals, and as possible professions for soldiers, although army size stayed smaller outside of war. It is worth noting that in the case of Europe in the nineteenth century, army careers were also a matter of imperial/colonial forces acting outside of Europe and its wars. So, the professionalised mass based standing army only really comes into its own in the twentieth century, with the two World Wars and the subsequent Cold War centred on the US and the USSR. In the US conscription continued to be a device for maintaining war-forces in the Korean and Vietnam Wars, but has since been abandoned, as military forces have become more a matter of technological rather than personnel inputs, and military posture is more about control of information and intelligence, rather than 'boots on the ground'. There has been a general move away from large forces and conscription, towards smaller, fully professionalised standing armies (Burk 2018).

We can look more closely at these changes through the lens of the various roles of combatants and the composition of forces. Four key terms help bring this out: aristocrats, militias, mercenaries, and eventually fully modern professionals (as just touched upon). The classic feudal role of aristocratic war leaders, the knight on horseback, was first weakened by the growing importance of longbow archery (e.g. the English victory at the Battle of Crecy, 1346), which was very effective against mounted knights, as well as the rise of the Pike Phalanx (or 'Schiltron'), in which a tight formation of infantry soldiers projected their pikes all around their formation, making them very difficult for mounted knights to attack. This technique of the Swiss infantry limited the destructive power of the mounted charge of knights, and became widely used. These innovations helped precipitate the military revolution and the growing importance of large infantries in ratio to cavalries, use of muskets and cannon, and the techniques of siege. Set-piece battles among generations of mounted nobles became less important – this was one element in the general transformation in the social roles of feudal nobility.

Aristocracies also became more civil and urbane, intermarrying, where necessary and advantageous, with rising merchant classes, and seeking new lines of profession in expanding government bureaucracies ('*noblesse de robe*'). Those that held fast to noble martial traditions did so by occupying the new official roles of military leadership as generals and colonels, often now trained in new and burgeoning military academies, and expected to bring an element of science and elite training to their practice. Paradoxically, while European aristocracies were 'demilitarised' in terms of their autonomous military powers within the dynastic systems they were part of, they were also more deeply integrated into the new militaries as a way of life. Whereas before, actual medieval military duty had been a seasonal practice according to exigent needs, balanced with other displays of elite status, under the new regime of standing armies and large-scale warfare, it became a full-time professionalised career. As Storrs and Scott keenly observe:

> The nobility's continuing military role had implications for its political and social position. It undoubtedly contributed to the biological extinction of some families, whose sons entered the army and either were killed in combat or did not marry. But the overall verdict must be rather more positive. The nobility had survived the challenge represented by the Military Revolution and indeed had adapted remarkably successfully to the new circumstances. This involved a reshaping of the nature of its military service by 1800, revealing that there was no inherent contradiction between nobility and military professionalism. The transformation also underlines that the nobility – or at least significant parts of it – was not inherently resistant to change. Its former 'feudal' service certainly had been redefined, with the mounted knight becoming an officer in infantry or cavalry regiments. The nobility, and particularly the numerically preponderant lesser nobility, had become a service caste, acting as officers in the state's permanent forces, their main military virtue being obedience. But a fundamentally personal relationship between ruler and elite remained central to this service. (Storrs and Scott 1996: 39)

In short, in the context of the present argument, competition among nobles was domesticated – refocused and subordinated to competition between states.

The term 'militia' is also worth examining (Prak 2015). We associate it primarily with the idea of the republic, and in medieval to early modern Europe, especially with the self-governing Swiss Cantons, northern Italian city-states such as Venice and Florence, and the Dutch Republic. But if we take militia to mean military forces mobilised from the general population, whether citizens of a republic or subjects of a monarchy, then it is a category that cuts across the monarchy/republic distinction. All medieval burghs placed obligations on town members to provide service in the defence of the community and in the keeping of public order and night watches. These were often associated with and organised through guild membership, and these could be recruited in times of dynastic warfare. Even the feudal military service of more rural populations of infantry were drawn from local populations that normally had some control over who they sent: those at the bottom were not integrated into the lord-vassal hierarchy of obligation in the same way as those above them. Of course, the great republican militias do epitomise the principle, but even their leadership tended to come from great and powerful families. There is a sense in which 'militia' simply designates the military service of those who are non-professionals, often conscripted in one way or another, and as such have played a role in large scale warfare throughout European history.

We often think of mercenaries as an early modern innovation, and indeed they became very important during the expansion of warfare around 1500–1700 (Tilly's period of 'brokerage'), but mercenaries played a role in medieval warfare as well, supplementing forces raised through the hierarchy of vassalage, or compensating for noble vassals' refusals to serve and call out troops. 'Mercenaries' have a bad name, understood as fighting forces with no underlying loyalty to those who they fight for, and motivated only by the best price for their service. Machiavelli (1985: 48–50) famously warned against republics relying on them for these reasons, and his warning has resonated through the modern historiography of warfare, which sees it as a transformation towards the ideal model of the nation state of citizens in arms, to which mercenaries were increasingly alien. However, this perspective tends to obscure the fact that mercenaries were an important part of the military revolution, not a vestigial element withering away, and this is not surprising when we consider that rulers caught up in escalating scales of warfare would need to find fighting forces when and where they could. David Parrott (2012) prefers to call the phenomenon more broadly 'military enterprise', that is, the role of private contractors in provisioning the needs of war. These included war leaders, usually from the landed aristocratic class, who would provide fighting forces for a fee, but it could also include other 'entrepreneurs' providing other necessary services, such as food supplies and transport. Parrott likens the practice to variable public-private partnerships, in which different deals could be made in terms of the combination of up-front payments, payments as services are delivered, and a final share in the rewards of war. Parrott questions the presumption of the low quality of mercenary soldiering, seeing this as an ex post facto denigration by those who championed the republican nation state. In fact, mercenaries were, almost by definition, professionals, often with long-term training and skill in the art of warfare, with motivation to do their jobs, even if pecuniary. Indeed, effective performance could bring honour and glory, and further opportunity. So even though they defy modern norms of citizen-based warfare, they played an important role in enabling the growing scale of military competition, and the process of professionalisation. Privatised 'military enterprise' is still with us today, e.g. in the Iraq and Afghan Wars, where the state buys in services (provisioning, security), however, the tendency now is for these services to be provided by private companies that are legally constituted in the same state for which they are providing services (Malešević 2019). Co-operation across the public-private boundary persists, but now largely contained within the national frame.

The concept of 'professionalisation' has run throughout the discussion of various kinds of military forces. It is a trend that one expects as warfare has become not a practice that defines a privileged caste, but a specialised full-time career associated with a division of the modern state bureaucracy. Much of the twentieth century was a story of the consolidation of the norm of professional-led armed forces, in careers 'open to all' within the modern state. As technological inputs increasingly predominate over the human, and voluntary rather than conscripted service has become the norm, even in wartime, forces have become smaller in personnel, and professionalism is the guiding principle throughout the organisation, not just at the top. The movement over this long 500-year period has been away from military action as the jealous preserve of a caste of nobles, in constant competition with each other, towards militaries as subordinated divisions of the modern state, providing necessary services to that state. Where martial capacities had been distributed among aristocrats and their networks of kin, clients, and their rural subjects, as well as urban-based militias, and mercenary forces, they are now unified, no longer fragmented. While there are intra-bureaucratic rivalries among armed services and other state divisions for the favour and resources allocated by the state, such competition is contained within this regulated sphere, not sanguinary: that kind of competition is reserved for conflict with the modern state's enemies. In the next section I look at aspects of the fully modern military-state relationship.

The Modern Military

The historical trajectory just outlined leads us to quite recent theoretical, even philosophical, questions about the relationship between the military and the modern state, especially in its liberal democratic form. The simultaneous institutional convergence, and functional differentiation of military and state powers, raises puzzles. In the social sciences of the military, this is known as the question of 'civil-military relations' (Brooks 2019, Feaver 1999, Owens 2017). The first term of the pair does double duty, because 'civil' covers both civilian government, and the idea of a wider society in which both government and the military are embedded. The relationships between these three points – military, government, society – define the field. It is a field that has normative but also empirical and comparative dimensions, which interpenetrate. Analysis of the diversity and possibilities of civil-military relations inevitably bear on how they *ought to be* related, in a world where so much power is concentrated in military hands. The field arose in a specific context, during the Cold War, in the wake of the expansion of western, and especially US military power in World War Two, in which standing armies poised for war around the globe had become the norm. While it tries to survey the wider world, it reflects the perspective of liberal democracy, and especially of the US, the heartland of its development. The field is multidisciplinary, but with particularly strong strands in political science, international relations, and sociology. Here I can do no more than scratch the surface and engage with some defining texts to outline the major conceptual issues relevant to the present discussion.

Peter D. Feaver has succinctly defined the 'civil-military problematique' as a paradox: 'The very institution created to protect the polity is given sufficient power to become a threat to the polity' (1999: 214). 'Who guards the guardians?', as the saying goes. The seminal and enduringly influential analysis of this problem was offered by political scientist Samuel Huntington in *The Soldier and the State* (1957), an analysis that continues to shape the self-understanding by military leaders in the US of their proper role (Brooks 2020). Huntington saw the US as having a predominantly liberal and antimilitary culture, which tended to impede the development of an adequately robust military that could respond to the functional pressures of the Cold War. Prescriptively, in order to create a sufficiently strong military that was nonetheless firmly under 'objective civilian control', Huntington emphasised the importance of the 'professionalism' of the military. He argued for a clear division of labour in which the civilian government controls all political decisions about when and why to go to war (or other military operations), but the military command is given its recognition as experts in military strategy, tactics, logistics, with authority over the practical conduct of war. The military is given autonomy within a circumscribed sphere of action, in a word, is rendered professional. This brings with it an ethos of military service, in which the role of the military is to remain apolitical, and carry out the commands of legitimate civilian government as effectively as possible. More recently Feaver (2003) has developed this line of argument in terms of a principal-agent framework borrowed from microeconomics. The problem is, how does the 'principal', the civilian government and the wider society, ensure that the 'agent', the military, carries out orders faithfully, without relying on intrusive and costly levels of oversight? This is a fundamental dilemma that neither Feaver, nor anyone, can resolve (cf. Cohen 2002, Davidson 2013). But it poses the empirical question of how much the subordination of the agent to the principal depends on an alignment of separate interests, versus more normative principles of duty and propriety. In fact, even in the best arrangements, control can never be exact. The principal relies on information the agent possesses, and is inevitably advised and influenced by them. Correspondingly, the agent always has scope to redirect orders and policy in the process of implementation: it is a problem of command that is characteristic of large, multipart corporate actors.

If Huntington focused on the government aspect of the civilian pole, the sociologist Morris Janowitz was more concerned with the societal aspect in his rejoinder to Huntington, *The Professional Soldier* (1960). Huntington was concerned with how the military could protect the liberal democratic way of life of the civilians; Janowitz was concerned with how the civil-military relationship itself could cultivate democratic values and civic virtue (Burk 2002: 12). Janowitz worked in a civic-republican tradition with a long history, in which military service is seen as an obligation of citizenship, one which levels and normatively binds society together, and the absence of which weakens society. Janowitz believed that military traditions were naturally conservative, and dangerously slow to keep up with the modern pace of political and technological change: they needed the influence of more dynamic civilian society to correct this tendency. While Janowitz respected the functional distinctiveness of the military profession, for him the problem was to promote the convergence of the interests and outlook of the military and the wider society, and prevent schism. To overcome this tendency Janowitz encouraged the use of conscription, and the location of ROTC (Reserve Officer Training Corps) programmes in colleges and universities, so as not to isolate professionalisation in specialised military academies. Janowitz argued that the model of the modern military should be the 'constabulary force'. Rather than being limited to the highly specialised skills of full war, kept on stand-by much of the time, Janowitz thought the modern military needed to be more like a police force operating in an international arena, using force as minimally as possible, but steadily engaged in keeping peace and advancing democratic values. While not really rejecting Huntington's institutional structures of military professionalisation and governmental control, Janowitz was concerned with the value integration of the civilian and military populations, and ensuring that military officers remained good citizens.

The threat of all-out nuclear war has perhaps abetted Janowitz's vision of the US military as a global police force regularly engaged in 'limited' warfare. But the end of the Cold War and the shift to an all-volunteer force in the US from 1973, requiring greater technical skills, has worked in the opposite direction, reducing the social integration of the military, as it becomes less of a duty and more of an occupation (Moskos 1977). The literature has become concerned with a 'cultural gap' between civilians and the military (Inbody 2015, Rahbek-Clemmensen *et al.* 2012). The members of the US military are 'disproportionately Republican (especially its officers), Southern, and rural relative to American society', and while polling shows that the American public generally holds the military in high regard, interviews and surveys have shown that soldiers disparage the 'dissolute and indolent character' of civilian society (Brooks 2019: 388). Such tensions can be exaggerated, but they suggest that Janowitz's anxieties were not entirely unwarranted.

So far, in keeping with its core literature, this has been a US-centric discussion. While writing this book Myanmar saw a military *coup d'etat* in February 2021, in which the military took into custody President Win Myint and State Counsellor Aung San Suu Kyi, along with key members of the National League for Democracy (NLD), other politicians, and some activists. This was followed by crackdowns on independent media, violence against and arrest of protestors, civil unrest in outlying ethnic regions, and the sentencing of Suu Kyi to four years in prison on trumped up charges. The military justified its coup by claiming a recent democratic election in which they lost seats was fraudulent. However, the 2008 constitution drafted by the military junta reserved three powerful ministries and a quarter of the Union Parliament seats to the military's control, so despite a general political and economic opening in 2011, and a landslide victory for the NLD (led by Suu Kyi) in 2015, the military never really relinquished control. In a familiar pattern, military leaders and their families have substantial control over the country's business sector through which they monopolise national wealth (cf. Kandil 2012, on Egypt). Myanmar's most powerful neighbour, China, has political and economic interests in the country, and limited interest in disrupting the given arrangement of power. Electoral losses in the recent election, and perhaps the cover of the global Covid-19 pandemic distracting other countries, seem to have triggered this overt reassertion of military power.

This event, like many others throughout history, reminds us that the current pattern of civil-military relations in stable liberal democracies is not the global norm. One of the first to focus academic attention on this fact was Samuel Finer in his book *The Man on Horseback* (1962). The book sought to analyse the conditions in different types of regimes that led to military coups, and broke ground for more international and comparative approaches to the issue. In both liberal democracies like the US, and powerful authoritarian states such as the USSR and China, the military is more fully under the control of civilian powers. But among the less globally powerful states, which Finer describes as 'autocracies' and 'oligarchies', the relationship is inclined to be less stable, and militaries often have considerable *de facto* if not *de jure* power. For Finer the question was – why do militaries ever relinquish power, given their advantages? Finer saw this as partly a developmental question. As societies become larger in scale, more complex in their civil society, and economically advanced, specific military skills become less adequate to the tasks of administration and political negotiation. But in regimes where the 'political culture' is less developed, there are propensities for militaries to seize and claim government, negotiate power with a civil sector, or sometimes maintain control from behind the scenes, while allowing the appearance of democratic rule (as in the recent history of Myanmar). There is now a large and expanded literature on, *inter alia*, the causes of coups, the strategies of autocratic rulers to offset the powers of their militaries ('coup-proofing'), and the 'defection' of militaries when they refuse orders to impose violence on civilian populations (see Brooks 2019: 381–384, Feaver 1999: 218). This briefly reminds us that concerns about how to improve civil-military relations, as opposed to dealing with coups, is perhaps the ultimate 'first world problem'.

All of this has bearing on a more theoretical and conceptual debate about the relationship between political and military forms of power. As we have seen, Michael Mann divides the analysis of social power into four 'sources': ideological, economic, military, and political. Mann sees the last two as quite distinct, defining military power as 'the social organisation of concentrated lethal violence' (2006: 351) and political power, which he identifies closely with the state, as 'centralised, territorial regulation of social life' (2006: 352). For Mann the currencies of military power are force and fear, whereas that of politics is effective authority. The strong state's political power is 'infrastructural', built into the fabric of society, in terms of widely accepted law and the distribution of governance through bodies in civil society. Military power is highly specialised and stands apart, even if nearby. More despotic states lack infrastructural power and thus have to rely more heavily on military power. Military and political/state power inevitably entwine, but they are analytically distinct.

But some have argued that these two are not as easily distinguished from one another as Mann claims. Most prominently, Gianfranco Poggi (2001: 180–185, 2006), echoing Weber, has argued that there are three basic forms of power: political, economic, and ideological. In other words, the 'goods' and 'bads' of society are allocated according to three principles: 'command' (politics), 'exchange' (economics), and 'custom' (ideology, or shared beliefs) (Poggi 2001:18). For Poggi military power is ultimately an aspect of political power, a means of enforcing commands, and something which underwrites the power of the modern state. The formidable ability to operate on human existential vulnerability, through fear of harm, is what backs up the commands of the state, ensuring internal order, and protection from external enemies.

The very definition of 'the state' sheds light on their differences. Mann, in the style of archaeologists and many historians, uses an historically extended concept of the state to include archaic empire/states such as those of ancient Egypt or Sumer. Poggi sees the state as distinctively modern, as defined by Weber's famous definition of it as 'A compulsory organisation ... [which] ... successfully upholds the claim to the *monopoly* of the *legitimate* use of physical force in the enforcement of its order' (1978: 54, original emphasis). This is something only really achievable in the modern era. Of course, the implication of the latter definition, as the wider study of civil-military relations and coups suggests, is that many things we call states today, in fact are not. A 'failed state' is not a kind of state, it's not any state at all. Only those states where the problems articulated by Huntington and Janowitz require attention, are true, full states. The military's concentrated capacity for violence may be constitutive of the modern state, and a key 'tool' or attribute of it, but it is not just a means for enforcing commands, but also, at least in theory, an underlying threat to the state. I suspect different guiding research questions are behind the disagreement between Mann and Poggi, and their conceptions of political and military power, and the state, reflect this. Poggi has always been specifically concerned with how the modern constitutional state emerged, and its nature and prospects (1978). It is interesting because it is 'something new under the sun'. Mann's purpose has been to devise a framework that would enable the widest possible field of analytic comparison, historically and globally, of the concatenations of power. In that wider frame, even if political and military power have a strong affinity, and tendency to entwine, conceptually hardwiring them together would be hobbling for the analysis of variation.

Conclusion

For my purposes, the distinction between military and political power is necessary in order to track the changes that have led to the 'modern state' as an 'actor'. The feudal social order we began this narrative with was a fragmented ongoing contest among kinship/patron-client clusters, periodically stabilising under the dominance of one of these, but always with the potential to break out into armed conflict. These clusters and the people who led them were the key social actors in regard to the allocation of authority and command. At the end (so far) of this story we have a community of states involved in international relations, and among the stronger of these, military power is largely effectively directed outwards, and subordinated to civil government internally. This internal division of labour, interdependence, and 'mutualism' between political and military power – limiting and regulating the competition between them – makes the powerful modern state the key actor on the world stage. It also creates space for a new kind of social order in which other forms of political, economic, and ideological competition, driven by new kinds of actors, can develop.

In Chapter 2 I argued that it is not so much 'societies' but rather forms of social organisation that evolve, and the peculiar thing about human social evolution is that unlike species, forms of social organisation can split apart, or fuse and meld with other organisations, taking on different functions in a larger entity. In the narrative of European history above, we saw diverse forms of social organisation oriented towards martial purposes – nobles and their retinues, urban militias, mercenary armies, etc. – coalescing by degrees into modern national militaries. At the same time these were becoming fused with absolutising monarchies and a few republics that were evolving towards modern statehood under competitive pressure from one another. The outcome was the close but highly functionally differentiated relationship between the military and the modern state. As a field of multiple, warring aristocratic households gave way to this process of subordination and integration, multiform feudal society eventually evolved into the nation state system, in which each state, by extending and consolidating its power *over* territory and various members, acquired more advanced powers *to* wage war and mobilise the resources under its domain. A new ecology, of the international state system, emerges.

5 *From Adventurers to Companies*

This chapter addresses the social evolution of the economic firm, the emergence and development of the modern company. It continues the argument that if we want to understand the growth of competition, in this and other arenas, we need to focus on the key competitors, how individual competition is aggregated into corporate competition. It needs to be acknowledged at the outset that this is the arena of human activity, the capitalist economy, that many regard as the epicentre of competition in the modern world. I have already put forward my view, that as important as the rise of capitalism is for modern history, competition and its transformations across society cannot be adequately understood as 'projections' from the capitalist economy. Substantiating that argument has to emerge from the book as a whole, but here, minimally, I warn against looking for that kind of argument, because it will not be forthcoming. After defining some key terms at the start, I will broadly track the evolution of the modern company through different phases, and then focus more closely on traditions of critique of the company form, concluding with more general reflections on companies as power actors, and the evolutionary effects of competition.

It will aid the presentation if I define two terms before proceeding: capitalism and the company. This is not a chapter about capitalism in general, but that concept defines the general context, so it is worth laying out how I think about capitalism at the outset (Hodgson 2015, Ingham 2008, Kocka 2016). We can begin by contrasting a minimal with more extended definitions of capitalism. Minimally capitalism is investing money to make more money, that is, profit. In this sense we can find capitalism, expressed especially through commerce and trade, in many times and places across human history. This was Weber's point when he distinguished between 'capitalism', plain and simple, and 'modern capitalism', characterised by historically specific institutional conditions, with rationalised organisation being central (Weber

2005: 56–59). Generally, when we inquire into capitalism we are interested in the 'modern', extended sense. We might also call this a 'societal' definition, in that we are now talking not just about an economic practice, or even an 'economy' in the narrow sense, but a principle of social organisation that tends to permeate social relationships. The entire society becomes oriented towards the competitive pursuit of profit. This is what capitalism was for Marx (1970: 20–22).

This extended conception of capitalism adds numerous key but variable characteristics:

1. *Labour power* is mobilised primarily through the market, as a commodity with a price. It becomes formally 'free' in the sense that the individual worker's labour is not tied down by claims from other non-market social relations. Both Marx and Weber understood the irony here, that this freedom is often wedded to the extreme insecurity and vulnerability of the worker who has no other means to survive except to sell their labour. Weber placed great emphasis on the fact that 'free labour' with a market price made it much easier for employers to make rational calculations about the profitability of their businesses (Weber 2005: 59–60). Because both the mobilisation of labour and the pursuit of profit are central to capitalism, there are strong competitive pressures towards the replacement of more costly with cheaper sources of labour, and the replacement of human labour power with machines.
2. There is extensive *commodification* of all that is produced and consumed, and constant pressure to bring more things into the sphere of commodification. Both physical and mental labour are sold on the market, manufacturing goods and providing services, and those goods and services are themselves commodities. Notably land, which is often fettered by the non-market claims of kin groups and states, comes more easily to market under capitalism. And monies themselves become commodities which can be bought and sold, particularly in regard to speculations about their changing exchange values.
3. Modern capitalism develops and grows in conjunction, interdependently, with *the modern state*. States and their legal systems must ensure stable currencies, the enforcement of property rights and contractual obligations, the regulation of business practices, and

increasingly, macroeconomic planning and adjustments, for instance, regulating interest rates, and taking on national debt in times of economic crisis.

4. Not surprisingly, I also include the growth of *corporations as key actors* in the marketplace. While in theory one can imagine a capitalism made up solely of individuals as exchanging actors, in practice it has always involved aggregations of individuals into corporate forms that can compete more effectively (cf. Coase 1937). Corporations as well are ultimately constituted through law and the state, not purely out of market forces. Moreover, they have a tendency towards monopoly control of markets. They are shaped by competition, but also try to limit competition where this is possible.

There are also some major historical patterns and tendencies associated with the rise of capitalism, which might be seen as defining further key characteristics, in somewhat broader terms than those stated above:

1. Tied to the importance of the corporation, is the growing *separation of work and production from the household*. For the vast majority of households under advanced capitalism, work is delivered elsewhere for a wage, and the household is a unit of consumption, but not production. Family farms and small businesses can be something of an exception, but most people are employed by large organisations in which they have little or no ownership (Perrow 1991). Even when 'working from home', the worker is subsidising the costs of the employer, and their household does not constitute assets of the business.
2. However pervasive, capitalism is not socially exhaustive, and often *articulates with non-market systems*. There are many kinds of social relationships that are never fully subsumed under the commodification of labour, especially those of caring, nurturing, and support within the household or kinship and friendship networks. This unpaid work, predominantly provided by women, in effect subsidises the costs of capitalism. Historically, especially in colonial contexts, this principle has operated in regard to large populations of rural agrarians (peasants) who provided for their own subsistence according to kin and community-based norms of distribution, but also seasonally provided wage labour to commercial agriculture

(e.g. picking coffee), at costs lower than it would take to sustain these workers' households only through wages.

3. Markets and capitalism have always seen *cycles of growth and collapse*, boom and bust. Some of these are moderate and some severe, and they are probably an inevitable aspect of dynamics of innovation and obsolescence that capitalist competition generates. The point is that this is an endogenous, not for the most part an exogenous feature of capitalism.
4. Finally, capitalism is *geographically concentrated and restless*. It has developed through a series of primary centres or 'cores' in which characteristic practices (banking, the factory) have been most advanced and the accumulation of wealth most intense, drawing more peripheral economies into capitalism's orbit (Arrighi 2010). The succession of these 'hegemons' – the north Italian city-states, the Netherlands, England/Britain, the US, increasingly China – is a basic part of the story of capitalist development, and how it articulates with geopolitics. Capitalism is increasingly 'global' and whether this pattern of state-based dominant cores will continue, or morph into one of multiple national cores embedded within a global class stratification based on capitalism, is a big and open question. (cf. Wallerstein et al 2013)

Let me sum up by elaborating two main points. The first is that modern capitalism and the modern state are deeply entwined. Although, with Karl Polanyi (1957), we might identify enduring tensions between the market and the state as institutions for provisioning society's needs, capitalism and the state have evolved together, and are highly interdependent. It is not so much a question of 'states versus markets', as of the variable forms that the relationship can take (Hall and Soskice 2001), and the distribution of power between organisational actors on both sides. The second point is that capitalism, in the extended sense, is not so much a 'system' as an historical process with systemic properties. It is an organising principle of our era, but not a terribly stable system. The theorisation of capitalism has been heavily shaped by the rise of industrial, factory-based capitalism and its associated class structures and large centralised companies, around the nineteenth century, driven especially by Britain. This is rather different from the mercantile and agrarian commercial capitalism that preceded it in the sixteenth to eighteenth centuries, and the more recent trend of 'finanancialisation', in which speculation on the values of commodities competes with the actual production of commodities as a strategy of wealth accumulation. And of course, the boundaries between these three abstracted historical periods of capitalism are permeable and hard to draw sharply. Like European feudalism before it, capitalism will have a historical trajectory, and it may be very difficult to pinpoint when it began, and when it ended (if it does). This is as much a matter of conceptual definitions as historical facts. Because modern capitalism developed as a rough system, in which people had contending interests for and against, in an age when democratic politics was increasingly organising people into interest-based parties, and literacy and public opinion enabled the contest of associated ideas, this encouraged a public discourse in which capitalism was presented as a system that populations could be called on to accept or reject, wholesale. The same goes for alternatives, often more theoretical than practical, such as socialism and communism. But the reality is that capitalism is an historical process we are caught up in, not a system we can easily opt into or out of: to say this is not to advocate passivity in the face of history, but rather to suggest that influencing the course of capitalism is more a matter of steering certain processes in certain directions, than one of choosing between systems.

Now let me add a few things about the company. The chapter charts the emergence of this form, but it may help us keep our bearings if we define the key attributes of the form as it eventually took shape. Formulating an 'ideal type', I highlight four key features of the fully arrived form of the company. First, *self-incorporation*. There are legal rules and systems of registration for setting up various kinds of companies, and these vary nationally, but the right of incorporation is not tightly controlled by the state, instead it is a generally available option for citizens to exercise, one that is encouraged. Second, *shareholding*. Ownership of the company rests in shares, distributed among shareholders, that can be bought and sold; share ownership normally involves some say in corporate governance. Third, *risk-limitation*. The company has a 'fund' of its own, separate from the personal funds of its members. Limited liability, the legal principle by which corporate investors risk only their invested capital, not the entirety of their personal wealth, makes it much easier to attract investment, and limited liability is just one side of the equation of 'entity shielding', the other being protecting the company from liability for the individual investor's debts accrued outside of that business (see Hansmann et al. 2006). Fourth, closely connected to the previous, is the theme that runs through this book – *juristic personality*. In order for economic firms to operate efficiently as agents in the marketplace, they must be more than a bundle of implicit contracts between their members, and between them and whomever the firm might do business with. Such loose assemblages are particularly unwieldy when they become engaged in legal action, generating multiple suits against individual persons. It is much easier to sue a single company than a network of individuals. The legal personality of the firm, as a fictive person in law with rights and liabilities, greatly facilitates the business of business, by allowing companies to be unified agents, whatever their internal divisions.

Precursors

The ideal type of the company just described took shape gradually. To what degree did it have predecessors outside of Europe, and how did this form coalesce? In general, the major corporate forms found outside of Europe, often with deep historical roots, were strongly shaped by dominant kinship structures, no matter how flexible and adaptive they were to circumstances. In India the *sreni*, an association of traders, merchants, and artisans that operated something like a medieval guild in Europe, establishing and policing membership rules of conduct (the *sreni dharma*), and litigating among members, flourished between about 800 BCE and 1000 CE. They were established through royal approval, had governance structures, and seem to have provided some charitable and money-lending services to members. Membership was partly hereditary, inasmuch as occupations were passed down from father to son, but could cut across caste boundaries, and there were mechanisms for individuals to join and leave (Harris 2009, Khanna 2018). In China, the 'clan corporation', a patrilineage-based organisation around shared business interests, evolved out of ancestral trusts that looked after the common resources for ancestor worship (shrines, graves, genealogical lists) and charitable and educational needs of the patrilineage. Members were generally from the same community of an agnatically related village or villages. Over time some lineages also took on the management of economic interests in agricultural production, domestic manufacturing, and trade, co-operating to pool assets, spread risks, and coordinate activities. In the Ming era (1368–1644) some powerful lineages became, in effect, 'contractual lineages' (Zhenman 2001), organised more in terms of common economic interests that could be bought into through shares, than kin relations among males. Teemu Ruskola (2018) argues that these should be seen as economic corporations that operated through the socially and politically sanctioned idiom of patrilineage, but were not narrowly kin-based. It would seem there was a continuum of forms of patrilineage-based organisations, embedded and disembeded in kin structures to varying degrees. At the end of the Qing Empire (1644–1911), China began to adopt forms of corporate law from the West (Chung 2015, Faure 1989, Harris 2009, Watson 1982, Zelin 2009). In the Islamic legal system, the closest correlate to the corporation was the *waqf*, a kind of unincorporated charitable trust. This was created by an individual endowing land or other fixed property for charitable or religious purposes. A trustee was appointed to look after the property in the interest of the beneficiaries, but there was little scope for these entities to evolve beyond their narrowly set initial purposes (Harris 2009, Kuran 2005). Although simple partnerships of a few people over limited time horizons were possible for merchants, there was no wider body of corporate law available to make these larger, more complex and more autonomous. Jared Rubin (2018) argues that the close relationship between Muslim rulers and religious authorities has meant that until recent times merchant interests were marginalised in the law, causing economic stagnation.

Across Eurasia, prior to the development of the modern corporation, the most important vehicle for mercantile activity was the *commenda* (González de Lara 2018: 71–77, Pryor 1977). Although this is a Latin term deriving from Italy, Ron Harris argues we should use it as the name for a typical nexus of contracts (2009: 610) that operated in and connected regional trade networks for centuries from the Far East to Northern Europe (cf. Abu-Lughod 1989). The origin of this form was in the *qirad* or *mudaraba* contract used by Arab traders working the caravan routes from South Arabia to the Mediterranean before the rise of Islam, although it was incorporated into Islamic law early on (Udovitch 1962). However, it was in late medieval Italy that the *commenda* became the most elaborated, and a vehicle for a socially wider base of investment for profit in long distance sea trade. The key characteristic of the basic form was that it was a written and legally enforceable contract between two parties, one the investor who put up capital in goods and/or cash to fund a journey (the principal), the other the travelling party who provided the expertise, information, and contacts necessary for trade, and took on the risk of the journey (the agent). In some cases the travelling merchant also invested some of their own capital. There was an agreement to split the profits, depending on how much each party had invested, usually with the greater portion going to the investor (2/3 to 1/3 was common). It was also possible to compound the contract by bringing in further third-party investors. The contract created a common fund of capital for the specific venture, and only that was liable to investors' claims. In some cases the travelling party could engage in further contracts (usually to take trade to more distant locations), thus becoming the principal in a second contract with a new agent. As Harris put it: 'The single *commenda* contract was not only a nexus of several contracts, but it was itself part of a complex web of contracts. Each of the parties to that contract could [be], and often was, a party to other *commenda* contracts' (2009: 611). With local cultural variations, this broad form ended up enchained from China to England, articulating overseas and overland trade. Harris argues that it was precisely this form of contracts between a relatively small number of individuals that allowed it to adapt locally and create links across vast civilisational distances – it gave trade a universal language.

In late medieval Italy, the most commercially advanced part of Europe at that point, alongside the *commenda*, the *compagnia* (from 'sharing bread') was evolving. Unlike the former, the latter was primarily used for land-based enterprises concerned with commerce and industry. Like the ancient Greco-Roman *societas*:

> it was a consensual agreement by which two or more partners, who might or might not be family, pooled their capital and labour for a common purpose or exploitation and shared the enterprise's profits and risks. The *compagnia*, however, had a separate fund distinct from the individual partner's own liable assets and operated under a joint name, as a firm, by which it conducted business. (González de Lara 2018: 78)

It is this 'separate fund' and 'joint name' that begins to anticipate the modern company, although its 'solidary' as opposed to 'limited' liability does not (cf. Weber 2003). However, this institution was still highly enmeshed in kin relations. In the thirteenth and fourteenth centuries many *compagnia* took the form of family firms, some of them, such as the Bardi, Peruzzi, and Acciaiuoli companies, became very large, involved in trading and finance over extended regions. The Medici Bank is a well-known example. Another variant, the *fraterna compagnia*, which became prominent in Venice in the fourteenth century, was basically an association of brothers (sometimes sisters were included in its earlier versions) over a couple of generations, managing inherited wealth through business investment. In the trading heydays of Venice and Genoa, commercial success involved a combination of strong state support for trading, in terms of protective convoys and overseas bases, and multiple forms of relatively small-scale and impermanent partnerships, rising and falling, but not coalescing into more permanent corporate structures (González de Lara 2018: 81–83).

I have already discussed the slow historical emergence of the idea of the corporation with juristic personality, in all its forms, in Chapter 3. Most advanced in England, this legal form was available for adaptation by the early modern period, and some of its established variants were more explicitly oriented towards commercial activities than others, such as the chartering of towns, merchant guilds, and livery companies. Companies chartered by the Crown, called 'regulated companies', were in effect merchant guilds granted monopolies over particular trades, in exchange for financing the state and collecting taxes. The Merchants of the Staple of London, dating from 1248, regulated the wool trade and its taxation for England, and was granted authority over Calais in France by Henry VI in 1466. The Company of Merchant Adventurers of London (formally established by Henry IV in 1407) also controlled the cloth trade, particularly broadcloth, and established trading ports in towns such as Antwerp. These competed with the Hanseatic League, not a company, but a Baltic confederation of merchant guilds and market towns seeking to control trade in its region, and who had been granted trading privileges in England. All three operated primarily in northern Europe, extending to Russia.

The next stage in the evolution of the company was shaped by the fiercely competitive expansion of European trade by sea to Asia (India, China, Japan, the Spice Islands of what is today Indonesia), and around the Atlantic, to Africa, North and South America, and the Caribbean. The Portuguese took the lead after they expanded Asian oceanic trade by establishing the Cape Route round the southern tip of Africa in 1497. The Portuguese trade in Asia was organised as an often violent and coercive sea-based colonial project under the *Estado Da*

India. The union of Spain and Portugal under one monarch (1580–1640), and the rule of Spain by kings from the House of Habsburg (1516–1700) meant that Portugal, Spain, and the Habsburgs constituted a major European power bloc, a concatenation of empires, for much of the sixteenth and seventeenth centuries. The Portuguese dominance of the Asian trade fed into the wealth and power of the Habsburgs in Europe in the sixteenth century and became an object of rivalry, especially for the Protestant English and Dutch. Early on in this context regulated companies in England were established to extend trade further afield, and because greater risks required wider investment bases, this led to a new form – the joint stock corporation. Early examples were the Russia (or Muscovy) Company (est. 1553), originally seeking routes to Asia but eventually focussing on whaling and fur, and the Levant (or Turkey) Company (est. 1581), seeking various eastern Mediterranean goods, but relying on the carrying trade of Venetians and Arabs. Neither of these companies were very successful (Turner 2018: 123–124).

There is wide consensus that the great chartered, joint stock companies of Northern Europe, especially the English East India Company (EIC) and the Dutch East India Company (VOC, for *Vereenigde Oostindische Compagnie*), were the most relevant direct antecedents of the modern corporation (Harris 2018, Phillips and Sharman 2020). But even here, because of their peculiar scale and close relationships to the states that produced them, we are still in the 'antechamber' to the company form we commonly live with today. Regardless of the colonisation of the Americas, around 1600, the main opportunity for profitable trading was still in the East, in the land of silk and spice, and these companies were set up by their home countries on a grand scale, with peculiar powers, in order to compete for this trade. These new forms of company, chartered by kings and parliaments, allowed much larger levels of joint stock investment with limited liability to be raised by wider bases of merchants and nobles. This was necessary to defray the considerable costs and risk involved in outfitting ships for such long-distance trade, which required a lengthy time for return on any investment. While early investments were on a voyage-by-voyage basis, this soon settled into a system of standing company capital to finance ongoing trade.

Phillips and Sharman (2020) emphasise the hybrid nature of these huge companies, arising in a time before the modern distinction between the state as a public institution, and companies as private ones, was well established. These were more like extensions of the state and its policies into areas it could not practically reach, thus they call them 'company-states' (following Stern 2008). As 'public/private' projects, they were preceded by 'privateers', individual captains and crews charged by monarchs to harry and plunder the ships and cargo of other empires, like Sir Francis Drake did to the Spanish in his circumnavigation of 1577–1580. But the goal of the English and Dutch states to open up steady trade to the Far East was a much larger project which, lacking the deep pockets of the Habsburgs, could be adequately financed only with joint stock private investment. Moreover, the Asian trade was distant, involving polities with which European rulers had little experience or influence: this posed a principal-agent problem which these companies addressed. Endowed with state-like powers in their charters, they not only had monopolies over certain trades, but powers to engage in diplomatic negotiations, establish territorial bases, administer justice, maintain armies and navies, and engage in war. This granted these companies great strategic leeway, but they had to use it in a context where their powers were quite limited, being strangers in lands ruled by others. Phillips and Sharman describe the role of the EIC and the VOC in the East not as one of colonial conquest, but of 'bespoke bargains' and 'diplomatic dexterity' in negotiating with local powers (2020: 205, *passim*). Although the EIC was established two years earlier, 1600 versus 1602, the VOC took the lead in competing with the Portuguese to dominate the Asian trade in the seventeenth century, but was eventually overtaken by the EIC by the eighteenth century. Both deployed means of war against local polities, and each other, although the VOC was more militarised in its approach, spending between a fifth and a third of its budget on military costs at its height (Phillips and Sharman 2020: 45). Through its insinuation into the structures of the Mughal Empire in India, the EIC eventually grew into an empire itself, ultimately generating suspicion in Britain towards its powers.

The company-state model was most profitable in the Asian trade, less so in the transatlantic trade, and the differences between the two are instructive. The sheer distance and complexity of the Asian context, and scale of operation required, was conducive to the formation of these Leviathan-like monopolistic companies. There were company-states in the Atlantic trade as well, notably the Royal African Company

(RAC) and the Hudson's Bay Company. The former played a key role in expanding English trade with Africa, especially the lucrative slave trade, eventually transporting around 188,000 individuals as slaves (Phillips and Sharman 2020: 85). But unlike the VOC and EIC in the East, the RAC was less able to protect its chartered monopoly from the incursions of much smaller slave trading partnerships, which could more easily enter the Atlantic trade, and became the predominant business form of the slave trade. The RAC also saw internal corruption, very high death rates from disease among its staff in Africa, and struggled to raise the capital to maintain the system of small forts along the African coast. It went bankrupt in 1752, and was replaced by the African Company of Merchants, supported by subscription, to maintain African outposts, which in turn were supporting the activities of the private traders. In contrast, the Hudson's Bay Company (HBC) survives to this day. Operating in the frozen north, heavily reliant on indigenous fur traders (especially the Cree at first), with a trade highly constrained by the seasons and melting of ice, and somewhat insulated from the imperial naval and military conflicts of the main Atlantic, the HBC was more able to maintain its monopoly in an environment too hostile for small traders. But the HBC was the exception. Generally, company-states in the Atlantic arena found it much harder to maintain dominance compared to the VOC and EIC in Asia.

The Florescence of Joint Stock Companies[1]

In 1832 Angell and Ames published the first comprehensive account of US corporate law. The preface begins:

> The reader does not require to be told, that we have in our country an infinite number of corporations aggregate, which have no concern whatever with affairs of a municipal nature. These associations we not only find scattered throughout every cultivated part of the United States, but so engaged are they in all the varieties of useful pursuit, that we see them directing the concentration of mind and capital to the advancement of religion; to the diffusion of literature, science and the arts; to the prosecution of plans of internal communication and improvement; and to the encouragement and extension

[1] This section, particularly in regard to the US, draws generally on: Gomory and Sylla 2013, Hansmann et al 2006: 49–60, Kaufman 2008, Micklethwait and Wooldridge 2005, Sylla and Wright 2013, and especially Wright 2011, 2014, 2018.

of the great interests of commerce, agriculture, and manufactures. There is a great difference in this respect between our own country, and the country from which we have derived a great portion of our laws. What is done in England by combination, unless it be the management of municipal concerns, is most generally done by a combination of individuals, established by mere articles of agreement. On the other hand, what is done here by the co-operation of several persons, is, in the greater number of instances, the result of a consolidation effected by an express act or charter of incorporation. (Angell and Ames 1832: v)

The divergence in practice from England that they observe was very real, and telling, in regard to why the US became the locus of further evolution of the corporate form, despite that form being inherited from England. To answer why it happened this way we need to go back to the early history of British colonisation of North America in the seventeenth century.

It's helpful to know that by the eve of the Revolution in 1776, three basic types of British colony in the Americas had evolved, distinguished primarily by how they were governed. All colonies were established by charters granted by the king, or sometimes the parliament, and ultimately under the sovereignty of the Crown, but what was granted in the charter varied. Royal (or 'provincial') colonies were under the direct control of the king, who appointed a Royal Governor, these included Massachusetts (incorporating Maine), New Hampshire, New York, and the southern colonies of Virginia, North Carolina, South Carolina, and Georgia. Proprietary colonies were in effect owned by patent-holders, a person, family, or small designated group, with autonomy and monopoly of governance, these included the middle colonies of Pennsylvania, Delaware, New Jersey, and Maryland. Charter colonies were established as self-governing bodies in which the free colonists collectively held the charter. At the time of the Revolution these were the New England colonies of Rhode Island and Connecticut.

However, at the start of the seventeenth century early colonisation was largely in the hands of two relatively short-lived joint stock companies: the Virginia Company and the Massachusetts Bay Company (Kaufman 2008, Wright 2018: 485). These were chartered by the king as companies with powers to set up colonies. The Virginia Company, modelled on the EIC and established in 1606 under a charter from James I, was composed of two 'sub-companies', the Plymouth

Company situated in New England, which subsidised the transportation and plantation of the Puritan Pilgrims from Leiden, and the Virginia Company of London based in Chesapeake Bay, and with its ruling council based in London. The Virginia Company attracted investment from merchants, politicians, and nobles, hoping to find another short route to Asia, goods such as precious metals and timber, and to stake territorial claims in the face of imperial competition from France and the Netherlands. The company was not profitable, and eventually both branches were sold at a discount to colonists. In 1624 James I revoked the company's charter and it became a royal (or 'crown') colony.

The Massachusetts Bay Company was formed in London in 1628 to trade in fish and furs. However, it was quickly co-opted, when Puritan members led by John Winthrop, its first Governor, bought out the other company members, and set out on a mission of establishing an independent Puritan commonwealth, sailing from England with the charter and seal of the corporation. So it persisted as a company colony for several decades, but somewhat detached from its original business purposes. Meanwhile, the British Isles became preoccupied with religiously charged civil war between Royalist and Parliamentary forces (1642–1651), leading to the defeat of the monarchists and the instalment of the Protectorate government of Oliver Cromwell (1653–1658). Under this 'benign neglect' the North American colonists were often left much more to their own devices. It was in this context that groups of religious dissenters from the Massachusetts colony established new colonies in what would become Providence Plantations, Rhode Island, and Connecticut. These colonies were originally established by their settlers through deeds with Native American groups, not directly sanctioned by the Crown or Parliament, and inherited the self-governing conventions of the company form, which prefigured, and has an affinity with, the model of the chartered colony. Thus Rhode Island and Connecticut today are often referred to as originating in the joint stock form of the Massachusetts Bay Company.

With the Restoration of the Monarchy in Britain under Charles II in 1660, the mother country increasingly tried to regain control of its distant colonies which had been evolving more independently, a trend that continued into the eighteenth century. Roger Williams had managed to secure a charter for Rhode Island from Parliament in

1644 during the dark days of war, which was replaced by a charter from Charles II in 1663. Connecticut had received a charter from Charles the previous year. Both charters largely preserved the *de facto* powers of self-governance for the colonists. In 1684 the Massachusetts Bay Company was formally turned into a royal colony, although in 1691 William and Mary gave the colony a new charter that reinstated many of its former powers, but grafted a Royal Governorship on top, making it something of a hybrid. All three retained their status as chartered colonies. In some sense the company model, governed by shareholders and directorates, seems to have provided practical guidance in ways to do autonomous governance in these colonies – they were more 'democratic'. Though the companies themselves fell by the wayside, the colonies carried on, with the 'company imprint' in their charters. By 1763, the other colonies, many of which had been established during the years of upheaval, were regularised into royal or proprietary colonies. However, these also developed considerable *de facto* self-governance due simply to their remoteness from Britain. They gave more ground to control by the 'centre' through appointed Royal Governors, or Patent-Holders, but still had to negotiate with the powers of the colonists and their elected representative *in situ*. The ideology of self-governance that fed into the formation of the US had its germination in the combination *de facto* autonomy based on sheer distance, and the idea of corporateness encoded in the company model, and transferred to the colonies themselves, especially the chartered colonies.

At the same time, during the colonial period the idea of legal incorporation was being normalised within the colonies, which often saw themselves as having their own powers of incorporation (Wright 2018: 485–491). Whether they had the authority to do so, apart from king and parliament, was ambiguous and contested, and the boundaries between looser associations and full incorporation was sometimes vague, but colonial corporations also tended to be relatively small scale and local, and civic in purpose, thus managing to fly under the radar. Municipal incorporations of cities, towns, and counties, and business corporations to build and run wharves and water utilities to serve the general public, were relatively uncontroversial. Also common were religious organisations, benevolent societies, mutual self-help organisations such as fire companies and mutual fire insurance schemes, libraries, and hospitals. The oldest North American corporation still in existence is the President and Fellows of Harvard College incorporated in 1650 (Kaufman 2008: 406); Yale was incorporated in 1745, and Dartmouth in 1769. Incorporation was a practical part of the wider American disposition towards forming associations for common purposes, which struck Tocqueville on his 1831 travels through the new country.

The British 'Bubble Act' of 1720, established before the devastating stock collapse of the South Sea Company later that year, appears to have originally served the purpose of protecting that company's monopoly and channelling capital into its coffers, by saying that no joint stock companies could be legally chartered except by the monarch (Turner 2018: 125–127). But after the collapse it became a bulwark against the formation of joint stock companies in general, which had become deeply suspect, and remained so in Britain for many years to come. The Act would not be repealed in Britain until 1825. In 1741 it was explicitly extended to the colonies, which put constraints on the formation of for-profit organisations in various areas such as fishing, whaling, trading, marine insurance, iron works, glass, works, mines, saw mills, and so on. Instead these 'for-profit quasi-corporate businesses' (Wright 2018: 488) constituted themselves as voluntary associations, or under time-limited statutes, in order to avoid legal complications. The Act was also used to prevent various bank ventures in Massachusetts, New Jersey, and Philadelphia in the later eighteenth century. But the practical pressures for incorporation around diverse purposes in the colonies, and less exposure to the crash itself, meant that it did not have the same dampening effect in the colonies that it had in Britain.

Unsurprisingly, the years of secessionist war, and the interim between the end of the war and the establishment of the new US constitution in 1787, disrupted processes of company formation. Under the new political order, the federal government was not given the power to charter corporations, that was reserved to the several states, which 'touched off a chartering spree at the state level that has not abated to this day' (Wright 2014: 25). The three states that had been charter colonies, Massachusetts, Rhode Island, and Connecticut, took an early lead in the expansion of incorporation practices between 1790 and 1810 (Kaufman 2008: 413–414). Motivated by opportunities for profit, and for serving the public good, incorporation flourished, and state legislatures became quite active in issuing special charters for various purposes. States and their politicians had an interest in improvements to their territories that would serve commercial ends and economic growth, and competed with one another to attract investment. Much joint stock was raised around general development projects such as canals, bridges, and turnpikes, to facilitate travel and trade. There were projects with more of an eye on speculation for profit, such as land development, the wonderfully named Dismal Swamp Company, in which George Washington was a major investor, being an example. Projects of extraction, manufacturing, insurance, and banking, all attracted investment, and corporations from before the Revolution, such as Harvard and other colleges, often had to seek new state charters to re-establish their legitimacy. Over the years 'general incorporation' laws developed that allowed potential companies to seek bureaucratic approval and registration without requiring specific enactment from state legislatures, a law to this effect in Connecticut in 1837 often being seen as the pivotal instance (Micklethwaite and Wooldridge 2005: 46). This eased the burgeoning workload on legislatures, and facilitated general economic growth. However, this was a gradual process with states first easing chartering in areas such as establishing churches or municipalities, and later for specific enterprises such as canals, with a general opening up for manufactures coming in the 1810s, and becoming widespread by the 1840s and 1850s.

It is of course important not to exaggerate the role of joint stock corporations in the economy as a whole. A large part of the economy was made up of small family farms, independent traders, modest business partnerships, that had little need for the powers of incorporation. Moreover, as Wright observes (2018: 480–481), despite Angell and Ames's emphasis on the growth of the 'aggregate' corporation, between 1801 and 1860 at least 2,575 'sole corporations' owned by one individual were established across thirty-five states, with a concentration on bridges, dams, ferries, port facilities, and turnpikes. Some of this development was funded by individuals with deep pockets, or with less formal ways of getting people to pool their capital. Moreover, it took time for business and infrastructural corporations to expand in relation to other 'non-profit' organisations. Looking at Massachusetts, by far the most active in incorporating in the early decades after independence, Kaufman (2008: 415–417) found that between 1781 and 1790, few incorporations were for infrastructural (4 per cent) or business

(3 per cent) purposes, the two largest areas being municipal (61 per cent) and religious organisations (15 per cent). By 1791–1800 the demand for municipal charters had more than halved, and that for religious organisations had almost doubled. Business incorporation had grown slightly to 4 per cent, but infrastructural corporations were now 24 per cent. This gives a sense of the strong early orientation of corporate growth towards development of economic infrastructure as promoted by state legislatures. In time however, facilitated by laws of general incorporation, the proportion of for-profit companies expanded dramatically. In the 1790s the number of corporations in the US increased around tenfold, and by 1860 it would have around 22,000 specially chartered business corporations, way beyond the number found in any other country (Sylla and Wright 2013).[2] Wright (2014: 49–65) finds that the annual issuance of special corporate charters by states grew from about five a year in 1790 to almost 1,000 a year in the 1850s. Over the same period, the total minimum authorised capital (MINAC) required yearly in the charters granted, grew from a few million USD to well over a hundred million USD a year in the 1850s. There were particular peaks in incorporation in the mid-1830s and mid-1850s, separated by a recession in the 1840s. Wright also distinguishes two periods, 1790–1829 and 1830–1860, noting a shift in what kinds of businesses were being founded and capitalised:

> Turnpikes were the most common form of enterprise in the earlier period, followed by manufacturers, banks, bridges, and insurers, while the most heavily capitalised corporations were banks, manufacturers, insurers, and canals. In the three decades before the Civil War [1861–1865], turnpikes and manufacturers remained the most common type of corporation, but railroads supplanted banks, bridges and insurers to take the third spot. In terms of capitalisation, railroads reigned supreme with over half the MINAC, followed by manufacturers, mining companies, and then banks and insurers. (2014: 61)

Wright's other key finding is that, contrary to any impressions of the southern states as mired in low economic growth due to slavery and

[2] Sylla and Wright (2013) have compiled a large comprehensive database of business companies formed between 1790 and 1860, using state legislative records. This misses those 'self-registering' corporations set up under general incorporation laws that were coming in over the period, which they estimate to be around another 8,000 in 1860. This leaves aside other forms of business such as sole proprietorships and traditional partnerships.

the plantation system, despite the northeast's early lead, by the 1850s the southern states were outstripping the northern ones in the number of specially chartered corporations established per head of population, and in their overall capitalisation (2014: 57–60, Sylla and Wright 2013: 656). We will return to the implications of the plantation system and the railroads for the scale and complexity of businesses in a moment.

But first let us underscore the distinctiveness of the US expansion of the corporate model compared to other countries (Sylla and Wright 2013: 661–665, Wright 2014: 74–79). As the epicentre of the rise of industrial capitalism we might expect the UK to have taken the lead in forming the modern company, but instead it ran behind the US. The 1720 Bubble Act, not repealed until 1825, placed a heavy restraint on company formation, therefore, much business of the early industrial period in Britain was organised in terms of partnerships based on families and close social networks. Businesses with larger capital requirements (e.g. turnpikes, canals, utilities, banks, insurers) could organise as unincorporated companies, but these encountered legal constraints that made it difficult for investors to trade shares freely, and they lacked legal personhood making all investors liable to legal action. Even for chartered joint stock companies, legal status was often ambiguous in the eighteenth century (Turner 2018: 128–131). The number of incorporated and unincorporated companies, and their total capitalisation, grew in Britain in the late eighteenth and early nineteenth centuries, but not at the same rate as the US. By comparison the British firms were far fewer, although some of the largest were much more heavily capitalised. Aware of these comparisons, and with the balance of power shifting from the older landed elites to commercial interests advocating liberal free trade, in 1844 Parliament allowed incorporation by simple registration, and in 1855 introduced general limited liability for corporations. This brought the UK more in line with the US. Nonetheless, a preference for the family-owned firm with family actively involved in management persisted in Britain through the nineteenth and well into the twentieth century.

France, like the US, had undergone a revolution, enacting a Code of Commerce in 1807 that enabled the formation of *société en commandite par action*, limited partnerships with tradable shares, and *société anonymes*, which were modern limited liability corporations. By 1867 it was possible for these to incorporate by simple registration: this law largely regularised and codified already existing business practices. Most smaller scale business and trade was done through *sociétés en commandite*, while the *société anonymes*, like many of the early US corporations, tended to be used for basic economic development, such as banking, insurance, transportation, and other public infrastructure (Rochat 2018: 253–255). Again, corporation formation lagged considerably behind the US. Other European countries such as Prussia/Germany and Sweden followed the same general path of corporate development, but lagging even further behind. Canada, the US's northern neighbour, despite cultural and geographic continuities, did not really begin to develop in this regard until after the US Civil War and its own independence in 1867. The US was the pace-setter in the development of the corporate form, using it to aggregate capital that was much more diffused among the population than in Europe, and spurred on by state-level competition to support economic expansion and infrastructures.

The New Leviathans

So far we have been discussing the crystalisation of the modern legal form of the corporation. From the middle of the nineteenth century the growth of the joint stock corporation entered a new phase, again led by the US, as the 'scale and scope' (Chandler 1990) of some of these corporations began to dramatically expand, setting the stage for the world of corporate dominance that we live in to this day. The great railroad corporations were the main drivers of this change (Chandler 1977, Perrow 2002: ch 5, Roy 1997: ch 4),[3] although corporate structures in retailing and manufacturing soon followed (Micklethwait and Wooldridge 2005: ch 4). The social change was profound. Charles Perrow observes that in the US in the early nineteenth century most people worked on farms, or as small traders, craftspeople, artisans, shopkeepers, if not as sole proprietors, in small organisations of five to twenty people. In 1820 only about 20 per cent of the gainfully employed worked for wages or salaries. Much work was family based, and factories employing 100 people or more were

[3] By the middle of the nineteenth century a great deal of corporate capital was concentrated in the development of railroads not just in the US, but also in Britain and France.

rare. Where these did arise, they had the capacity to dominate local communities and their labour markets (Perrow 2002: 4, 227).

The most conspicuous exception to this, and qualification to my assertion at the outset that capitalism mobilises labour largely through the market, was plantation slavery in the burgeoning cotton south. The 1850 census indicated that 1,479 plantations had over 100 slaves, with 187 of those running from 200 slaves to over 1,000 (Chandler 1977: 64). These were big operations, that employed 'overseers' to organise and control the enslaved workforce, included early stages of production using mills and gins, relied on bank credit to meet expenses and expand, and engaged in simple forms of bookkeeping to monitor income and expenditure, although without clear distinctions between household and business, and limited in internal calculations of costs relative to income (Chandler 1977: 64–67). Older debates about whether slavery-based operations could be regarded as 'capitalist', given the absence of wage labour (Genovese 1965) have largely resolved towards the position that the plantation economy of the US South and the Caribbean was indeed capitalist, but of a historically particular kind (Clegg 2020, Kocka 2016: 65–70). It was an expanding economy. The combination of cheap land for expansion towards the west, new and more 'productive' strains of cotton and processing technologies, the proliferation of small slave trading partnerships competing with one another, and rapidly expanding markets for textiles, were all factors. These combined with the fact that free labour was in short supply (why not start one's own farm or business?), so the costs of purchasing and maintaining slaves was not prohibitive given all these factors and the opportunities for profit. Contrary to the popular image of an economically inert, agrarian, antebellum South, from the late eighteenth century to the mid-nineteenth century the slave plantation economy developed rapidly, sweeping southwest, from emphasis on tobacco in Virginia, to the expansion of the cotton south through the Carolinas, and west to Louisiana and into Texas (Olmstead and Rhode 2018). As we have seen, towards the end of that period company formation in the South was beginning to outstrip the North. Anyone living through this period would have seen a dynamically growing economy, with designs on the territories further west, something we know worried many northerners, and combined with principled anti-slavery (McPherson 1988: ch 3).

So while the slave plantations were often very large in scale, prefigured some aspects of modern industrial organisation and management, and were manifestations of a competitive global industry, they were largely, in effect, family businesses, and never achieved the next level of corporate organisation – this arrived with the railroads. Alfred Chandler's monumental and influential study *The Visible Hand* (1977), which emphasised the 'managerial revolution in American business', argued that the railroads brought a shift from multiple small scale businesses coordinated through the market, to a few very large scale businesses that internalised multiple functions into complex divisional structures, requiring an internal hierarchy of professionalised managerial staff, who displaced owners as corporate leaders (cf. Berle and Means 1932).[4] These operations required massive amounts of capital, much of it met by foreign investment from Britain. The railroad industry played a key role in the expansion of the New York Stock Exchange by the 1850s. The sheer complexity of the task of building up a single network of transportation, with uniform standards (e.g. rail gauges), teams running and repairing the engines, others controlling traffic through a network of stations in telegraph communication and dealing with passengers, still others dealing with wholesalers seeking to ship their goods, led to the first vast corporate bureaucracies with divisional structures, in which managerial hierarchies trumped the market in terms of the power to coordinate complex economic activity. This scale and complexity drove other innovations, in record keeping, accounting, and financial control through treasury functions. Throughout, Chandler places a strong emphasis on the skills of managers to envision and reorganise business activities (Teece 2010). Other areas of business followed suit: a national telegraph system evolved interdependently with the growth of the railroads; an increasingly integrated transport system stimulated the growth of the mass production and distribution of all kinds of commodities. Retailers and new wholesalers tended to move first, taking advantage of new mass marketing and distribution opportunities to set up mail order businesses, such as Sears Roebuck, and establish chain stores in multiple cities. Manufacturing followed, especially with the shift from steam to electric power-driven machines, producing standardised products on a much greater scale, with the likes of Carnegie (steel) and Ford (cars) eventually building great business empires (Chandler 1977,

[4] Because of their scale and requirement for 'immanent domain' railroad companies were usually incorporated by special state legislation, rather than under general registration.

Mickelthwait and Wooldridge 2005). While many small businesses and family firms remained (to this day), these now became minnows within a business ecology dominated by whales. All large organisations, in both the private and public sector, and in government, became characterised by managerial hierarchies within complex divisional structures, seeking integration and efficiency (Perrow 2002: 196).

Chandler's insights were largely historical, with a light touch in regard to theoretical explanation. His argument suggests a kind of organisational functionalism, in which organisational change in business is attributed to a 'natural' drive to increase organisational capacities, and achieve efficiencies. Exploiting basic technological innovations (coal, steam, electricity), organisations grow in complexity in order to dominate their environments. In terms of classic arguments about the relative efficiencies of 'markets' versus 'hierarchies' (i.e. organisations) in allocating resources (Coase 1937, Williamson 1975), Chandler argues that at this point in history the balance of power shifts decisively towards the 'visible hand' of organisational complexity and managerial skills. One of the strongest challenges to this thesis has come from William G. Roy's *Socializing Capital* (1997), which criticises Chandler's emphasis on efficient control of market environments, arguing that it misses the wider political economic context of corporate and state power. Roy looks at corporations not so much as market actors, but as legal forms, as bundles of property relations and as vehicles for the concentration of capital. He is concerned with the implications of the legal form we have discussed: joint stock, limited liability, and what happens when the agency of corporate juristic personality becomes detached from a narrow group of owners/directors. Thus, Roy focuses on the massive extension of ownership in the corporation through public shares sold on stock markets, large investment banks, and the tendency of large firms to have substantial shares in each other,[5] all of this made viable through limited liability. As ownership becomes more dispersed and detached from

[5] The legality of corporations owning stock in other corporations was a contested issue, but by the late nineteenth century states were passing new laws that allowed this practice, creating the possibility for a 'holding company' which existed just to own shares in other companies. New Jersey's early liberalisation of its laws in this regard in 1888–1889 made it a mecca for incorporation, which Connecticut and Delaware soon emulated (Perrow 2002: 210–211, Roy 1997: 150–153).

corporate control, the peculiar class of corporate managers gain strategic power over their organisations, now mobilising capital on a much greater scale, and able to achieve national monopolies. Corporate power for Roy is realised not in efficiency, but in the ability to dominate markets through sheer size[6]. Charles Perrow (2002) might be seen as striking a middle path between Chandler and Roy. If Chandler's approach errs on the side of portraying firms as self-constituting agents, and Roy tends to see them as systemic effects of wealth concentration through structures of property, Perrow prefers to specify organisations as actors with interests, which shape institutional structures, rather than just being the products of those structures. He sees society as constituted by organisations, both private and public, and especially by large ones which 'are seen as recalcitrant tools fashioned by particular elites' (2002: 234). Invested with the agency of real persons, they are agents in their own right, pursuing power in particular organisationally defined ways.

Compared to Chandler, both Roy and Perrow place greater emphasis, as I have, on the legal constitution of corporations as a necessary precondition for the rise to dominance of larger firms, and as large firms developed, the legal parameters of incorporation evolved further to accommodate them. Both Roy and Perrow see a divergence from an earlier form of incorporation around the beginning of the nineteenth century that was oriented as much to non-economic aims and public goods (i.e. charities, religious organisations, community development), as to private economic purposes. In short, as the size and scale of corporations grows, private interests come to dominate over public ones (Perrow 2002: ch 2, Roy 1997: ch 3,). To this day, large economic firms dominate the now globalised capitalist economy, although their strategies for doing so have continued to evolve. From

[6] Basic to Roy's critique of Chandler is that Chandler has an innocent view that neglects power, whereas Roy is correcting for that in his analysis. I am not sure the charge entirely holds up. I argued in Chapter 2 that power involves two dimensions, power as the capacity 'to' do things, and power as control of some 'over' others, and that these have complex evolutionary interdependency. It seems to me that Roy somewhat reduces power to 'power over', that is, the power of capital over society, failing to appreciate that what Chandler offers is a concrete account of how a new form of 'power to', the power of large complex firms to capture markets. One might wish that Chandler had put more of a moral gloss on his account, but he is giving an account, without any elaborate theoretical apparatus, of how power developed in the realm of corporations.

the 1970s many large companies began a reverse movement, trimming down by outsourcing many supply chains that they had previously internalised under the 'Fordist' model (Harvey 1991). As John Kay observes, recent trends are moving away from raising large amounts of public stock to put it at the disposal of corporate leaders: 'over the last two decades, less money has been raised on the stock markets of Britain and the US than has been taken out through acquisitions for cash and "share buybacks"' (2021: 31). Instead, today's mega-corporations such as Apple and Amazon have a very different corporate strategy – 'capitalism without capital'. These companies' balance sheets consist mostly of cash, with very little outside equity or material assets. Other smaller companies rent them operational space, manufacture their products, and distribute or deliver them. They control intermediation among producers and consumers, and have distinctive organisational capabilities in the technical knowledge, expertise, and skills of their owners and staff. Meanwhile, the finance sector has become less about raising equity for the non-financial economy, and more about strategic opportunities for profit within the exchanges of the financial sector itself (Kay 2015, see also Philippon 2019). These latest developments are beyond the scope of this book, which is more concerned with the great transition in competition and corporate forms between the eighteenth and nineteenth centuries. But the observation is that time doesn't stand still, and competitive pressures continue to shape and reshape corporate form.

The Tradition of Critique[7]

I have focused on long term morphological change, the emergence of the modern corporate form, however, there has of course been a tradition of commentary, often highly critical, on these institutions and processes, which I turn to examine now. The outcry noted previously, over the *Citizens United v. Federal Election Commission* decision to recognise corporations as persons with rights to free speech, in the form of political donations, has a long prehistory. In 1612, in the case of the Sutton's Hospital, the jurist Sir Edward Coke noted unease

[7] This section draws especially on: Maier 1993, Harvard Law Review 1989, Roy 1997: 51–55, Perrow 2002: 33–35, Wright 2014: 27–48, Micklethwait and Wooldridge 2005: 33–36, and Wood 2009: 459–468.

with these uncanny persons: 'they cannot commit treason, nor be outlawed or excommunicated, for they have no souls' (quoted in Micklethwait and Wooldridge 2005: 33). Nonetheless, he upheld the personhood of the corporation in question. In *The Leviathan* (1651), Thomas Hobbes warned of the threat to sovereignty in the ambitions of great 'towns' and 'corporations', describing the latter as 'many lesser commonwealths in the bowels of a greater, like worms in the entrails of a natural man' (Hobbes 1994: 218).

In the eighteenth century, Adam Smith was notoriously critical about joint stock companies. Apart from banking, insurance, and some public works, which could not otherwise be organised and funded at scale, Smith saw these as constraints on trade, which posed insuperable principal-agent problems:

> The directors of such companies, however, being the managers rather of other people's money than their own, it cannot well be expected, that they should watch over it with the same anxious vigilance with which the partners in a private copartnery frequently watch over their own. ... Negligence and profusion, therefore, must always prevail, more or less, in the management of the affairs of such a company. (1981[1776]: 741)

Smith suggests that such companies can rarely compete against 'private adventurers' in foreign trade, except when enjoying monopoly privileges. Smith's scepticism was widely held in the early decades of the US, and fed into the decision of the Constitutional Convention not to grant Congress and the Federal government the power to charter corporations. This was jealously reserved to the states themselves. Early debates, reflecting the nature of the US secession from Britain, were often framed in terms of an opposition of 'republican' and 'aristocratic' values. Corporations were associated with the monarchical power to bestow privileges, not democracy. This distinction was made even in regard to the creation of municipal corporations:

> Those who fought proposals to incorporate Boston in the 1780s and in 1792 insisted that incorporation would 'destroy that equality which ought to subsist in all republics'. Its proponents were 'in their hearts ... inveterate enemies of republicanism' who favoured the 'introduction of aristocracy – a government of all others ... the worst'. (Maier 1993: 61)

Echoing Hobbes's warning, such corporations were also sometimes seen as raising problems of sovereignty, as instituting 'republics within republics', although defenders argued that repetition of republican form at different levels was precisely the right way for a new republic to meet its governance needs (Maier 1993: 62–64). Similar criticisms of the reinstitution of aristocracy and threats to republican sovereignty were made in regard to economic corporations, especially large projects such as Alexander Hamilton's Society for the Establishment of Useful Manufactures, and the Bank of North America. Judges responded to these anxieties about corporate powers by increasingly defining certain acts of corporations as '*ultra vires*', trying to define more sharply the limits of their powers. Another check on the joint stock company was the vote-weighting of shares, such that large shareholders got fewer votes per share than small shareholders (Hilt 2013).

As the editors of the Harvard Law Review (1989) observe, this pro-republican and anti-aristocratic language tended to map on to class fractions and emerging party positions (which we explore further in the next chapter). Skilled artisans, organised in small shops as masters, journeymen, and apprentices, felt particularly threatened by the power of incorporation. Angered by accusations that they were seeking a corporate charter from the state to form a producer co-operative, one group of journeymen proclaimed in 1835:

> 'We entirely disapprove of the incorporation of Companies, for carrying on manual mechanical business, inasmuch as we believe their tendency is to eventuate in and produce monopolies, thereby crippling the energies of individual enterprise, and invading the rights of smaller capitalists'. (HLR 1989: 1897)

Such artisans often cast themselves as the backbone of an independent citizenry, crucial to the integrity of the republic. Their idealised path was to work for a master until they could set up as independent businessmen with their own shop, an ambition threatened by the corporate organisation of manufactures. In the 1830s and 1840s Jacksonian Democrats, more aligned with the rural agrarian economy, tended to invoke the language of republican freedom and independence to claim that corporations were contrary to 'the genius of our institutions' (HLR 1989: 1893). The Whigs, who later fed into the Republican Party, were more based in a growing small business class, and more inclined to defend the corporate form. Contrary to the Democrats, they more often argued that precisely because there was not an aristocratic class monopolising wealth, incorporation gave those of modest means the opportunity to pool resources and counterbalance the power of state governments.

> Thus, Calvin Colton, in the pamphlet in which he launched the influential concept of the 'self-made man', linked corporations both to social equality and popular sovereignty. He described how 'by a division of the capital into small shares, and securing to men of small means equal chances, [corporations] are well adapted to a democratic state of society'. (HLR 1989: 1895)

Despite the Whig counterargument just noted, examples of protestations against the dangers corporations in the early nineteenth century abound, and many, including Roy and Perrow, have read these as evidence of a broad anticorporate culture in the US, especially in regard to business, prior to the rise of the railroads. Robert Wright (2014: 27–48) acknowledges the strain of distrust and critique, but emphasises the ambivalences. Apart from principled objections to the corporate form, it was manifestly the case that corporate interests were often advanced through political corruption, lobbying and bribing politicians and state legislatures, and this contributed to their unpopularity. Nonetheless, criticisms tended to respond to specific crises, such as panics, cooling during better times. Raging against corporations was also a vote-getter in political elections, ramping up the rhetoric. And, 'as it turns out, many people who criticised one corporation were stockholders or directors in another: in early America, all corporations were bad, except one's own' (2014: 37). Early Americans were confronted with a classic paradox of power, in a new setting. The people could limit the power of corporations by tightly controlling them and limiting their numbers through law and the states, but this tended to amplify state power and opportunities for corruption. Alternatively, they could try to democratise participation, allowing corporations to multiply, counterbalancing state power, and checking each other through competition. Ultimately, the latter strategy won out, no doubt for a combination of reasons, including narrow corporate interests, and principled beliefs in the social value of corporations, but also due to the sheer rate of economic development and expansion and the demand it created for the corporate form.

Conclusion

This account of the evolution of the modern company is one thread in a wider analytic history of competition. It is good to remind ourselves that in the American case, the narrow economic story is of a piece with the arrival of democracy in the broad Tocquevillian (2000) sense, of an expanding equality of conditions and opportunities, at least for free, European descended men. Democracy, not just as the formal institutions of government, but as the effect of a society in which the right to rule is no longer inherited, moral authority is not monopolised by a church, and the power to associate for common purposes is widely available. I conclude by reviewing with a sharper focus on the ideas of power actors, evolving, in competition.

Companies are a particular kind of power actor, aggregating individuals into an organisation with agency to carry out certain activities. We saw how in the premodern era, in various cultural contexts across Eurasia, entities resembling corporations were nonetheless deeply embedded in family and kinship networks, even if they sometimes developed a degree of autonomy, as with the Chinese clan corporations. Much commerce across this area was driven not by such organisations, but by various kinds of trading partnerships, summed up in the concept of the *commenda*. Trade travelled along a vast web of such interlocking partnerships, which were also often kinship based. Such trade, largely in luxuries, no doubt involved competition between various groups and organisations, but power ultimately resided in the hands of the territorial dynasts whose tastes commerce served.

With the expansion of sea travel and the imperial ambitions of European dynastic states, companies as extensions of state power took on new forms. The regulated companies that had been designed to capture monopolies in European international trade gave issue to new forms. Most conspicuously the massive 'company-states' of the VOC and the EIC that sought to displace the Portuguese in the East Indian trade, still largely focused on luxury goods. But the company form was also used in the Atlantic trade, and to establish colonies in New England. In this phase the striking fact is the interpenetration of the company and the state, as companies form quasi-governments to pursue state sponsored objectives. But the British company-colonies also develop their own traditions of replicating the form of incorporation to meet various purposes (towns, colleges, wharves, etc.).

After the American Revolution, the environment of expansion, opportunity, and inter-state competition creates a new spur to the incorporation process, and soon companies rapidly multiply. A new ecology of corporations develops, in which over a few decades the defining 'traits' of the corporation standardise and become more codified: juristic personality, limited liability and asset shielding, widespread shareholding, and general or self-incorporation. By the middle of the nineteenth century the stage is set for the new expanded corporation, professionally managed, with complex internal structures, led by the rise of the railroads. Meanwhile, under similar economic pressures, European states were following suit, with their own variations, not too far behind.

It is striking that the study of economics and business is one area where there is a distinct strain of applying evolutionary theory (e.g. Nelson and Winter 2002, Wilson and Gowdy 2013). It lends itself to this approach precisely because one can easily model companies and their practices developing in an economic environment as species with traits within an ecology. I've briefly traced the evolution of the company form, now let me look more closely at the dynamics of competition and evolution, especially in the American 'fluorescence'. A critical factor in this case is the two-dimensional nature of competition in this context. On the one hand, the powers of incorporation were reserved to states, which competed with each other to develop the infrastructures of their own economies, to expand their tax bases, and to attract corporations, their investment, and associated legal fees. On the other hand, the citizens themselves, an unusually mobile and expanding population, were in competition for their own livelihoods, and in some cases, opportunities to grow wealthy. Participation in companies was one way to do this. This double dynamic, from states above and citizens below, created exceptional pressures towards company formation.

Let me finish by returning to some of the key processes of evolutionary competition laid out in the Introduction. Certainly, this multiplication of company formation meant that many were formed but fell by the wayside and were 'eliminated' either by direct competition from other firms, or other hazards of economic life. This is the economy 'red in tooth and claw' as it were. But at the same time as they are instruments of competition, companies are also manifestations of co-operation; they pool people's money, resources, and energies towards common ends: that may be profit, but it may also be community improvement, charitable work, or some complex combination of these. As I've said, competition is a major stimulus to co-operation. The company form, for all its limitations and abuses, is one answer to how people aggregate their power while maintaining their independence from the state. It is a response to the power dilemma posed by democracy. Moreover, companies do not exist in environments of sheer eliminationist competition, they often depend on each other in complex patterns of mutualism, providing for each other's needs. When they do compete over the same market terrain, the effect is often differentiation and 'adaptive radiation', not just elimination. The rise and consolidation of the company as a corporate form happened because it proved a powerful vehicle for combining and channelling competitive energies towards productive ends. The overweening power of extremely large corporations, from the railroads to 'Big Tech', and the tendency to exploit workers with little bargaining power, are indeed profound problems. But these are not universal properties of companies. These are questions related to the entire balance of power in society, not necessarily intrinsic to the corporate form. In the path charted here, the corporate form of the economic firm moves from being relatively small alliances of kin and friends operating as partnerships in the interstices of states, to extensions of state power and imperial ambitions, to widely cultivated vehicles of economic development in modernising states, routinising competition within fields of law.

6 *From Factions to Parties*

In this chapter we move our attention to the domain of politics, and the emergence of the key competitive organisational form, the political party, and party systems. In real life there can be no clean separation of economics and politics, as both involve the distribution of power. But by focusing separately on the stories of the company and the party, and setting these side by side, we can gain a certain analytic purchase on what both unites and distinguishes these spheres in modern liberal society. While economics and politics interpenetrate, sometimes in murky and corrupt ways, the key objects of competition differ significantly. In the economy the object is market position, its viability and profitability. In politics the object is the legitimate authority of administrative, decision-making position. Struggles for customers and voters may both require 'sales-pitches', organisational strategies, and deliver forms of power into the hands of those successful in these struggles. But neither of these key resources, market versus administrative position, can be reduced to the other, so the expertise in pursuing them tends to differentiate.

I begin with conceptual framing, by examining the varied and somewhat ambiguous legal status of parties, contrasting it with the 'company' in the previous chapter, and considering the importance of party systems for party competition. The two core sections of the chapter provide an historical narrative of the prehistory and then emergence of the modern mass party, inevitably focussing again on Britain and the early US in the eighteenth and nineteenth centuries. I then widen out the discussion through an excursus on two other areas of the state's activities where the formalisation of competition in this period is conspicuous, first, and, in more depth, in the rise of conventions of adversarial law, again associated, especially, with the British and American common law tradition, and then briefly in regard to competitive appointment to civil service posts. At the end I consider the relationship between elite competition and party competition, before returning to the book's overarching themes of collective agency and social evolution.

But first, the question of 'party law'. This term can refer narrowly to laws concerned with establishing and regulating political parties, or more widely to all those laws in a system that bear on the operation of parties (Janda 2005: 3–4, Karvonen 2007, Müller and Sieberer 2006: 435). Party law tends to be more explicit, and more likely to be incorporated into written constitutions, the later those constitutions were created. More recent democratic and constitutional states have been modelled on predecessors, attempting to institute a version of the 'full package'. Such formalisation is associated with 'constitutions written after periods of one-party dictatorship', and Germany post-1949 is understandably a 'heartland' for current developments of party law (Müller and Sieberer 2006: 438). The US, unambiguously the origin point of fully modern party systems, makes no mention of political parties in its constitution, for the obvious reason that there was no original intention that these be part of the political system at the time – indeed parties, understood as factions, were seen as a threat to the new system. We will unpack this story below.

Kenneth Janda (2005) suggests that bodies of explicit party law, concerned with the institution and regulation of parties, overlap with three other bodies of law regulating the conduct of elections, campaigning, and political finance, and in some systems these latter constitute most of the legal status of parties. In his cross-national survey Janda notes that legal and constitutional silence about parties can either be inhibiting, providing no legal ground, or permissive, as in the case of the US. He identifies five broad approaches to party law: (1) *Proscription* disallows some possible bases for founding parties, such as on religion, language, race, or ideology (e.g. in the Italian case, forbidding the reorganisation of the dissolved fascist party). (2) *Permission* explicitly affirms citizens' rights to form parties, with minimal prescription as to how this is to be done (e.g. members must be citizens). (3) *Promotion* seeks to encourage party formation, for instance, through public subsidies for parties, or systems of proportional representation conducive to smaller parties. (4) *Protection* – at the extreme this can involve securing the power of a single party by forbidding others, but it can also involve protecting larger parties by restraining ballot access for smaller parties, or punishing elected representatives who defect from their party ('crossing the floor').

(5) *Prescription* can range from broad constitutional requirements that parties be internally democratically organised (Germany, Spain, Portugal), to micromanaging criteria that must be met to legitimately register and function as a party. Altogether these approaches convey the diversity of ways in which states, and dominant powers within them, seek to legally frame and manage political parties.

This raises fundamental questions about what political parties are, how they come into being, and where their boundaries lie. Here the contrasts with the corporations examined in the previous chapter are instructive. We saw that the ideal type of modern corporation, although many of its features were longstanding, coalesced most rapidly in the first half of the nineteenth century in the US. The first modern party system takes shape in that same period, and in the same place, but political parties, their membership and purposes, are very different from corporations. Indeed, they are more 'associations' than corporations; they emerge into a legal world that tends to treat them somewhat like corporations, but cannot fully. The difference here has to do with the relationships between civil society and the state, between social movements and the organisations that advance them, and between private and public spheres.

If we think of civil society as that zone of society outside the state in which people form opinions and pursue their interests, economic, political, or otherwise, either as individuals or by forming alliances, networks, associations, and organisations, then it becomes apparent that political parties have a peculiar relationship to both civil society and the state. When out of governmental power, they function more like civil society or social movement organisations, mobilising people around shared interests and sets of ideas. When in power in government, they become functional parts of government, components of its organisation. Correspondingly, their connections with their social bases tend to weaken, and their inevitable failures in wielding power, and internal divisions, become more exposed. Meanwhile, parties out of power are thereby 'closer to the people', cultivating those ties in order to win support for elections and get into government. In a democracy political parties' function like dredges, that sink into civil society in search of support and legitimacy for a governing agenda, and then drag that back into government, rejuvenating it in the process. They provide a key mechanism through which private interests are translated into public interests, and brought to bear on the public power of the state (Schattschneider 1975). Thus, the analysis of parties frequently makes important distinctions between a core of party activists made up of politicians and other professionals, a wider party membership, and a voting constituency that may or may not be members (e.g. Key 1964). It is this chain of relationships that links the party-in-the-state to the party-in-civil-society.

Political parties are organised actors that concentrate and focus the diffuse agency of a population, both responding to and cultivating issues of public concern around which to mobilise. But this does not lead to the kind of juristic personality that corporations have, precisely because the boundaries between leaderships, formal organisations, and followers and supporters, are necessarily fluid. Corporations have an executive in a directing board, and owners usually as shareholders. They are generally organised to pursue relatively focused goals in the economy, and are distinct actors from their customers and clients. Parties by contrast, blend into the wider population, formulating and promoting broad and evolving political agendas. Indeed, the core conundrum of political parties is that they must represent the partial interests of their core supporters, while also claiming to best represent the nation as a whole. While they may have core organising bodies that are incorporated and can be the objects of legal action (e.g. fairness in hiring), you can't sue an entire political party. Allowing for the considerable cross-national variation touched on above, generally parties are constituted through a process of formal registration (like companies), and are bound by particular rules of financing, such as limits on donations and/or public recording of donors, and of promotion, such as not trespassing on other party names and logos in pursuit of votes. So although they may have central bodies that are incorporated and have juristic personality, parties as a whole are unincorporated (Johns 1999, Müller and Sieberer 2006). Having said this, being constituted and regulated as actors by party law, neither are they simply patterns of private association. They are a hybrid that falls somewhere in between the company and the club (Persily and Cain 2000: 777–779).

Designed for political competition, parties by definition come in sets of rivals, in party systems, and the nature of those systems affects the dynamics of competition. The literature on party systems is extensive, generating numerous different cross-national typologies (Mair 1997a, Wolinetz 2006). Party systems evolve and change over time, and many new ones came into being after the most recent democratic transitions in Latin America, Africa, and Eastern Europe. Although there are stable generalisations, for example, that electoral systems based on single member plurality tend to promote two-party systems, and systems of proportional representation tend to promote multiple parties, even this needs qualification in particular cases. Sartori's (1976) influential typology defined a continuum, from single-party states, through states that allow multiple parties, but one is hegemonic or at least 'predominant', setting the parameters of action for the others, to systems where two parties predominate and tend to alternate power, to multi-party systems characterised by coalitions with some parties dominant, down to highly atomised systems. We can agree with Sartori that a single-party system is no 'party system' at all, while recognising that this hardly eliminates competition, it simply drives 'undomesticated' power competition into the internal dynamics of the single party. At the other end, highly atomised 'systems', by definition, lack systematicity. Most of the action, which is to say capacity to manage the process of political competition, is in the middle range of systems dominated by two to a few sizable parties, with 'third' and other minor parties arrayed around a central dynamic, sometimes able to shift the balance by changing the electoral arithmetic or entering into governing coalition. Other factors, besides the number and relative sizes of parties, and the electoral system itself, can affect the competitive dynamics of party systems, and party struggles to get control of government. Sartori also emphasises the difference between 'centripetal' relations between parties in a system, where parties orient to a centre-ground, and 'centrifugal' relations, where parties polarise to ideological extremes. Allegiances to parties may or may not be aligned with major social cleavages in regard to class, ethnicity, race, region, or religion, and support for parties can intensify or slacken according to the social and political climate. But unlike companies, for which the arena of competition is more or less divisible and expandable, political parties compete to deliver a single good, control, or at least influence, over government, to a constituency, and ultimately to an entire national population. Thus, the viable number of parties in a system is always quite limited, compared to the complex ecologies in which corporations operate.

E. E. Schattschneider (1975), who took a 'realist' approach to US politics, provided an enduring argument about the importance of political parties for the development of democracy. Schattschneider saw conflict as natural to society, and politics as the process by which certain conflicts are selected out of many, and made central to political dispute, marginalising other conflict issues in the process. He saw politics as the socialisation of conflict, turning relatively private axes of conflict into public matters, and parties as the primary means of doing this. In doing so, the weaker party always has a motive for expanding the scope of politics through promoting certain conflicts, which has been central to the expansion of franchises and the nationalisation of politics. Party competition 'provides the people with an opportunity to make a choice' (1975: 137), it domesticates national political conflicts. This chapter proceeds very much in the spirit of Schattschneider's insights (cf. Mair 1997b).

The Prehistory of Parties (Britain)[1]

The earliest applications of the term 'party' in politics are found in British history in the late seventeenth century through to the eighteenth century. The idea also appears in the politics of the British North American colonies in this period, but as we will see, is profoundly altered in the first half of the nineteenth century, as the idea of democracy in the new republic took practical shape. So, there is a kind of 'founder effect' in the history of the modern political party. The idea starts in Britain, is transplanted to North America, and then evolves rapidly once the social and political environment is transformed by revolution, secession, and constitutional innovation.

Throughout the eighteenth century the terms 'party' and 'faction' were used interchangeably as names for groupings aligned around shared political and ideological interests. Today these terms have become quite distinct, factions being rather loose alliances that appear in almost any organisation and institutional setting, and parties being relatively formal organisations designed for democratic competition, as outlined above. The history of early parties in Britain is too complex to do full justice here, but I explore the prehistory of political parties to emphasise the novelty of the modern form that eventually emerged. I will schematically cover the British political history of the period, but my primary aim is to show that the things commonly called 'parties' in

[1] This section draws on: Dickson (2002), Hill (2002), O'Gorman (1982), Plumb (1967).

the literature, are better understood as 'factions', in order to appreciate the significance of the change in question. In this section I focus on Britain in the eighteenth century, the next section picks up the American story before and after the Revolution.

In the American colonies there was a fundamental break and 'new beginning' in the structures of government and constitution (even if the leading elites remained largely the same). In Britain, the story of political factions-cum-parties played out over the messy, piecemeal migration of the political system away from aristocracy and towards democracy, including a long period often known at the time as 'mixed government', that is, one that combines principles of monarchical, aristocratic, and democratic rule. In practical terms in the British case, this was a combination of a monarchical executive, and a constraining and enabling parliament representing various constituencies, aristocratic, ecclesiastical, but also commercial and common. The Glorious Revolution of 1688/1689 was basic in cementing this pattern in Britain, and the American constitution, with its separation of presidential executive, bicameral legislative, and judicial powers, can be seen as an effort to establish a kind of mixed government in the absence of formal institutions of monarchy and aristocracy. As Sartori and others have noted, while this period in Britain saw parliamentary factions rather than parties, the presence of 'responsible government' in which ministers were held accountable by a parliament, was a factor conducive to the formation of factions, and eventually parties (1976: 16–21, Scarrow 2006: 17–18).

The original 'parties' in the British system, the Tories and the Whigs, took their names from epithets that emerged during the War of the Three Kingdoms (including The English Civil war) (1638–1651) and then crystallised around shifting factional interest in the latter part of the century. The 'cavaliers', loyal supporters of Charles I, were ancestors of the Tories, and the 'roundhead' parliamentary forces were ancestors of the Whigs, but these were contending forces during a period of civil war, not parties. Eventually, what mainly divided Tories and Whigs were principled conceptions of the appropriate distribution of power between the monarch and parliament, Tories preferring a more autonomous (and virtuous) monarch, the Whigs preferring to see the monarch as bound by agreement to limits set by parliament. More pragmatically, both parties struggled to influence monarchs, and win their favour: this was the more 'factional' face of the system. So these were factions immersed in a system of monarchical patronage, at the same time trying to affect the basic terms of that patronage, the terms of monarchical rule. That they took shape at all indicates that the monarch did have to rely on support from below, and negotiate contending interests. Monarchs have always had to do this in their relations with rivalrous nobles, but unlike older feudal aristocracies, the Whigs and Tories were only partly defined by landed and lineage interests, they were also defined by competing ideas about religion, commerce, and the very nature of authority. Broadly, the Whigs were associated with nobility and the peerage, tied into London merchant networks, supportive of protectionist policies, distrustful of Catholic religion, supportive of religious non-conformers, and inclined towards constitutional reform. The Tories were associated with the gentry class of relatively large landholders who took in rents from tenant farmers, were entitled to have coats of arms but were not part of the peerage, were more committed to Episcopalian and sometimes Catholic religion, and were more conservative in regard to preserving the traditional status and power of the monarchy. These factions mapped on, imperfectly, to an evaluative distinction made primarily by Tories, between a 'court party' of Whigs enjoying power and the monarch's favour in the court in London, and a 'country party' (in the sense of 'the country as a whole') of Tories defending what they saw as the national interests against the corrupt patronage networks around the court. 'Country party' was a self-ascription, 'court party' an accusation.

This division first became really clear during the 'Exclusion Crisis' (1678–1681), in which the Whig faction sought to exclude the Duke of York (later James II and VII), King Charles II's younger brother, from eligibility to succeed to the throne, due to his Catholicism. Two bills to this effect were prevented by Charles' dissolutions of parliament, and key Whig leaders either fled the country or were imprisoned for treason when a pro-republican plot against the king was revealed. On his brother's death, James did reign briefly, 1685–1688, but amid plots to overthrow him, and widespread distrust of his Catholic sympathies, the Whigs eventually prevailed, deposing James in the Glorious Revolution of 1688, and replacing him with the invited William of Orange, who was married to James' daughter, Mary, thus securing a Protestant monarchy. Beneath the Protestant-Catholic conflict, was the constitutional innovation of a parliament having established the power to appoint a monarch, and bind them with legal terms, such as those laid out in the Bill of Rights of 1689, as conditions of office. The divine right of kings was being replaced with a more 'contractual' understanding of the relationship between King and Parliament, and subjects more generally. Many Tories abhorred this; for many Whigs it was essential.

One factor clearly distinguishing this from a modern party system is that throughout this period, the two factions tended to prosecute national politics through alliances with outside powers, the Tories with France, and the Whigs with Holland, as in the case of the Glorious Revolution. And while the price for being caught, or not prevailing, could be high, the strategy was relatively normal. During the reigns of William and Mary (1689–1702), and their successor Anne (1702–1714), monarchs tended to try to balance the forces of the two factions, although sometimes favouring the Tories because, despite their distrust of court circles, they were more inclined towards royal authority. With the death of Anne and the Hanoverian succession of George I, the Whigs came into favour in the ministry, and used their position to exclude the Tories from the patronage networks of public offices in the church, army, navy, civil service, and court of law. This began a long period known as the 'Whig Supremacy' (1714–1760) (Dickson 1973). One response of some Tories in this period was to become attracted to Jacobitism, and get involved in plots to restore the Stuart line, most notably in the Jacobite Rebellions of 1715 and 1745, but also in recurring abortive plots. Although representatives of both factions continued to be elected to the Commons and sit in the House of Lords, and fought over matters of policy there, the dominance of the Whigs sent many Tories abroad in search of support to subvert the monarchy and its government.

Meanwhile, Robert Walpole became the first 'Prime Minister' in 1721, and this signalled a move towards a more stable parliamentary structure effectively managed by a parliamentary leader. In the middle years of the eighteenth century there was convergence on a moderately whiggish political view, and from the 1750s to the 1780s the distinction between Whigs and Tories largely dissolved and ceased to be a core axis of power struggles in government (Namier 1957). Correspondingly, under George III (1760–1820) divisions tended to revolve around more personalistic factions following contending leaders in parliament (Bedford, Chatham, Glenville, Rockingham), all working under the Whig mantle in one way or another. The gradually emerging British two-party system was at this point still not really organisationally distinct from elite patronage networks more generally, and thus, party distinctions could simply fade and go out of focus.

Throughout the eighteenth century the political discourse on parties and factions was largely critical. One's opponents fomented faction, while one's own group represented loyalty to tradition, institutions, principles, and the nation. Nonetheless people were fully aware of the practical existence and operation of 'parties'. By the late eighteenth century some intellectuals were beginning to make more pragmatic and realist arguments about the role and possible necessity of political parties in modern, at least partially, democratic politics. Sartori notes that while the terms 'faction' and 'party' were often used interchangeably, there was a tendency to see party as indicating divisions over principles, whereas factions were more a matter of allegiances among 'concrete groups' (1976: ch 1). Viscount Bolingbroke, a key articulator of the court/country party distinction, spoke positively of the need for a country party with which he associated himself, but only to stand up, at times of crisis, for the national interest which was threatened by the factional interests circling around the court. Ideally, parties and factions should not be necessary. David Hume (1985: 54–72, 493–501; Phillipson 2011) began to speak more pragmatically about parties in the 1740s and 1750s. Hume didn't make a clear distinction between the terms 'faction' and 'party', instead devising an overarching typology distinguishing between those based on 'interest', 'affection', and 'principle'. In other words, they can instrumentally pursue largely material ends, be based on emotional ties to families or persons, or advance entrenched ideological positions. Hume saw the last of these as a distinctly modern innovation, and one particularly driven by the pernicious effects of sectarian religion. But all three, especially those based on interest, were perhaps a necessary evil of modern politics in a mixed government. The first full-throated argument for parties came from Edmund Burke, who argued in his *Thoughts on the Present Discontents* (1770) that while factions are indeed pernicious, these needed to be distinguished from parties proper, which were a necessary means of making connections among politicians in order to advance shared principles and pursue common interests. For Burke kings confronted a choice, either governing through a web of self-interests and personalistic patronage, that is, factions, or through parties which have public support for relatively coherent agendas:

> Party is a body of men united for promoting by their joint endeavours the national interest, upon some particular principle in which they are all agreed. For my part, I find it impossible to conceive that any one believes in his own politics, or thinks them to be of any weight, who refuses to adopt the means of having them reduced into practice. It is the business of the speculative philosopher to mark the proper ends of Government. It is the business of the politician, who is the philosopher in action, to find out proper means towards those ends, and to employ them with effect. (Burke 2007: 54)

In contrast to Bolingbroke's rather high-minded notion of the country party in opposition, Burke realistically acknowledged that politicians and their parties are corruptible, but in this theirs is like any other human practice:

> Every profession, not excepting the glorious one of a soldier, or the sacred one of a priest, is liable to its own particular vices; which, however, form no argument against those ways of life; nor are the vices themselves inevitable to every individual in those professions. Of such a nature are connections in politics; essentially necessary for the full performance of our public duty, accidentally liable to degenerate into faction. Commonwealths are made of families, free Commonwealths of parties also; and we may as well affirm, that our natural regards and ties of blood tend inevitably to make men bad citizens, as that the bonds of our party weaken those by which we are held to our country. (Burke 2007: 52)

But Burke's opinions on parties remained eccentric for some time. In the next section we cross the Atlantic to North America, beginning with the same climate of ideas, but following them on a new trajectory triggered by the exigencies of setting up a constitutional republic, and making it work.

The Formation of Modern Mass Parties (the US)[2]

The political culture of the British North American colonies in the mid-eighteenth century inevitably had many continuities with the mother country, including traditional conceptions of social hierarchy, as well

[2] This section draws generally on: Bridges (1984), Crotty (2006), Hofstadter (1969), Holt (1999), Howe (2007), Kruman (1992), McCormick (1966), Parsons (2009), Renda (1995), Watson (2020), Wilentz (2005), and Wood (2009).

as a common literature and set of ideas flowing in either direction. After the social and political upheavals of the mid-to-late seventeenth century, the Crown had sought to reassert and formalise its powers in the colonies. Nonetheless, social structures were also quite different in the colonies, more shifting and fluid. The absence of an indigenous landed nobility was a fundamental difference. Some aristocrats were present, appointed in royal government and the military for instance, but there was no indigenous noble class. That said, there was an upper class of large landholders and merchants who saw themselves as part of a 'natural' aristocracy, destined for social leadership by dint of property, learning, and worldly experience (Onuf 2012). Leading figures in the Revolution would come from this class. These white, European descended men wielded formal, legal power over women, African slaves, and indentured servants from Europe. This, rather than the noble-commoner distinction, was the most fundamental divide in the colonies. Despite a certain pragmatic egalitarianism and independent-mindedness among the 'free', fed by the rapid growth and mobility of the population, people could be quite status conscious, especially in the more urban settings. However distant the king, it was still a monarchical society with an in-built sense of hierarchy. People were sensitive to titles of rank (Mister, Esquire, Yeoman), and important institutions such as the military, the Anglican Church, and the colleges were quite codified in marking status differences. Like Britain, hierarchy was expressed through interlocking vertical chains of obligation and patronage, creating clientelist networks that cut across the finer horizontal distinctions of status (Wood 1991: 11–76).

This setting was no more conducive to the modern idea of parties than Britain. As Hofstadter puts it, 'First, parties had to be created; and then at last they would begin to find a theoretical acceptance' (1969: 39). Hofstadter finds occasional sympathetic words to the idea of parties in the colonial writings of the period, but no systematic defence. Burke's argument was novel and marginalised on both sides of the Atlantic. If anything, the colonials leaned towards the Bolingbroke view, of a legitimate party existing only in temporary opposition to the corruption at the core, around the court. The colonials often had a rather romanticised conception of their inheritance as 'free Englishmen', who had reasserted their freedoms through the English Civil War and the Glorious Revolution, freedoms that must be jealously guarded against the backsliding and corruption of monarchs and their placemen and hangers-on. This was an attitude that eventually predisposed to the Revolution; a Burkean conception of parties required a system of political representation which did not yet exist.

To a degree the divisions of Whig and Tory, though more remote, were echoed in the American colonies in the eighteenth century. With their own local forms of government, and lacking parliamentary representation, matters of party, in the sense of these factions, were less directly salient. However, the colonists drew on a body of writings by people such as Algernon Sydney, James Harrington, and the authors of *Cato's Letters*, bolstering their sense of the dangers of tyranny and the usurpation of the traditional rights of English liberty. Much of what they inherited were common ideas of the time regarding natural rights and the contractual nature of government, along with core anxieties about the dangers of standing armies, national debts, and political corruption. These were themes that ran across the Whig/Tory boundary, but by the time they reached American shores, they tended to coalesce in a radical Whig view that thought that the reforms of the Glorious Revolution did not go far enough in securing liberty, and for some, that the work of the English Civil War and the ideal of the commonwealth, were incomplete. By the time of the Revolution, in the colonies Whigs were restyled as 'Patriots', and Tories as 'Loyalists' (Bailyn 1992: 33–54; Middlekauff 2005: 136–138).

After the Revolutionary War, a new, written constitution was hammered out by the constitutional convention, and then presented to the people of the states for ratification. In the *Federalist Papers* (1787), designed to encourage ratification in New York, paper No. 10 by James Madison, famously argued that a degree of party and faction in politics was unavoidable, but that a large republic, contrary to common assumptions at the time, could manage these dangerous divisions by distributing power widely among the separate states, and among the branches of government: the presidential executive, the House of Representatives reflecting the actual population in the legislature, the Senate representing the States on an equal basis, and the Judiciary, supposedly standing at some remove from the rest. In Madison's vision, such institutional variability and dispersion would make it very difficult for any majority faction to seize power and tyrannise the whole, at least in any sustained way (Madison 2001). George Washington's two terms as the first president (1788–1796) occluded nascent party divisions, but he saw the divisions between

'Federalists' (e.g. Alexander Hamilton, John Adams) and 'Anti-Federalists' (e.g. Thomas Jefferson, James Madison) looming, and in his farewell address warned that:

> All combinations and associations ... with the real design to direct, control, counteract, or awe the regular deliberation and action of the constituted authorities ... serve to organize faction; to give it an artificial extraordinary force; to put in the place of the delegated will of the nation the will of a party, often a small but artful and enterprising minority of the community. (quoted in Kruman 1992: 509)

My focus is on the transition between what have been called 'first party system' (1796–1828) and 'second party system' (1828–1860), pivoting on the presidential election of Andrew Jackson in 1828 (McCormick 1966, Parsons 2009). As just suggested, in the early decades of the US, the main division was between Federalists who saw a larger role for the federal government in fostering trade and supporting commercial interests, and the Anti-Federalists who favoured greater political autonomy of the states and the agrarian and slaveholding economy. But the leading figures on both sides of the first party system generally saw themselves as part of a natural aristocracy (though they would have rejected that term), highly educated and civilised, and born to lead the new nation. And both sides saw themselves as legitimately representing the interests of the whole society; they generally all espoused anti-party views, and resisted the idea of political campaigning, expecting instead to be called to office by their peers. After John Adams' presidency (1796–1800) the Federalist faction was increasingly marginalised as the opposition led by Jefferson generally attracted a wider social base of support across the country, but one still very deferential to patrimonial elites. In this pre-party era, the followers of Jefferson variously styled themselves 'democrats' and more often 'republicans', and have often been called the Republican Party, but recent historians have tended to label them 'Democratic-Republicans' to mark their precursor relationship to what became the Democratic Party in the second system, from the presidency of Andrew Jackson in 1828.

It wasn't until the next generation confronted the problems of political succession and routinisation, in a political system fundamentally based on popular election and not inheritance, that the idea of parties and a party system gradually became normalised. A paradigmatic figure here was Martin Van Buren, the son of a tavernkeeper of modest means, who became a key operator in New York State politics, rising to become a member of the New York Senate (1813–1820), New York Attorney General (1815–1819), US Senator for New York (1821–1828), and briefly Governor of New York in 1829. After that he held several posts in President Jackson's cabinet, before becoming Vice President, and going on to become the eighth President in 1837, after Jackson. Known as 'The Little Magician', Van Buren was the prime example of the new politician, and a major advocate of professionalised party-based politics that used the congressional caucus to strategically coordinate party mobilisation across the various states, thereby leading to a more integrated national party system. He espoused an ethos of gentlemanly respect across party lines, unlike the rancour that often characterised the previous generation, and solidarity, discipline and compromise within parties, to assure their political efficacy. Describing the 'Albany Regency', the dominant group that controlled the New York Democratic-Republican Party under Van Buren's leadership (c. 1817–1825), Hofstadter says that their:

> rationale for the party appears not to have been derived from theoretical writings but rather from an awareness of past American experience with party conflict and from efforts to cope with contemporary realities. It was one of those pragmatic American innovations, based upon experience and experiment, which one usually finds keyed closely to changing institutional necessities. After more than a generation of party-building by anti-party thinkers, there had at last evolved a rationale for parties which made it unnecessary for politicians to apologize for doing what the necessities of their trade plainly required them to do, and which now made it possible for them to say why forming and managing parties were acts of service to the liberal state. (1969: 252)

The first full-blown party system in the world, the one that laid the template for others to follow, emerged gradually through piecemeal adaptation to a new political environment, not directly out of some ideological vision of how to organise democracy.

It is worth noting that the formalisation of parties ran alongside the gradual decline of a more traditional martial discourse of political conflict. Politics and militarism were domesticated together. It took some time before this new model, rather than outright contests of force, could seep into the popular imagination. The country had already seen two small armed tax revolts militarily supressed: Shays' Rebellion (1786–1787) just before Washington's presidency, and the Whisky Rebellion (1791–1794) during it. Washington was also wary of unrest fomented by the numerous 'Democratic Societies' (1793–1796) that flourished in the wake of the French Revolution, advocating more radical forms of republicanism and democracy (Hofstadter 1969: 92–94). Cedric de Leon (2010) has argued that under the first party system the US never made the shift to a truly civil conception of politics. The threat of the remobilisation of continental armies and dissolution of the union often lurked in the background of the political contest, and persisted in the social memory. With the 'second party system' that emerged out of the efforts of Van Buren and others, a new generation was mobilised into what were now organised mass parties, and an important part of how this was done was by modelling party activity and discourse on militias. Parties borrowed military terminology: enlistment, brigades, and campaigns, using public drills and parades to show a mass presence on the streets. They styled themselves as mass mobilisations, potentially violent, in defence of a state under threat of corruption and usurpation, and they played upon the idea of 'regenerative war' as a necessity for vital democracy (as Jefferson once put it, 'the tree of liberty must be refreshed from time to time with the blood of patriots and tyrants'). The new generation involved in mass democratic politics had missed the experience of the Revolutionary War, but that was still part of the language through which they understood the political process as a whole. This was a kind of ideological stepping-stone on the path to the fuller routinisation of the party system. This reinforces my argument about the domestication of military competition being a precondition for the elaboration of competition in political, economic, and ideological spheres.

The actual shift to a national party system, the second party system, hinged on the presidential elections in 1824, of John Quincy Adams, and 1828, of Andrew Jackson. By 1823 the Federalists were in disarray, and Democratic-Republican President James Monroe, who had little influence over the House of Representatives, which was becoming the actual centre of national legislative politics, failed to lobby effectively on behalf of a successor. Thus the 1824 election became a contest between four candidates from within the Democratic-Republican field: Andrew Jackson, John Quincy Adams, William H. Crawford, and

Henry Clay. The main contest was between Tennessean Jackson, portrayed as a salt of the earth war hero from the battle of New Orleans (1815), and Adams from New England, the highly educated and politically experienced son of the one Federalist president, John Adams. The younger Adams had come over to the Democratic-Republicans about a decade earlier, but was always something of an outsider. Jackson's demotic appeal tended to run much deeper than the more dispassionate and cerebral support for Adams. Both ran in the traditional mode of the 'mute tribune' (Hudson 2009: 76–77), standing back from the fray and allowing others to make the case for them. In Jackson's case this included the adept tactical support of Van Buren, which would prove even more effective in the next election. Although Jackson won the plurality of the popular and electoral college votes, 152,901 and 99 to Adams's 114,023 and 84, without a majority the election was decided by the House of Representatives, and Clay, as Speaker of the House, manoeuvred the result to Adams's favour, and was subsequently appointed Secretary of State under Adams. This was seen as a 'corrupt bargain' by Jackson and his followers, engendering considerable bitterness towards the Adams presidency, which was seen by many as yet another victory of corrupt elites over true democracy, and further weakened the legitimacy of the older, pre-party patrician model of elite-led politics. When the next election came, the gloves were off.

With the next election in 1828, in which Jackson confronted the incumbent Adams, party organisation and campaigning strategies took a leap forward, and historians frequently see this as the start of the Democratic Party, although campaigning under that mantle didn't really begin until Jackson's re-election in 1832. Van Buren became even more central to the 1828 campaign, bringing machine-like strategies honed in New York State to the national stage. Parsons (2009: 134–142) has emphasised four innovations associated with Van Buren's leadership. First, partisan newspapers were increasingly coordinated among a network of publishing editors, coordinating political messages (and sometimes slander) across the country. Improving post roads and congressional franking privileges enabled the dissemination of newspapers and pamphlets. The Adams campaign was seriously outgunned on this front. Second, was the organisation and coordination of the voters. Previously a key tactic had been the congressional caucus as a means of getting party members in the House and Senate to align their efforts behind candidates and messages. With this election a much wider field was brought in, harnessing various local 'committees of correspondence' and 'Hickory Clubs' ('Old Hickory' was a nickname for Jackson), which organised 'conventions' of delegates from various towns, which in turn sent delegates to state conventions. Conventions involved speeches, the proposal and adoption of resolutions, with their activities being reported on through a sympathetic press. The Adams campaign followed suit, but its conventions were drier affairs, lacking the popular enthusiasm of the other side. Third, was money. To cover costs such as printing and events, large donors and banks were increasingly solicited in the New York-Philadelphia area, and fund-raising events such as dinners were organised. Adams's supporters followed suit. And fourthly, particularly in Jackson's case, the 'mute tribune' approach was abandoned, and the candidate became an active campaigner himself, networking among fellow politicians to consolidate support, and making public statements. Adams remained more aloof, believing the president should avoid such partisan activity. More generally, the issue of patronage, of those in power parcelling out offices to their faithful supporters, sometimes called the 'spoils system', had long been an issue in politics, and many presidents, like Adams, sought to overcome divisions by offering posts to those on either side of the main divide. But with the hardening of political parties, the idea of rewarding the party faithful once in office became more normalised, a basic resource in party consolidation and control.

Jackson won the 1828 election with 647,276 popular votes and 178 in the Electoral College, to Adams's respective 508,074 and 83. From the previous election voter turnout increased from 17 per cent to 57 per cent, and it stayed at or above 69 per cent for the rest of the century (Parsons 2009: 182–184). As Parsons sums up:

> Before 1828 voters took more interest in state and local elections than they did in the presidency. Afterward the pattern was reversed. Van Buren was right: increased partisanship meant increased competition, increased competition meant increased awareness of the issues, and the voters responded accordingly. Most agree that the era of mass political parties began with the election of 1828. (Parsons 2009: 184)

This was the beginning of the second party system. The consolidating Democratic Party led this change, but the new opposition, drawing on strains from both the old Federalists and Madisonian dissenters from the Democratic-Republicans, soon followed suit, regrouping first under the mantle of 'National Republicans' in opposition to Jackson, and then under the name of 'Whigs', a term that rhetorically suggested resistance to Jackson's 'kingly' and 'tyrannical' approach to the presidency, frequently defying the Congress by means of the veto. However, the Whigs often lost votes to smaller single-issue parties such as the 'Anti-Masons' and the nativist 'Know Nothings', and to 'antiparty' northern Evangelicals, natural allies because of the party's New England puritan roots, who sometimes resisted parties as worldly competitors for moral authority (Formisano 1969, Holt 1999: 1–18). Despite the fact that the Democrats held six out of eight presidential terms during this period, a truly national political system had emerged in which both parties contested, often fiercely, in most states and regions. Older patterns of 'sectionalism', in which single parties (in the older sense) dominated sets of states in New England, the Mid-Atlantic, and the South, were greatly reduced. The Whigs, still associated with wealthier commercial classes, continued to advocate for a federal state active in economic development, and enjoyed support in all areas, especially among community leaders in market and commerce-oriented towns, both north and south. For a time both parties contended over economic issues, holding the deeper divisions over the institution of slavery at bay. But as the issue of whether slavery would be allowed in the western territories became more pressing by the 1850s, the slavery issue – whether the national future was to be dominated by a slave-holding aristocracy dominating both black and white, or small-holding, small-business white middle class – displaced economic development issues. As well, by that time much of the 'whiggish' developmental policy was more widely accepted, although Democrats preferred to pursue these ends more at the state than the federal level, as the rapid growth in corporations in the south in this period, mentioned in the previous chapter, indicates. In effect, competition over the fate of the western territories, and thus the nation as a whole, overwhelmed all other politics, subsuming the party system for the period of the Civil War. This led to the 'third party system', from the election of Lincoln in 1860 on, as the Whigs and other smaller parties were absorbed by the new Republican Party. After the war a national two-party system of Republicans and Democrats took hold and operated into the next century, once again 'sectionalist', with Republicans dominant at the federal/presidential level, and allied with a national business class, and southern politics after reconstruction largely yielded to the elites of the 'solid south' and the segregationist Democratic Party.

In the antebellum years, as the actual institution of political parties, born of practicality, bedded in, their theoretical justification began to follow (Hofstadter 1969: 252–271). Alexis de Tocqueville preferred the great early parties representing fundamental principles around the concentration (Federalists) versus dispersion (Jeffersonians) of power, over the more instrumental, interest-based parties he saw forming in the 1830s. Tocqueville's more subtle appreciation of what was taking shape is found somewhat separately in his treatment of 'political associations', the undercarriage of political parties, and how they operated to coordinate wills and opinions in a democratic society (Tocqueville 2000: 166–172, 180–186, 496–500). Indigenously, Francis Leiber's *Manual of Political Ethics* (1838–1839), Jabez Hammond's *History of Political Parties in the State of New York* (1843), and Frederick Grimke's *The Nature and Tendency of Free Institutions* (1848), all espoused, like Burke, the necessary virtues of political parties. As Grimke put it: 'when opinions have to pass through a great number of minds before they are reduced to practice, society does not experience a violent shock as it does on their sudden and unpremeditated adoption. Factions stir the passions of men, but parties introduce the conflict of opinions' (1968: 175). All these thinkers followed Van Buren in recognising 'the value of opposition itself as a cohesive force' (Hofstadter 169: 226). In a way Van Buren echoed the argument of Adam Ferguson (1966[1767]), who had seen martial conflict as a basic force promoting social solidarity, which he was worried would be weakened by commercial 'civil society'. But by transposing conflict to the realm of civil politics, between parties, conflict could be harnessed without the cost of bloodshed. Looking the other direction, Van Buren and these authors anticipated mid-twentieth century theorists of social conflict, such as Max Gluckman (1954) and Lewis Coser (1957), who emphasised the integrating effects of social conflict, seeing it as functional for society.

The preceding is a largely narrative account, but why did it happen this way? Some of the answer lies in changes in the underlying material and structural conditions. The rate of demographic change was phenomenal, with overall populations doubling about every twenty years, spreading over half the continent. 'Between 1790 and 1820 New

York's population quadrupled; Kentucky's multiplied nearly eight times ... In a single generation [European] Americans occupied more territory than they had occupied during the entire 150 years of the colonial period' (Wood 2009: 2). While small farming remained the foundation of the economy, rapid market integration was happening across the country, on farms and in cities, though more intensively in the northern 'free' states, where industrialisation was more significant than in the southern states dominated by the slave plantation economy. Everywhere developments in communications – roads, canals, railroads, postal services, telegraphs – were assisting geographic mobility and commerce, pulling the country together into a more unified field of exchange and discourse. All these factors contributed to the breakdown of the older patrician order, and the need for new ways, such as parties, to coordinate popular politics.

More broadly, as emphasised in previous chapters, the traditional European authority structures, of kin-based, monarchical-aristocratic rule, and the ideological authority of an established church, were largely absent. Without these there was a kind of vacuum into which rather abstract ideals of republicanism and democracy were inserted and cultivated, in a somewhat ad hoc manner. While these were developing, a kind of 'natural aristocracy' of American elites established before the Revolution held things in place, through the first party system, but this could not last. Because of this, the newly minted federal constitutional structure itself, rather than kingly/courtly favour, was the primary object of political competition. In lieu of a king, the presidency became a primary focus of attention; an office to be captured, by a party, rather than a person to be appeased. The office calls forth the person, rather than the person inheriting the office (or being elected to it by a narrow aristocratic elite). At the same time, the houses of congress, especially the House of Representatives, and the state level governments, were also foci of competition, and democratic power required predominance in multiple branches of government. The key point is that the personalism that permeated the power complex of monarch, nobles, and merchants in Britain, structured around crown, court, ministers, and commons, was supplanted in the US by a more open institutional terrain of various levels and branches of government, to be populated by contending interests. Even though presidents were symbolically important, and charismatic leaders like Jackson mattered, the strategy was one of mobilising support from below, for networks of 'activists' to seek to occupy government by election.

The model of formal, competitive party politics emerged first in the US in this period, eventually spreading to Europe and beyond, as other political systems shifted towards democracy. In Britain the parent soon followed the child, with the extension of the franchise in 1832 transforming the earlier competing patronage networks of Whigs and Tories into a system of more modern parties focused on winning parliamentary power. This process was further accelerated by the 1867 and 1884 extensions of the franchise, and by the late nineteenth century Liberals had replaced the Whigs as a modern party, and labour and socialist parties were forming (Hawkins 2018). Across continental Europe in the nineteenth century change was slower. In varying sequences, shifts to more parliamentary government and franchise extensions stimulated party development, but parties were not widely normalised until the twentieth century (Scarrow 2006). Caramani (2004) describes the gradual territorial and vertical integration of party systems in Western Europe, the next frontier of the party system after Britain, across the nineteenth century. In the early days of developing democracies and party systems there were many 'silent elections' where seats were held uncontested over many years, usually by local notables (Caramani 2003). It was not until after World War One that multiparty competition on a national scale was widely established. From the 1830s to the 1920s, suffrage expanded and high barriers to entry into the political contest came down, and a new national mass party politics based more on economic cleavages tended to replace more localised territorial politics between conservatives/Catholics and liberals/radicals. Parties developed centralised but nationwide strategies of competition with their opponents, furthering national ideological integration. To follow the process further is beyond the scope of this book, but it was the critical shift in the US in the late 1820s that established the model that would increasingly be imitated, albeit with substantial variations, across the globe.

Excursus: Adversarial Law and the Civil Service

Another striking example of the institutionalisation of competition in the domain of law and the state, linked to British and American history in this same period, is the rise of adversarial legal systems, in which trials are structured as a contest between parties represented by lawyers. In Chapter 3 we saw the classic distinction between the continental civil law and English common law traditions (Herzog 2018), noting how the latter was particularly conducive to the idea of juristic personality. Adversarial law also has a special affinity with the common law tradition. The civil law tradition is centred on a judge or magistrate who collects evidence and adjudicates between contending parties, whereas in common law judges take a more detached role, and the prosecution of cases is led more by lawyers representing parties in an adversarial contest. This distinction is to a degree reproduced within the common law traditions in the distinctions between 'civil' and 'criminal' law, the former being more 'judge-led' and the latter more 'lawyer-led'. Adversarial, lawyer-made law came to the fore in Britain and the US from the seventeenth to the nineteenth centuries in separate but parallel and related histories.

In Britain, and more specifically England, because of Scotland's distinct legal tradition, an adversarial legal system emerged in stages out of medieval traditions of magistrate-led law. Before and throughout the seventeenth century, criminal law indictments were made in the name of the monarch, whose prosecutors were allowed legal counsel and able to take witness testimony under oath. But legal counsel and the right to call witnesses was denied to prisoners. This began to change following the Glorious Revolution with the Treason Trials Act of 1696, which was a response to the abuse of legal power by the Stuart kings in persecuting their Whig opponents. The act allowed those accused of treason to be represented by legal counsel, setting a precedent for the expansion of this right to all accused, in a broader context of spreading Lockean ideas of individual rights. As the role of criminal prosecutors increased in the context of law protecting property in an expanding economy, and a system of substantial rewards for 'thief-takers' (i.e. bounty hunters) became prone to abuse and corruption, judges found it ever more prudent to allow legal counsel to defendants, until this became the norm (Langbein 2003).

From the middle of the eighteenth century, under the influence of figures such as William Garrow (Hostettler 2006), and an increasingly lawyer-led legal culture centred on London's Old Bailey, the role of legal defence grew, especially after about 1780. During this period, as lawyers took ever more prominent roles in prosecution and defence, rules of evidence were increasingly formalised. However, it was not until the Prisoner's Counsel Act of 1836 that the right of prisoners to have counsel address the jury directly was established. At issue during this transition was whether inquisitorial (judge-led) or adversarial (lawyer-led) law was more subject to manipulation, and/or better at revealing the truth. Both are open to abuse, and historians of law continue to debate the merits of the two systems to this day (see for instance Langbein (2003) versus Hostettler (2006)). But the wider point is that as the British political system slowly democratised, and middle classes expanded, and opportunities for civil as well as criminal dispute increased with an expanding market economy, the old connections between trial as the support of monarchical and aristocratic interests gave ground to the more individualised and populist dynamics of an adversarial system (see also May 2003).

The American legal system inherited some of this British (English) history, including strong Whig sentiments in opposition to overweaning control of law by government magistrates. In the colonial period there was considerable variation across colonies, but Courts of Chancery, led by appointed colonial governors, operating in an inquisitorial style, were common, and objects of opposition and distrust in the revolutionary era. Amalia D. Kessler (2017) unearths a somewhat forgotten 'equity' legal system based on the collection of written testimonies on either side to be reviewed by a judge, that operated in a more judge-led fashion in the antebellum period, providing a means of dispute resolution in a rapidly expanding society and economy. Nonetheless, in the same period, parallel to this, as various states sought to better codify their legal systems, much greater attention was paid to legal procedure, interpreted in the context of ideas about the English common law tradition. Kessler describes a developing legal culture in nineteenth century America in which leading lawyers saw themselves as civic republicans, dedicated to oratorical skills uniquely displayed in public trials, featuring cross-examination before a jury. As Kessler puts it:

> Valued by lawyers because they facilitated republican self-display, these techniques also came to be viewed (both by many lawyers and the public more generally) as fostering a form of socially beneficial competition. This adversarial competition between warring litigants was, in turn, vaunted as vital for preserving and promoting a distinctively American commitment to freedom, encompassing both political liberty and free enterprise. (2017: 200)

Kessler argues that the parallel 'equity' system was increasingly eclipsed after the Civil War by the adversarial system partly because it had become a forum for ameliorating racial injustice in the Reconstruction period, and this was opposed in a society reconstituting a racial caste system post-slavery.

I simply conclude this section by noting that in addition to the emergence of party systems and adversarial legal systems, the competitive principle was also becoming more institutionalised in the basic process of appointment to government posts in the army and civil service. When one tracks the use of the term 'competition' in encyclopaedias in the nineteenth century, one becomes aware of a period when there were raging controversies about the need to replace older patterns of patronage as the route to office with more justifiable systems of competitive examination.[3] In Britain this change was advanced particularly by the establishment of the Civil Service Commissioners in 1855, as envisioned in the Northcote-Trevelyan report commissioned by Gladstone a few years earlier. The report advocated that appointment should be based on merit according to performance in open competitive examinations. This in turn influenced the development of the civil service in British India, and was further imprinted on the popular imagination by Sir George Otto Trevelyan (not the same Trevelyan) in his book *The Competition Wallah* (1864),[4] previously serialised in *Macmillan's Magazine*, which sought to comment critically on British colonial relations in India. The key point here is that this shift is another example of addressing the declining legitimacy of patronage networks based in aristocratic society with the institutionalisation of competition, to render the growing government bureaucracy more legitimate.

Conclusion

To wind up this discussion I will do three things. First, address an outstanding issue about how the competition of parties relates to underlying competitions between elites. Second, return to a core theme of this book, of how individual agency is aggregated into forms of

[3] For example, the entries on 'competition' in the *Chambers Encyclopaedia* of 1876 and the ninth edition of the *Encyclopaedia Britannica* of 1878.

[4] A 'competition wallah' was a man recruited to the Indian Civil Service in the decades after the establishment of competitive examinations for that career.

collective agency, in the present case, the path from real persons, through parties, to the agency of the ultimate fictive person – the state. Third and last, return to the core theme of social evolution, and how the case discussed above exemplifies key evolutionary processes.

It should not be thought, based on the account in this chapter, that I am arguing that elites were somehow replaced by political parties. That would be naïve. As an episode in the domestication of competition, political parties overlay, and to a degree formalise and regulate the political process, but they can't replace underlying distributions of interests, including those with disproportionate power due to their advantageous positions in economic, social, and governance networks and organisation. But the role of elites, how they pursue their interests, is fundamentally altered by the rise of liberalism and democracy and expanded popular access to the political process (Mosca 1939).[5] Elites must somehow work through this new system. Indeed, the account above is one of older, more aristocratically based elites and newer commercially based elites turning to the wider populace despite themselves, with the help of new 'mid-level' operators like Van Buren, building up the party system as a new venue through which to both pursue and legitimate their power and interests. Notable is the fact that the social networks, connections, and patronage, often kin-based, that are sinews of premodern elite power, persist in the interstices of modern democratic politics, now embedded within the institutions and organisations of party government. My view of this situation is neither rose-tinted, nor cynical. Democracy is strongly influenced, though not entirely controlled, by elites, whose efforts must nonetheless negotiate a system of popular rule, which has an unpredictable dynamic of its own.

The term 'elites' gets used in many different ways (Kahn 2012). We can easily reject overly conspiratorial conceptions in which all power is imagined to be held in very few hands, and we can minimally accept that all complex forms of organisation require forms of leadership, through which some subset rules over the wider group, and controls its

[5] Mosca's idea of the 'political formula' argued that political authority is legitimated by being grounded in abstract principles, and he made basic distinctions between 'supernatural' or 'autocratic' formulas associated with aristocracies in which authority radiates down from above, and 'rational' or 'liberal' formulas associated with democracy, in which authority radiates up from below.

own organisational reproduction, to some degree. The serious study of elites lies in between these poles. G. William Domhoff's (2014) long-term studies of power in the US construct a useful model in which a 'power elite' made up of overlapping networks of corporate leaders, policy planners, and the social upper class, achieve a degree of 'class domination' over the rest of society, managing to get their interests, particularly in regard to major corporations, large banks, agribusiness, and commercial real estate, prioritised in legislative agendas. However, Domhoff is clear that there are divisions of interest within this power elite, between these varied economic interests, between more liberal and conservative wings, and historically between northern and southern elites, which have changed but endured from the colonial times to the present. Domhoff's story is largely one of how they succeed in maintaining alliances despite these divisions; how collective interests usually trump sectional elite interests. Richard Lachmann (2000) argues for the primacy of elite over class conflict in determining the fate of states. Taking a longer-term transnational comparative perspective, drawing on world-systems theory, Lachmann emphasises that conflicts among elites, variously resulting in triumphs, defeats, and stalemates, are key to understanding the rise and fall of power in both cities and states. When inter-elite competition trumps co-operation at the national level, the ability to rule and direct states in the international arena weakens. This leads him to the pessimistic view that the US is now in permanent decline, with its elites unable to coordinate their interests and instead cannibalising rather than rebuilding state resources and powers (2020). These theories are largely beyond the present argument, but they are not incompatible with it. My argument is about how a set of competitive institutions associated with liberal democracy took shape. How elites use and abuse those institutions is an important but separate question.

I have argued that one of the core sociological questions is about how individual agency gets aggregated into forms of collective agency (in ways that ultimately imply leadership and elites). Parties are a particularly telling example of this process. Economic corporations do the same thing, but as I've suggested above, they are bounded and private (even if their stock is sold on a public market). To do their work political parties must be, in principle, open for membership, or support, to all citizens, and they must aim to gain or at least influence public power in the form of government. They run from the very bottom of the chain of agency, the individual citizen, through parties, to the very top – the state. So parties, in the widest sense, are unincorporated and lack juristic personality, but they aim towards the state, which we might regard as the ultimate juristic person. And this is so in two senses. First, that it provides the legal framework through which incorporation and the proliferation of such bodies, both for-profit, as emphasised in the previous chapter, and not-for-profit, as is more central in the next chapter, are made possible. Secondly, that the international community of states answers to and is constituted by no higher body, but instead operates in relative 'anarchy' loosely regulated by negotiated agreements and the hegemony of particularly powerful states (Hall 1996). However poorly enforced, the internationally recognised idea of sovereignty constitutes states as actors on the world stage, and assumes that, one way or another, they get their legitimacy from within and below, however weakly this claim may correspond to reality. This is not to totally disregard the efficacy of other organisations in the international arena, such as transnational corporations, NGOs, and international governance bodies. But when push comes to shove it is powerful sovereign states, with militaries and economic clout, that mainly influence the course of events.

Competitive party systems are important because they provide individuals, communities of interest, and elites, the means, however imperfect, to channel their agency into the largest form of collective agency available on the planet. States are legitimated by many different forms of nationalism and bases for national identification in the world, whether religion, ideology, or sheer performative success in the international struggle for power. Not all rely on the formalised democratic 'voice of the people' that party systems provide. However, for liberal forms of society, this enchainment of agency from person to state, has been central to how states are legitimated, and constrained, as collective actors. There is no guarantee that this complicated system won't break down, and pass away as a social form from the Earth, but if it does, my contention is that the same will be happening to liberal societies as an historical form.

Finally, I want to make explicit the evolutionary processes involved in the case examined here. Despite their comparative lack of 'closure', like corporations, political parties are particularly amenable to an evolutionary and adaptationist analysis, because they exist in a population of similar entities locked into competitive relationships, constantly borrowing and adapting in search of the advantage. The transition from factions to parties in the British-American context is a classic example of how a set of cultural and institutional elements can undergo rapid change when transposed into a new context with new problematics of power. In effect a new species of organisation emerges, 'designed' to maximise political support in this new environment. Parties are prime examples and complex forms of co-operation, both within parties and between parties and other civil society entities, inculcated by intense competitive pressures. As in symmetrical 'arms races' in nature, parties are forced to match each other in their tactics and organisational strategies. Meanwhile, a 'competitive exclusion principle', especially in a population which, as we said at the outset, has narrow limits on how many members it can have, forces parties to differentiate and appeal to different interests, values, and beliefs, to merge if they are too similar, or to form mutualistic relationships of support. This is not to say that historical change is entirely explained by endogenous processes of adaptation. Relatively exogenous political and economic shocks can alter the environment and call forth adaptation. Party competition over national policy in regard to the extension of slavery to the western territories was one of the precipitates of the American Civil War over slavery (Holt 1999). Here the second party system is closely entwined with the events that led to the war and the emergence of the third party system of northern Republicans and southern Democrats. By contrast the fifth party system associated with FDR, the New Deal, and a realignment of working-class support for the Democratic party, was precipitated by major events starting well outside the party system: the Great Depression, and World War Two. These events and the ensuing and post-war expansion exogenously reshaped the circumstances for party competition and evolution. The social evolutionary paradigm helps us see how social forms, such as parties, compete to adapt, and also respond to contingent historical circumstances.

7 From Churches to Universities

This is the last of the internal historical chapters, turning to what, in Mann's model, would be called 'ideology'. That term is being used as a label in its broadest sense, as large social patterns of ideation and processes of idea creation, not in the narrow sense of a set of ideas justifying a political agenda. At various points terms such as culture and discourse would work just as well. As I've already indicated in the introduction to Part II, the issue of competition in this sphere is quite different from that in the spheres of the military, economy, and politics, because of its peculiarly unbounded nature. The goods that people compete over in those other spheres are by their nature more limited. But when people compete over claims to the truth, it is very easy for alternative claims to proliferate, especially when those claims are about moral truths rather than matters of fact. The arena of such claim-making is not limitless, people have only so much attention and energy, but the non-material, discursive nature of truth claims, makes them relatively cheap to produce and disseminate, unless these processes are being tightly policed by the state. The proliferation of truth claims is a diagnostic feature of liberal society.

Another difference relates to the discussion in Chapter 3, in which I emphasised the decline of authority in the forms of monarchy, aristocracy, and religion. We have seen how the rise of modern companies and political parties, in different ways, involve the weakening hold of social networks based more narrowly on kinship and patronage, and the formation of corporate forms based more on voluntarist membership and mass participation (shareholding, voting). It is not an absolute shift, there are still family firms and political 'dynasties', but true to a significant degree. The decline of religious authority is a conditioning factor in these historical shifts, but is less directly relevant to the emergence of these new corporate forms out of earlier kin networks. With ideology, understood as the making to truth claims, it is different. Here the decline of religious authority is centrally important, because of the Church's attempted monopoly on truth claims about morality, metaphysics, and the natural world. The unravelling of this authority that we touched on in Chapter 3, helps create the space for the proliferations of truth claims we associate with the growth of scientific debate and literacy-based public opinion. And this is why, in this chapter, I have treated the shift from churches to universities, from religious authority to science-and-scholarship-based authority, as emblematic of the shift under discussion as a whole. As already suggested, the arena of truth-claiming extends well beyond this particular institutional and organisational frame, permeating society, media, and public discourse. But looking at the rise of universities, as with that of national militaries, companies, and parties, gives us an anchor for the wider discussion.

I will use the concept of 'civil society' as a wider frame for the entire discussion. This is a labile concept that gets used in many ways. Michael Edwards (2014) has reasonably emphasised three different dimensions of the concept: civil society as 'associational life', as 'the public sphere' of discourse and debate, and as a vision of 'the good society'. While I am not here concerned with making explicit normative arguments about the value of civil society (see Chapter 9), the first two dimensions do capture something basic to my approach. On the one hand, as in previous chapters, we are interested in how modern collective forms of agency take shape, and the idea of 'associational life' captures this dimension. On the other hand, as I have been emphasising, the process of making truth claims ('ideology') points us towards an idea of the 'public sphere' defined by contending arguments and beliefs. I will go into the idea of civil society and these two aspects in greater depth in the next section.

The chapter is structured in three main sections. First, an elaboration of what is meant here by civil society and why it's useful, developing the distinction just made between corporate agency and truth claiming. Second, I offer an episodic history of entwined formations of the European university and modern civil society, as infrastructures through which ideational competition is increasingly institutionalised. I trace this process from the founding and florescence of medieval universities, through a slight detour of the emergence of civil society and the Enlightenment, and back to the expansion of modern university systems in conjunction with nation building over the last 200 years. The narrative tracks the rise of modern universities out of the seedbed of the church to become central institutions, of knowledge production, authority, and legitimation, somehow suspended between state and civil society. Chapter 8 extends the discussion by considering how the idea of competition itself operates as 'culture'. Here I am primarily concerned with the emergence of core institutions that sustain discursive competition over ideas in general.

The Two Sides of Civil Society

I start with a bit of ground clearing, addressing general issues in the conceptualisation of civil society and how I am using it. Minimally, civil society is a social structural concept. As Ernest Gellner once put it, it 'is first of all that part of society which is not the state. It is a residue' (1990: 303). But of course, this 'residue' is the substance of society itself; it contains individuals but these individuals have the capacity to associate, organise, and mobilise around shared interests and convictions. A civil society must provide the legal means to do this, and social atomisation is not compatible with it. In providing this capacity, civil society as a whole acts as a counterweight, or set of counterweights, to the power of the state. At the same time, none of these organisations and groupings can be overly coercive – people must be able to join and leave as they see fit. For this reason, militia-like self-organisation, like Black Shirts, street gangs, and crime organisations, while they might emerge from civil society, are, with their coercive power, a threat to it. Our story of the unification of military power and its subordination to the state is of a piece with the emergence of civil society. I would also distinguish civil society from the ties of kinship that exist in all societies, no matter how attenuated. This is an important and indispensable part of the 'residual', but because we cannot easily choose our families, this part of the social structure is also beyond civil society in the strict sense. So, with a nod to Hegel, I am inclined towards the 'sandwich' image of civil society as that which lies in between kinship and the state (Keane 1988: 46), but as I've just indicated, the substance of what lies there, matters (see Bobbio 1989, Gellner 1996).

The concept is not merely structural, but also historical. Earlier usage of the term in seventeenth- and eighteenth-century Europe tended to see it as an emergent form of society based on the rule of law rather than armed force, one stimulated by the growth of commerce and consumption. It was this emergent historical form, rather than the idea of a structural part or 'zone' of society distinct from the state, that first caught the imagination. Although the appellation was sometimes attached to the ancient polities of Greece and Rome, many understood that these were actually very different kinds of societies, based much more deeply on shared kinship, communal rituals, and martial obligations. And similarly, while societies of considerable scale and complexity, with a degree of pluralism based on kin groups, village communities, religious bodies, or whatever, can be found all over the world across history and cultures, the peculiar pattern and balance of forces laid out above are a distinctive emergence of European-derived societies. Civil society is unavoidably attached to the specific story of European transformation that this book is about.

Now let me turn to the two aspects of civil society that will particularly concern us below – first as a population of artificial agents occupying that middle range between state and kinship, and then as an arena of competing truth claims. The 'structural' conception of civil society outlined above leaves unstated what kind of organisations can occupy the 'middle range'. Many have seen it rather strictly as an arena in which people mobilise around explicit political and moral causes, social movements and campaigning groups being characteristic. I find this too narrow. In the previous chapter I argued that political parties are peculiar organisations designed to traffic between civil society and the state, not fully of one or the other. I would also argue that in the broadest sense, businesses are occupants of civil society, even if their purposes are relatively non-political.[1] Thinking this way helps us break down an artificial conceptual divide between 'business' and 'cause-oriented' organisations, which is important because the line is blurry. Many charities, campaigning organisations, and so on, are large employers, with large amounts of capital, and legal personhood (more below). Many businesses are oriented towards 'positive social change', such as 'green' solutions to global warming. The boundary between 'public' and 'private' sectors, towards serving social versus private goods, is not always clear. Perhaps more significant is the divide between voluntary versus paid and professional work in these

[1] Of course, through lobbying and other connections some powerful businesses, though not formally part of the state, develop 'cosy' relationships with the state, for example, those able to monopolise defence contracts.

organisations, and the degree to which organisations depend on each, which again corresponds to their power. This suggests a different sense of the private/public distinction, corresponding more to leisure versus work, or amateur versus professional. Although we need to be mindful of the historical association of charitable voluntarism with middle-to-elite classes, with more leisure time at their disposal, charity and philanthropy have tended to become the province of large organisations. Because I dealt with business corporations in Chapter 5, the focus here is more on those kinds of organisations oriented towards social causes and what is normally understood as 'the public good' rather than private interests. But I consider this to be a domain of civil society, not the whole thing. In Bourdieu's terms civil society is a vast concatenation of social fields in which people, through organisations, compete and co-operate over particular aims and objects, material and ideal, public and private. This broad conception of civil society helps us see the underlying continuities in the social organisation of human agency into corporate forms.

So, civil society is an arena of power in which various corporate bodies compete with one another for position and influence, across various social fields. These bodies coordinate and focus diffuse social agency. It is not just a domain of virtuous struggle against the powerful, but one within which there are many power struggles. Sometimes the locus of mobilisation is 'from below', of people socially marginalised in various ways (although movement leadership often requires some social and cultural capital). At the same time, civil society organisations, especially in their philanthropic guise, also express elite power, and bolster dominant social order, including corporate power (Hall 2013). Legal personality operates here as well, but as with political parties, again along a continuum from loose patterns of association, with no legal dimension, to elaborate incorporated legal forms, such as non-profits, trusts, and charities (Gentry 2015). Many organisations evolve and travel along this continuum, beginning as looser associations of the like-minded around a given cause, to becoming more formalised and institutionalised, as they deepen and extend their powers, and deal with problems of their own social reproduction. While specifics vary from one legal jurisdiction to another, this generally involves a shift from unincorporated to incorporated legal status. This pattern is especially true of organisations that emerge and crystallise out of social movements.

Institutions of religion and learning are ambiguously placed in terms of civil society. The medieval Catholic Church long predates the emergence of modern civil society, but with the Reformation, the proliferation of churches and sects, and secularisation and general 'privatisation' of religion, the religious domain becomes more 'of' civil society, and less the awkward partner of the state. It becomes more a field of competing corporate actors, attracting the faithful on a voluntary basis (although there is still a socially heritable component in some cases), and often emphasising public campaigning around social and moral causes. This transformation is also signalled by the fact that modern religious organisations often have the legal status of charities, helping to assimilate them, for purposes of governance, to the broad structures of civil society. Universities are also difficult to place, combining and cutting across many aspects of civil society. Like churches, the institutional form has a premodern history. Because they are generally longstanding, in some cases 'ancient', not an organisational response to current politics and normative issues, and not normally joined by students or employees for charitable motives, it is easy to write them out of civil society. In terms of legal form, some are private sector businesses, but many are technically charitable enterprises (like churches), subject to some governmental regulation. But as we discuss in the historical sections below, they are closely bound up with ideological trends and movements in wider society, with the articulation of knowledge about natural, aesthetic, and moral worlds.

The main point here is to appreciate a complex organisational ecology in which businesses, charities, non-profits, social movement organisations, religious organisations, universities, all interact, co-operate, and compete. A 'field of fields' in Bourdieu's terms, populated by artificial actors. These all largely operate in between the control of kin groups from below, and of the state from above, although there will be interpenetration with these, to varying degrees, and churches and universities have a special relationship to the state. On one side, the study of civil society is the study of this organisational ecology.

On the 'truth claiming' side it is a matter of social cognition. Around the eighteenth century the social process of making claims to truth changed profoundly, responding to institutional changes that had been building for several centuries. This is the Enlightenment and a whole set of associated ideas and dispositions: scepticism about received beliefs, questioning traditional authority, relying on the evidence of one's own senses and experience, in Kant's famous phrase: *sapere aude*, 'dare to know', to trust one's own judgement (Kant 1991: 54). I think Ernest Gellner's subtle argument about this 'cognitive transformation' is useful to think with (1991: 70–90). Pared down, it says that across human history there is a fundamental shift from one mode of cognition to another. Originally the moral order of relatively small societies is underpinned by a unified conceptual system expressed in symbols, rituals, and cosmologies, while the practical material world is understood through relatively unintegrated sets of task specific knowledge (in regard to hunting, curing, shelter making, etc.). But in the socially complex modern world understandings of the moral order have fragmented and become less conceptually integrated, while understandings of the natural world and its operations have become increasingly integrated, into a single conceptual system underpinned by empiricism and science. Gellner sees agrarian civilisations (e.g. medieval Europe), as occupying a middle point between these two ideal typical extremes, characterised by unstable attempts to rationally integrate knowledge about the natural and moral orders (as we saw in Chapter 3). This broad shift is the macro-historical context for the rise of civil society as a new arena for making truth claims, and a new mode for testing and validating truth claims. As the capacity of the church to impose its moral authority weakened, so did its claims to more general authority over knowledge and learning.

My emphasis on what I call 'truth claiming' might seem narrow and overly specific – might not 'knowledge production' or 'ideation' do just as well? I do this to focus attention on the competitive aspect, with the assumption that the truth is a limited good: not everyone can make successful claims. Whether it is limited by accuracy in correspondence to reality, or because people can entertain only so many truth claims at a time is a secondary question (I think both of these are true). Whether truth claims encounter each other in sheer 'might makes right' terms, the most effective rhetoric wins, or in terms of most accurately 'hitting the mark' of correspondence with reality, there is a struggle to win, to prevail, to establish the dominant view. I recognise that a vast amount of the discourse that takes place in public (narrowly or widely) doesn't have this competitive form, and simply proliferates options to satisfy personal tastes. Modern religion in secularised liberal society hovers on the boundary, exemplifying the fact that claims can either be presented and treated as matters of personal preference, or as existential matters of universal truth. Whether truth claims become competitive is contextual. But when what is at stake is the coordination of collective action, and ultimately individuals and corporate bodies must choose between various courses of action, the implications of truth claims regarding or bearing on those actions becomes more acute. Truth claim competition happens over questions of 'what is the case', over 'what we ought to do', to strategically achieve ends, and 'what we ought to ultimately value', to inform those ends. The practical interpenetration of these very different kinds of truth, lead to constant disputes in modern liberal society, both about matters of fact, and about matters of principle.

Probably the most influential idea for thinking about this aspect of civil society as an arena of truth claiming has been Habermas's 'public sphere' (1991), which he defined as 'a realm of our social life in which something approaching public opinion can be formed' (1974: 49).[2] However, Habermas's concept was somewhat narrower than this might suggest, because he was particularly concerned with the foundations of rationally informed bourgeois democracy, not the entire realm of modern ideation in general. He saw it not as a sphere of individual autonomy and independence from the state, but rather as a process in which the 'public' (eligible citizenry) took control of the rational argumentation that shaped government policies, through such things as public discussion in coffee houses and literate debate in newspapers. The public sphere is oriented to the state, appropriating a part of the state's public power and authority that had grown with absolutist forms of monarchy. It is worth noting two historical points of Habermas's argument. First, that he sees Britain in the eighteenth century as the first example of a public sphere (1991: 57), which accords with the argument I have been making. And second, he sees the public sphere as a phase of political development specific to the era around the eighteenth century, especially in Britain, France, and America. Like Reinhard Kosseleck's (1989) contemporaneous 'sattelzeit' (saddle period) in which a great wave of new concepts is articulated in society, the public sphere is historically bounded. In Habermas's argument, the growth of capitalism and the rise of the

[2] I engage with Habermas's original concept as a baseline for defining what I mean by the truth claiming aspect of civil society. I leave aside the extensive elaborations and criticisms of his concept (e.g. Calhoun 1994, Emden and Midgley 2012).

twentieth-century welfare state replaces the public sphere as a process of rational public opinion formation within bourgeois society, with a brute and irresolvable contest among conflicting interests in industrial and post-industrial society (1974: 55). Habermas's pubic sphere is consistent with his thesis about the 'crisis of legitimation' and governability in twentieth-century society (1973). The public sphere is something we have lost and that can be restored only at a higher level after the resolution of the basic structural conflicts of capitalist society.

When I describe an arena of truth claiming as an aspect of civil society, I am posing a concept that includes but is much wider than Habermas's public sphere. Struggles over knowledge relevant to state policies are included, but so are struggles over things less easily legislated, for instance, religious beliefs, moral principles, and interpretations of historical events. Truth claims oriented towards the state operate in a wider, churning sea of contending claims about moral order and reality itself. While I disregard matters of personal preference that lead to no significant conflict, I include all those relatively public contentions over the truth of matters, whether or not these are oriented to the state's policies. And while struggles over truth claims generally take a discursive form, reason blends with rhetoric, emotion, and prejudice, getting the upper hand only some of the time. The underlying rationalism of Habermas's idea is not assumed here.

The decline of centralised religious authority, as a kind of public authority, has been, to a degree, substituted by socially sanctioned secular modes of authority based on scientific methods, expertise and scholarship, often housed and sustained by universities, but not confined to them. But the stabilisation this institutional foundation brings is delicate, and easily disrupted by the cacophony of truth claims more widely generated and sustained by numerous forms of communication media, written and spoken, printed and electronic, visual and aural. Note that my argument in the previous chapter about the unexpected rise of political parties in the early nineteenth century is also about how Habermas's public sphere took a more concrete competitive form, institutionalising and routinising the entrenched competition that he saw as eventually unravelling the public sphere. Whereas Habermas was more concerned with the democratic function of the public sphere, I am more concerned with an arena of competitive claims to represent the truth, about all manner of things, that is the necessary concomitant of a society which has loosened centralised control over truth claims.

Even those more socially sanctioned ways of claiming authority, such as science, are fundamentally based on formalised competition, not mere positional authority.

The rest of this chapter tries to trace the long history of public authority over truth, dominated first by religion and the church, but shifting towards the situation of the twentieth century, in which universities, with their key role in sustaining research and science, have become dominant. This long shift moves through the intervening period of the Enlightenment, in which civil society, in the sense outlined above, took shape, and which is pivotal for the transformation towards the new balance of power between religion and science, between churches and universities. Thus, the historical sketch has a tripartite structure – medieval, Enlightenment, and after in the late nineteenth and twentieth centuries – and takes the form of a long institutional shift that passes through a critical period. Throughout I highlight questions of corporateness, in the juristic sense, and truth claiming, and how these change over time.

The Medieval Church and University[3]

Many threads lead in to the European university tradition that began in the Middle Ages. The peripatetic schools and texts of ancient Greece, the Christian monastic traditions that preserved Latin texts and literacy after the fall of the Western Roman Empire, the recovery of ancient texts, Greek, Roman, and Arabic through the influence of the Islamic world on Europe via its southern regions. This brought new access to ideas on law, politics, medicine, chemistry, mathematics, and algebra, sustained through the European 'dark ages' by the Islamic Caliphate, which had its own major centres of learning, such as *al-Qarawiyyin* (est. 859) in Morrocco, and *Al-Azhar* (est. 972) in Cairo.[4] More directly in institutional terms, schools attached to cathedrals and under the authority of bishops, with the purpose of cultivating an educated clergy, were part of the general goals of the Catholic Church, and common by about 1100. These were particularly concentrated in France and the Low Countries, and focused on teaching the

[3] In this section I have generally drawn on: Cobban 1975, De Ridder-Symoens 1992, Haskins 1957, Moore 2019, Pedersen 2009, Riddle 1993, Schachner 1962.

[4] Both were established as madrassas, becoming universities in the 1960s.

classical liberal arts curriculum of grammar, rhetoric, and logic (the *trivium*), and less systematically, arithmetic, geometry, astronomy, and music (the *quadrivium*). At the same time there were also private and itinerant teachers circulating in this environment, the most famous being the scholar, theologian and poet, Peter Abelard (1079–1142).

But the true beginnings of the modern university lie in the period of economic and urban growth, and legal expansion, of the eleventh and twelfth centuries in continental Europe. Two contrasting first instances are usually emphasised: Bologna and Paris. Exact founding dates are uncertain, but by the twelfth century Bologna had become a centre of legal training, many of its teachers' resident citizens. Students came from all over Europe, and to protect their interests as students and consumers of city resources, formed a corporate union, to which the general legal term for such bodies, *universitas*, was applied (Cobban 1975: 22–23). It was much like a students' guild, and the city commune had an interest in attracting their business. By contrast, the University of Paris grew out of the cathedral school a little bit later, and primarily offered training in theology. At Paris, formal organisation was based more on the corporate body of masters (teachers) who often came from beyond the city, although in time the term *universitas* came to refer to masters and scholars (students) collectively. Along these two different paths, both cases exemplify a key innovative characteristic of the university, a sign of its times, that is, its corporateness, on the model of the guild, as a body with a distinctive set of privileges and protections in law (Baldwin 1972: 8–9, Hyde 1972). Bologna enjoyed the patronage of Emperor Frederick Barbarossa from 1155, and, when they came into conflict with citizens, King Phillip (II) Augustus of France offered his support and protection to the students of Paris in 1200. The burgeoning universities generally enjoyed the patronage of a pope, a prince, or towns themselves (especially as the economic attractions became clearer), and sometimes more than one of these.

The early thirteenth century saw a wave of new universities established at Salerno (possibly the previous century), Oxford, Montpellier, Cambridge, Salamanca, Padua, Naples, Toulouse, Orleans, and several others rose for a while and then disappeared. New universities were sometimes established when students, in conflict with city residents, decamped *en masse* to other neighbouring towns (e.g. Padua and Cambridge). By the thirteenth century there were around twenty universities distributed in a band from southern Italy, through France, to southern England, and along northern Spain. By 1500 there were over seventy, extending geographically to Lisbon, Aberdeen, Uppsala, and Cracow (Verger 1992). The multiplication of universities in Europe over this period was an effect of Europe's peculiar situation of having an overarching Christian culture with a distinctive supporting bureaucracy, the Church, with its own domain of law, and yet a plurality of secular domains, competing with each other for prestige, income, and personnel for their own expanding secular bureaucracies.

What was studied? The growth of medieval universities out of previous institutions of learning involved the extension of the liberal arts mentioned above, which was the main fare of those studying for a bachelors, to specialisations at higher degree level in theology, medicine, and law. Universities in the thirteenth century were more commonly called *studium generale*, indicating the greater breadth of studies increasingly available. Particular universities had specialisations, such as Bologna in law, Paris and Oxford in theology, and Montpellier and Salamanca in medicine. Many students led itinerant lives between universities, and many never graduated. Nonetheless, there was a growing demand for well-trained scholars with mastery of Latin and writing, and especially civil and canon law. Particularly in Italy, where law was a dominant subject, but also in places such as Oxford, specialisation in the *ars dictandi*, the science of rigorously procedural letter-writing, was in high demand. Not just in the formal civil law that was spreading throughout the continent, but also in diplomacy, official communications between institutions, and other areas of business and government intrinsic to growing cities (Cobban 1975: 220–223, Moraw 1992). For elite transactions the world was increasingly a written world, and the universities supplied the skills and men (it was a male domain) to support this process.

This was a time before 'civil society' proper, and yet it makes sense to ask in what ways what was to come was prefigured. First, while the church, in its alliances with various worldly rulers, monopolised authoritative spiritual knowledge and had the power to enforce its truth claims, we know that there were heterodox beliefs and religious movements throughout the Middle Ages, and other dissenting movements. There was a limit to how far church orthodoxy could penetrate into illiterate peasant communities and more remote hinterlands, and specific local conflicts sometimes generated counter-ideologies expressed in supernatural idiom (Cohn 1970). It would be a mistake to presume the ideology of the church to be absolutely hegemonic. But it was the prevailing power, and dissenting views demonstrated the limits of its effective reach, rather than a zone of society in which dissent was formally tolerated and even encouraged.

Conversely, neither were the new universities merely zones of pedantic learning and intellectual conformity. The relatively fused Church-University nexus was an arena of intellectual conflict and debate, of struggles over not just what is true, but of how we determine truth. In this arena these struggles took the form of both public intellectual contests among actors, and more formalised, institutionally bounded procedures (Collins 2000: ch 9). In regard to the former, two indicative figures stand out, Abelard and Ockham. Abelard built up his great reputation as a scholar and debater in the period just before the universities had begun to be truly established. He moved around the French intellectual sphere defined by monastic and cathedral schools, and populated by several figures in this milieu, who also taught logic and rhetoric independently of these institutions. Abelard's text *Sic et Non* (Yes and No, or, For and Against) placed next to each other passages from Christian commentary on the Bible that reached opposing conclusions. His point was not to undermine the authority of the Bible, but to show that simply relying on authorities resolved nothing. One needed to learn the skills of exegesis and logical analysis, at which he was a master, to truly engage with biblical texts. Abelard is known for his contribution to what has come to be called the debate between 'nominalism' and 'realism'. Put simply, against 'realists' such as St. Bernard of Clairvaux, who argued in Platonic fashion that abstract, general terms such as 'blue', 'horse', and 'love', must correspond to actually existing 'forms' to which they refer, Abelard as a 'nominalist' argued that general terms rest only on the particulars they abstract from, they are just names constructed out of human experience. Without going into theology, it is apparent that this basic philosophical difference about the relationship of language to reality, which persist to this day, has implications for how one might conceive of God, and our knowledge of God. Abelard's approach became known as 'the new learning' or the '*via moderna*', and flowing into the universities, was often condemned by church figures, such as Stephen the Bishop of Tournai in a letter to the Pope sometime between 1192 and 1203:

> The studies of sacred letters among us are fallen into the workshop of confusion, while both disciples applaud novelties alone and masters watch out for glory rather than learning. They everywhere compose new and recent

> *summulae* and commentaries, by which they attract, detain, and deceive their hearers, as if the works of the holy fathers were not still sufficient, who, we read, expounded holy scripture in the same spirit in which we believe the apostles and prophets composed it. … Contrary to the sacred canons there is public disputation as to the incomprehensible deity; concerning the incarnation of the Word, verbose flesh and blood irreverently litigates. (in Thorndike 1944: 23)

Despite such efforts of church and university authorities to control the scope of dissent through the prescription of learning, axes of debate such as this persisted. Shortly after Abelard's time there was a new infusion of Aristotelean texts on logic and other matters, as well as other classic sources, thanks to the influence of translations from Arabic. This fed into a new dominant orthodoxy, broadly in line with the realist position, with the great synthesiser of Aristotelean logic and Christian teachings being St. Thomas Aquinas (1225–1274). Still, a new generation of nominalists returned, exemplified by the English philosopher and theologian William of Ockham (c. 1287–1347). 'Given' at an early age to the London Greyfriars (a Franciscan house), he studied at Oxford and developed a reputation for his heterodox views, being called before a provincial Franciscan meeting in Bristol to defend his views in 1323, and then before the Pope and a commission of theologians in Avignon the next year. Ockham was never charged with heresy, but his researches while in Avignon led him to the view that Pope John was himself a heretic, and in 1328, he slipped out of Avignon with some friends, for which he was excommunicated. He eventually found refuge in Munich under the protection of the Holy Roman Emperor, then in conflict with the Pope, where he turned to writing on political matters. Ockham was an extreme case, who lived and wrote at the margins of the university-based culture, but like Abelard, he indicates the way volatile public dispute was generated within the sphere of medieval church-based learning (Spade and Pannacio 2019).

Even within the much more controlled confines of university training, disputation was cultivated, as essential to the practice of the medieval scholar. Core to university teaching were lectures and disputations. Lectures were given to those training at both master's and bachelor's levels, and generally involved the teacher reading and commenting on prescribed texts, and answering questions. 'Disputations' were public debates usually on designated topics, tending to use syllogistic forms of argument, and demonstrating mastery in deploying authoritative texts. The practice varied among institutions, but generally bachelor's students progressed from attending disputations, to participating in them during the last two years of their four years of study. With questions set and proceedings overseen by a master, a bachelor would respond to the question, and then to interrogations of his response, coming first from the master, then other bachelors, and perhaps other students, with the master summing up, perhaps further in lectures in the following days (Leff 1992: 325–328). Although often fairly procedural, according to some accounts, debates could become quite wide-ranging and heated, releasing cooped-up intellectual energies (Cobban 1975: 213–214, Schachner 1962: 322–323). In particular, extraordinary '*de quolibet*' disputations held mainly in faculties of theology, allowed any topic to be debated, including ecclesiastical and political issues. In general disputations seem to have run the gamut from fairly routine and hidebound affairs, perhaps more so as medieval scholasticism bedded in, to much more lively and probing events. But the point is that however formalised and constrained, the art of intellectual competition was being cultivated in the university training environment, in ways that must have spilled over into wider intellectual conflicts such as those engaged by Abelard and Ockham. While far short of Habermas's public sphere, we can see a certain antecedent, in the pursuit of truth through a community of discourse (cf. Collins 2000: 643).

Finally, I have defined civil society as that zone where people escape the direct constraints of the state on the one hand, and kin-based obligations on the other – where people are relatively free of these encumbrances. Medieval Europe was a world where principles of kinship, and the potentially intrusive powers of church and state, were pretty pervasive. But one of the distinguishing features of the church, the monastic orders, and the universities was their relative detachment from the kin-based social order, and the uneasy autonomy of the church from the power of various secular rulers. This was not civil society, but the sphere of the urban universities was one in which *men* were empowered as individuals to pursue their own interests and ends, and to play a role in the formation of 'opinion', to a much greater degree than was possible in many walks of medieval life. It provided a somewhat circumscribed foretaste of what would happen when literacy became more widespread, and the grips of states and churches on people's minds loosened.

Interlude: The Enlightenment and the Emergence of Civil Society

Some of the seeds of the Reformation can be found in the medieval debates between realists and nominalists. The violent international conflict and division within the church and its eventual subsidence, touched on in Chapter 3, set the stage for the next episode in our story, the Enlightenment, the growth of civil society, and a new context for the development of the university. With the universal authority of the medieval church fragmented and weakened, struggles over truth claims could now be held outside its formal boundaries, even if often alongside and in compatible terms, according to the regnant territorial brand of confession. The invention of the printing press, the spread of vernacular translations of the bible, and growing literacy among elite and middling urban classes, were important conditions for the great transformation of communication, ideas, and social organisation in the late seventeenth and eighteenth centuries that we call the Enlightenment.

In keeping with our two-sided conception of civil society, I will start with the new associational and organisational patterns that were emerging, before turning to the discursive truth claiming aspects, bearing in mind that this is an analytic separation. The florescence of new forms of association supporting the exploration and exchange of ideas in this period is well known (Im Hof 1994: 105–154; Robertson 2020: 351–400). But it is perhaps useful to distinguish between those settings that supported somewhat looser and more fluid social intercourse, and those organisations, more and less formal, that were more programmatic and purposive. In the former case, much has been made of coffee houses as venues where middle- and upper-class men could discuss business and politics, read newspapers and periodicals, sometimes aloud, and debate issues of the day. These began to appear in and around London in the 1650s, and spread quickly around Europe. Sometimes they became the meeting places of, and associated with, specific political groupings. They were sites for the formation of public opinion, but also businesses selling a fashionable commodity, and places to practise the art of polite conversation and social interaction (Robertson 2020: 358–360). Similarly, though centred on the elite culture of Paris and France more widely, the 'salon' was another important context of association among middling and upper classes, more especially bringing together leading figures in the worlds of philosophy, literature, science, and government. Frequently organised by an aristocratic and erudite hostess, while they brought together some of society's most knowledgeable people, and were venues for intellectual discussion, they were more about social networking and opportunities to display wit and learning, than about addressing the big issues of the day (Im Hoff 1994: 113–117, Robertson 2020: 360–363). Coffee houses and salons facilitated social networks and traffic in ideas, but were not what we might call civil society actors.

By contrast, academies, societies, and clubs provided more focused activities, having not just customers or guests, but members organised around common purposes. Academies (sometimes called 'societies') were generally communities of the learned organised beyond the confines of the university, early ones dating from the first half of the seventeenth century, and often with royal patronage. They were generally dedicated to the advancement of scientific inquiry, particularly in areas of natural science, but also regarding language, literature, and history, in effect creating space for investigations that were marginalised in the universities by the dominance of theology and law as topics of study (Im Hoff 1994: 108). Such academies spread across Europe, the most distinguished usually being based in capitals, but with smaller versions often found in the provinces. On a somewhat more modest scale were local reading societies which promoted literary discussion in regular meetings and built up membership libraries. These became common in provincial English cities. The division between 'academies' and 'societies' isn't always strict, but the latter term tended to associate with organisations set up to focus on practical improvement in areas such as agricultural knowledge and practice, arts and manufactures, and economics more generally. These were often set up and led by local notables with a material interest in economic development. A noticeable aspect of these academies and societies is that they often promoted their ends in learning and improvement through formal competitions in which awards were given out for the best essay on a set topic,[5] or achievements in cropping, drainage, textiles, brewing, or other technological solutions to practical problems (Im Hoff 1994: 110, 124–125, Staum 1985). Also present in the mix were societies with charitable and moral aims, such as poverty relief, abstinence, anti-slavery, and promotion of the bible and 'Christian knowledge'. Smaller

[5] Such as Rousseau's First and Second Discourses: on the Arts and Sciences, which won in 1750, and on Inequality, which did not, in 1754.

and more informal localised groups of acquaintances organised around common interests were often called 'clubs'. Ritchie Robertson uses Adam Smith to illustrate the spectrum of organisations a learned person, almost always a man, might be involved in:

> as professor of moral philosophy at Glasgow from 1752 to 1764, he belonged to numerous enlightened societies in both Glasgow and Edinburgh. He helped to form the Literary Society of Glasgow, which lasted from 1752 until about 1803 and met on Fridays during the university sessions. He belonged to another club which dined on Saturdays, and on another weekday he attended the Political Economy Club, founded by Provost Andrew Cochrane to discuss commercial improvement. On his frequent visits to Edinburgh he attended meetings of the Philosophical Society, the Select Society and its offshoot, the Edinburgh Society for the Encouragement of Arts, Science, Manufactures and Agriculture in Scotland; he was also among the original members of the Poker Club, founded in 1762 to discuss the question of a Scottish militia. (2020: 366)

These face-to-face social settings were just one arena in which ideas, and controversies, were cultivated. Although spoken discourse, and attention to it, was central to the Enlightenment, the expansion of the written word was of great material significance. Expanding freedom of the press, especially in Holland and Britain, was crucial. A key event here was the British Parliament's allowing the 1662 Licensing of the Press Act to lapse in 1694, thereby freeing publishers from the restrictions of the Stationer's Company, which had held a government granted monopoly on publishing. This came under pressure from leading figures such as John Locke and John Milton, and led to the rapid expansion of London and regional newspapers and other periodicals, such as the culturally influential *Tatler* and the *Spectator* in the early eighteenth century. As already mentioned, many societies maintained libraries for their members, and the publication of books and pamphlets also flourished, many addressing controversies of the day. Although often facing stronger legal restrictions, the countries on the continent followed suit in this expansion of written discourse (Im Hoff 1994: 150–154). As Robertson also observes, publications were also sustained by 'the Republic of Letters', the epistolary networks that linked the learned across Europe into fields of common inquiry, into a 'virtual public sphere' (2020: 373–389). With roots in Renaissance humanism, these networks linked scientists, literati, and major librarians across Europe and beyond. Leibniz corresponded with over 1,000 individuals in multiple languages, 'some 50 of whom stayed in touch for 20 years ... Benjamin Franklin is estimated to have sent and received around 15,000 letters during his lifetime' (2020: 375).

Across the Atlantic the American colonies had their own version of the florescence of associational life. We can see fairly direct parallels to European associational civil society of the Enlightenment, but often with more of a self-help ethos, in contrast to the semi-elite 'noblesse oblige' of the European improvement societies. Benjamin Franklin's (1709–1790) 'Junto', based in Philadelphia, was a prime example:

> 'a club for mutual improvement' composed of ambitious journeymen – a scrivener, a surveyor, a shoemaker, a joiner, a merchant's clerk, a book binder, a printer, a maker of surveying instruments. The group met weekly to debate issues of morals, politics and natural philosophy and through this experience, as Franklin noted, acquired not only 'better habits of conversation' but also a capacity for self-controlled, goal-directed behaviour. (P. Hall 1992: 19)

The club spawned many branches. The first Great Awakening (1730–1755) caused many parish congregations to split over matters of faith, multiplying the number of churches, many of which started their own missionary, educational, and other charitable projects. Freemasonry was imported from England in the early eighteenth century, its combination of brotherhood and esoteric knowledge appealing especially to the colonial elites. Volunteer fire companies for mutual protection also served as social nodes, as did many other mutual benefit societies.

The history of the corporation is particularly pertinent to the development of civil society in the colonies and early US. Because of the unique political path of detaching from the sovereignty of the British homeland, the evolution of the corporation played out in a particularly fraught way, as an object of struggle in the reconstitution of social power. Peter Dobkin Hall, authority on the history of philanthropy and non-profit organisations in the US, has perceptively analysed this story (1984, 1992: 13–83, 2013).[6] Hall argues that in the colonial period of the seventeenth and eighteenth centuries, power was very much concentrated in the hands of notable families, particularly in

[6] Also, on the history of civic activity and voluntarism in the US, see Clemens 2010, 2020.

New England and cities such as Boston. Known to historians as the 'Standing Order' (Field 1998), this elite group exerted social control through puritan churches and monopolisation of government offices. Hall describes them as an 'alliance of merchants, magistrates and ministers' (1984: 16) tying together power networks through leadership across the economy, government, and religious institutions. These families were particularly influential through the clergy leadership of Congregational, Unitarian, and Presbyterian churches and their various outreach projects. The disruption of their colonial power monopoly, by accelerating social change and population growth in the eighteenth century, but especially by the Revolution and consolidation of a new constitutional order at the end of the century, was a spur to finding new ways to protect their interests and to exert control over society. After the Revolution this social group was generally aligned with the Federalist faction, with its stronger northern commercial interests, which as we saw in Chapter 6, was increasingly marginalised by the more southern Jeffersonian faction of Democratic-Republicans, which was more effective at mobilising wider bases of popular support in politics. The Standing Order's relationship to the development of the eleemosynary sector post-revolution was a part of their strategy for maintaining their power and influence, despite being increasingly shut out from federal government.

As we observed in Chapter 5, the early development of corporations in colonial and then independent America, was not clearly focused on the development of a 'private' business sector. Most early corporations served the collective needs of economic development (wharfs, roads, bridges, canals) and eleemosynary purposes (religion, education, hospitals), and there was distrust of the corporate form. Before independence their legal basis was uncertain, but nonetheless derived from English law, and they were often seen as devices of aristocratic control. As the new state developed its own legal system, heated debates (as we saw) about corporations ran through the antebellum period. The Jeffersonians and later Jacksonians, viewed corporations with suspicion, as efforts by private interests to lay claim to and monopolise public resources (land, utilities, charitable activities). Thus, they preferred to keep such bodies under the close scrutiny of the state governments. The Federalists and New Englanders on the other hand, promoting the growth of corporations, saw it as a matter of mobilising private resources and wealth to serve the public good. So, the early legal struggles over the definition and status of the corporation were driven only in part by resistance to business interests *per se*. The power competition between the two great elite factions from before the Revolution, the southern planter 'aristocracy', and the northern commercial 'aristocracy', was a more fundamental driver. By investing heavily in the institutions of public good – colleges, hospitals, schools, religious societies – the northern elites were able to put their stamp on the development of American high culture, and the social reproduction of their own elite strata, despite their marginalisation from federal power.

The idea of the 'trust', paradigmatic for many large-scale non-profit corporations, became central to these struggles for control. Eventually courts, including the Supreme Court, came to the view that such corporations were not gifts of the state, but rather private contracts between donors and the trustees, that needed to be protected from too much public/state interference. Here again the contest we saw in Chapter 3 between theories of corporations as juristic persons, that see them either as gifts of the state or as having a certain natural autonomy to be protected, is being tested, with a version of the latter eventually winning out. One of Hall's major points is that we need to see the growth of the corporation as a product of the joint development of the consolidation of power in both the world of business and the eleemosynary sector, with the latter perhaps leading the way in processes of legal change (1984: 95–124). The northern commercial elites took the lead in regard to both kinds of corporations, but it was only with time and legal struggle that the corporation for business profit, and the non-profit corporation serving public goods, clearly diverged.

This is why the history of American colleges is so central to this legal history. The old New England elites were major benefactors of the older colleges, such as Harvard, Yale, and Princeton, the governance of which was a point of ongoing conflict, as the new states, after the Revolution, sought to exert more control, treating them as public bodies, answerable to government officials in terms of budgets and activities, and placing political appointees on their governing boards. But private supporters saw this as interference, and sought greater legal autonomy from the state. By contrast, New York State maintained very restrictive laws on the funding of charitable organisations including universities, and thus in the early antebellum period Columbia College was massively outstripped in growth by the other New

England colleges, and only enabled to catch up when New York reformed its laws in the late nineteenth century (Hall 1984: 120–121). For the same reasons, New England's charitable institutions generally tended to outgrow those of New York and other states. The *Dartmouth College v. State of New Hampshire* decision of 1819 was critical in this story, because it established the strong legal precedent that the college was constituted by a private contract (the trust) between donors and trustees as individuals, and not as an arm of the New Hampshire state government. In this way its autonomy in its own governance was greatly strengthened. Thus, elite struggles over the control of eleemosynary organisations, perhaps as much as the pursuit of business interests, was basic to the consolidation of the legal corporate form (Hall 1992: 28–31).

To widen the frame for a moment, various dimensions of competition are at work here. The competition between the northern and southern elites was a driver of corporate evolution, as each group sought to control this legal form. This dovetailed with the competition between the newly established state governments, as each sought economic and cultural development in ways that involved all kinds of corporations. Added to this was the peculiar 'free market' of the American religious environment, in which multiplying denominations competed for members, also through charitable and outreach organisations, especially as states disestablished the churches privileged in their colonial foundings. The organisational infrastructure that evolved, of religious, charitable, and educational corporations, of course competed over material resources (land, endowments, etc.), but also became the platforms, along with the press, and the emerging political parties, that supported the competition among ideas about religion, science, politics, and social and moral order.

The Rise of Universities[7]

As the preceding analysis suggests, much of the Enlightenment took place outside the confines of universities. This is especially true of England and France. Nonetheless, in other countries, such as Scotland, Holland, and parts of Italy and Germany, university

[7] This section draws especially on Anderson 2004, Collins 2000, Moore 2019, and Rüegg 2004.

professors were key figures in the Enlightenment (Anderson 2004: 20). In the eighteenth century, although divided by the Reformation and the will of the relevant sovereign into Protestant and Catholic, universities were still ecclesiastical institutions, largely teaching the liberal arts curriculum and training the great professions of clergy, law, and medicine (Rüegg 2004: 4). In the core powers of England and France, change in the universities was slow to come, but in the 'periphery' enlightened absolutism took the lead, as rulers sought to modernise their relatively backward countries by supporting agricultural and industrial sciences, civil and military engineering, improvements in medicine, and understandings of political economy. Some of this took place in reformed universities, and some in new specialised academies in areas such as engineering and medicine, often with particular focus on military applications. Such moves tended to knit together older aristocracies and newer bourgeoisies into a class of bureaucratic servants of the developing state. In Central and Eastern Europe, where the bourgeoisie was less developed and there were fewer relatively independent corporate bodies, the ground was clearer for 'enlightened' rulers to push through such reforms.

Piedmont, Prussia, and the Habsburg Empire, were leaders in this process (Anderson 2004: ch 2). In Piedmont, starting with the reform of Turin University in 1729, there was a move to create a more unified educational system with colleges at the top and schools below, a pattern followed by many absolutist systems. Here there was a particular concern to counterbalance the power of the Jesuits and their institutions, a policy which also began in Portugal in 1759, and reflected the desire of Catholic monarchs to nonetheless strengthen their state powers against those of Rome. Somewhat similarly, in Prussia the University of Halle was founded in 1694 to wrest control of religious teaching from orthodox Lutheranism into the hands of the state, and became a centre of pietism. The new University of Göttingen (est. 1737), seeking exceptional talent from around Germany, offered high salaries, status, and intellectual freedom, planting seeds of the modern role and identity of the academic. At Göttingen, philosophy taught in German, and covering diverse newer sciences of history, philology, geography, statistics, and economics, was foundational, and helped displace the traditional dominance of theology and law persisting from the medieval period. Other principalities and jurisdictions in the German lands, both Protestant and Catholic, followed suit.

Prussia led the way in introducing civil service entry examinations, systematising the path from schools to universities, and defining both as institutions of the state (in the legal code of 1794). It is not coincidental that both Piedmont and Prussia would eventually become the cores of the forming Italian and German nation states in the nineteenth century. The Habsburg Empire picked up on this same pattern of reforms under the reigns of Maria Theresa (1740–1780) and especially her son Joseph II (1780–1790). The dissolution of the Jesuit order in 1773 by Pope Clement XIV left a vacuum in these largely Catholic lands that the state stepped into. Although bringing many of the same reforms as in Germany, the Habsburg state used its bureaucratic power to impose more political loyalty and conformity, and seemed to reach deeper into the lower middle classes and peasantry to construct its new bureaucratic personnel (especially in Austria). Outside the absolutist orbit, urban elites controlled and reformed universities in Holland and Switzerland. Portugal, Spain, and southern Italy tended to lag behind, more encumbered by Catholic institutions. The key point in all this is that the relative 'backwardness' of those regions not as caught up in the rise of northern European commerce (much of southern Europe having lost its earlier lead), and with less developed civil societies, meant that activist absolutist states took the lead in developing the university as a strategy of modernisation and state integration.

Two processes defined the shift from the late eighteenth to the early nineteenth century: the French Revolution and ensuing Napoleonic conquests, and the rise of the 'Humboldtian model' and the prestige and influence of the German universities. The initial effect of the French Revolution was to abolish twenty-four universities in France, and the Napoleonic Conquest further reduced numbers across Europe, altogether from 143 in 1789 to eighty-three in 1815 (Rüegg 2004: 3). The 'Napoleonic model' echoed earlier absolutist trends in its centralisation. In place of universities (restored in 1895) was a system of secondary schools (*colleges* and *lycees*) and the *grandes écoles*, which sought to build the new society and supply it with necessary talents through an almost military discipline and close state control of the curriculum and degree awarding under the overarching body of the Imperial University (the only corporation re-founded after the Revolution, and one definitely a creature of the state). Under this regime the path to an academic career became much more systematised in terms of degrees necessary for certain attainments, and promotion by competition and examination. Despite aspects of the Napoleonic model being projected throughout the continental empire, and indirectly to the Spanish Empire, only in Romania was its effect lasting, its basic tendency towards centralisation and state control already in motion due to Enlightenment absolutism, as just discussed.

The influence of what has been called the Humboldtian model, based on the ideas of Wilhelm von Humboldt, put into practice at the newly established University of Berlin in 1810, and radiating throughout the German universities, has been broader and more lasting. The model called for the unity of research and teaching, seeing professors not as transmitters of established knowledge in their fields, but as discoverers of new knowledge, passing on the skills and culture of scientific inquiry to degree candidates. Here science is meant in the German sense of *Wissenschaft*, in other words broadly to include all kinds of disciplined scholarly inquiry, not just the 'hard' or 'natural' sciences. Like Kant, Humboldt emphasised the philosophical underpinnings and unity of all knowledge, and the emerging German approach was often contrasted with the French model, more concerned with 'specialisation'. Humboldt emphasised the importance of the autonomy of the scholar, free from state interference, and the freedom of teachers to teach as they saw fit (*Lehrfreiheit*), and for students to choose and direct their own studies (*Lernfreiheit*) (Anderson 2004: ch 4, Charle 2004: 44–53, Rüegg 2004: 4–13). Importantly, and somewhat in contrast to the French system, the German reforms managed to preserve much of the medieval corporate autonomy of the university, while also building these institutions into the national development of German states. For instance, while rulers had a say in professorial appointments, it was also the case that training and election of candidates, and the curriculum they taught, was very much under the power of the universities (Anderson 2004: 60, Rüegg 2004: 14). This exceptional corporate autonomy in the German universities was probably aided by taking place in a culturally and linguistically integrated zone, a market for professional academics, that was politically fragmented, playing one ruler off against another.

While attached to Humboldt's name because of his significant role in educational reform and innovation, his ideas were in line with wider German ideas, and other leading German intellectuals such as Kant, Fichte, and Schleiermacher, all published statements of principles regarding how universities should be organised. And the somewhat idealised image of the model just offered continued trends from eighteenth-century Prussian reforms already discussed, and is itself partly a retrospective construction from the late nineteenth century, as the model became more internationally influential. Moreover, the distinctions between the Napoleonic and Humboldtian models, while real, can be overdrawn. Both were parts of state centralising projects, that sought to build and equip new middle classes and professionals, forging modern national identities in the process. Both were part of the general state bureaucratisation of learning involving new ministries of education, the expansion of competitive examinations, and the formation of a new class of professional academic intellectuals, sustained by specialised journals and academic conferences. The elite patronage of eighteenth-century Enlightenment intellectuals was increasingly replaced by state patronage through university employment. The French process was triggered by national revolution, while the German process underwrote gradual territorial unification across the nineteenth century. National rivalry drove both convergence and differentiation in these systems.

In his magisterial *The Sociology of Philosophies* Randall Collins treats the rise of the German universities, and more specifically, German philosophical idealism, as a pivotal process in the emergence of modern intellectuals and their emancipation from the authority of religion (2000: 618–687). Enlightenment thought mostly took place outside the confines of the church and the universities, sustained by the civil society milieu discussed above, promoting a practical scientism, social reform, and turning away from the totalising worldview of theology. But German transcendental idealism, running from Kant's categorical imperative to Hegel's world spirit embodied in the Prussian state, sought precisely for a total regrounding of morality and science in the very conditions of knowledge, adapting various versions of a God-concept in order to do so. In effect the reformed universities were becoming the new, state-aligned institutions for the promulgation of ultimate knowledge and authority, in place of the church. The latter, in German lands, was divided between Protestants and Catholics, Lutherans and pietists, and various patron sovereigns, whereas the universities were becoming a system. In keeping with his larger argument about the history of intellectuals, Collins sees this process as reflected in social networks of idealist intellectuals and professors, competing to articulate rival versions of the philosophical trend in a particularly overcrowded arena of contenders. Just as the rise of the original universities absorbed and domesticated the dynamics of theological and philosophical contention, the post-Reformation modern universities, particularly in the Humboldtian model, became a new state-linked arena for the competitive production of authoritative knowledge. Only now, this new institutional framework, especially in the 'West', sat within a wider arena of ideological competition, sustained by the organisations of civil society – media, charities, non-profits, campaigning organisations, and so on – which also drove contests of ideas and values.

Although there is still much that can be said about the social evolution of the modern university, this takes us to the key point of transition, once again concentrated around the move from the eighteenth to the nineteenth century in Europe and America. I will round out this section by briefly sketching the subsequent history of the growth of national university systems, with a strong influence from Humboldt's model, and more recent globalisation of the university model.

The early nineteenth century to the mid-twentieth century saw the global spread of the universities. There were two periods of reduction in numbers in Europe. First in France and the territories occupied by Napoleon, as part of the rationalisation of educational systems, making them more serviceable to the needs of the modern state. And second, as a result of conquest under the Third Reich, closing down many universities in Germany and its occupied countries. But despite these episodes, the overall trend was growth in numbers of universities and students, as well as the growth of specialised institutions oriented to more practical training in agricultural, industrial, and military fields. Beyond Europe, colonial powers planted universities in Latin America, Asia, and Africa to train clergy and indigenous elites. Later the establishment of communist governments in the Soviet Union and China led to the expansion of universities, again designed to stimulate productive skills in the mass of the population, and to socialise new elites. By the late nineteenth century the Humboldt model was spreading beyond Germany and the Habsburg empire, to other parts of northern Europe, including Britain, partly because of the growing prestige of a unifying Germany as an intellectual leader in cultural and natural sciences. In the US the colonial and early national universities had been frequently aligned with religious denominations, and oriented to a more classical education of elites, but as the system grew in the late nineteenth century the Humboldt model was increasingly adopted. The leader of this trend was the founding of Johns Hopkins in 1876, explicitly on the Humboldt model of combining teaching with the cultivation of independent research. After World War Two, under US occupation and the Marshall Plan to help rebuild war-torn Europe, the American version of Humboldt's vision was reimported back into Europe, influencing the subsequent revival of the university sector there.

Having said this, by this point the idea of the university as a national promoter of research and high-level teaching was widely generalised, whatever its roots in Berlin and Prussia. It, combined with extensive primary and secondary education, and a host of 'short-cycle' specialised training institutions, made up a basic part of the strategy of nation building in this period (Gellner 1983: 35–38). Universities were part of the international competition for productivity and prestige that continues to this day. Earlier elite doubts about the value and risks of educating working classes were gradually replaced by a kind of 'human capital' vision in which increasing literacy and general education was part of increasing the strength and capacities of the nation as a whole. Through the teaching of history and other disciplines schools and universities played a role in moulding national identities out of disparate populations. At the more elite level the universities, still serving a relatively small minority of the population, contributed to national prestige in the cultivation of the arts, humanities, and sciences (increasingly including the social sciences in the twentieth century). And as access to universities expanded in the twentieth century, through their credentialism they were increasingly involved in the validation of a class structure in which those doing more 'cognitive' kinds of work in professional and service sectors were better paid, and enjoyed a certain social prestige on that educated basis. Universities were key to both international competition, including the Cold War rivalry of the US and the USSR, and internal competition to move upwards in the class structure.

At the same time, especially in their more Humboldtian versions in the 'West', they were becoming core institutions of the liberal democratic form of society, in which the values of academic freedom and open debate over ideas were promoted, sanctioned, and to a degree, also contained and controlled. As universities grew, the value of intellectual competition was encoded not just in the activities within the walls of the university, but in wider academic arenas of intellectual competition, such as peer reviewed journals, conference debates, and professional associations. Intellectual and scholarly activity across times and cultures has always been defined by rivalry over ideas and proposed explanations for phenomenon (Collins 2000), but in this new modern context it was happening within an institution much more inclined to explicitly cultivate such rivalry as one of its core aims. This competition over hard-won ideas can never be fully disarticulated from the competition to carve out career paths and professional identities. The struggle over ideas, when situated in a stable institutional context, is also a struggle for advancement and status within that institution. And this of course took place within a wider and compatible culture of competition over ideas, beliefs, and values, in which the institutions of civil society, newspapers, and other media also provided arenas for these struggles, interacting with social movements, religions, and national party politics. The university sector grew in dialogue with the wider civil society, a point that became abundantly clear in the late 1960s as continuing student expansion and political unrest around issues such as the Vietnam War and inequalities based on race and sex often came to a head on campuses.

As is well known, influenced by figures such as Newton and Bacon, the modern period saw the consolidation of science and the experimental method, to form both a practice and a world view (Berry 1997: ch 3, Henry 2008, Ritchie 2020: ch 2). Quasi-sciences such as astrology and alchemy were increasingly displaced. The Enlightenment marked the spread of this worldview, much of which took place outside the universities in the academies and societies of eighteenth-century civil society. As David Wootton (2016: 92–93, and *passim*) has observed, the rise of science was driven by a new spirit of competition to discover truths about the world, increasingly signalled from the late seventeenth century by intense priority disputes over those discoveries amongst mathematicians, experimenters, and explorers. By the nineteenth century, with the growth of the Humboldtian model, and fuller integration of universities into nation building projects, modern science and its competitive norms found a home in the universities, which could provide space for pure scientific thinking, and over time provided greater material support for experimental science in terms of labs and funding. As secularisation tended to privatise the religious worldview, and constrain the power of churches, universities grew in power under the patronage of states and supported the consolidation of a secular-scientific worldview, at least in elite and middle-class circles. The ancient marriage of church and state was largely dissolved, replaced by a new marriage of university and state, a new way of combining authority over ultimate knowledge and worldly power. However, it was not just the rise of 'hard' science regarding the workings of the natural world that was going on here. The study of humankind itself, its aesthetic and moral beliefs, was also at stake. To the longstanding humanities of the older universities, which had operated in dialogue with religious beliefs, was added the new idea of 'social sciences', which multiplied and grew, especially across the twentieth century, often outstripping humanities such as literature, philosophy, and history. While the hard sciences often stand aloof from questions of moral authority, falling silent where religion dared to tread, the humanities and social sciences are different. So frequently concerned with such things as ultimate sources of meaning, and the causes of deep social problems, they inevitably court moral authority, transforming knowledge about how the world is, into knowledge about how it ought to be. These disciplines, sustained by universities, have become the seedbeds of moral critiques and justifications of society, colonising an ideological space once more firmly held by religious authorities.

If the period from roughly 1800 to 1945 was the heyday of university expansion as a part of nation building, the period since 1945, and especially since the 1960s, might be viewed as the era of the globalisation of the university. In a series of writings John W. Meyer and colleagues (e.g. Frank and Meyer 2007, Ramirez and Meyer 2013, Schofer and Meyer 2005) have put a bold interpretation on a set of undeniable trends. These trends include: the vast expansion in the global number of universities, to the point that even countries like Samoa and East Timor have universities; the expansion of the number of students worldwide engaged in higher education, including previously excluded groups, especially women; huge multiplication of the number of topics and majors that can be studied in most universities; the global mobility of large sectors of the student population, especially at postgraduate level; the internal organisational change in universities to make them more like other large bureaucratic corporations, with large specialised administrative, managerial, and service staff; and moves towards transnational standardisation, such as the Bologna Process in Europe.[8]

[8] To give a sense of where we have come to, according to Palfreyman and Temple: 'There are more students than ever before: over 150 million in over 17,000 institutions around the world, and this number is growing all the time – with over thirty million students in China; some thirty million in India; more than twenty million in over 4,000 universities and colleges within the US; and more than two million across 150 or so institutions in the UK' (2017: 2).

Meyer argues that one might have expected the universities to fragment with increasing complexity of the division of labour, unable to keep pace with such change, instead replaced by numerous more specialised training institutions. But on the contrary, they have largely adjusted to and reflected this complexity by expanding in scope (allowing for the coexistence of more specialised education and training). For Meyer they are prime examples of his thesis of 'world society' (2010) – that against the trends of differentiation within and between societies, there are also strong tendencies towards the isomorphism of institutions across societies, exemplified by the universalisation of science, trends towards democratisation, notions of international law as exemplified in the idea of human rights, and shared norms and strategies in regard to economic development. My emphasis on the spreading form of the corporation, which includes universities, fits well within Meyer's paradigm of institutional isomorphism. Meyer sees the globalisation of the university model not simply as the pragmatic extension of an institution of national power (though it is that), but as a key element in the globally converging institutionalisation of a set of values linked to institutions, involving rationality, science, and the idea of a 'knowledge society'. Just as the medieval matrix of church and university provided an overarching rational frame within which knowledge and truth claims could be made and disputed, in a 'shrinking' world, a global institutional framework is now developing on the basis of science and secular learning. Just as the Christian and Latin-literate professors and students of old were 'citizens' of a wider Europe, today's scholars, who are an increasing portion of the global population, whatever their nationality, inhabit an essentially global cosmopolitan culture of norms and institutions. Whatever the national divisions, and axes of competition, the university is now an instrument of a kind of universal society, according to Meyer and colleagues.

It is difficult to deny that the model of the modern university is instrumental in the universalisation of many values and norms of knowledge. However, this argument seems to see all knowledge, practical and moral, as essentially moving together towards an integrated form. Democracy, individualism, liberalism, empiricism, and science seem to move together as a package. If we recall Gellner's assertion noted earlier in the chapter, that the modern age, in a reversal of previous times, is characterised by an integration of practical, scientific knowledge about the material world and how it works, but simultaneously fragmented in its capacity to unify societies through shared moral concepts, then we might be less sanguine than Meyer. Whether a universal global culture of science and empiricism necessarily entails cultures of liberalism, individualism, democracy, and human rights, would seem to be less than resolved. The former might be just as compatible with more authoritarian systems of values. The tendency Meyer identifies towards 'isomorphism' can be understood in terms of what have been called 'symmetrical arms races', in which competition leads social forms to converge, as all parties develop similar features as they strive towards the same winning strategy. But this may happen on some fronts and not others. Social change for Meyer seems to be more progressive and functionalist, and less agonistic, than my perspective on competition would suggest.

Conclusion

Once again, as with modern militaries, companies, and political parties, we have tracked the growth and transformation of an originally European form, to the point of its global spread. Competition is operative in various dimensions: among human actors, real persons, over ideas, among universities, corporations, competing for students and prestige, and among states competing with other states for economic development and, again, prestige. The university is an arena of intellectual competition, an agent in its own right engaged in competition, and a product of political and economic competition. I have only edged up to the present, but many readers will be keenly aware of this last dimension. While I have suggested that universities, somewhat like political parties but for different reasons, are suspended between civil society and the state, bear in mind my earlier claim that civil society includes the business world and economic interests and actors. In capitalist societies these are often the most powerful actors in civil society. Increasingly in the present era, as universities have become more numerous and larger, more a part of international competition and less a matter of the social reproduction of relatively small elite classes, they have borne an ever-larger burden to directly serve the interests of the state and the economy. They have become much less the redoubt of an intellectual class, and more a component in national strategies of economic development, weakening the fabled

Humboldtian ideal. This has led to defences of the older, more purely intellectual and autonomous purposes of the university (Collini 2012), and critiques of tuition-driven economic competition (McGettigan 2013), and of the socially stratifying and psychologically fatiguing effects of societies that place so much emphasis on a university education as a way of 'getting ahead' (Markovits 2020). Universities have undergone a degree of 'institutional capture' by states and big business in recent years, perhaps reducing their peculiar autonomy within civil society.

In this chapter, in order to centre the idea of the university, I have been able to give only limited attention to the phenomenon of civil society, focussing primarily on its emergence in the Enlightenment period, but not following through on the obvious fact that civil society becomes a fundamental aspect of liberal society thereafter. So let me emphasise that while universities have become major players in such societies, with a sanctioned role to play in the production of authoritative knowledge, including the status of endless public experts on all manner of social issues, they do not monopolise truth claims in liberal societies. The general openness of public discourse, made possible when the state reins in its policing of thought, and when the economy provides numerous innovative ways to communicate ideas, means that these core institutions of authority are nonetheless surrounded by a sea of ideas with other bases, religious, spiritual, ideological, experiential, anti-establishment, and sometimes conspiratorial. As for the church before them, absolute monopoly of belief is impossible, and competing ideas inevitably emerge from the interstices of society. The means for the production and dissemination of truth claims has exploded in the modern era, especially in the internet age, meaning that university-based knowledge and authority must be advanced in a very different and unpredictable environment.

Universities generate social power. With their stewardship of science, they generate practical knowledge about how the world works, increasing human understanding of and mastery over the physical world. But they also generate beliefs, more tenuously grounded, about the true nature of humans and society, and these feed into beliefs about ultimate values and the best moral order (Pinker 2002). These beliefs play a role in society's power over itself, its ability to coordinate diverse perspectives around shared visions of society. But in a liberal society, these visions are chronically contested, countered by alternatives.

Universities are also social actors. Despite the vast expansion in numbers, the potential global population of universities would appear to be limited. They could never be as numerous as commercial companies in general, because they require substantial initial capital, and offer basically the same asset, education, to a population largely limited by generation and class resources. They operate in a rather specialised ecology. While these actors are corporations with specific social and business aims, at the same time they are staffed in large part by academics who often are less inclined to see the particular university that employs them as a vessel for their agency, but instead as an arena (and perhaps a temporary base) within which the collectives that *do* matter to them and their sense of agency – research teams, theoretical schools, academic disciplines – must operate. There is a certain disjuncture between the agency of the university-incorporate, and the self-image of the academic as an autonomous intellectual and agent, which generates tensions within these institutions. And finally, universities, as we have seen, evolve. As I've suggested, competition in this field has increased numbers, diversified universities and other higher education organisations into different markets ('adaptive radiation'), and at the same time led to convergences in organisational forms as they compete in globalising markets under shared notions of science and scholarship. Meanwhile, at the level of ideas and truth claims, bodies of research and theory, which are never fully bounded by corporate organisational forms even if they rely on them for their practical reproduction, compete for attention and followers (Collins 2000). This happens within the narrow confines of academic practice, but also more widely in the 'public sphere'.

PART III

The Wider View

From this point on I want to pull back and view the subject from a broader perspective, one that looks at competition as shaping a general kind of culture, and that grapples with some of the normative questions about competition that I have largely left aside so far. These are the purposes of the last two chapters. Here I will offer an overview of the materials offered in Part II, to help synthesise the several chapters.

Most fundamentally, I argue that these four narratives 'add up', they analyse the formation of a package of institutions (military, economic, political, ideological) characteristic of the modern age, and especially of liberal forms of society. Indeed, this gives us a more concrete and less idealised understanding of what we mean by 'liberal society'. Although there are separate developmental processes in each institutional sphere, they converge in their respective elaborations of the corporate form, and in their corresponding formalisations of competitive principles and processes (allowing for the 'contrary movement' of the military case). They form what I have called 'systematically competitive society'. And, their convergence is not entirely contingent, but rather involves the perennial problem of power – how do societies generate authority and legitimacy once commitments to supernatural beliefs, kinship-based obligations, and traditionalism more generally, have weakened? Institutionalised competition is a dominant modern alternative. It is also the story of the rise of law as an expanding and deepening principle of social integration and power legitimation. It helps illustrate what Weber meant by the growth of legal-rational legitimacy, and the rationalisation of society. Competition across Europe among states, churches, and other institutions, led to a massive expansion and refinement of organisational power, which called for new principles for the legitimation of that power. Competition in its more raw and uncontrolled forms, including a lot of war, stimulated the harnessing of competition as an idea, as an explicit way of managing power.

Having emphasised this convergence, each of the four institutional domains has a different dynamic in terms of the domestication of competition. Military power undergoes unification and subordination to the state, limiting internal competition and focussing military practice on geopolitical competition between evolving empires and nation states. The economy also develops, and economic actors evolve, under the stewardship of the growing modern state and its legal reach and innovations. Older forms of trading partnerships are overtaken by newer forms of corporation with juristic personality, and these become the 'heavy lifters' of the industrialising capitalist economy. Democracy, unable to find any other means for aggregating the popular will into political agendas to shape government, increasingly calls forth political parties and party systems. In the realm of truth claims, the authority of religious institutions is gradually transferred to the university system, through the intermediate disruption of the Enlightenment. In this context new modes of non- or anti-religious thought were first cultivated largely outside the church-university matrix, but eventually became re-grounded in the modern university context, as science and secular scholarship. But the domain of ideas is chronically unbounded and over-productive, especially in the conditions of communication that characterise modern liberal society.

Another theme, somewhat in the background, and perhaps needing to be highlighted, is that the institutionalisation of the corporation as a legal person, goes hand-in-hand with the sharper definition of the individual, as a legally defined 'real person' and the bearer of rights and duties. The domestication of competition is driven by the growth of both 'real' and 'fictive' populations of competitors. And these are not just two different 'levels', individuals realise their agency by investing it in larger, more powerful and organised agents, corporations of all kinds, including the ultimate agent, the modern state. The competition of corporations is the competition of individuals writ large, but it is also the case that the competition of corporations, of all kinds, in all spheres, compels and inculcates individual competition. Real and fictive personhood provides a kind of matrix through which these forces interact.

The vast social changes thus described, I treat as social evolution, because the change is directional, and has general effects on social morphology. The modern corporate form, while not exhaustive, nevertheless permeates social organisation, sharpening the definition of different parts of society, and abetting growth in social scale. These corporate forms, rather than 'societies', become the key objects of social evolutionary pressures and competition, and the reason we often talk as though societies evolve, is because in the modern age they are generally housed in the ultimate corporate form, the state. Precisely because of its artificiality, that is its disconnection from the biological constraints of kinship, the corporate form is more malleable, more adaptable to different contexts. Thus, it differentiates and radiates. It has to be re-emphasised that this is a history of 'the West' and the liberal form of society as it came about, and how aspects of it have spread globally. It is not a prognostication about the future, nor a claim about historical necessity in the past, but rather an analysis of a key process in recent centuries, with a specific aetiology, involving historical contingencies. We can imagine many things having gone differently, but they didn't.

The last two chapters do two things. Chapter 8 in a sense picks up from Chapter 7, asking how the idea of competition informs a kind of culture, or worldview. Chapter 7 was primarily concerned with the way institutions involved in truth claiming have been transformed, building competition more systematically into that process. Chapter 8 is more concerned with how the *idea of competition* is explicitly institutionalised, to become a governing idea in the culture of liberal society. Chapter 9 turns to the normative dimension, posing some of the moral lessons we might take away from this study. In regard to competition, it elaborates my view that to 'critique' something is to distinguish between its good and bad, or at least better and worse, forms. It asks what conditions are necessary for competition to be a benefit to society, and what conditions tend to undermine this value. Compared to previous chapters in the next two there is a change of tone. They are not historical, but rather an analysis of an abstracted cultural and moral system. The emphasis is less on surveying bodies of literature, and more on laying out key issues as I understand them, engaging with a few helpful thinkers along the way.

8 *The Culture of Competition*

If Chapter 7 focused on transforming institutional bases for competitive truth claiming, from churches to universities, this chapter is more concerned with competition as ideology, broadly defined. It is about how the idea and practice of competition gets elaborated, forming part of a wider culture of competition. I begin by clarifying how I think about culture, making analytic distinctions between two senses of culture: as an organising principle, and as a system of representations. In this chapter the focus is more on the latter. Within that heading, the rest of the chapter explores its topic through three further analytic lenses. First, culture as a pattern of legitimating beliefs; second, culture as a pattern of performative practices; and third, bringing together the first two, competition as a form of ritual that binds together liberal society. Taking a cue from Mary Douglas (1982), I argue that far from modern 'disenchanted' society being evacuated of ritual, it is saturated in the ritual form of competition, which does a lot of the legitimating work that rituals have done in all societies.[1]

The Culture Concept

In his famous ethnography *The Nuer* the anthropologist E. E. Evans-Pritchard said '*cherchez la vache*' – look for the cow (1969[1940]: 16). This was a play on the sexist saying '*cherchez la femme*', look for a woman if you are trying to explain the origins of troubles.[2] The Nuer are semi-nomadic pastoralists, Nilotic people of the South Sudan, where they are the second largest ethnic group after the Dinka. Evans-Pritchard's point was that cattle are absolutely central to the culture of the Nuer as pastoralists. Not only were they the central form

[1] This chapter develops ideas explored previously in Hearn (2014b, 2016a).

[2] This phrase is normally traced to Alexandre Dumas' 1854 novel *The Mohicans of Paris*, but also more generally as a prominent theme in pulp fiction detective novels and films.

of wealth, and thus power, but the idea of the cow ran through Nuer culture, including the regulation of intergroup relations as bride wealth at marriage, ideas of supernatural authority, the naming of children, and the reckoning of the seasons. The cow was both an essential part of the material basis of the social order, and a potent symbol for making sense of that order. Since Evans-Pritchard's study the Nuer way of life has been impacted by Sudan's independence in 1956, resistance to oil exploration, recurring warfare, increasing importance of guns in the region, the separation of South Sudan from Sudan in 2011, and the growth of a population internationally dispersed as refugees. But cattle remain central to their way of life.

The motto of this book might be: '*cherchez le concurrence*' – look for the competition, in the same spirit of identifying a conceptual key for unlocking the culture. Of course the culture in question, that of liberal forms of society, is of a vastly different scale, cutting across divisions of ethnicity and nationality that we normally associate with culture. Nonetheless there is a spreading pattern of core institutions, organisations, and ideas, that warrant the label 'culture' as a way of understanding that patterning. I highlight two senses of culture, out of many.[3] First, culture is an organising principle, binding together the disparate parts of any social formation into a reasonably functional system, through core institutions: culture is an aspect of social organisation. Second, in more ideational terms, culture is a system of representations, a complex of symbols and meanings, stories people tell themselves about themselves. Both angles are important for understanding competition as culture.

In a sense I have already demonstrated what I mean by culture as an organising principle in the substantive historical chapters of Part II. I have argued that modern liberal society involves the corresponding transformation of competition across institutional spheres, enabled by the rise of corporate personhood. Military competition is subordinated to states and oriented outward to the international arena of states, within states economic competition is fostered through the proliferation of companies and framing law, political competition is channelled into political parties in a democratic framework, and ideological competition over truth claims is grounded in universities, operating in a wider field of civil society. This is not an exhaustive description of

[3] For a fuller critical discussion of the concept of culture, see Hearn (2017: 53–56).

everything that might be labelled culture, but rather a core institutional pattern that characterises a general type of society. The more that pattern has coalesced as a package, the more any particular case is 'of' that type.

This conception is reminiscent of the idea of 'cultural cores' put forward by the anthropologist Julian Steward (1972: 5–6, 37). Steward was a leading figure in cultural ecology and neo-evolutionary social theory that I discussed in Chapter 2. Drawing perhaps obliquely on Marxian notions of material determination, Steward was interested in how certain sets of social, political, and religious institutions, things like kinship structures, combined with available technologies to enable the group to extract a living from its environment. He saw these as primary, and distinguished them from 'secondary' features of culture that were less central to organising subsistence activities, more historically contingent, often the result of diffusion and borrowing from other groups. For Steward, identifying these core functional relationships between institutions, livelihoods, and environments, was basic for being able to make cross-cultural comparisons between types.

I argued previously that one of the limitations of the cultural ecological approach to social evolution was that as societies become more complex, and the relations between them more interdependent, it becomes impossible to identify a clear relationship between 'subsistence activities' and an 'environment'. When I define a complex of competition-oriented institutions, I am saying these are core to a certain strategy for creating and legitimating authority within that type of system, so that it can persist as a system. These systems are housed in relatively successful nation states, that manage to sustain themselves through economic and political exchanges with other nations states, and through sufficient military power and alliances to protect their basic integrity. The community of states and their political, economic, and military relations, *is* the environment.[4] There are many cultural variations, in language, religion, and so on, that distinguish the state-societies of this broad liberal type. But what they share is this basic cultural core which determines their basic survival strategy.

[4] Albeit underneath it all there still holds a collective relationship between humanity and the natural world, from which we derive our subsistence, which is consequential, and can become unbalanced.

The other sense of culture is as a system of representations. This chapter is more concerned with this second sense; but the main features of culture as representations tend to correspond to what I have called, echoing Steward, the 'cultural core', they are not independent. While ideation and symbols can enjoy a certain malleability and contingency that social institutions and organisations do not, they get their deeper and more enduring meanings precisely from how they correspond to, respond to, and render tractable, those core organising principles that govern people's lives. Arthur Lovejoy's study of *The Great Chain of Being* (1960) described an ideological construct of the European Middle Ages that claimed that the inorganic and organic worlds, and the ranks of human society, all followed a permanent, God-given hierarchical order, a 'great chain'. The reason this idea was important to late medieval philosophy and theology was that it legitimated the given cultural core of institutions whose decline I have stressed throughout this book: heritable monarchy, aristocracy, and the church. Such cultural accounts could not serve an emerging society presumably based on equality, mobility, and individual autonomy. Such a society needs to be legitimated by very different sets of ideas, that speak to the determining force of its new core institutions. Look for the competition.[5]

Within this second sense of culture as ideation and representation, there is a further conceptual division that structures the body of this chapter: that is between bodies of beliefs that legitimate the social order, and performative practices that demonstrate the social order to its members. In an essay on 'religion as a cultural system' (1973: 87–125) Clifford Geertz elaborated his influential idea that cultures should be understood as systems of symbols, and that the practice of studying them is fundamentally a work of interpretation. There he added, thinking especially about religion, that these systems of symbols, or at least parts of them, are at once both descriptive and prescriptive, providing both 'models of' reality, and 'models for' how to act on that reality:

> Unlike genes, and other nonsymbolic information sources, which are only models *for*, not models *of*, culture patterns have an intrinsic double aspect: they give meaning, that is, objective conceptual form, to social and

[5] As I have argued, it is not that premodern feudal society lacked competition, but apart from elite martial culture, it was not a broadly legitimating concept.

psychological reality both by shaping themselves to it and by shaping it to themselves. (1973: 93, emphasis in original)

Geertz's approach, while often rich in its 'thick descriptions', had a tendency to lose touch with the material underpinnings of social power, the 'cultural core' as I have expressed it above. Nonetheless, if Geertz is broadly correct, that culture as a system of symbols and representations seeks to provide both models of how the world works, and of how we ought to act in it, this idea returns us to the is/ought problem. How do cultures bridge the divide between description and prescription? One has a sense that for Geertz the great virtue of culture is that it manages this synthesis. We might ask if this is always so, and especially in the case of liberal forms of society, which preserve so many tensions between viewpoints. The very idea of 'culture' grinds against that of 'liberalism', the one suggesting the mental holism of a community, the other the mental diversity of a bundle of individuals. After examining these two senses of culture as representation, I bring them back together in a consideration of the relevance of the concept of ritual.

Culture as Legitimating Beliefs

A signal feature of liberal society is the relative openness to ideological dispute and change. I discussed in the previous chapter how the modern university evolved to provide a core platform for disputation over truth claims, as a dominant institution within a wider public sphere of truth claiming in civil society. Now I want to look more closely at the system of ideas themselves, that help justify the institutions.

On the one hand, new beliefs developed and spread that placed limits on previously dominant claims to power and authority. Tolerance of religious dissent and pluralism gradually became normalised, religious institutions were disestablished in some cases, and religious belief became subject to 'market' competition between churches, sects, and prophets seeking believers (Finke and Stark 1998). Older patterns of heritable noble status were either rejected or seriously curtailed. Wealth and social connections of course continued to pass down through some noble families, but more importantly, legally protected intergenerational transfer of property allows for new concentrations of wealth in family lineages (Piketty 2014). In a way, European notions of heritable status were generalised and ideologically reconfigured in forms of ethnic, racial, and colonial stratification, placing Europeans as a whole at the apex of a system of 'races'. But the long-term ideological trend in liberal society has been against these forms of stratification as well, however incomplete that process may be. The point is that recognising religious authority is increasingly at the choice of the believer, or can be rejected altogether, and that no lineage or strata has a monopoly claim on the right to rulership, however materially and ideologically advantaged it might be.

On the other hand these rejections of older legitimating beliefs are matched by new positive assertions about the proper basis of beliefs, and for contending claims about the truth. First, with complex roots in the history of Christian thought (Seidentop 2014), the assertion of claims to freedoms of conscience, thought and speech. And second, with the rise of empirical science, the assertion of the authority of demonstrable evidence from the external world (Wootton 2015). Note how these move in opposite directions, the former asserting the inward autonomy of the individual mind, the latter the outward authority of shared experience. This is an uneasy balance. Any attempt to synthesise these ideas needs to overcome their contrary movement by construing truth claiming as a social process, carried out among notionally equal and autonomous individuals. Jonathan Rauch calls this 'liberal science', meaning a cultural pattern for legitimating belief, not a narrow philosophical school. According to him it is based on two 'rules' (2013: 46):

- 'No one gets the final say' – the process of truth seeking is open ended.
- 'No one has personal authority' – no one is in a privileged position to decide the truth.

For Rauch this is at once a minimal definition of the practice of science, and at the same time a statement of the key principles of liberal society. It puts truth claims in a permanent state of competition. Its inherent indeterminacy in regard to truth makes it unstable for at least two reasons. First, these principles, by their nature invite challenge, even to themselves as principles. Liberal societies exhibit many attempts to 'have the final say' and to claim 'personal authority'. The rules of the game allow challenges to its fundamental rules, at least as proposals that can be openly expressed. Second, though they may define the broad 'rules of the game' in practice, this does not prevent some people from seeking or claiming more foundational authority through basic ontological or epistemological claims. And however indeterminate its underlying legitimating principles, science is often socially positioned as an ultimate source of authority, because those are the terms in which many people conceive of truth, and because political leaders still need external authoritative sanction. What they once sought in the authority of the church, they now seek in the authority of science.

Given these conceptions of liberal culture and science as grounded in a competitive contest among ideas, it is intriguing to note that one of the distinctive forms of social theory such societies have generated in recent decades, is 'game theory'. It will be recalled that James Coleman was a game theorist (1989). Game theory models social interaction as a set of strategies carried out by rational actors, using certain underlying assumptions about human interests to predict behaviour. Such models can then be tested against actual behaviour in various natural and experimental settings. Sophisticated game theory recognises that human rational action takes place in conditions of limited knowledge, and that not all human motives are self-interested (Gintis 2017). One of the key questions of game theory is when and why do people choose to cooperate, or not (Bowles and Gintis 2011). The paradigm has influenced research across many of the areas we have been concerned with in this book – warfare, politics, economics, ideology. My point here is not to go deep into the pros and cons of game theory, but rather to point out the striking isomorphism here. A society that increasingly conducts its social business as a controlled, competitive game, that repeats the formalisation of competition across many domains, providing both individual and organisational actors with various rule-governed frameworks for pursuing their ends, will inevitably become more susceptible to analysis on the model of a game. This is not to say that such a model isn't applicable to other times, places, and non-liberal cultures. Some aspects of rational self-interest are highly generalisable, and most of the time societies provide reasonably stable frameworks within which it is possible to strategise. But it is to suggest that the articulation of this model as a fundamental explanatory framework (in contention with other theories) is in some sense characteristic, perhaps even symptomatic, of systematically competitive society. There is an 'elective affinity'. As the 'great chain of being' was to medieval social hierarchy, so 'game theory' is to liberal society; although liberal society being what it is, there is a greater proliferation of ideological challengers.

Rauch draws inspiration from Karl Popper (1902–1994). We can read Popper's philosophy of science and society (see Shearmur and Stokes 2016) as an indicative manifestation of the wider cultural pattern of liberal society. Early on Popper set out to challenge the paradigm of science as 'inductivism', that is, producing generalisable statements about reality on the basis of particular observations that support those statements. Popper argued that what makes science a distinctive practice is not that it is a collection of statements built up on observable facts, but rather that its claims, scientific theories, are formulated in such a way that they could be refuted by empirical tests. Thus, his account of science rests not on the validation of claims by evidence, but the openness to potential 'falsification' of claims. In other words, science is not the building up of an authoritative and unchallengeable body of knowledge, but a practice of knowledge production based on the ongoing competition among truth claims. For Popper these views about science were connected to views about preferable social orders. Popper advocated what he called the 'open society' (1945), in which people are free to criticise intellectual and political authorities, and social improvement is pursued through cautious reforms, revisable in the face of new evidence. Correspondingly he was critical of what he called philosophical 'holism' (1957), the quest to build an ideal and complete society, which he associated with figures such as Plato and Marx (see Stokes 2016). Again, ongoing competition among ideas about society and how to improve it is basic to this perspective.

However influential, Popper's specific approach to questions of science and society have had a mixed reception in academia and wider society. As Ernest Gellner pointed out, while Popper sought to lift his principle of falsification above crude positivist empiricism, it rather assumes such a cold, objective reality against which theoretical claims can be measured. Without a gap between reality and our claims about it, and treating the former as the final court of appeal about the latter, falsification risks becoming a self-enclosed game of theoretical refutation, unconstrained by anything external to it. The competition among claims rests on this mundane assumption of a natural and regular world (Gellner 1974: 174–175, Hall 2011: 217–221). The point, however, is that Popper's accounts of science and the open society work as general descriptions of practice, of how scientists understand what they are doing, and how citizens of liberal societies would justify those societies. His philosophy is itself, whatever its flaws, a cultural manifestation, summing up a particular 'model of and model for'.

Culture as Performative Practices

All cultures provide contexts for the performative demonstration of core ideas and values. In modern liberal societies, especially today, this fact is complicated by the sheer multiplication of communication media as channels for such performances. 'Live' performances in theatre and the arts, are now augmented by broadcast media such as radio and television, which have in turn been overtaken by interactive online social media. The platforms for performance proliferate, as do the opportunities for truth claiming.

Of course, many cultural performances, especially in the arts, do not take the form of competition, but rather through literature, drama, music, dance, and so on, narrativise and otherwise represent social ideas and feelings. This may include representations of conflict and competition, among characters in drama for instance, but competition isn't intrinsic to the form itself. However, the modern institutionalisation of the arts has introduced many formalised venues of competition, for prizes, awards, and so on, that set aesthetic standards and contribute to professional ranking (McCormick 2015, Stark 2020). So while the artform itself and individual artistic productions may not be concerned with competition, the social practice gets partly managed through competition. The same could be said of fields besides the arts, such as academia, where scholarly work pursued at least partially for its own intrinsic merits, nonetheless gets channelled into arenas of formalised competition, for funding and other forms of recognition (Lamont 2010). And of course, all these activities are subject to the wider competitive pressures of multiple markets, for jobs and other resources.

However, it is particularly relevant here that for many forms of public performance, competition *is* intrinsic to the practice, and gives the performance its narrative forms, and sense of drama. One need only think of the proliferation of television entertainment of this kind, in which viewers tune in to watch contestants compete to be the best dancer, singer, chef, or housemate. The drama is ready-made in the competitive format, in which shows conclude with the tense revelation of winners and losers, and demonstration of the joy in, and acceptance of, those appointed roles. And these performances have their corollary in the small, everyday activity of household games – cards, Monopoly, Trivial Pursuit and so on – entertainments being augmented or replaced by new media forms such as online gaming. Competition in this format of entertainment and amusement, with relatively low consequences for spectators and participants, saturates daily life. However critical we might be of competition, it is a normal part of everyday life which many people participate in on an everyday basis, in these relatively harmless forms.[6]

The arena of sports is probably the most emblematic case of the institutionalised cultural performance of competition, so I will look at it more closely. Here again, there is a spectrum from sports as a leisure activity among friends and children in school on up to sports as a highly professionalised, multi-national, high stakes industry. Modern sports are public dramas, performances that encode social values, teaching lessons about fair play, teamwork, and how to be good winners, and good losers. Indeed, Geertz's most famous essay, 'Notes on a Balinese Cockfight' (1972), demonstrating his 'thick descriptive' approach to symbolic analysis, argued that these competitive events surrounded by gambling and status rivalries provided a view into the nature of Balinese culture.

One reason to focus on sports is simply that there is a research tradition, a 'sociology of sport'. But one of the most curious things about this tradition is how little it is concerned with the phenomenon of competition *per se*. It is of course there in the background, but most attention is given to how sports play a role in reproducing and articulating conflict around structures of stratification, of race, class, and gender (Carrington 2013, Frey and Eitzen 1991, Washington and Karen 2001). C. L. R. James's seminal *Beyond a Boundary* (1963), scrutinised cricket in the Caribbean as an arena in which colonially framed conflicts of class and race were 'played out', with West Indians both appropriating the game, and asserting a counter-identity through

[6] This is not to deny that certain practices, such as online gaming and gambling, can become addictive and harmful. But we are unlikely to indict the entire complex of competition-based leisure and entertainment because of these pathological tendencies.

it. Here the competition of the game is an arena through which wider social conflict is expressed.

Another prominent theme has been the transformation of modern sports under pressures of 'commodification, rationalization, bureaucratization, quantification, commercialization' (Frey and Eitzen 1991: 507), mediatization, and corporatization. Many have identified a critical period from about 1890 to 1930 in which certain sports became highly professionalised and institutionalised, in line with the consolidation of working- and middle-class cultures in industrial societies (Markovits and Hellerman 2001; Patterson, Tomlinson and Young 2011: 560–561). More recently the story is one of the global growth of sports as media entertainment and big business. In this context it is interesting to note that it is the competition among corporate entities for sports generated revenues, between universities in the US, between cities rivalling to host major stadiums, that is often the focus (Noll and Zimbalist 1997, Sage 2011), again, rather than competition within the sport itself.

In Chapter 2 I noted the relevance for this book of Pierre Bourdieu's notion of social fields as arenas of competition, even though he doesn't pay close attention to the concept of competition itself. His influential programmatic article on the sociology of sport (1988) bears this out. There he emphasises the role of sport as a context in which class habitus, including its bodily dimension, is cultivated and reinforced, and the given system of sports as a social space corresponding to wider social structures. Bourdieu's comparisons to the fields of music and dance emphasise the performative rather than competitive aspects. More intriguing as a point of comparison for the present study is the work of Norbert Elias, whose treatment of sport falls within his overarching thesis of a 'civilising process' (1994). This is particularly apparent when considering the question of the modern rise and institutionalisation of sports (widely defined to include such things as fox hunting) (Elias and Dunning 1986). Elias emphasises an 'affinity' between this process and wider themes already addressed in this book: the pacification of aristocratic martial power, and the growth of a more civil form of parliamentary politics in the wake of civil war. The latter is particularly associated with the English case, which Elias sees, as I do, as an historically contingent but consequential development. He emphasises the formalisation of sports and their national standardisation as supported by new clubs and associations formed for the purpose in the eighteenth century. Thus, his account also fits with my narrative of the Enlightenment as a florescence of civil association. As he puts it: 'The "parliamentarization" of the landed classes of England had its counterpart in the "sportization" of their pastimes' (Elias 1986: 34). And these two processes fit into the broader themes of 'pacification' and 'civilisation' in Elias's work.

An important part of Elias's approach is his emphasis on the bodily manifestation of impulse control, the way humans learn to regulate the combined physiological and psychological capacities to build-up and then release emotional and psychic tensions, in ways that are both satisfying and disciplining. He views sports, and leisure pastimes more generally in this light, as mini symbolic dramas, that build up tension and lead to a climax and resolution. Thus, a play, or a symphony concert, have the same narrative form as a sporting event. However, in the latter, there is a 'mock-battle' or contest between teams or individual competitors, and this is what supplies the drama. In highly civilised society such events serve a certain organic need for excitement, while doing so in a controlled and non- or minimally destructive way, at the same time teaching participants and spectators how to manage and process those impulses in a socially acceptable, even productive way. This is the context in which Elias and Eric Dunning (1986) make sense of the propensity towards violence in some sports, particularly among football fans and spectators. The staged violence of the game easily spills over into the real, uncontrolled violence of the riot.

There are clear parallels between what I have argued and what Elias is arguing. However, there are also significant divergences. Elias is interested in the correspondences between developments in norms, behaviours, and habitus, on the one hand, and political and social institutions, and ultimately the state, on the other. He sees a single process in which people gain greater control over their own behaviour at the same time that states gain greater effective control over their citizens/subjects and territories. He offers a somewhat Freudian account of psychological change wedded to a more structural account of political change. He wants to avoid an image of either 'micro' or 'macro' levels driving change in the other, and views this instead as a single, unified process. However, it is not always clear what is causing these changes altogether. Is it part of a deeper evolutionary tendency towards pacification and social integration? How contingent are the changes of the last 500 years or so, and why were they triggered first in

Europe, especially, in different ways, in England and France? I am not sure Elias ever gives a clear answer to these questions.

I see the formalisation of sports as part of the general process of the 'domestication of competition' put forward in this book. However, I am more inclined to see it as a symbolic expression of the deeper changes going on at the level of political and economic power. For me sports and all kinds of leisure competitions provide a context for the relatively 'safe' dramatisation and celebration of a key dynamic of modern liberal society, and also a means for the socialisation of the young into norms and values appropriate to a world routinely shaped by competition. Functionalist arguments that sport is an arena of socialisation can be challenged on the basis that the values inculcated are reproduced generally in society, regardless of people's participation in sports (Frey and Eitzen 1991: 506). But if we consider sports not just as a matter of direct participation, but as an arena of cultural representation for both participants and spectators, it becomes less a matter of individual socialisation, and more a matter of the culture demonstrating itself to itself. Sport is one kind of cultural drama, with competition at its core.

Elias sees the civilising process as a synchronised, society-wide transformation. Unlike Elias, I see the domestication of martial competition, subordinating it to the state, as a precondition for other domestications in politics, economics, and the realm of thought, ideas, and beliefs, rather than a parallel development. More fundamentally, I see competition itself as a mode of legitimation of the power order, not simply an aspect of socialisation and social control. It is an historically emergent strategy for solving the eternal problem of the greater 'power to' of the social group entailing greater 'power over' of the whole to its parts, which perennially meets with resistance. Elias saw changing 'balances of power' (1978: 15, 74) as a factor in the great transformation he was trying to understand, and it might be that he would have been receptive to me couching the 'civilising process' in these terms of the delicate balance of power to and power over.

Competition as Ritual

The preceding is a relatively quick sketch of how competition has come to permeate modern liberal culture. For the rest of this chapter I want to focus the discussion by looking more closely at the concept of ritual, because ritual is often seen as one of the diagnostic manifestations of culture, providing a window into its inner mechanisms. However, it is sometimes claimed that ritual is characteristic of premodern society, and a less significant part of how modern societies work, with their greater individualism and stronger organisational, bureaucratic, and legal means to shape behaviour. At the same time, modern nation states are replete with cultural and political rituals, from flag and independence days, to political rallies, that play some role in generating national solidarity (McCrone and McPherson 2009, Tsang and Wood 2014). And such societies contain many institutional arenas, religious and otherwise, in which ritual practices, as normally understood, play an important role.

In her fascinating if speculative study, *Natural Symbols* (1982), written amid the anti-conformist countercultural movements of the late 1960s, Mary Douglas argues that critiques of ritualism are more structural and cyclical, than indications of a unidirectional secular decline of ritual. Drawing on the ideas of Basil Bernstein (1971), she finds an affinity between ritualism and tightly bounded social groups, with strong norms of reciprocity, and rule-bound behaviour. Likewise, Douglas associates anti- or weak ritualism with more fluid and less bounded social groups, where ego must negotiate a shifting set of social relationships and appropriate norms for them. For the former, cosmological beliefs present a fixed order that one must observe, while for the latter they present a personal relationship between the individual and the supernatural. In the former, one is 'justified by works', by performing the rituals, in the latter it is more a matter of 'inner faith'. In the anthropological literature, the former is associated with larger, more sedentary societies with relatively rigid kinship structures, while the latter is associated with smaller, more mobile foraging societies with looser and shallower kinship ties. Douglas thinks all societies need symbols and rituals, but recognises that they go through cycles of building up ritual practices to bolster social relations, and generating counter-movements of anti-ritualism in search of authenticity, as rituals become mere conventions. In the western European context, the Protestant Reformation against the Catholic Church is the ultimate example, and perhaps haunts Douglas's study. The questions her analysis poses for ritualism in modern liberal society are whether there is: (a) a long-term trend away from ritualism; (b) a tendency for ritualism to become enclosed in tighter bounded communities, while wider society is relatively un-ritualised; and/or (c) a moving tension between ritualism and anti-ritualism across society as a whole, as it wrestles with the tensions between the needs for fixity and fluidity.

In another argument that grapples with estrangement from ritual, and the role of ritual in traditional and modern societies, Adam Seligman and colleagues (2008) have suggested that all societies confront permanent problems of social tensions and divisions. For them ritual is an ongoing task of overcoming this situation through the positing of subjunctive, 'as if' worlds, in a way similar to the imagining, and suspension of disbelief, involved in play. They see participation in such imagining as creating conditions that cultivate shared empathy. Working against this principle is the constant call for 'sincerity', predominant in the modern period, which rejects ritual and seeks to overcome division within the world, and between self and world, through authentic connections. They see a permanent and insuperable tension between these two principles. The authors draw on non-western traditions of thought, particularly Chinese, to get an alternative perspective on ritual. Nonetheless, their problematic, of ritual versus sincerity, is again heavily inscribed with the Catholic versus Protestant division in the western Christian tradition.

In what follows I consider what the idea of ritual, in the context of modern liberal society, might tell us about the role of competition in knitting together society. I follow Douglas, and Seligman et al., in their claims that ritual is enduringly relevant, although I am less concerned to make the case for the social value of ritual. Instead, I am more concerned with how competition as ritual helps to legitimate and naturalise the social order, and its distribution of power.

Before considering competition as ritual, I begin by looking at the basic, widely recognised standard features of ritual that are highlighted across various theories (Bell 1997: 138–170, Rappaport 1999: 23–68, Wuthnow 1987: 98–109):

- *Formalism:* While having some scope for improvisation and spontaneity, rituals are defined by their formulaic, rule governed nature. There is generally a script of some sort, an order of words and actions, and standards for how they must be performed for the ritual to be effective.
- *Expertise:* While some rituals are conducted by everyday actors, in many cases there are 'ritual specialists' who have appointed roles

and authority to officiate, and may have special abilities, to make the ritual valid.

- *Separation/sacredness:* The event itself is clearly demarcated, there is a before and after, and while it is going on, there is an absorption of participants, both actors and observers, in the event. It takes place in a kind of liminal time that is set apart from daily life, and that ends in some kind of resolution.
- *Performativity:* On the one hand public rituals, both religious and secular, often dramatise core ideals and values, encoding these in symbols and narrative forms, that seem to attach the given social order to a more fundamental cosmology. On the other, many rituals perform actions, transforming social statuses, such as from child to adult.

I want to look more closely at the last two, separation and performativity. Durkheim (1965) thought of ritual as marking a boundary between sacred and profane worlds, that the sacred gets its symbolic power by being ritually 'set apart' from the mundane world, and thereby heightened. He hypothesised that through intense communal focus in ritual on the symbols of the clan totem, or god, the participants were in fact worshipping their society itself, and sanctioning its social rules and order. I question the adequacy of this thesis as a basis for a general understanding of ritual. While the principle of 'separation' operates in some cases, it is by no means a universal or comprehensive account. Rather, ritualism is often distributed along a gradient, from the high pitched, rare, and marked off communal rituals of the kind Durkheim emphasised, through smaller scale, more frequent and local rituals, on down to mundane daily practices observed by individuals. This is more a question of differences of degree than of kind. Ritual, especially in larger scale societies, takes the form of a complex of formalised activities distributed through society, not something always 'set apart'. In the realm of religion, the once in a lifetime Hajj connects to daily prayers, and the observance of rules of diet and dress; rituals of Baptism and the Eucharistic Mass connect to confessions, Sunday services, and rosary prayers. In Aztec society, the great rituals of human sacrifice of war captives, understood as a way of maintaining ecological and cosmological balance, were matched by minor personal and household daily rituals of autosacrifice, letting small amounts of blood by piercing soft tissue with a thorn, and offering these at household alters. All are equally exotic or mundane depending on one's perspective. The point is that ritual gets its force not simply by being set apart and heightened, but by such rituals being connected in a chain of understanding, on down to routine practices, so that the ritual complex permeates daily life.

As I've suggested, the performative aspect of ritual has two dimensions. As dramatisation and display of core values informing social order, the ritual performance tends to happen on a grander public scale, with the entire community potentially acting as the audience. Think of national holidays, investitures, flyovers, marches, and parades. Even household-based rituals such as Christmas, with their secularisation and family variations, nonetheless are replicated 'across the land' at the same time, and anticipated and participated in publicly throughout the season. The ritual somehow attempts to symbolically square the circle between the need for family and communal caring, concern and reciprocity, and an extensive consumer driven economy in which people are enmeshed. In the more instrumental sense of performative, rituals of a standard format are generally engaged in by smaller groups, and exemplify what J. L. Austin meant by 'doing things with words' (Austin 1975). The specific ritual actions, often in the form of liturgical words, effect changes in people. Through various ceremonial performances, immigrants become citizens, the accused become convicts, lovers become married partners, princes become kings, and so on. The ambiguities of social relationships are cleaned up by formally moving people from one status to another, according to the proper ritual (Van Gennep 1960).

Randall Collins is one of the few who have tried to provide a thoroughgoing analysis of how ritual works in modern secular society, with his theory of 'interaction ritual chains' (2004). Finding Durkheim's emphasis on the 'set apart' ritual inadequate to explain solidarity in modern complex society, he incorporates Erving Goffman's more microsociological concern with everyday social interaction. He accepts Durkheim's claim that rituals work by generating emotional intensification, 'effervescence', among participants, contributing to social solidarity. But in complex, highly differentiated societies full of tension and conflicts, rather than the big communal ritual, Collins emphasises long and relatively independent chains of smaller scale, often secular rituals in which social bonds are strengthened through emotional intensification. Thus, the sinews of ritual bind the whole together, without needing to supply the encompassing apex ritual for society as a whole that Durkheim's approach seems to require. It may be that my treatment of competition as ritual has things in common with Collins's, but in my view his concern to rethink the dynamics of the emotional intensification of social bonds through ritual leads him to neglect Durkheim's other concern, which was with how societies generate the authority of the social whole over its members. The outcome of ritual for Durkheim was not just tighter social bonds, but a hypostatised image of society as the ultimate source of power and authority, society as its own God. Ritual is not just an institution through which power is constructed and implemented (Bloch 1989), although it is that. It also characteristically addresses the very question of the nature of power and the order of the cosmos. The close association between ritual and religion affirms this point, as ritual so often involves gaining access to supernatural forces, and by the same token, acknowledging the ultimate transcendent power behind order in the world. Ritual presents an image of how the cosmos is ordered, where power lies, and the means for tapping into that power and applying it. It is a 'model of' and a 'model for'.

Now let me turn to competition as ritual in liberal society. Competition is concerned with power, shaping how conflict is managed, resources distributed, and authority allocated in almost every institutional sphere. From science, to politics, to economics, *the idea* suffuses how activities are organised, both consciously and habitually. But precisely because it is *a method* of organising activity, from grand contests for national power to daily entertainments, it also manifests itself in the form of rituals, and a ritual complex, running the gamut of society. I return to the basic features of ritual outlined above, as they apply to 'competitions', that is, formalised competitive events:

- *Formalism:* Competitions are rule governed, and must follow the rules if they are to be legitimate. Violation of the rules can invalidate the event and its outcomes. They normally follow set sequences, like a liturgy. There is scope for improvisation by actors within the form, but only within limits.
- *Expertise:* Competitions also tend to rely on specialists to make the event work, such as referees, who not only officiate but also ensure the rules are followed, and appointed judges who are qualified to validate outcomes (about which more below).

- *Separation/sacredness:* Competitions are temporally demarcated, again in a kind of immersive and liminal period in which participants can lose themselves temporarily. While it may be a conceptual stretch to call these periods 'sacred', there can be a heightened, intensified, shared experience associated with them.
- *Performativity:* Competitions also exhibit the duality of performativity, providing a dramatisation of a core principle of how society works, while at the same time transforming statuses, most conspicuously, from contenders, to winners and losers.

We easily recognise the parallels in highly formalised events such as sports, as discussed above, but the form itself permeates society in less readily recognisable forms: any election, adversarial court cases, bidding for business contracts, competitions for funding and awards, job interviews, house auctions, and so on. All exhibit some or all of these properties.

However seriously they take the worldviews of their subjects, almost all theories of ritual include some idea of latent and manifest functions. Some have argued that religious rituals, such as cyclical feasting, actually serves to stimulate food productivity (Rappaport 1968); many rituals have been viewed as serving to psychologically manage social structural tensions (Turner 1967); and Durkheim's theory claims the supernatural beliefs expressed ultimately serve to generate social solidarity. My analysis of competition as ritual similarly claims that the myriad forms of competitions in daily life, that help achieve various pragmatic ends, add up to an overall image of the social order, one verified by the deep institutional embedding of competition this book has been about. The argument is that rather than supernatural rituals having practical effects, practical rituals have not so much supernatural effects, as cosmological implications, which are experienced as instantiations of an almost inevitable, pervasive, and naturalised social order.

How does competitive ritual do this? I argue it does this partly by blurring certain conceptual boundaries, between 'is' and 'ought', 'nature' and 'artifice', 'might' and 'right'. Through multiple forms, with variant ways of resolving outcomes, competition rituals as a complex combine and confuse principles of human judgement, and natural fact. A brief typological analysis of competition ritual forms helps show how the ritual complex helps achieve this ideological synthesis. The key question is how are the outcomes arrived at and resolved. At one end outcomes are resolved through performance before some form of experts with the authority to make judgements (judges, juries, panels, committees). A judgement is made by the experts about who 'ought' to win (which of course is also a decision about who 'ought' to lose). At the other end, outcomes are largely resolved through the performance of the competitors themselves. Apart from contextual judgements about whether all have acted within the rules, the rules themselves provide the criteria by which winning and losing is decided – the highest score, first over the finish line, the greatest annual return to shareholders, and so on. Between these two types, resolved either by authorised experts or sheer performance, there is an intermediate type, in which competitors perform, but the judgement is made not by a narrow group of experts, but by wide populations aggregating their judgement through voting. In a move particularly characteristic of democracies, the populace as a whole become, briefly, the experts. Together these three types define a spectrum of competition rituals: (1) resolved by experts, particularly characteristic of ideational competition, as in the arts and sciences; (2) resolved by wider interested and qualified populations, characterised by elections, and integral to democratic politics; and (3) resolved in the performance of the competition itself, particularly characteristic of many sports, and economic competition in the marketplace (see Figure 8.1).

This is, of course, a heuristic abstraction. There are intermediate or hybrid forms of competition ritual: entertainment show contestants are judged by panels of experts mixed with audience votes; courts can combine the decisions of juries and judges; many sporting events (boxing, gymnastics) are judged by expert panels. And more recognisably ritualised competitions shade into the more mundane competitions of daily life and work. This is precisely the point, competition is part of a ritual complex that permeates daily life in liberal society, the 'high rituals' devolving into almost unnoticeable forms. There is a fractal-like repetition of form throughout society. Moreover, the more formal competition rituals are surrounded by the general ethos of competition they help generate, which is not neatly contained in the ritual form. Across the board, where designated authorities make outcome decisions, this is normally presented not as personal preference or favouritism, but as the capacity to recognise the best

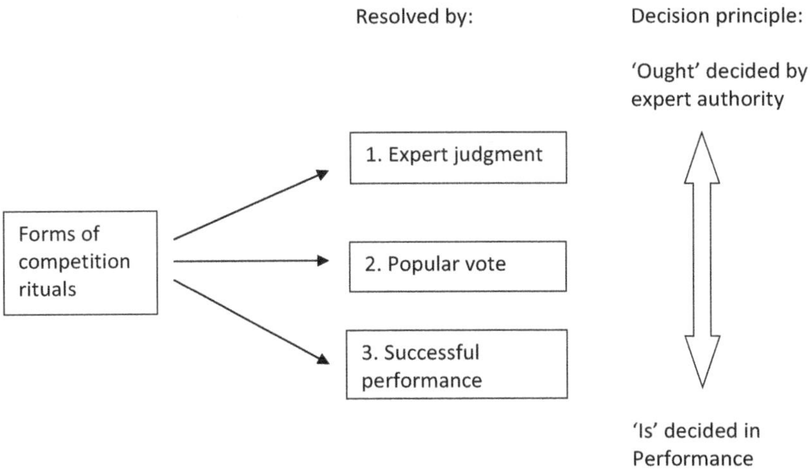

Figure 8.1 A typology of competition rituals (adapted from Hearn 2014b: 73)

performances – as a judgement still grounded in the actual performance. When competitions normally resolved through the competition ritual itself are ambiguous and have to go to adjudication, this is normally viewed as compensation for a failure of the process. Thus, artificial authority is naturalised, and natural competition is domesticated. The irrevocable modern gap between what is, and what ought to be, is bridged by ritual.

Let me conclude this discussion of competition as ritual with two broad contrasts, first between this as a specifically modern ritual complex contrasted with more traditional or premodern ones, and then between this complex as it manifests in liberal forms society in contrast with more authoritarian forms.

We can see a certain trace of the slow epochal shift from agrarian to industrial-capitalist society in the rise of competition and what it is slowly displacing – commensality. Historically, cross culturally, food has been central to at least some of the rituals in almost all societies. Ritual commensality, the sharing of food in ceremonies of feasting, is widespread, occurring in relatively small, acephalous tribal societies, on up to very large agrarian civilisations. And the obverse, fasting, is also frequently an element in an annual ritual cycle. In premodern societies, food is the most critical resource, its abundance or scarcity directly relevant to social and political stability. Thus, its distribution, through channels of kinship, patronage, and alliance, is commonly buttressed by ritual form, and its symbolism, in the sharing of common substance and nurturance, powerfully evokes social solidarity. But what power does this symbol have in modern society, where food is widely abundant rather than scarce, to the point that it is often cheap and wasted? Food scarcity persists in parts of the affluent world, but not to the point of its risk structuring the wider society. Ritual meals, such as those associated with Thanksgiving in the US, and Christmas, persist, but with a greatly reduced symbolic load. In modern affluent society, what is scarce is opportunity itself, for income, for advancement, for position, for markers of status. The scarcity of these goods is not natural, but an artifact of the institutions that produce them, various bureaucratised hierarchies, with fewer positions as one moves towards the top. This scarcity is understood not as an expression of the anger of the gods, but as a feature of a naturalised (though artificial) social order, variously attributed personal limitations, or structural flaws in that social order (see Chapter 9). In such a society competition itself becomes the freighted symbol, ensconced in ritual, and food recedes into the background.[7]

Finally, I would posit that some, but significantly not all, of this ritual complex applies to more authoritarian regimes. Sports and academic contests, as cultivators of excellence, and competitions as minor entertainments, are found in all kinds of modern societies, liberal and illiberal, democratic and authoritarian. But to the degree that social goods are distributed through governmental and elite patronage, and less as a response to democratic pressures, we should expect the middle range of the diagram above to be somewhat evacuated, leaving either sheer authority or sheer performance as the decider, and perhaps a more lax attitude towards maintaining the 'rules of the game'. Where central authority limits opportunities to compete over market domination, over political power, and over true beliefs, we can expect the ritualisation of competition to be more circumscribed and underdeveloped, perhaps yielding to more communal rituals of social solidarity, on both mass and interpersonal scales.

[7] In terms of this analysis, we might regard gambling, from lotteries to Las Vegas, as a kind of ritual of inversion of the social order, in which instead of competing, people surrender themselves to chance, although the compulsive gambler often thinks they can bring competitive techniques to the game.

Conclusion

As I suggested at the outset, this chapter is an attempt to sketch the major outlines of a culture of competition. The number and variation of what I have called 'competition rituals', and their spread from the grandiose to the trivial, makes it impossible to be comprehensive. But that is the point, that endless repetition of form helps naturalise that form. For much of this book I have been arguing the centrality of competition to the basic logic of major institutions, of economics, politics, and truth claims. Here I have looked at how competition also permeates daily practices. Competition informs basic liberal philosophical norms about how truth claims are legitimately made, and beliefs upheld, but as a performative practice, it also provides a core dramatic form through which the dynamics of human relationships are represented, and outcomes of competitive relations determined. It is a relatively peaceful means of allocating the social goods we fight over, while also sanctioning those allocations as grounded in first principles, and validated by proper ritual observance. None of this is to offer a judgement about whether such allocations are just, this is merely an analytic description of how the system works. In the next and final chapter I turn to the question of when and why we might be critical of the workings of competition.

9 *The Critique of Competition*

As I said in the Introduction of this book, it is my expectation that some who read it will want a more glowing endorsement of the virtues of competition, and others will miss a more full-throated indictment of its evils. I aim to disappoint equally. This book takes a middle path. For me, to critique something is to assess its virtues and vices, its pros and cons, not to simply praise or condemn. A critic sees intrinsic value in the thing they critique (music, art … society), but makes distinctions, according to clear criteria, between better and worse instances of the thing in question. Doing this requires maintaining a distinction between what is, and what ought or ought not to be. This is why I have bracketed off the criticism of competition until now in this final chapter, in order to first have a clearer picture of what I am being critical of. When we start from the impulse to praise or blame, it clouds our perception, leading us to see only those aspects that support the case we want to make. I want to know, as realistically as possible, what I am dealing with. Moreover, in this chapter I am not simply interested in competition as an object of criticism, but also in how domesticated competition supplies the very terms of reference for social criticism.

In his book *Power: A Philosophical Analysis* (2002: 36–46) Peter Morriss makes a very useful distinction between three contexts in which we have a need for a concept of power. In practical contexts, we want to know what our powers are, and their disposition in regard to the powers of others, so we can make judgements about what we can and cannot achieve. We want to know what's possible. In moral contexts, we need to know about power in order to assign responsibility to agents for their actions, good or bad. Those with power over their actions can be held responsible for them, and those without, cannot. In evaluative contexts, we judge not persons, but social systems. It may well be that a given system distributes power and other goods in ways we regard as bad or harmful, and that we can envision a better way of doing it. This does not in itself indicate that anyone is responsible for these flaws, that we need to assign moral responsibility. The system's flaws may be unattributable to any specific actors, or to so many in such small degrees that such attribution would be meaningless. Morriss's point is that we easily confuse the moral and evaluative contexts, assuming that because we evaluate some social arrangements negatively, there must be someone to blame. My aim in this final discussion of competition is to evaluate it, in Morriss's sense of that term, and also its implications for social power.

I have argued that the domestication of competition involves harnessing a given aspect of social existence, rivalry over limited goods, and bringing it into the orbit of human intention and culture. It takes something natural, and renders it artificial. The Italian philosopher Giambattista Vico (1668–1744) is remembered for his *verum ipsum factum* principle, that the creator knows and thus understands their own work (Lollini 2012, Vico 1988: 45–47). He saw limits to our ability to understand nature, because it is God's work, not our own, but as the authors of civil society and social institutions, humans can understand their society and history. This may be ambitious, given how society evolves out of a complex maelstrom of intention and accident among myriad actors. But there is surely some truth to the idea that to the extent that human institutions are deliberately constructed, we can have some insights into how and why they work. Competition becomes domesticated through a mixture of unplanned adaptations and intentional design. It is part of a social system that we can evaluate, and to some degree modify, according to our understanding. We needn't put blind faith in the 'spontaneous order' (Hayek 2013: 34–52) we find ourselves in, as long as we avoid a hubristic confidence in our powers of craft. To the degree that we have made competition, we can change it.

In what follows I take the view that domesticated competition, whatever its faults, has a positive role to play in society. I recognise the considerable distance between what I claim are the normative implications of domesticated competition, and what is the case regarding actual competition in the real world. The discrepancy is the point. I am examining the underlying moral implications of competition, when taken seriously and neither worshipped nor demonised, and how those implications correspond to actual practice.

Level Playing Fields and the Image of the Game

In the previous chapter we saw that the ritualisation of competition often takes on its most heightened and symbolic role in the forms of games, sports, and formal contests that seek to entertain. The image of the 'game' encodes all sorts of normative standards, of fairness, good conduct, and proper order, that are internal to the practice of games, and if society as a whole is 'like a game' then those standards tend to follow. The idea of a game here is very serious. It implies not something light and diverting, but the conditions for limiting incivility, cheating, exploitation, violence, and abuse. This is why the ritualisation of competition is so important. It is doing normative and ideological work, telling us a story about how we ought to interact.

We also noted the logical fit of game theory to a society in which competition is highly formalised. However, game theory also directs our attention to the limitations of competition as a legitimating ideology, because in actual social life there is always a question of the boundary, of what falls inside and outside of the 'game' in question. With the formulaic games and contests that permeate society, the boundaries of the competition are relatively clear. But for whole societies, bounded by states, the 'rules of the game' are much less clear and strict, let alone in the more anarchic international sphere. It is this wider, real-world context, outside theoretically defined 'games' that classic game theory often disregards, or assumes is constant, not containing information relevant to the outcome of the game. Game theory tends to assume a 'level' starting point, locating differences in the strategic decisions of players (social actors) inside the game.[1]

As ever with ideology, there is a traffic in half-truths. The pervasive image of the rule-bound game promotes the idea that society itself is a rule-bound game, its outcomes arising from within those rules, with people winning or losing according to how well they've played the game. But despite being heavily populated by actual ritualised games,

[1] It is true that sophisticated forms of game theory allow for the imperfection and unevenness of information available to players, continuous games with no clear end, games in which strategies evolve thereby changing the game, and stochastic outcomes where factors other than the player strategies randomly enter the decision field (Breen 2011, Maschler, Solan and Zamir 2020). All of these grapple with the ambiguous boundaries of 'real' games, but they do so by introducing new factors into the game context, not by theorising what is outside of it.

and further integrated through informal social conventions, the overall rule-boundedness, and fairness of society, depends on the state and its policies. It is truer to say that people opt into, or are drawn into, various practice-specific competitive games in their life pursuits, but that their lives as a whole only loosely conform to the image of a rule-bound game. Yes, they live largely under shared laws, however unevenly applied, but these are situationally applied to manage social conflict, they do not contain and delimit people's lives and livelihoods, the way a real game sets the parameters of action.

The key deception here is the claim that liberal society presents its members with a 'level playing field', a rule-bound game within which to pursue their values and interests. In fact, given the vastly uneven distributions of power among social actors, both individual persons and corporate organisations, and the loose definition of the rules of engagement, the playing field is far from level. The competitions people engage in at the larger level of lives lived in a society, under a state, are relatively 'red in tooth and claw', conducted in something closer to a 'state of nature', in which competition has not been fully 'domesticated'. This is about holding competitive liberal society to account. If I am right and competition is central to how such societies are legitimated, then competition, and whether it is sufficiently domesticated across society, become criteria by which to evaluate society.

The point here is that if domestication lifts competition up to a more civilised level, and harnesses the process for a more general social benefit, then there is a problem with institutionalising it within certain domains of society (regulated markets, democratic politics, etc.), but not in society as a whole, for the citizen as a member of the state. What are the implications? Most fundamentally, that for society as a whole to be a 'fair' game, and the state a legitimate referee, there needs to be two things. First, sufficient equality of access and opportunity to enter the game on a level footing with other contenders – 'a level playing field': there must be a reasonable hope of success. And second, sufficient limitations of risk posed by outcomes, such that people have reasonable incentive to play the game. Few would choose to play a game if the cost of losing was death – as in gladiatorial combat, which was compelled. The conditions for a society pervasively legitimated by domesticated competition include a foundational level of support and opportunity for all, and limitations on concentrating the benefits of competitive success into permanent advantage such as monopoly for a few. The implications are broadly social democratic.

Now of course in real-world games such as sports the participants are never exactly equal, and this can be a determinant of outcomes. But there are efforts to keep contestants reasonably well matched, for instance, through league rankings, and to keep the costs of losing and rewards of winning within limits. Nonetheless, success attracts investment, and can tend to 'lock in' the superior position of some actors, such as top ranked sports teams. This suggests the need for either the regular redistribution of the rewards of winning, to prevent the undermining of genuine competition by the lock-in of advantage, or the strict separation of distributions of relevant resources from the matter of competition outcomes. In other words, competing just for the 'honour of winning' but with no monetary reward. The honour of winning is intrinsic to the outcome, and cannot be alternatively distributed in the same way as monetary rewards. However, there is honour in participating in the game, 'fair and square', in making one's best effort, in supporting the good of the practice itself, regardless of who wins. While a world with no material incentives is implausible, one in which the uneven distribution of the material rewards of competition is reduced, and greater emphasis placed on the symbolic rewards, is possible, especially in more affluent forms of society.

Returning from sports analogies, the upshot is that a society that has become heavily dependent on competition for the legitimation of power distributions risks delegitimation if the very conditions of competition seem to undermine its purposes, if the 'ritual' is invalid because necessary conditions have not been met. It is not enough for there to be many competitions to engage in according to one's inclinations and resources, the overarching game of competitive society in general needs to have a reasonably level playing field for competition to do its legitimating work. Increasingly, that is not the kind of society we live in. A society with large and growing distances between the very rich and the very poor, in which those in the middle are struggling to keep their foothold there (Alverado et al 2013, Mayor and Machin 2018, Sayer 2016, Stiglitz 2013), is becoming one in which people are simply not all in the game, or at least not all in the same game.

In the *Wealth of Nations* Adam Smith observed that high rates of profit among a few capitals was a sign of a poorly functioning, 'underdeveloped' economy. When the competitive market economy is functioning well, he believed, profitability is reduced to a minimum and more widely distributed among economic actors (1981: 87, 105–115). The conditions of competition matter fundamentally. The best condition for productive competition is a 'flat-as-possible' distribution of resources and wide opportunity for entry. This is not only a matter of 'levelling up' but also of 'levelling down'.[2] To prevent competition from becoming ceremonial, mere form, everyone must have real 'skin in the game'. If the super-wealthy ultimately risk very little, distributing their risk strategically over numerous games, the actual practices of which they have very little invested in, then they are not really 'in the games' but just using them as opportunities. A seriously competitive society will have to countenance putting limits on the accumulation and concentration of wealth. If the very poor have limited access to well-governed, domesticated competition, they too, for opposite reasons, have less invested in the overall societal 'game'. The distension of society into a three-part structure, three sub-societies, which are not involved in the same shared sphere of competition, ultimately undermines the moral order. When competition becomes central to the legitimation of that order, some levelling of the playing field, in the sense of relatively equal distributions of opportunities to participate, become essential to the social order.

A perhaps unexpected implication here is that a truly competitive society, in the sense of domesticated competition, far from being based on 'natural' free markets, would need to use the means of the state to institutionalise competition, and level the playing field, as much as possible.[3] Such strident pursuit of systematic competition has the potential to justify an oppressively controlling and ultimately authoritarian state. Conversely however, a more market-based and 'open'

[2] 'Levelling up' is a favoured phrase among UK politicians, as it suggests making society more equal without actively threatening extreme concentrations of wealth. If I am right this is an unsustainable avoidance of the real problem, if the goal is to level the playing field of society. Levelling cannot be achieved only from one end.

[3] Again, a more legally constituted arena of competition was the key idea of the ordoliberals (Gerber 2001), but their concerns were more narrowly with the capitalist economy. And the contrary dystopian view of a state driving competition more deeply into all kinds of practices where it does not belong has been central to many critiques of neoliberalism (Brown 2015, Davies 2017). But the idea that real competition requires general social levelling, as a basis for a critique of inequality, is less often entertained.

society (in Popper's terms) will have to set limits on competitive outcomes in order to preserve competition. The argument put forth here recommends the permanent search for the *via media*, in which there is wide access to opportunities to compete, and limits to how much success enables social actors to distort the process, but at the same time, a society where individuals do not become cogs in a competitive machine orchestrated by the state. This is not something that can be institutionally designed once and for all, but rather requires a balance of forces between cultural understandings, societal norms, legal frameworks, and state structures, which can be delicate and difficult to achieve.

Ultimately the idea of a 'level playing field' has to be complex. In all kinds of practices there are gradations of skill and expertise that mean that some will be more suited to compete against each other than others. Tiers of competitive arenas can make good sense, and can be part of keeping competition as level as possible. But to the extent that distributions in society as a whole are legitimated by competition, everyone must have a reasonable place in the encompassing 'game' of society and the economy, including stable work and decent living standards. And no one should be able, through disproportionate wealth and power, to stand outside and above the basic game that everyone else is obliged to play. Coming back to Vico's *verum ipsum factum*, it is not legitimate to retreat into the 'naturalisation' of competition, the idea that competition is merely natural and 'nature knows best', because the forms of competition in question are human creations, which we must take responsibility for, and which we can recreate.

Spheres of Competition

If the previous section is about a certain requirement of the game, relative levelness, then this section is about the boundaries between games. To make my argument I draw on Michael Walzer's ideas of 'spheres of justice' (1983) and 'the art of separation' (1984). Walzer was addressing debates about the nature of justice, how best to distribute social goods, that had been stimulated by John Rawls's *A Theory of Justice* (1971) and Robert Nozick's *Anarchy, State, and Utopia* (1974). Rawls argued that a redistributive welfare state could be justified on the basis of what social arrangements people would be likely to choose, from behind a 'veil of ignorance', not knowing what their personal fate might be. He thought this would lead people to rationally support a social order in which the only inequality tolerable was that which would contribute to the prosperity and wellbeing of all. Nozick, with whom Walzer co-taught a course leading to their respective books, took a more libertarian approach, treating individual liberty as the guiding principle, and one more central to justice than equality. Walzer resisted trying to deduce a just social order from a single overarching principle. Instead, he argued that to understand by what principle social goods should be distributed we need to recognise that there are different kinds of goods, suited to different kinds of distributive principles. Some goods, such as commodities whose consumption largely concerns private individuals and groups, can be distributed through free exchange in the market, with reasonable fairness. Other goods should be distributed on the principle of desert. Promotions, accolades, and public offices should be distributed according to some means of reaching a reasoned judgement about qualification, whether by committee review, popular vote, or some other way of aggregating judgements. And still other social goods are so fundamental that a principle of basic human need is the appropriate criterion, and it makes sense for a centralised redistributive agency such as the state to take action in provision. This is a very general sketch of the argument, which explores many variations and nuances of how social goods get distributed, and those distributions justified. Walzer's notion is one of a 'complex equality', of a theory that provided a guide to how we might assess fair distributions of social goods, but one that would always be imperfect, working with the uneven grain of actual evolving society. A key idea however, was that serious problems arise when the distributive principles of one sphere interfere with those of another. Some things cannot or should not be bought and sold for the going price – love, public offices, people. Many consumer goods have to be distributed according to personal preference – assessing deservingness would be irrelevant. Relying only on markets, or the authoritative assessment of desert, to adequately distribute essential goods to all those in need – basic food, housing, healthcare, education, simply does not work (cf. Keat 1993).

Along similar lines, I would argue that we need to think in terms of appropriate 'spheres of competition', and that many problems arise when arenas of competition trespass on each other's boundaries, distorting each other's practices. We need to think of competition not as a general and somewhat amorphous principle of action, but rather as something that takes shape in regard to specific practices, defined by specific goods. The good of market competition should be the general provision to meet wants and needs. The good of democratic competition should be wise and skillful governmental leadership. The good of intellectual and scientific competition should be refined and improved understandings and explanations.

Every practice is defined by its own telos, the ends and goods towards which action is oriented. The immediate telos of the hundred metre sprint for each runner, is to cross the finish line first, or as close to that as possible. But also, to do so unaided by performance enhancing drugs. The latter intervention may enable a contestant to win, but it undermines the wider telos of the practice. Because the telos, the 'good' to which the practice is oriented, is not simply winning, but pushing the boundaries of unaided human bodily performance. There may be a proper place for performance enhancing drugs in some practices, and a proper competition amongst experts to find their best design, but this competition should not be allowed to trespass on the competition among the runners. The reason for raising this is that boundaries between various competitive practices are routinely transgressed, perverting the practices in question. The prosaic example of the sprinters just given involves surreptitious cheating to achieve the end, in a way that once exposed is widely recognised as wrong. But the problem is more complex than this for two reasons. First, because it is not just a matter of using unfair means to achieve agreed ends, but of the competitive practice being diverted to ends other than those it ought to be oriented to. Second, because the 'ought' I have just invoked is always contentious, and those who believe that 'the ends justify the means' are less likely to be troubled by the confusion of practices I claim is problematic.

Nonetheless, let me start by elaborating my claims above, that markets, democracy, and science each have a telos, an orientation to a defining good. If we agree that the good that markets aim for is the general provisioning of people's wants and needs, then we assess them by how well they achieve this end. The justifying end is to supply consumers, as citizens, with goods and services. But we know that markets also provide an arena for the accumulation of wealth, often on a vast scale. And market actors, individuals and corporations, the providers, not the provisioned, enter into competition with each other to dominate markets and secure incomes, in struggles to consolidate their own strength as actors, rather than to provision consumers. This kind of competition, even when it does not result in clear cases of monopoly or oligopoly, distorts the basic practice and orients it away from its telos. The practice of democracy supposedly brings political visions and talents to the fore, forcing competitors to place themselves before the jury of the electorate. Here the outcomes are always more fraught, because unlike private purchases, the people choose collectively, and many will be disappointed with the outcome. Nonetheless, in a stable democracy people accept these disappointments the same way they accept their team losing a game. But again, we also know that political campaigning involves the mobilisation of ever larger resources, and that to even enter and stay in the game, candidates must compete for these resources. Indeed, this competition often precedes and determines actual electoral choice, and it distorts the pattern of obligations away from their proper end, from serving the electorate as promised, to serving funders as owed. In science the good is not the attainment of final truths, but the steady winnowing and improvement of truth claims through competition among ideas, so that they have better purchase on reality. Scientific truth is always provisional. But successful truth claims that become widely accepted also bring status, prestige, and other material opportunities, and these can easily become ends in themselves. The competition for status can lead to basic sins – the falsification of data, plagiarism – but it also has the potential to distort research purposes in the first instance, to the search for findings people want to hear, to the avoidance of research that might yield unwelcome findings. These are just some of the most obvious examples of how competition in these three practices can get diverted from its proper end.

This line of criticism will mean little to anyone committed to a sheer egoistic pursuit of power. If the aim is simply to win by whatever means, such transgressions are of no significance, apart from the material risks of social disapproval and sanction. It is also possible to disregard these boundaries out of a notion of pursuing a 'greater good'. Not egoism, but value commitment overrides one's sense of proper conduct. If the highest ideal is the supremacy of your social group, or service to and glorification of some transcendental ultimate good, then these spheres of competition may only be means to an end, with no morally binding internal logic. This returns us to the image of the game, a form that is in its very nature rule-bound, and requires disciplined commitment to those rules, and the game's purposes, to work. A world of heavily institutionalised competition, if people are genuinely committed to those competitions, is a morally strenuous world. It is a world that brings together the two great traditions of moral thought, revolving around 'right' and 'virtue' respectively (Nussbaum 1999). Valuing domesticated forms of competition implies, in the mode of Kantian deontology (Korsgaard 2012), a duty to obey and live by the rules. Domesticated competition, unlike natural occurring competition, is rule-constituted. Those committed to the forms of competition that permeate liberal society need to constantly ask themselves, what are the rules of this game, and am I following them? On the other hand, as we have seen in reviewing the multiple temptations that distract us from the telos and goods specific to practices, the social role of the competitor is one that requires certain virtues, such as fortitude, honesty, fidelity, propriety, and magnanimity. The game cannot rely simply on the moral force of rules, or their material enforcement. The good competitor desires to play the game fairly, according to its internal goods. The inclination and commitment of the social actors involved is what animates the competitive practice in the first instance, what puts the rules in motion. Far from the state of nature, domesticated competition relies on virtuous agents submitting themselves to rule-governed practices, and observing the boundaries of those practices.

In Chapter 2 I argued that all social actors are oriented the acquisition of power, at least in the modest sense of enough power to meet their needs. The assumption that we are power-seeking creatures, although not insatiably power-hungry creatures seeking domination over others, underlies this book. The good of having the requisite power to pursue one's aims is the precondition for the pursuit of other, more practice-specific goods. Power is the underlying universal currency. This may pose an 'Achilles' Heel' for the argument just laid out, or at least point to why the boundaries are so often transgressed. For that transgression involves the parlaying of some kinds of power (wealth, status, influence) into other kinds. The attraction of power-in-general probably underwrites a permanent temptation to translate any given arena of competitive practice into a means to acquire more fungible forms of power. All we can do to counteract this is to agree to police each other, and do our best to learn to be good.

The Evolving Balance of Power

It is not just that the good of the practice suffers if confused with ends external to it. A corollary of this idea of separate spheres of competition is that a degree of institutional autonomy is necessary to help protect those distinctive ends. Liberal society relies on a distribution of power among the persons, groups, organisations and institutions out of which it is composed. A standing tension between various forces and interests gives it its dynamism and helps offset concentrations of power. The idea of the 'balance of power' is associated with the discipline of international relations and the study of interstate relations, but properly understood, it is one of the most basic and general ideas in social science (Beloff 1968: 4, Hearn 2016b). Wherever there are multiple actors, whether individual persons or organisations, on up to the state, there are balances of power. And the dynamics of all kinds of social settings involve the shifting and stabilising balances of power among social actors. I consider the idea of power balances in four contexts: citizens, civil society, government, and then in the four domains of power that have structured this book.

The decline of aristocracy corresponds to the rise of citizenship, the idea that all members of society are fundamentally equal, at least before the law, if not in their personal endowments (Dunn 2006: 114–117). Tocqueville's claim that democracy was irreversible was based on his observation of the expanding 'equality of condition', by which he meant the opportunities afforded to non-elites by expanding church and legal bureaucracies, the growth of trade, increasing literacy, and so on (Tocqueville 2000: 3–15). This made the aristocratic monopoly of power impossible, even in old Europe, let alone post-revolution America. Class and other forms of social stratification may distribute power unevenly among citizens, but the idea of citizenship does not legitimate these inequalities. Some institutions such as slavery and caste, will exclude some people from claiming the rights of citizenship. But with the aid of law, citizens hold some power over each other, and collectively over their state.

The pluralism of civil society, composed of voluntary associations serving diverse and competing interests and projects, also distributes power. From businesses serving private consumer preferences, to charities serving their understandings of the public good, civil society organisations are corporate actors, citizens writ somewhat larger, the better to pursue their ends. While the landscape of civil society is lumpy, with some very big players, and many smaller players, it is also open and evolving, with new formations entering, and older ones expiring. Together the organisational actors form an ecology of balancing forces, holding each other in check (Bobbio 1989).

The same era that saw the rise of the citizen and civil society saw the development of new ideas about how best to construct government to prevent the undue concentration of power. Montesquieu argued in the *Spirit of the Laws* (1989[1748]) not just that executive, legislative, and judicial functions of the state need to be differentiated and counterbalancing, but that a more organic balance between various institutional interest groups (commoners, nobility, clergy, magistrates) needed to be maintained: 'power must check power by the arrangement of things' (1989: 155). David Hume similarly extolled 'mixed government' in which monarchical and republican principles (king and parliament) created a 'mutual watchfulness and jealousy' (1985: 12). And these ideas fed into the US constitution as shaped by the *Federalist Papers*. James Madison's *Federalist No. 10*, argued not only for the counterbalancing of the branches of government, but also that a large federal system of states would itself provide counterbalancing forces, making it difficult for any single faction to commandeer the whole (2001[1788]).

The idea of power balancing suffuses liberal society, from citizens, to civil society, to the constitution of government. It also helps us understand the relationships between the four major spheres of institutional power dealt with in this book. Military, economic, political, and ideological power institutions need to maintain a certain uneasy distance, in order to do their respective jobs. Each one has a distinctive kind of relationship to the others.

This is clearest in the case of the military, where this particularly volatile form of power has engendered the discourse around 'civil-military relations' (Brooks 2019), discussed in Chapter 4. Here it is not so much a matter of counterbalancing and autonomy, as ensuring that the military remains subordinate to civilian government. As I've argued throughout, this subordination is a precondition for the institutionalisation of competition in the other spheres. The military is there to guarantee national security, fight wars when needed, and provide some supplementary emergency services. But there are constant risks that its unique subordination to the state, and autonomy from the rest of society, will be transgressed. For instance, it provides a unique and necessary market for state-of-the-art weaponry and supporting technologies, and can easily become a captive and manipulated market for certain industries. As a kind of subsociety with its own ethos and culture, it tends to have an elective affinity with traditionalist and rightward political parties (Brooks 2019: 388). This is in the nature of democratic representation, but too close a relationship risks blurring the line between politics and the military.

The modern liberal state is deeply dependent on the capitalist economy and its key actors to generate legitimating prosperity and sustain tax bases big enough to support the government. Correspondingly, the state provides the macroeconomic, legal and peaceful conditions necessary for the market economy to operate. This interdependence conduces familiar problems of revolving doors between big business and government careers, and of the business community pressuring politicians and government through professional lobbying (Domhoff 2014). The reliance of politicians on private funding to run campaigns, and further remunerative temptations while in office, can distort their roles as representatives of citizens.

Universities are hindered in their function as arenas for the free cultivation of knowledge and contestation over truth if their efforts are subordinated to the interests of business and government. To the degree that they are seen as a social cost that must be legitimated either by what they contribute to economic innovation and growth, or by how research serves the solution of governmentally defined problems, this erodes their autonomy. If the university is defined entirely in terms of external instrumental purposes, its capacity to serve as a locus of relatively detached reflection on society itself, and as a community committed first and foremost to a method of inquiry, is compromised. Somewhat like the military, universities are not just susceptible to capture by business and governmental interests, but also to ideological capture by political party aligned worldviews (Adekoya, Kaufman and Simpson 2020: 44–70). This is especially true in the humanities and social sciences, which have inherited a moral voice and authority once monopolised by the clergy and churches.

The more these separate institutional spheres become fused, the more they form a single entity that hoards power, reserving it to the social stratum that commands positions across these institutions. This runs contrary to the historical trends that generated these distinctive institutional spheres in the first place. The emergence of liberal society, with its peculiar propensity for creating a distributed balance of power among relatively separate institutional spheres, and a proliferation of competing corporate actors within those fields, is an historically contingent social evolutionary process. It did not come about by any grand design or inevitable causal trajectory in history. Although there were periods of innovative constitutional thought that shaped its emergence, no great legislator brought it into being. Rather, it took shape precisely because there was a power vacuum, a crisis of traditional modes of power and authority, that made space for various institutional and organisational adaptations. Liberalism and democracy tend to become established where there are multiple centres of power that need to cooperate, but none of which can effectively dominate the rest (Zinnes 1967: 272). But there are no guarantees that such relative pluralism will endure. Social evolution can just as easily lead towards monopolies, and the fusion of separate spheres under the dominant power of a state, with not just military, but also economic and ideological practices and agents effectively subordinated to central power.

The final point here, once again, is that if a relative balance of powers in society helps legitimate that society, then it may be necessary to use law and policy to help insure its preservation. Once those balances become basic rules of the game, then the principles of levelling and autonomy explored above apply. Liberal society may emerge from historically contingent balances of power, but require more concerted action as it matures to maintain its openness, and to prevent it from congealing into a new form of tight hierarchy.

Criticism from Within

The aim of this chapter is to articulate a position of critical reflection on liberal society that begins from where we are (Walzer 1993). This is sometimes called 'immanent critique', an approach that traces back to Hegel and Marx, and carries on through various modern branches of 'critical theory' (Antonio 1981, Browne 2008, Stahl 2013). With many variations, the basic idea is that social criticism cannot begin from some outside, 'transcendental' position, that judges society according to higher principles. This is the position often attributed to Kant, who sought to ground all human morality in the analysis of 'pure reason' (Kant 2012: 56–72). Instead, it must begin with society as it is, exploring its ideological premises, its internal contradictions and inconsistencies, as clues to how to improve society. Of course, any position which presumes to evaluate society, whether from without or within, assumes some kind of distance from the taken for granted common sense of that society. But an internalist approach assumes that social change for the better must be evolved out of that same common sense. Basic to this perspective is that society is complex and plural, containing tendencies that are in tension with each other, and that strategies for change and reform involve developing some of these tendencies over others, from within.

The term 'reform' here raises another issue. Much of the tradition of thought premised on 'immanent critique', eschewing reform, has ultimately set its sights on revolutionary change, specifically the total transformation of capitalist society into something new to follow, often some form of communism. There is a difficult disjuncture between critique from within, based on existing resources, and an end that is so utterly different from that starting point that it can barely be defined in its terms. Even if, as Marx did, you locate the end of the given social order in its irresolvable contradictions, this still leaves few clues as to what a new order, without these contradictions, will look like. I travel on the other fork in this road, as a reformist who thinks that the accumulation of relatively minor changes from within, can eventually lead to profound changes in the structures of society. This is the most viable and surefooted way to proceed, with a view to change, not to topple. Social evolution is often presented as the 'gradualist' opposite of revolution. But in fact, it proceeds through both these routes, sometimes manifested as steady cumulative change, and at other times as the radical collapse and revision of society. Both reform and revolution imply a normative critical standpoint that guides efforts after social change. The reformist, however, only seeks to change certain parts of the world, finding other parts satisfactory. The revolutionary on the other hand, seeks a total transformation, root and branch, that changes almost everything. But the more our analysis of the actual world aims at an ultimate, normatively based overhaul of that world, the more difficult it becomes to maintain a conceptual boundary between is and ought, between descriptive and prescriptive practices, as all that is described becomes grist for the prescriptive mill. The reformist finds it easier to maintain the distinction.

I have argued throughout this book that competition is not external, but internal to society, in various ways. It is not something alien that comes in from outside. In a world where there are inevitable scarcities, there will be natural ('wild') competition between rivals for scarce objects – resources, status, power. No society entirely escapes this. The domestication of competition involves harnessing this social conflict, routinising, ritualising, and institutionalising it. An important part of this process is the creation of new corporate actors who can carry on competition at larger scales, for greater gains. And as we have seen, this takes place in multiple spheres of power contestation, ideological, political, economic; each internalising and institutionalising competition in its own distinctive way and forms. And within those larger spheres, multiple narrower social fields of competition take shape. Precisely because it is so pervasively embedded in modern liberal society, competition is a suitable object for internal social critique, whether reformist or revolutionary. But for the reformist, practising internal critique, it is not simply a disease to be excised from the social body, but a resource to be drawn on and developed in specific ways, and discouraged in others. Domesticated competition is already about how people organise their social relations, it is already norm-laden, and thus a propitious site for critical scrutiny.

If competition as such encodes certain criteria of judgement as I have suggested, of level playing fields, and unmolested orientation towards its proper telos, then the more we assess society as a whole according to these criteria, the more it is envisioned as a large competitive game. But far from being brutally eliminationist, this form of competition is highly civil, and can be further assessed according to how civil and productive its effects are. Competition, especially in its more ritualised forms, offers a dramaturgical resource for thinking about moral order. It provides a story about how society ought to be, against which wider actual society can be measured. It teaches us how to channel social conflict, show mutual respect for opponents, work in teams, to excel in a practice, accept defeat and triumph gracefully, respect and play by the rules, and so on. It models a productive balance between rule structured behaviour and spontaneity. The high drama of competitive entertainments – sports and games – are not just distractions, or sublimations of our darker impulses. They are more like contained experiments in social order.

It is from these rituals of competition that our natural language of moral critique derives. It is part of the common sense of liberal society, expressed in both 'high' and 'popular' cultural forms. At the high end, let me return to and elaborate the still influential formulation of John Rawls's idea of 'justice as fairness' (2001). Rawls based his concept of justice on 'the idea of society as a fair system of social co-operation over time from one generation to the next' (2001: 5). This in turn rested on assumptions of the freedom and equality of individuals, derived from the thought experiment of the 'original position' in which it is hypothesised that abstract individuals, with no knowledge of what their actual situation in the world would be, not even their own preferences and notions of 'the good', would choose to live in a world where goods and opportunities were as widely distributed as possible. Rawls advocated a form of 'political liberalism' (1996) in which the state acts as a referee, securing baseline conditions for divergent and competing visions of the good life. His theory was a highly abstract justification of actual liberal social democracy, and its idealised potential. Whether or not you find this theoretical route to justification satisfactory, my point is that the influential model that Rawls produced is also an image of the competitive game, supporting various conceptions of the good, and requiring a relatively level playing field. As I said in the Introduction, co-operation is not the antithesis of competition, but one of its most basic effects. Rawls tended to sidestep the question of competition, but was sensitive to the need to support a pluralistic society in which there can be multiple conceptions of the good and diverse orientations to them. In a formalised competition, rivals share the same image of the good, but it is a good which cannot be shared. But because the competition is a social form that can be repeated, begun anew, and because the stakes are limited to the game, the indivisible nature of the goal, of winning, is not final. The claim is not that the world is actually like this. People in liberal capitalist society, as presently constituted, experience baseline inequalities that are cumulative and undermine their re-entry into various competitive games, shunting people into disadvantaged lives. The claim is that our objections tend to invoke this falling short of the ideal model. We say 'that's not fair', people are not being 'given a fair chance', it's 'one rule for them, and another rule for us'. For all his rather dry abstraction, Rawls was attuned to the basic language of liberalism, the idea of fairness as the ultimate measure of legitimacy. I merely suggest that he under appreciated the degree to which the pursuit of fairness, in an open and evolving society, has to take the form of rule-governed competitive practices.

When we turn away from the high theory of liberalism, to everyday life, the basic image is again confirmed. While writing this book a government report on the state of football in the UK, called the *Fan Led Review of Football Governance* (Crouch 2021), led by MP Tracey Crouch, was published. Among several issues, the report addressed the concentration of wealth and power in a few successful football clubs, and how this tended to undermine the wider social practice of football in smaller clubs, as a community-based activity generating social goods beyond club revenues. So, one part of the report's criticisms is that the good of the practice of football was being distorted by other ends such as concentration of power and profit. One of its most basic proposals was to institute, in effect, a tariff on the more prosperous clubs, to redistribute resources down to the small clubs and help maintain their viability and social good. It was a proposal to 'level the playing field' at a higher level than the actual football pitch.

I harbour no illusion of being able to 'rectify' society according to the principles of 'level playing fields', and a 'separation of spheres'. Social reality is a complex accumulation of unintended consequences, and society is not neatly 'designed'. The social world is ultimately a universe of evolving power struggles going in and out of balance. However, it matters what ideals we measure society against. Even if they can never be realised in full, they can influence the course of events. If such ideas, taken as criteria of assessment that enable true critique, help us to think more sharply about our dissatisfactions, then that is something. The point is not to imagine we can overhaul society, dreaming Jacobin dreams (Chirot 2020, Yack 1992). It is to foreground the existing tools by which particular groups of people might choose to judge particular arenas of practice, from local elections, to disciplinary debates, to the licencing of economic activities. I for one would prefer a world where the distribution of wealth and power is much flatter (though not entirely flat), and various productive social practices, both material and intellectual, were less prone to distortion by ends external to them. Competition offers risks, but also benefits in regard to these problems.

Conclusion

I began this chapter with two premises. First, that social criticism needs to aim at evaluating the workings of society, in order to improve them, not at laying blame for its flaws. Second, echoing Vico, that to the degree that society is something humanly made, it is susceptible to our analysis and improvement. And in the previous section another related premise has surfaced, that social criticism needs to emerge from within a society's ideological, conceptual, and cultural resources. Positive social change must involve drawing out and developing resources that are already present, not simply visions of how things ought to be. Together these frame the understanding of what it means to do social criticism that guides this chapter. I have consciously concentrated the discussion of 'ought', of normative critical evaluation, in this chapter, rather than have it run through the book. Let me pick up on three themes from earlier chapters to help connect this discussion to the rest of the book. These are: the nature of modern authority and legitimacy, the liberal nation state, and competition as a central component in the culture of liberal societies.

In Chapter 3 I traced the crisis of authority and legitimacy, the decline of traditional notions of heritable rights to power and religious validation of the social order, that created space for the principle of institutionalised competition to emerge. Law came to the fore, displacing religion, creating the more rule governed context that also brought forth and consolidated new corporate actors, including the ultimate actor, the modern state. My emphasis above on organic social criticism taking the form of complaints about fairness, understood through the image of the game, is identifying an outcome of this long history. As decisions about how power and resources get distributed shift from a setting of the traditional and supernatural, to one of competitions within positive law, the mode of justification of those distributions shifts from claims about divine favour and longstanding precedent, to claims about fairness within the rules of the game. The abstract model of the game becomes a handy theoretical tool for analysing social behaviour, but this ultimately is of a piece with this grand historical shift in how societies achieve legitimacy.

Once again, this is a specific history, of the 'rise of the West', and the formation of modern liberal society, as housed in the political form of the nation state. Several lines of argument in this chapter lead up to and then stop at the level of the nation state. There is a good reason for this. Such states are the ultimate arbiters of modern law, framing most of the 'rules of the game' for those who live within them. There is a sphere of international law, but it is more tenuous and less surely enforceable. The European Union is an exceptional case where the law of the Union has been allowed to overwrite law at the national level, and that is why the question of whether it is unworkable and undemocratic, or must ultimately lead to a very large modern state in the full sense, is a live one. It is ambiguous as an object of social critique, because its presence as the ultimate containing social actor above the level of the nation states is ill-defined. The basic form of modern social life is that social actors, as real persons, are invested in fictive corporate actors in order to better pursue their various ends, and those in turn are governed by the ultimate fictive corporate actor, the state. If such state-societies are legitimated not by Gods or sheer might, but by the even-handed enforcement of the rules of the game amongst civil competitors, then the coherence and sovereignty of this ultimate actor really matters.

In Chapter 8 I argued that competition is a deeply embedded cultural form in liberal societies. Through its pervasiveness and varying degrees of ritualisation, it becomes a kind of ubiquitous, abstracted representation of the underlying social order. Thus, it becomes a part of the ideological resources available for developing an 'immanent' critique of society from within. It is already a cultural idiom through which society understands itself, and therefore is uniquely suited as a focus for evaluative discussion and debate about where and how society goes wrong. The idea of 'fairness' is rendered substantive through an idiom that allows us to talk about how level the playing field is, and whether the boundaries of competitive 'games' are properly observed. In this kind of systematically competitive society, we culturally evaluate that system according to how well it instantiates the rules of the game, and we morally judge social actors according to whether they exhibit virtues or vices as players of the game. The normative language of the game, however metaphorical, reflects the substantive structure of society as an arena of social actors, obliged to compete with one another, for both harmful and beneficial ends.

Finally, let me note that this has been an assessment of systematically competitive liberal society as a broad type, and its intrinsic moral and cultural resources for generating criticism about itself, and arguing about how things *ought to be*. It may appear more sanguine than

I intend about the actual state of competition-based liberal institutions in the world today. In fact, there are good reasons to be worried about the faltering capacities of universities and civil societies to negotiate truth-claims, of party-systems to negotiate access to governing power, of capitalist economies to widen rather than narrow access to opportunities, indeed, of liberal society to maintain its place in the course of history. I will turn to these worries about the state of the world *as it is* in the Conclusion.

Conclusion

I have tried to sum up my argument at various points along the way. Here I will do that one more time for the book as a whole, and then offer some final reflections on the somewhat besieged state of domesticated competition in the present, at the time of writing. I will not try to predict the future, but I will try to assess the state of health of liberal society, using competition as a diagnostic.

Citizens of liberal democracies live in a form of society saturated with competition. It is deeply built into our organisations, institutions, and culture. It is so integral to how we deal with social conflict, with divergent interests, that we must learn how to work with it, with critical awareness. It is not something we can abandon, or get around. Moreover, this domesticated kind of competition brings benefits, as a spur to achievement, and an alternative to more brutal forms of conflict. It can and does become dysfunctional and pathological, as many recent critics of neoliberalism and meritocracy have emphasised. But it is not a recent development, it is a perennial aspect of social relations, now highly elaborated in modern liberal society. That is why we need a realistic understanding of competition, so we can bring out its benefits, and limit its injuries.

A focus on competition provides a way of understanding what has often been called 'the rise of the West', linked to the historical emergence in that context of the modern nation state. I have tried to show that the institutionalisation of competition across military, economic, political, and ideological spheres is intimately tied to the development of major forms of large-scale organisations, and organisational ecologies. At the global level, states and their militaries, the ultimate political form, position themselves in the relatively ungoverned arena of geopolitics and international relations. However, this book has been primarily concerned with the institutionalisation of competition below this level, within states and their civil societies. There the emergence of the legal form of the corporation has been critical, providing the organisational infrastructure of the capitalist economy, democratic politics, and struggles over knowledge, ideology, and public opinion in the public sphere. I have targeted the modern firm, political parties, and universities as exemplars of this process, but have also shown that these develop in a wider field of organisations devoted to charitable, moral, and discursive purposes, all caught up in competition in one way or another. In all of this the underlying claim is that this complex of competition and competitive forms emerged for a reason. Domesticated competition provides a rule-governed means of allocating power and resources, while justifying those allocations at the same time. In the emerging form of liberal society, in which claims to authority based on inherited right and religious tradition were faltering and being demoted, the institutionalisation of competition provided a way to legitimate allocations of social goods. This could appear legitimate because competition seems to naturally reward native abilities, and yet also legitimate because it is a human made institution that we ourselves have created and chosen.

Because this kind of competition is basic to the structure of liberal society, to how it works, liberal culture reflects this, in effect endlessly cogitating on the competitive form through performance and ritual. We don't just pragmatically allocate goods through competition, we glorify the form itself in all kinds of games and entertainments, that become encapsulated dramatisations, and validations, of the social order. To be received as salient, any critique of such a society must at least begin by working within its own structural and cultural terms to evaluate it. It must examine the contradictions, tensions, and implications of a competitively based society, asking where, specifically, competition goes wrong. I have argued that there are practice-specific spheres of competition, each with their own telos, and that when the boundaries between spheres are transgressed, ends are distorted and problems ensue. Moreover, if competition legitimates the social order, then at the largest extent of the state-society there must be some general balance of power among society's members, and the array of organisational forms that give it structure, such that everyone can be 'in the game' on a relatively 'level playing field'. This is not a call for equality or justice in the abstract, but rather for a practical commitment to dispersing power and opportunities widely enough that competition can genuinely adjudicate emerging distributions, rather than simply validate established concentrations of power.

I think that the argument I have made is demonstrable from the historical record, viewed from my perspective on the institutionalisation of competition. However, I have been quietly guided by the theoretical premises laid out in Chapter 2. All social life involves the constant play of power, the development of human capacities to do things, and the growth of organisational forms that are able to do greater things, generally by forming internal organisational structures and chains of command. Power over increases power to. Power becomes manifest as agency – the agency of individuals, generally invested in the agency of corporate groups with the capacity to be social actors. Broad categories of social types – races, sexes, classes – lack the capacity to concentrate power and agency, to become real actors in history: this requires organisation. The story I have told is one of a new ecology of corporate actors taking shape, as the very terms of authority and legitimation that had supported previous forms of kin-based and religious corporate actors went into decline. Such broad parallel changes in social morphology, while clearly historical processes, I think warrant the term social evolution. This helps specify the broad pattern of changes, the domestication of competition, out of the welter of historical contingency that is always with us.

There are good reasons to worry that institutionalised competition is losing its capacity to negotiate and legitimate power and authority in liberal societies (cf. Fukuyama 2022). In the realm of beliefs and ideas in public discourse, an increasingly cavalier attitude towards truth prevails, signalled by terms such as 'alternative facts' and 'fake news'. To the degree that these are simply signals of contestation over the truth, there is little danger, but where they indicate a loss of confidence in the presumption of a shared underlying truth, they raise severe problems. Such a presumption provides the basic structure of a competitive 'game' of truth claiming, where dispute aims towards common understanding. While highly formalised methods and criteria of proof, as found in the physical and natural sciences, tend to have this basic structure 'hardwired' into the practice, the social sciences and humanities are less tightly bound by shared methods and rules of practice. Arguments more often rely on interpretation and subjective judgement, and at the extreme, on the 'lived experience' of the researcher. Some parts of the human sciences concern humans as meaning-using creatures, and so, some interpretivism is unavoidable when we want to understand motivation and social action. But this means that a commitment to a hypothesis of shared truth is even more crucial for binding this kind of science together as a practice. The more this shared ground is in doubt, the more the competition over ideas and interpretations dissolves, replaced by mere positional struggles within institutions over which discourses will dominate. In recent decades theoretical trends such as postmodernism and poststructuralism have tended towards a deep scepticism about underlying truth, which leads to a highly instrumental attitude towards truth, as being not what people make claims about, but simply the label for those truth claims that succeed in dominating beliefs. This can be a difficult distinction, but the former encodes a commitment to common understanding, to a shared 'game', while the latter presumes a kind of state of nature, a 'war of all against all'.

In universities, especially in the social sciences and humanities, this divergence has played out as the increasing polarisation between an older, more 'realist', 'objectivist', and 'naturalistic' pursuit of true interpretations, and a newer preference for 'social constructionism', 'subjectivism', and a primary commitment to the moral messages of arguments. In the latter case research can become not so much the pursuit of truth, as the pursuit of 'social justice' (Haidt 2016). Thus, fields of study influenced by identity politics often see the purpose of research and writing as the emancipation of, or at least struggle on behalf of, various identity groups. I am not criticising political struggle as such, which is inevitable and necessary. But to the degree that universities and their various sciences become zero-sum contests over ideological supremacy and institutional turf, rather than collective, ongoing, rule-governed competitions in search of truth, they cease to be either sciences, or universities.

This divergence has its corollary in wider public discourse sustained by various modern media. In an atmosphere of deep distrust towards public truth in some quarters, with people 'siloed' in networks of mutually reaffirming messages about reality, and deeply distrustful of messages from outside those silos, productive public debate about truths, both material and moral, breaks down. Domesticated competition in the realm of ideas and beliefs risks devolving into a more wild, anarchic contest.

This febrile atmosphere of public debate has become associated in liberal democracies with political movements of populist distrust towards 'elites' and government, and the intensifying polarisation of leftward and rightward political views. The prime example at the time of writing is the US, with a two-party system in which the extremes in each constituency have a preponderant influence on the positions and policies of the parties as a whole. The ability of the system to articulate a politics of the centre, in which the aim is to shape opinion in the centre-ground, has weakened (Lilla 2018). Such centrism needn't be a symptom of stifling conformism and compromise. In the sphere of democratic politics, the idea of the value of a central consensus, no matter how hard won, serves the same function as the presumption of truth in the sciences. It is the shared goal that unifies the 'game'. Opposing views must struggle to define the centre-ground, where it lies, and to orient the wider society to it. But once this ceases to be the goal, again, the domesticated competition of democracy gives way to an all-out struggle for domination, with no holds barred. Donald Trump's appropriation of the Republican Party, and his refusal, along with his followers, to accept the outcome of the 2020 US presidential election, threatens genuine democratic competition. It denies the legitimacy of the central game of politics. The system has not failed so far, but it is under severe strain.

Capitalism has always had anticompetitive tendencies towards monopoly and oligopoly working against the dispersion of power in expanding markets. As we have seen, the modern corporation is partly a product of this tendency, as firms seek larger scopes and scales of operation, and dominant positions within markets. Successful competition in the economy leads towards anticompetitive practices on the part of those who achieve market dominance, unless counteracted by government action, the unpredictability of the market, or strategic and innovative competitors. There is a genuine tension between these contrary forces, but a central dynamic of the economy is that some corporate actors manage to concentrate power in their own hands, accumulating both power to, and power over. Without a strong separation between the powers in the economy and those of the state, and without the capacity of the latter to police the former and break up concentrations of power, the capitalist economy will tend towards control by a few major actors, and thereby stagnate. The troublingly concentrated powers of 'Big Tech', 'Big Pharma', and 'High Finance' are continuing evidence of this perennial problem of capitalism.

In societies which are concatenations of complex organisations, there will be multiple systems of hierarchy according to skill, expertise, and seniority. Social complexity inevitably brings a degree of inequality. Sometimes hierarchy is also due to socially privileged access to entry and promotion within those organisations, but if this were eliminated, the other principles would still create a degree of stratification, even if there are opportunities of mobility within organisations. This kind of inequality can be regulated and justified by fair structures of competition. However, to the degree that inequality does not result from the inner logic of various organisations but rather, as in the age of aristocratic rule, from an inherited status with limited opportunities for escape, the wider system is delegitimated. The tendency in capitalist liberal democracies, especially in the anglosphere, towards the concentration of great wealth in an elite at the top, relative stasis in the middle class, and a persistent and growing class of the un-, under-, and precariously employed, undermines the idea that all are engaged in the same open field of competition. Those at the top may be inclined to rationalise their success and think that all are in the same game, but to those further down this is less plausible, and it will appear that they have been summarily relegated to the minor leagues and shut out from the larger game. Although individuals can sometimes make themselves exceptions, achieving great feats of social mobility, as a general rule opportunities for such mobility, as determined by such things as family wealth and class, are maldistributed. The result of this failure to ensure the conditions of fair competition is to sow alienation from, and distrust towards, the wider society among those who feel they have been excluded.

As I have emphasised throughout, the international arena of geopolitics by its nature is less domesticated, more wild. The collapse of the Soviet Union and the end of the Cold War allowed some to imagine a world in which globalised commerce would tie together a community of liberal democracies, and liberalism and democracy have been making steady advances. But the power of autocracy has also been consolidating, particularly in China and Russia, and some in the 'West' now proclaim the value of 'illiberal democracy', with reduced tolerance for a diversity of values and ideology, and a newfound faith in the tyranny of majorities. We may be heading towards a new 'cold war', with China taking the place of the USSR, and a new cast of states negotiating paths between east and west. And China's novel combination of global capitalism and single-party rule make it a very different geopolitical rival to the West than the USSR was. As in the previous

Cold War, all sides have an interest in limiting the extent of conflict, and even more this time in sustaining a global capitalist economy. Whether this geopolitical tension will reinvigorate domesticated competition within the liberal democratic sphere, or dampen it in search of internal social stability, is an open question. A deeper question is whether the marriage of internal autocratic rule with external capitalist competitiveness in the global arena, the Chinese model, is a new corporate form of the modern state that will outcompete the more haphazard model of internally competitive and dynamic liberal societies that produce enough statehood to hold things together, but often lack a strategically consistent presence in the international arena. If states are now the ultimate corporations acting in the global market, then corporate discipline may trump democracy as their organising principle.

As mentioned in a footnote in Chapter 2, general theories of social evolution, not just among humans, but among all species, grapple with the question of the boundary between a society of organisms, and an individual, internally complex organism (Birch 2017, Bourke 2011). Is a colony of ants, or a coral reef, a society or a single organism? At what point does an aggregate of mutually supporting single-cell organisms transform into a single multi-celled organism? At some point in this transition co-operation and subordination displaces competition, and cells get permanently differentiated into those that reproduce (germ cells) and those that simply serve specific functions within the whole, but cannot reproduce.

In the study of human social evolution there is a corresponding problem. I emphasised in Chapter 2 that our powers of communication and language, and corresponding recognition of 'other minds', makes us a highly individuated species. Using social coordination to achieve greater collective power is a challenge, and the solution, forms of social organisation with authority over and legitimacy among members, is difficult to construct. Like the transition from single-celled to multi-celled organisms, the long process of transition from societies assembled out of kin groups, to one assembled out of legally constituted corporate actors, is a major transition in human social evolution, and human sociality itself. The more these new 'bodies', including the state, become the ultimate competitors, the more actual individuals become significant, not as competitors, but as functional components within those larger competitive beings. But if this is the case, then competition is thereby weakened as a legitimator of the distributions of social power in the given social order. The logic of social organisation will need to assign people to their place in the system and minimise internal conflict and competition. It may be that the liberal competitive society I have been talking about, with its heightened individualism, and its ability to unleash social energies while keeping their more destructive tendencies in check, has just been a passing phase on the way to new, more tightly bound forms of social organisation. Forms we associate with terms like bureaucracy and autocracy. Forms that are ultimately 'selected' for their competitive capacities at the level of the global economy and geopolitics, while supressing or muting competition lower down the scale. This raises a disturbing image that has permeated folk mythology, especially in science fiction – Invasion of the Body Snatchers, the Cybermen, the Borg, the Matrix – in which the individual is fully subordinated and subsumed in the whole.

On the other hand, there are reasons to doubt that intractable human individuality, which I have located in the nature of our species, not simply the modern era, can ever be fully reprogrammed by new forms of social organisation. Most despotic forms of rule achieve their ends not by controlling every aspect of people's inner and outer lives, which would be too costly, but by using sanctions to define certain 'no go' areas, especially those that would challenge the given power structures. Individuality rumbles on, beneath the surface, in private. The idea of domesticated competition that I have explored in these pages, is about harnessing and limiting social conflict, channelling it along more productive paths, that beneficially serve a larger social order. It is about a balance, a midpoint between conflict as anarchic disorder, and a controlling order that allows no room or vent for conflict. It is about a form of society in which there is a balance of power among numerous separate spheres of competition, in which none fully dominates the others. It is about a liberal society which is not the ideal of certain philosophers, but the practical if substantially unintended achievement of average human beings. Despite the worries about our current state essayed above, I will hope that the domestication of competition can continue to serve human purposes, and maintain that delicate balance.

References

Abu-Lughod, Janet L. (1989). *Before European Hegemony: The World System A.D. 1250–1350*. New York: Oxford University Press.

Adams, Julia (1994a). The Familial State: Elite Family Practices and State-Making in the Early Modern Netherlands. *Theory and Society* 23(4): 505–539.

(1994b). Trading States, Trading Places: The Role of Patrimonialism in Early Modern Dutch Development. *Comparative Studies in Society and History* 36(2): 319–355.

(2010). The Unknown James Coleman: Culture and History in Foundations of Social Theory. *Contemporary Sociology* 39(3): 253–258.

Adekoya, Remi, Eric Kaufmann, and Thomas Simpson (2020). *Academic Freedom in the UK: Protecting Viewpoint Diversity*. Westminster: Policy Exchange.

Allen, Amy (1998). Rethinking Power. *Hypatia* 13(1): 21–40.

Alverado, Facundo, Anthony B. Atkinson, Thomas Piketty, and Emmanuel Saez (2013). The Top 1 Percent in Economic and Historical Perspective. *Journal of Economic Perspectives* 27(3): 3–20.

Anderson, Benedict (1991). *Imagined Communities: Reflections on the Origins and Spread of Nationalism*. 2nd ed. London: Verso.

Anderson, R. D. (2004). *European Universities from the Enlightenment to 1914*. Oxford: Oxford University Press.

Angell, Joseph K., and Samuel Ames (1832). *Treatise on the Law of Private Corporations Aggregate*. Boston: Hilliard, Gray, Little and Wilkins.

Antonio, Robert J. (1981). Immanent Critique as the Core of Critical Theory: Its Origins and Developments in Hegel, Marx and Contemporary Thought. *British Journal of Sociology* 32(3): 330–345.

Armitage, David (2007). *The Declaration of Independence: A Global History*. Cambridge, MA, and London: Harvard University Press.

Arora-Jonsson, Stefan, Nils Brunsson, and Raimund Hasse (2020). Where Does Competition Come From? The Role of Organization. *Organization Theory* 1: 1–24.

Arrighi, Giovanni (2010). *The Long Twentieth Century: Money, Power and the Origins of Our Times*. Updated ed. London: Verso.

Asad, Talal (1983). Anthropological Conceptions of Religion: Reflections of Geertz. *Man, n.s.* 18(2): 237–259.

Asch, Ronald G. (2003). *Nobilities in Transition, 1550–1700: Courtiers and Rebels in Britain and Europe*. London: Hodder Education.

Austin, J. L. (1975). *How to Do Things with Words*. 2nd ed. Cambridge, MA: Harvard University Press.

Bailyn, Bernard (1992). *The Ideological Origins of the American Revolution*. Enlarged ed. Cambridge, MA, and London: Belknap Press of Harvard University Press.

Baldwin, John W. (1972). Introduction. In J. W. Baldwin and R. A. Goldthwaite (eds), *Universities in Politics: Case Studies from the Late Middle Ages and Early Modern Period*. Baltimore, MD, and London: Johns Hopkins University Press. Pp. 1–15.

Ball, Terrance (1993). Power. In R. Goodin and P. Pettit (eds), *A Companion to Contemporary Political Philosophy*. Oxford: Blackwell. Pp. 548–557.

Batrinos, Menelaos L. (2012). Testosterone and Aggressive Behavior in Men. *International Journal of Endocrinology and Metabolism* 10(3): 563–568.

Beetham, David (1991). *The Legitimation of Power*. Basingstoke and New York: Palgrave Macmillan.

Bell, Catherine (1997). *Ritual: Perspectives and Dimensions*. Oxford: Oxford University Press.

Beloff, Max (1968). *The Balance of Power*. London: George Allen and Unwin.

Bendix, Reinhard (1964). *Nation-Building and Citizenship*. London: John Wiley and Sons.

(1978). *Kings or People: Power and the Mandate to Rule*. Berkeley: University of California Press.

Berle, Adolf A., and Gardiner C. Means (1932). *The Modern Corporation and Private Property*. New York: Commerce Clearing House.

Bernstein, Basil (1971). *Class Codes and Control, Vol. 1, Theoretical Studies towards a Sociology of Language*. London and New York: Routledge.

Berry, Christopher J. (1997). *Social Theory of the Scottish Enlightenment*. Edinburgh: Edinburgh University Press.

Birch, Jonathan (2017). *The Philosophy of Social Evolution*. Oxford: Oxford University Press.

Blaut, James (1993). *The Colonizer's Model of the World: Geographic Diffusionism and Eurocentric History*. New York and London: Guilford Press.

Bloch, Marc (1961). *Feudal Society, Volume 1: The Growth of Ties of Dependence*. L. A. Manyon (trans.). Chicago: University of Chicago Press.

Bloch, Maurice (1989). *Ritual, History and Power: Selected Papers in Anthropology*. London: Athlone Press.

Bloor, David (1976). *Knowledge and Social Imagery*. London: Routledge & Kegan Paul.

Bobbio, Norberto (1989). *Democracy and Dictatorship: The Nature and Limits of State Power*. Minneapolis: University of Minnesota Press.

Boucher, Douglas H. (ed.) (1985). *The Biology of Mutualism: Ecology and Evolution*. New York: Oxford University Press.

Bourdieu, Pierre (1988). Program for a Sociology of Sport. *Sociology of Sport Journal* 5: 153–161.

(1991). *Language and Symbolic Power*. Cambridge: Polity Press.

(1996). *The State Nobility: Elite Schools in the Field of Power*, with the collaboration of M. de Saint Martin. Cambridge: Polity Press.

(2005). *The Social Structures of the Economy*. Cambridge: Polity Press.

Bourke, Andrew F. G. (2011). *Principles of Social Evolution*. Oxford: Oxford University Press.

Bowie, Nikolas (2019). Book Review: Corporate Personhood v. Corporate Statehood. *Harvard Law Review* 132: 2009–2040.

Bowles, Samuel, and Herbert Gintis (2011). *A Cooperative Species: Human Reciprocity and Its Evolution*. Princeton, NJ, and Oxford: Princeton University Press.

Breen, Richard (2011). Game Theory. In P. Bearman and P. Hedtröm (eds), *The Oxford Handbook of Analytical Sociology*. Oxford: Oxford University Press. Pp. 619–638.

Brenner, Reuven (1987). *Rivalry, in Business, Science, among Nations*. Cambridge: Cambridge University Press.

Breuilly, John (1993). *Nationalism and the State*. 2nd ed. Manchester: Manchester University Press.

Brewer, John (1989). *The Sinews of Power: War, Money and the English State, 1688–1783*. New York: Knopf.

Bridges, Amy (1984). *A City in the Republic: Antebellum New York and the Origins of Machine Politics*. Cambridge: Cambridge University Press.

Brooks, Risa A. (2019). Integrating the Civil–Military Relations Subfield. *Annual Review of Political Science* 22: 379–398.

(2020). Paradoxes of Professionalism: Rethinking Civil–Military Relations in the United States. *International Security* 44(4): 7–44.

Brown, Keith M. (2011). *Noble Power in Scotland from the Reformation to the Revolution*. Edinburgh: Edinburgh University Press.

Brown, Wendy (2015). *Undoing the Demos: Neoliberalism's Stealth Revolution*. New York: Zone Books.

Browne, Craig (2008). The End of Immanent Critique? *European Journal of Social Theory* 11(1): 5–24.

Brubaker, Rogers (1992). *Citizenship and Nationhood in France and Germany*. Cambridge: Cambridge University Press.

(1996). *Nationalism Reframed: Nationhood and the National Question in the New Europe*. Cambridge: Cambridge University Press.

Brubaker, Rogers, and Frederick Cooper (2006). Beyond 'Identity'. In R. Brubaker (ed.), *Ethnicity without Groups*. Cambridge, MA: Harvard University Press. Pp. 28–63.

Burk, James (2002). Theories of Democratic Civil–Military Relations. *Armed Forces and Society* 29(1): 7–29.

(2018). Military Mobilization in Modern Western Societies. In G. Caforio and M. Nuciari (eds), *Handbook of the Sociology of the Military*. 2nd ed. Switzerland: Springer Nature. Pp. 101–120.

Burke, Edmund. (2007[1770]). *Thoughts on the Present Discontents*. Project Gutenberg eBook no2173. At www.gutenberg.org. Transcribed from the 1886 Cassell & Company edition.

Buss, David M. (1999). *Evolutionary Psychology: The New Science of the Mind*. Boston: Allyn and Bacon.

Calhoun, Craig (ed.) (1994). *Habermas and the Public Sphere*. Cambridge, MA: MIT Press.

Canovan, Margaret (2005). *The People*. Cambridge: Polity.

Caramani, Daniele (2003). The End of Silent Elections: The Birth of Electoral Competition, 1832–1915. *Party Politics* 9(4): 411–443.

(2004). *The Nationalization of Politics: The Formation of National Electorates and Party Systems in Western Europe*. Cambridge: Cambridge University Press.

Carr, E. H. (1961). *What Is History?* New York: Vintage Books.

Carrington, Ben (2013). The Critical Sociology of Race and Sport: The First Fifty Years. *Annual Review of Sociology* 39: 379–398.

Centeno, Miguel A., and Joshua N. Cohen (2012). The Arc of Neoliberalism. *Annual Review of Sociology* 38: 317–340.

Cerny, Philip (2010). The Competition State Today: From *Raison d'Etat* to Raison du Monde. *Policy Studies* 31(1): 5–21.

Cerny, Phillip (2016). In the Shadow of Ordoliberalism: The Paradox of Neoliberalism in the 21st Century. ERIS–European *Review of International Studies* 3(1): 78–92.

Chandler, Alfred D. Jr (1977). *The Visible Hand: The Managerial Revolution in American Business*. Cambridge, MA: Harvard University Press.

(1990). *Scale and Scope: The Dynamics of Industrial Capitalism*. Cambridge, MA, and London: Belknap Press of Harvard University Press.

Charle, Christophe (2004). Chapter 2: Patterns. In W. Rüegg (ed.), *A History of the University in Europe, Volume III: Universities in the Nineteenth and Early Twentieth Centuries (1800–1945)*. Cambridge: Cambridge University Press. Pp. 3–80.

Chirot, Daniel (2020). *You Say You Want a Revolution? Radical Idealism and Its Tragic Consequences*. Princeton: Princeton University Press.

Chirot, Daniel, and Thomas D. Hall (1982). World-System Theory. *Annual Review of Sociology* 8: 81–106.

Chung, Stephanie Po-yin (2015). From Ancestral Tong to Joint-Stock Company: The Transformation of the Yip Kwong Tai Tong in South China, 1830s–1960s. *International Journal of Asian Studies* 12(1): 79–105.

Cippola, Carlo M. (1965). *Guns, Sails and Empires: Technological Innovation and the Early Phases of European Expansion, 1400–1700*. New York: Minerva.

(1980). *Before the Industrial Revolution: European Society and Economy, 1000–1700*. 2nd ed. New York and London: W. W. Norton.

Clegg, John (2020). A Theory of Capitalist Slavery. *Journal of Historical Sociology* 33(1): 74–98.

Coase, Ronald H. (1937). The Nature of the Firm. *Economica, n.s.* 4: 386–405.

Cobban, A. B. (1975). *The Medieval Universities: Their Development and Organization*. London: Methuen and Co Ltd.

Cohen, E. A. (2002). *Supreme Command: Soldiers, Statesmen and Leadership in Wartime*. New York: Simon and Schuster.

Cohen, Yehudi (1971). Adaptation and Evolution: An Introduction. In Y. Cohen (ed.), *Man in Adaptation: The Institutional Framework*. Chicago and New York: Aldine Atherton.

Cohn, Norman (1970). *The Pursuit of the Millennium: Revolutionary Millenarians and Mystical Anarchists of the Middle Ages*. Revised and expanded ed. New York: Oxford University Press.

Colagouri, Claudio (2012). *Agon Culture: Competition and the Problem of Domination*. Whitby, ON, Canada: de Sitter Publications.

Coleman, James S. (1974). *Power and the Structure of Society*. New York: W. W. Norton and Company.

(1989). Simulation Games and the Development of Social Theory. *Simulation Games* 20: 144–64.

(1990). *Foundations of Social Theory*. Cambridge, MA, and London: Belknap Press of Harvard University Press.

(1993). The Rational Reconstruction of Society. *American Sociological Review* 58(1): 1–15.

Collini, Stefan (2012). *What Are Universities For?* London: Penguin.

Collins, Randall (2000). *The Sociology of Philosophies: A Global Theory of Intellectual Change*. Cambridge, MA, and London: Belknap Press of Harvard University Press.

Contamine, Phillipe (ed.) (2000). *War and Competition Between States.* Oxford: Oxford Scholarship Online.

Cosandey, David (1997). *Le Secret de l'Occident: Du Miracle Passé au Marasme Present.* Paris: Arléa.

Coser, Lewis (1957). Social Conflict and the Theory of Social Change. *British Journal of Sociology* 8(3): 197–207.

Crotty, William (2006). Party Origins and Evolution in the United States. In R. S. Katz and W. Crotty (eds), *Handbook of Party Politics.* London: Sage. Pp. 25–33.

Crouch, Colin (2011). *The Strange Non-Death of Neoliberalism.* Cambridge: Polity.

Crouch, David (2005). *Tournament.* London: Hambledon Continuum.

Crouch, Tracey and contributors (2021). *Fan-Led Review of Football Governance: Securing the Game's Future.* Crown copyright, Open Government Licence v3.0. Retrieved from: www.gov.uk/government/publications/fan-led-review-of-football-governance-securing-the-games-future, on 15 February 2022.

Daly, Jonathan (2015). *Historians Debate: The Rise of the West.* London and New York: Routledge.

Darwin, Charles (2003[1859]). *The Origin of Species and The Voyage of the Beagle.* New York: Alfred A, Knopf/Everyman's Library.

Davidson, J. (2013). The Contemporary Presidency: Civil-Military Friction and Presidential Decision-Making: Explaining the Broken Dialogue. *Presidential Studies Quarterly* 43(1): 129–145.

Davies, William (2014). Neoliberalism: A Bibliographic Review. *Theory, Culture and Society* 31(7–8): 309–317.

(2017). *The Limits of Neoliberalism: Authority, Sovereignty and the Logic of Competition.* Revised ed. London: Sage.

Dawkins, Richard (1989). *The Selfish Gene.* Oxford: Oxford University Press.

Dawkins, Richard, and J. R. Krebs (1979). Arms Races Between and Within Species. *Proceedings of the Royal Society of London, Series B, Biological Sciences* 205(1161): 489–511.

Dawson, Christopher (1958). *Religion and the Rise of Western Culture.* New York: Image Books.

de Leon, Cedric (2010). Vicarious Revolutionaries: Martial Discourse and the Origins of Mass Party Competition in the United States, 1789–1848. *Studies in American Development* 24:121–141.

De Ridder-Symoens, Hilde (ed.) (1992). *A History of the University in Europe: Volume I, Universities in the Middle Ages.* Cambridge: Cambridge University Press.

Dennett, Daniel C. (1995). *Darwin's Dangerous Idea: Evolution and the Meaning of Life*. New York: Simon Schuster.

Desilver, Drew (2019). Despite Global Concerns about Democracy, more than Half of Countries are Democratic. Pew Research Center. Retrieved from: www.pewresearch.org/fact-tank/2019/05/14/more-than-half-of-countries-are-democratic/, on 3 November, 2020.

Deutsch, Karl W. (1953). *Nationalism and Social Communication*. 2nd ed. Cambridge, MA: MIT Press.

Dewald, Jonathan (1996). *The European Nobility, 1400–1800*. Cambridge: Cambridge University Press.

Dewey, John (1926). The Historic Background of Corporate Legal Personality. *Yale Law Journal* 35(6): 655–673.

Diamond, Jared (1997). *Guns, Germs and Steel: A Short History of Everybody for the Last 13,000 Years*. London: Vintage.

Dickson, H. T. (1973). *Walpole and the Whig Supremacy*. London: English Universities Press.

(2002). The British Constitution. In H. T. Dickson (ed.), *A Companion to Eighteenth- Century Britain*. Oxford: Blackwell.

Domhoff, William G. (2014). *Who Rules America? The Triumph of the Corporate Rich*. 7th ed. New York: McGraw-Hill.

Douglas, Mary (1982). *Natural Symbols: Explorations in Cosmology*. Revised ed. New York: Pantheon Books.

Duina, Francesco (2011). *Winning: Reflections of an American Obsession*. Princeton: Princeton University Press.

Durham, William H. (1990). Advances in Evolutionary Culture Theory. *Annual Review of Anthropology* 19: 187–210.

Durkheim, Emile (1964). *The Division of Labour in Society*. New York: Free Press.

Dunn, John (2006). *Setting the People Free: The Story of Democracy*. London: Atlantic Books.

Earle, Timothy K. (1987). Chiefdoms in Archaeological and Ethnohistorical Perspective. *Annual Review of Anthropology* 16: 279–308.

Edwards, Michael (2014). *Civil Society*. 3rd ed. Cambridge: Polity.

Elder-Vass, Dave (2008). Searching for Realism, Structure and Agency in Actor Network Theory. *British Journal of Sociology* 59(3): 455–473.

Elias, Norbert (1978). *What Is Sociology?* New York: Columbia University Press.

(1986). Introduction. In N. Elias and E. Dunning (ed.), *Quest for Excitement: Sport and Leisure in the Civilizing Process*. Oxford and New York: Basil Blackwell. Pp. 19–62.

(1994). *The Civilizing Process*. Oxford: Blackwell.

Elias, Norbert, and Eric Dunning (1986). *Quest for Excitement: Sport and Leisure in the Civilizing Process*. Oxford and New York: Basil Blackwell.

Emden, Christian J., and David Midgley (eds) (2012). *Changing Perceptions of the Public Sphere*. New York and Oxford: Berghahn.

Emirbayer, Mustafa, and Ann Mische (1998). What Is Agency? *American Journal of Sociology* 103(4): 962–1023.

Evans-Pritchard, E. E. (1969). *The Nuer: A Description of the Modes of Livelihood and Political Institutions of a Nilotic People*. New York: Oxford University Press.

Faure, David (1989). The Lineage as a Cultural Invention: The Case of the Pearl River Delta. *Modern China* 15(1): 4–36.

Feaver, Peter D. (1999). Civil-Military Relations. *Annual Review of Political Science* 2: 211–241.

(2003). *Armed Servants: Agency, Oversight, and Civil-Military Relations*. Cambridge, MA: Harvard University Press.

Ferguson, Adam (1966). *An Essay on the History of Civil Society*. Edinburgh: Edinburgh University Press.

Ferrone, Vincenzo (2015). *The Enlightenment: History of an Idea*. Princeton and Oxford: Princeton University Press.

Field, Peter S. (1998). *The Crisis of the Standing Order: Clerical Intellectuals and Cultural Authority in Massachusetts, 1780–1833*. Amherst: University of Massachusetts Press.

Finer, Samuel E. (1962). *The Man on Horseback*. Boulder: Westview.

(1997a). *The History of Government II: The Intermediate Ages*. Oxford: Oxford University Press.

(1997b). *The History of Government III: Empire, Monarchies, and the Modern State*. Oxford: Oxford University Press.

Finke, Roger, and Rodney Stark (1998). Religious Choice and Competition. *American Sociological Review* 63(5): 761–6.

Fisher, Nick, and Hans van Wees (eds) (2010). *Competition in the Ancient World*. London: Bloomsbury.

Fligstein, Neil, and Doug McAdam (2011). Toward a General Theory of Strategic Action Fields. *Sociological Theory* 29(1): 1–26.

Formisano, Ronald P. (1969). Political Character, Antipartyism and the Second Party System. *American Quarterly* 21(4): 683–709.

Foucault, Michel (1980). *Power/Knowledge: Selected Interviews and Other Writings, 1972–1977*. New York: Pantheon.

(1990). *The History of Sexuality: An Introduction, Vol. 1*. New York: Random House.

(2000). *Power, Essential Works of Michel Foucault, 1954–1984*, J. D. Faubion (ed.). New York: New Press.

(2008). *The Birth of Biopolitics: Lectures at the College de France, 1978–1979*. Basingstoke: Palgrave Macmillan.

Fracchia, Joseph, and Richard C. Lewontin (2005). The Price of Metaphor. *History and Theory* 44(1): 14–29.

Frank, Andre Gunder (1969). *Latin America: Underdevelopment or Revolution*. New York: Monthly Review Press.

Frank, David John, and John W. Meyer (2007). University Expansion and the Knowledge Society. *Theory and Society* 36: 287–311.

Freese, Jeremy, Jui-Chung Allen Li, and Lisa D. Wade (2003). The Potential Relevances of Biology to Social Inquiry. *Annual Review of Sociology* 29: 233–256.

Frey, James H., and D. Stanley Eitzen (1991). Sport and Society. *Annual Review of Sociology* 17: 503–522.

Fukuyama, Francis (2022). *Liberalism and Its Discontents*. London: Profile Books.

Futuyma, Douglas J. (2013). *Evolution*. 3rd ed. Sunderland, MA: Sinauer Associates, Inc.

Gane, Nicholas (2014). The Emergence of Neoliberalism: Thinking Through and Beyond Michel Foucault's Lectures on Biopolitics. *Theory, Culture and Society* 31(4): 3–27.

(2019). Competition: A Critical History of a Concept. *Theory, Culture and Society 37*(2): 31–59.

Geertz, Clifford (1963). The Integrative Revolution: Primordial Sentiments and Civil Politics in the New States. In C. Geertz (ed.), *Old Societies and New States: The Quest for Modernity in Asia and Africa*. New York: Free Press. Pp. 105–157.

(1972). Deep Play: Notes of a Balinese Cockfight. *Daedalus* 101(1): 1–37.

(1973). *The Interpretation of Cultures*. New York: Basic Books.

Gellner, Ernest (1974). *Legitimation of Belief*. Cambridge: Cambridge University Press.

(1983). *Nations and Nationalism*. Cornell: Cornell University Press.

(1990). *The Civil and the Sacred*, The Tanner Lecture on Human Values, Delivered at Harvard University, March 20–21, 1990. Retrieved from: https://tannerlectures.utah.edu/lecture-library.php, on 15 February 2022.

(1991). *Plough, Sword and Book: The Structure of Human History*. London: Paladin.

(1996). *Conditions of Liberty: Civil Society and Its Rivals*. London: Penguin.

Genovese, Eugene D. (1965). *The Political Economy of Slavery: Studies in the Economy and Society of the Slave South*. New York: Pantheon Books.

Genschel, Philipp, and Laura Seelkopf (2015). The Competition State: The Modern State in a Global Economy. In S. Leibfried et al., (eds), *The Oxford Handbook of Transformations of the State*. Oxford: Oxford University Press/Oxford Handbooks Online. Pp. 237–252.

Gentry, Anna (2015). Corporate Personhood and Nonprofit Director Duty of Obedience: Legal Implications that Necessitate Expanded Standing to Sue. *George Mason Law Review* 23(1): 165–198.

Gerber, David, J. (2001). *Law and Competition in Twentieth-Century Europe: Protecting Prometheus*. Oxford: Oxford University Press/ Oxford Scholarship Online.

Gerkin, Heather K. (2014). Boden Lecture: The Real Problem with Citizens United: Campaign Finance, Dark Money, and Shadow Parties. *Marquette Law Review* 97(4): 904–923.

Gierke, Otto von (1900). *Political Theories of the Middle Age*. Cambridge: Cambridge University Press.

Gintis, Herbert (2017). *Individuality and Entanglement: The Moral and Material Bases of Social Life*. Princeton: Princeton University Press.

Gluckman, Max (1954). *Rituals of Rebellion in South-East Africa*. Manchester: Manchester University Press.

Goldstone, Jack (2000). The Rise of the West–or Not? A Revision to Socio-economic History. *Sociological Theory* 18(2): 175–194.

(2009). *Why Europe? The Rise of the West in World History, 1500–1850*. New York: McGraw-Hill.

Gomory, Ralph, and Richard Sylla (2013). The American Corporation. *Daedelus* 142(2): 102–118.

González de Lara, Yadira (2018). Business Organization and Organizational Innovation in Late Medieval Italy. In H. Wells (ed.), *Research Handbook on the History of Corporate and Company Law*. Cheltenham: Edward Elgar. Pp. 65–87.

Goody, Jack (1983). *The Development of the Family and Marriage in Europe*. Cambridge: Cambridge University Press.

Gough, Ian, et al. (2008). Darwinian Evolutionary Theory and the Social Sciences. *Twenty-First Century Society* 3(1) 65–86.

Greene, Jack P., and Philip D. Morgan (eds) (2009). *Atlantic History: A Critical Appraisal*. Oxford: Oxford University Press.

Greenfeld, Liah (1992). *Nationalism: Five Roads to Modernity*. Cambridge, MA: Harvard University Press.

Grosby, Steven (2001). Primordiality. In A. S. Leoussi (ed.), *Encyclopedia of Nationalism*. London: Transaction.

Grossi, Paolo (2010). *A History of European Law*. Chichester: Wiley-Blackwell.

Habermas, Jürgen (1974[1964]). The Public Sphere: An Encyclopedia Article. *New German Critique* 3: 49–55.

(1975). *The Legitimation Crisis, T. McCarthy*. (trans.) Boston: Beacon Press.

(1991[1962]). *The Structural Transformation of the Public Sphere: An Inquiry into a Category of Bourgeois Society*. Cambridge, MA: MIT Press.

Haidt, Jonathan (2016). Why Universities Must Choose One Telos: Truth or Social Justice. Heterodox Blog, retrieved at: https://heterodoxacademy.org/blog/one-telos-truth-or-social-justice-2/, on 16 February 2022.

Haldén, Peter (2020). *Family Power: Kinship, War and Political Orders in Eurasia, 500–2018*. Cambridge: Cambridge University Press.

Hall, John A. (1986). *Powers and Liberties: The Causes and Consequences of the Rise of the West*. Berkeley: University of California Press.

(1993). Nationalisms: Classified and Explained. *Daedalus* 122(3): 1–28.

(1995). In Search of Civil Society. In J. A. Hall (ed.), *Civil Society: Theory, History, Comparison*. Cambridge: Polity. Pp. 1–32.

(1996). *International Orders*. Cambridge: Polity.

(2011). *Ernest Gellner: An Intellectual Biography*. London: Verso.

Hall, Peter A., and David Soskice (eds) (2001). *Varieties of Capitalism*. Oxford: Oxford University Press.

Hall, Peter D. (1984). *The Organization of American Culture, 1700–1900: Private Institutions, Elites, and the Origins of American Nationality*. New York: New York University Press.

(1992). *Inventing the Nonprofit Sector, and Other Essays on Philanthropy, Voluntarism, and Nonprofit Organizations*. Baltimore: Johns Hopkins University Press.

(2013). Philanthropy, the Nonprofit Sector and the Democratic Dilemma. *Daedalus* 142(2): 139–158.

Hansmann, Henry et al. (2006). Law and the Rise of the Firm. *Harvard Law Review* 119(5): 1333–1403.

Hardin, Garrett (1960). The Competitive Exclusion Principle. *Science, n.s.* 131(3409): 1292–1297.

Harling, Philip, and Peter Mandler (1993). From 'Fiscal-Military' State to Laissez-Faire State, 1760–1850. *Journal of British Studies* 32(1): 44–70.

Harris, Ron (2006). The Transplantation of the Legal Discourse on Corporate Personality Theories: From German Codification to British Political Pluralism and American Big Business. *Washington and Lee Law Review* 63(4): 1422–1478.

(2009). The Institutional Dynamics of Early Modern Eurasian Trade: The *Commenda* and the Corporation. *Journal of Economic Behavior and Organization* 71: 606–622.

(2018). Trading with Strangers: The Corporate Form in the Move from Municipal Governance to Overseas Trade. In H. Wells (ed.), *Research Handbook on the History of Corporate and Company Law*. Cheltenham: Edward Elgar. Pp. 88–118.

Hartmann, Eva, and Poul F. Kjaer (2015). Special Issue: A Sociology of Competition. *Journal of Social Theory* 16(2): 141–145.

Harvard Law Review (1989). Editorial: Incorporating the Republic: The Corporation in Antebellum Political Culture. *Harvard Law Review* 102(8): 1883–1903.

Harvey, David (1991). *The Condition of Postmodernity*. London: Wiley-Blackwell.

(2005). *A Brief History of Neoliberalism*. Oxford: Oxford University Press.

(2007). Neoliberalism as Creative Destruction. *Annals of the American Academy of Political and Social Science* 610 (March): 22–44.

Haskins, Charles H. (1957). *The Rise of the Universities*. Ithaca and London: Cornell University Press.

Hastings, Adrian (1997). *The Construction of Nationhood: Ethnicity, Religion, and Nationalism*. Cambridge: Cambridge University Press.

Hawkins, Angus (2018). Political Parties. In D. Brown, G. Pentland and R. Crowcroft (eds), *The Oxford Handbook of Modern British Political History, 1800–2000*. Oxford: Oxford University Press. Pp. 247–265.

Hayek, F. A. (2013). *Law Legislation and Liberty*. London and New York: Routledge.

Hearn, Jonathan (2006). *Rethinking Nationalism: A Critical Introduction*. Basingstoke: Palgrave Macmillan.

(2009). The Origins of Modern Nationalism in the North Atlantic Interaction Sphere. *Sociological Research Online* 14(5): 147–160.

(2012). *Theorizing Power*. Basingstoke: Palgrave Macmillan.

(2014a). On the Social Evolution of Power To/Over. *Journal of Political Power* 7(2): 175–191.

(2014b). Competition as Ritual and the Legitimation of the Liberal Nation State. In R. Tsang and E. T. Woods (eds), *The Cultural Politics of Nationalism and Nation-Building: Ritual and Performance in the Forging of Nations*. London: Routledge. Pp. 68–83.

(2016a). The Culture of Competition in Modern Liberal Societies. *Humanities: Christianity and Culture* 48: 31–54.

(2016b). Inequality, Liberal Society, and the Balance of Power. *Revue Internationale de Philosophie* 70(275): 109–128.

(2017). *Salvage Ethnography in the Financial Sector: The Path to Economic Crisis in Scotland*. Manchester: Manchester University Press.

(2021). Reframing the History of the Competition Concept: Neoliberalism, Meritocracy, Modernity. *Journal of Historical Sociology* 34(2): 375–392.

Hechter, Michael (2000). *Containing Nationalism*. Oxford: Oxford University Press.

Henrich, Joseph (2021). *The Weirdest People in the World: How the West Became Psychologically Peculiar and Particularly Prosperous*. New York/London: Penguin Books.

Henrich, Joseph, Robert Boyd, and Peter J. Richerson (2008). Five Misunderstandings about Cultural Evolution. *Human Nature* 19(2): 119–137.

Henry, John (2008). *The Scientific Revolution and the Origins of Modern Science*. 3rd ed. London: Red Globe Press.

Herzog, Tamar (2018). *A Short History of European Law: The Last Two and a Half Millennia*. Cambridge, MA and London: Harvard University Press.

Hill, Brian (2002). Parliament, Parties and Elections (1688–1760). In H. T. Dickson (ed.), *A Companion to Eighteenth-Century Britain*. Oxford: Blackwell. Pp. 55–68.

Hilt, Eric (2013). Shareholder Voting Rights in Early American Corporations. *Business History* 55(4): 620–635.

Hobbes, Thomas (1994[1650]). *Leviathan, with Selected Variants from the Latin Edition of 1668*. E. Curley (ed.). Indianapolis and Cambridge: Hackett Publishing Company, Inc.

Hobsbawm, Eric (1992). *Nations and Nationalism Since 1780: Programme, Myth and Reality*. 2nd ed. Cambridge: Cambridge University Press.

Hobson, John M. (1994). *The Eastern Origins of Western Civilisation*. Cambridge: Cambridge University Press.

Hodgson, Geoffrey M. (2007). Meanings of Methodological Individualism. *Journal of Economic Methodology* 14(2): 211–226.

(2015). *Conceptualizing Capitalism: Institutions, Evolution, Future*. Chicago and London: University of Chicago Press.

Hodgson, Geoffrey M., and Thorbjørn Knudsen (2010). *Darwin's Conjecture: The Search for General Principles of Social and Economic Evolution*. Chicago: University of Chicago Press.

Hoffman, Philip T. (2017). *Why Did Europe Conquer the World?* Princeton, NJ: Princeton University Press.

Hofstadter, Richard (1969). *The Idea of a Party System: The Rise of Legitimate Opposition in the United States, 1780–1840*. Berkeley: University of California Press.

Holt, Michael F. (1999). *The Rise and Fall of the American Whig Party: Jacksonian Politics and the Onset of the American Civil War*. Oxford: Oxford University Press.

Hont, Istvan (2005). *Jealousy of Trade: International Competition and the Nation-State in Historical Perspective*. Cambridge, MA, and London: Belknap Press of Harvard University Press.

Hostettler, John (2006). *Fighting for Justice: The History and Origins of Adversary Trial*. Winchester: Waterside Press.

Howe, Daniel Walker (2007). *What God Hath Wrought: The Transformation of America, 1815–1848*. Oxford: Oxford University Press.

Hroch, Miroslav (2000). *The Social Preconditions of National Revival in Europe: A Comparative Analysis of the Social Composition of Patriotic Groups in the Smaller European Nations*. New ed. New York: Columbia University Press.

Hull, David L. (1990). *Science as a Process: An Evolutionary Account of the Social and Conceptual Development of Science*. Chicago and London: University of Chicago Press.

(2001). *Science and Selection: Essays on Biological Evolution and the Philosophy of Science*. Cambridge: Cambridge University Press.

Hume, David (1975). *Enquiries Concerning Human Understanding and Concerning the Principles of Morals*, L. A. Selby-Bigge and P. H. Nidditch (eds). 3rd ed. Oxford: Clarendon Press.

(1978). *A Treatise of Human Nature*, L. A. Selby-Bigge and P. H. Nidditch (eds). 2nd ed. Oxford: Clarendon Press.

(1985). *Essays Moral, Political and Literary*. Indianapolis: Liberty Fund.

Hunt, Shelby D. (2000). *A General Theory of Competition: Resources, Competences, Productivity, Economic Growth*. Thousand Oaks: Sage Publications.

Hunter, Michael (2020). *The Decline of Magic: Britain in the Enlightenment*. New Haven and London: Yale University Press.

Huntington, Samuel P. (1957). *The Soldier and the State*. Cambridge, MA: Harvard University Press.

Hutchinson, John (2000). Ethnicity and Modern Nations. *Ethnic and Racial Studies* 23(4): 651–669.

Hyde, J. K. (1972). Commune, University, and Society in Early Medieval Bologna. In J. W. Baldwin and R. A. Goldthwaite (eds), *Universities in Politics: Case Studies from the Late Middle Ages and Early Modern Period*. Baltimore and London: Johns Hopkins Press. Pp. 17–46.

Im Hof, Ulrich (1994). *The Enlightenment: An Historical Introduction*. Oxford: Blackwell.

Inbody, Donald S. (2015). *The Soldier Vote: War, Politics and the Ballot in America*. New York: Palgrave Macmillan.

Ingham, Geoffrey (2008). *Capitalism*. Cambridge: Polity.

Jacob, Frank, and Gilmar Visoni-Alonzo (2016). *The Military Revolution in Early Modern Europe: A Revision*. London: Palgrave Macmillan.

James, C. L. R. (1963). *Beyond and Boundary*. New York: Pantheon Books.

Janda, Kenneth (2005). *Political Parties and Democracy in Theoretical and Practical Perspectives: Adopting Party Law*. Washington, DC: National Democratic Institute for International Affairs.

Janowitz, Morris (1960). *The Professional and the Soldier: A Social and Political Portrait*. Glencoe: Free Press.

Jenkins, Richard (2002). *Pierre Bourdieu*. 2nd ed. London: Routledge.

Jepperson, Ronald, and John W. Meyer (2011). Multiple Levels of Analysis and the Limitations of Methodological Individualisms. *Sociological Theory* 29(1): 54–73.

Jessop, Bob (2002). *The Future of the Capitalist State*. Oxford: Polity Press.

Johns, Gary (1999). Political Parties: From Private to Public. *Journal of Commonwealth and Comparative Politics* 37(2): 89–113.

Johnson, Allen W., and Timothy Earle (2000). *The Evolution of Human Societies*. 2nd ed. Stanford: Stanford University Press.

Jones, Eric. L. (1981). *The European Miracle: Environments, Economies, and Geopolitics in the History of Europe and Asia*. London and New York: Cambridge University Press.

(1988). *Growth Recurring: Economic Change in World History*. Oxford: Clarendon Press.

Jones, Gareth S. (2012). *Masters of the Universe: Hayek, Friedman and the Birth of Neoliberal Politics*. Princeton: Princeton University Press.

Kaesler, Dirk (2017). Universal Rationalization: Max Weber's Great Narrative. *Irish Journal of Sociology* 25(3): 315–323.

Kahn, Shamus Rhaman (2012). The Sociology of Elites. *Annual Review of Sociology* 38: 361–377.

Kalberg, Stephen (2005). Max Weber: The Confrontation with Modernity. In S. Kalberg (ed.), *Max Weber: Readings and Commentary on Modernity*. London: Blackwell. Pp. 1–47.

Kandil, Hazem (2012). *Soldiers, Spies and Statesmen. Egypt's Road to Revolt*. Brooklyn, NY: Verso.

Kant, Immanuel (1991). *Kant: Political Writings*, H. S. Reiss (ed.). Cambridge: Cambridge University Press.

(2012). *Groundwork of the Metaphysics of Morals*, M. Gregor and J. Timmermann (eds). Revised ed. Cambridge: Cambridge University Press.

Karvonen, Lauri (2007). Legislation on Political Parties: A Global Comparison. *Party Politics* 13(4): 437–455.

Kaufman, Jason (2008). Corporate Law and the Sovereignty of States. *American Sociological Review* 73(3): 402–425.

Kay, John (2015). *Other People's Money: Masters of the Universe or Servants of the People?* London: Profile Books.

(2021). RIP PLC: The Rise and Fall of the Listed Company, and Where–for Better or Worse–Private Equity Will Lead Business Next. *Prospect Magazine*, April 2021. Pp. 30–35.

Kayiklik, Abdurrahman (2019). How Elizabeth Warren Is Reviving the Concession Theory of the Corporation. *Columbia Law School's Blog on Corporations and the Capital Markets*. Retrieved at: https://clsbluesky.law.columbia.edu/2019/11/01/how-elizabeth-warren-is-reviving-the-concession-theory-of-the-corporation/#_ftnref14, on 1 November, 2019.

Keane, John (1988). *Democracy and Civil Society*. London: University of Westminster.

Keat, Russell (1993). The Moral Boundaries of the Market. In C. Crouch and D. Marquand (eds), *Ethics and Markets: Co-operation and Competition within Capitalist Economies*. Oxford: Blackwell. Pp. 6–20.

Keesing, Roger M. (1983). *Elota's Story: The Life and Times of a Soloman Islands Big Man*. Chicago: Holt, Rinehart, Winston.

Kennedy, Paul M. (1987). *The Rise and Fall of the Great Powers: Economic Change and Military Conflict from 1500 to 2000*. New York: Random House.

Kessler, Amalia D. (2017). *Inventing American Exceptionalism: The Origins of American Adversarial Legal Culture, 1800–1877*. New Haven and London: Yale University Press.

Key, V. O. Jr (1964). *Politics, Parties and Pressure Groups*. New York: Cromwell.

Khanna, Vikramaditya (2018). Business Organizations in India Prior to the British East India Company. In H. Wells (ed.), *Research Handbook on the History of Corporate and Company Law*. Cheltenham: Edward Elgar. Pp. 33–64.

Kocka, Jürgen (2016). *Capitalism: A Short History*. Princeton: Princeton University Press.

Kohn, Hans (1967). *The Idea of Nationalism*. New York: Collier.

Korsgaard, Christine M. (2012). Introduction. In M. Gregor and J. Timmermann (eds), *Immanuel Kant's Groundwork of the Metaphysics of Morals*. Revised ed. Cambridge: Cambridge University Press. Pp. ix–xxxvi.

Koselleck, Reinhard (1989). Social History and Conceptual History. *Politics, Culture and Society* 2(3): 308–325.

Krugman, Paul (1994). Competitiveness: A Dangerous Obsession. *Foreign Affairs* 73(2): 28–44.

Kruman, Marc W. (1992). The Second American Party System and the Transformation of Revolutionary Republicanism. *Journal of the Early Republic* 12(4): 509–537.

Kumar, Krishan (2010). Nation-States as Empires, Empires as Nation-States: Two Principles, One Practice? *Theory and Society* 39(2): 119–143.

Kuran, Timur (2005). The Absence of the Corporation in Islamic Law: Origins and Persistence. *American Journal of Comparative Law* 53: 785–834.

Kymlicka, Will (1999). Misunderstanding Nationalism. In R. Beiner (ed.), *Theorizing Nationalism*. Albany, NY: SUNY Press. Pp. 131–140.

Lachmann, Richard (2000). *Capitalists in Spite of Themselves: Elite Conflict and Economic Transitions in Early Modern Europe*. Oxford: Oxford University Press.

(2020). *First-Class Passengers on a Sinking Ship: Elite Politics and the Decline of Great Powers*. London: Verso.

Lamont, Michèle (2010). *How Professors Think: Inside the Curious World of Academic Judgment*. Cambridge, MA: Harvard University Press.

Langbein, John H. (2003). *The Origins of Adversary Criminal Trial*. New York: Oxford University Press.

Latour, Bruno (1986). The Powers of Association. In J. Law (ed.), *Power, Action and Belief: A New Sociology of Knowledge?* London: Routledge & Kegan Paul.

Leff, Gordon (1992). Chapter 10: The Faculty of Arts. In H. De Ridder-Symoens (ed.), *A History of the University in Europe: Volume I, Universities in the Middle Ages*. Cambridge: Cambridge University Press. Pp. 307–336.

Lesser, Alexander (1961). Social Fields and the Evolution of Society. *Southwestern Journal of Anthropology* 17(1): 40–48.

Lewins, Tim (2015). *Cultural Evolution*. Oxford: Oxford University Press.

Lilla, Mark (2018). *The Once and Future Liberal: After Identity Politics*. London: Hurst and Company.

Littler, Jo (2018). *Against Meritocracy: Culture, Power and Myths of Mobility*. London: Routledge.

Lollini, Massima (2012). On Becoming Human: The *Verum Factum* Principle and Giambattista Vico's Humanism. *MLN (Modern Language Notes)* 127(1): S21–S31.

Lovejoy, Arthur O. (1960). *The Great Chain of Being: A Study in the History of an Idea*. New York: Harper.

Lukes, Steven (2005). *Power: A Radical View*. 2nd ed. Basingstoke and New York: Palgrave Macmillan.

(2006). *Individualism*. New ed. Colchester: ECPR Press.

Macfarlane, Alan (1978). *The Origins of English Individualism: The Family, Property and Social Transition*. New York: Cambridge University Press.

(1987). *The Culture of Capitalism*. Oxford and Cambridge, MA: Wiley-Blackwell.

Machiavelli, Nicolo (1985). *The Prince*. Chicago: University of Chicago Press.

Madison, James (2001). No. 10: The Same Subject Continued. In G. W. Carey and J. McClellan (eds), *The Federalist*. Gideon Edition. Indianapolis: Liberty Fund.

Maier, Pauline (1993). The Revolutionary Origins of the American Corporation. *William and Mary Quarterly* 50(1): 51–84.

Maine, Henry Sumner (1986). *Ancient Law: Its Connection with the Early History of Society and its Relation to Modern Ideas*. USA: Dorset Press.

Mair, Peter (1997). E. E. Schattschneider's The Semisovereign People. *Political Studies* 45: 947–954.

(1997). *Party System Change: Approaches and Interpretations*. Oxford: Clarendon.

Maitland, Frederick W. (1900). Translator's Introduction. In Otto von Gierke (ed.), *Political Theories of the Middle Age*. Cambridge: Cambridge University Press. Pp. vii–xiv.

(2003). *State, Trust and Corporation*. D. Runciman and M. Ryan (eds). Cambridge: Cambridge University Press.

Major, Lee Elliot, and Stephin Machin (2018). *Social Mobility and its Enemies*. London: Pelican Books.

Malešević, Siniša (2019). From Mercenaries to Private Patriots: Nationalism and the Private Military Contractors. In O. Swed and T. Crosbie (eds), *The Sociology of Privatised Security*. Cham, Switzerland: Palgrave Macmillan/Springer Link. Pp. 45–66.

(2019). *Grounded Nationalisms*. Cambridge: Cambridge University Press.

Mandeville, Bernard de (1988[1732]). *The Fable of the Bees or Private Vices, Publick Benefits*, 2 Vols, With a Commentary Critical, Historical, and Explanatory by F. B. Kaye (reprint of 1863 ed.). Indianapolis: Liberty Fund.

Mann, Michael (1984). The Autonomous Power of the State: Its Nature, Causes and Consequences. *Archives Européennes de Sociologie* 25: 185–213.

(1986). *The Sources of Social Power, Vol. 1: A History of Power from the Beginning to A.D. 1760*. Cambridge: Cambridge University Press.

(1988). *States, War and Capitalism*. Oxford: Blackwell.

(1992). The Emergence of Modern European Nationalism. In J. A. Hall and I. C. Jarvie (eds), *Transition to Modernity: Essays on Power, Wealth and Belief*. Cambridge: Cambridge University Press.

(1993). *The Sources of Social Power, Vol. 2: The Rise of Classes and Nation States, 1760–1914*. Cambridge: Cambridge University Press.

(2004). *The Dark Side of Democracy: Explaining Ethnic Cleansing*. Cambridge: Cambridge University Press.

(2006). The Sources of Social Power Revisited: A Response to Criticism. In J. A. Hall and R. Schroder (eds). *An Anatomy of Power: The Social Theory of Michael Mann*. Cambridge: Cambridge University Press. Pp. 343–396.

(2013). *The Sources of Social Power, Vol. 4: Globalizations, 1945–2011*. Cambridge: Cambridge University Press.

(2016). Have Human Societies Evolved? Evidence from History and Pre-History. *Theory and Society* 45(3): 203–247.

Mannheim, Karl (1993). Competition as a Cultural Phenomenon. In K. H. Wolf (ed.), *From Karl Mannheim*. New ed. New Brunswick and London: Transaction Publishers.

Markovits, Andrei, and Steven L. Hellerman (2001). *Offside: Soccer and American Exceptionalism in Sports*. Princeton, NJ: Princeton University Press.

Markovits, Daniel (2020). *The Meritocracy Trap*. London: Penguin Books.

Marsden, Peter V. (2005). The Sociology of James Coleman. *Annual Review of Sociology* 31: 1–24.

Marx, Karl (1970). *A Contribution to the Critique of Political Economy*. New York: International Publishers.

Maschler, Michael, Eilon Solan, and Shmuel Zamir (2020). *Game Theory*. 2nd ed. Cambridge: Cambridge University Press.

May, Allyson N. (2003). *The Bar and the Old Bailey, 1750–1850*. Chapel Hill and London: University of North Carolina Press.

McClosky, Dierdre (2006). *The Bourgeois Virtues: Ethics for an Age of Commerce*. Chicago: University of Chicago Press.

McCormick, Lisa (2015). *Performing Civility: International Competitions in Classical Music*. Cambridge: Cambridge University Press.

McCormick, Richard P. (1966). *The Second American Party System: Party Formation in the Jacksonian Era*. Chapel Hill: University of North Carolina Press.

McGettigan, Andrew (2013). *The Great University Gamble: Money, Markets and the Future of Higher Education*. London: Pluto Press.

McNeill, William H. (1982). *The Pursuit of Power: Technology, Armed Force, and Society since A. D. 1000*. Chicago: University of Chicago Press.

(1998). World History and the Rise and Fall of the West. *Journal of World History* 9(2): 215–236.

McPherson, James M. (1988). *Battle Cry Freedom: The Civil War Era, 1848–1865*. Oxford: Oxford University Press.

Mesoudi, Alex (2011). *Cultural Evolution: How Darwinian Theory Can Explain Human Culture and Synthesize the Social Sciences*. Chicago and London: University of Chicago Press.

Meyer, John W. (2000). Globalization: Sources and Effects on National States and Societies. *International Sociology* 15(2): 233–248.

(2010). World Society, Institutional Theories, and the Actor. *Annual Review of Sociology* 36(1): 1–20.

Meyer, John W., John Boli, George M. Thomas, and Francisco M. Ramirez (1997). World Society and the Nation-State. *American Journal of Sociology* 103(1): 144–81.

Micklethwaite, John, and Adrian Wooldridge (2005). *The Company: A Short History of a Revolutionary Idea*. New York: Modern Library.

Middlekauff, Robert (2005). *The Glorious Cause: The American Revolution, 1763–1789*. Oxford: Oxford University Press.

Miller, David (1995). *On Nationality*. Oxford: Oxford University Press.

Mirowski, Philip and Dieter Plehwe (eds) (2009). *The Road from Mont Pelerin: The Making of the Neoliberal Thought Collective*. Cambridge, MA: Harvard University Press.

Mokyr, Joel (1990). *The Lever of Riches: Technology, Creativity and Economic Progress*. Oxford and New York: Oxford University Press.

Montesquieu, Baron de (1989[1748]). *The Spirit of the Laws*, A. M. Cohler, B. C. Miller and H. S. Stone (eds). Cambridge: Cambridge University Press.

Moore, John C. (2019). *A Brief History of Universities*. Cham, Switzerland: Palgrave Macmillan/Springer Nature.

Moraw, Peter (1992). Chapter 8: Careers of Graduates. In H. De Ridder-Symoens (ed.), *A History of the University in Europe: Volume I, Universities in the Middle Ages*. Cambridge: Cambridge University Press. Pp. 244–279.

Morriss, Peter (2002). *Power: A Philosophical Analysis*. 2nd ed. Manchester: Manchester University Press.

Mosca, Gaetano (1939). *The Ruling Class, Elementi di Scienza Politica*, A. Livingston (ed.). New York: McGraw-Hill.

Moskos, Charles C. (1977). From Institution to Occupation: Trends in Military Organization. *Armed Forces and Society* 4(1): 41–50.

Müller, Wolfgang C., and Ulrich Sieberer (2006). Party Law. In R. S. Katz and W. Crotty (eds), *Handbook of Party Politics*. London: Sage. Pp. 435–445.

Murkand, Sharun W., and Dani Rodrik (2020). The Political Economy of Liberal Democracy. *Economic Journal* 130 (April): 765–792.

Murray, Williamson, and Macgregor Knox (2001). Thinking About Revolutions in Warfare. In M. Knox and W. Murray (eds), *The Dynamics of Military Revolution, 1300–2050*. Cambridge: Cambridge University Press. Pp. 1–14.

Namier, Lewis (1957). *The Structure of Politics at the Accession of George III*. 2nd ed. London: Macmillan.

Nelson, Richard R., and Sidney G. Winter (2002). Evolutionary Theorizing in Economics. *Journal of Economic Perspectives* 16(2): 23–46.

Nolan, Patrick, and Gerhard Lenski (2006). *Human Societies: An Introduction to Macrosociology*. 10th ed. Boulder and London: Paradigm Publishers.

Noll, Roger G. and Andrew Zimbalist (eds) (1997). *Sports, Jobs, and Taxes: The Economic Impact of Sports Teams and Stadiums*. Washington, DC: Brookings Institution Press.

North, Douglas C., and Robert P. Thomas (1973). *The Rise of the Western World: A New Economic History*. Cambridge: Cambridge University Press.

Nozick, Robert (1974). *Anarchy, State and Utopia*. New York: Basic Books.

Nuciari, Marina (2018). The Study of the Military: Models for the Military Profession. In G. Caforio and M. Nuciari (eds), *Handbook of the Sociology of the Military*. 2nd ed. Cham, Switzerland: Springer Nature. Pp. 35–60.

Nussbaum, Martha C. (1999). Virtue Ethics: A Misleading Category? *Journal of Ethics* 3(3): 163–201.

O'Brien, Patrick K., and Philip A. Hunt (1993). The Rise of a Fiscal State in England, 1485–1815. *Historical Research* 66: 129–176.

O'Gorman, Frank (1982). *The Emergence of the British Two-Party System, 1760–1832*. London: Edward Arnold.

Olmstead, Alan L., and Paul W. Rhode (2018). Cotton, Slavery and the New History of Capitalism. *Explorations in Economic History* 67: 1–17.

Onuf, Peter S. (2012). Jefferson and American Democracy. In F. D. Cogliano (ed.), *A Companion to Thomas Jefferson*. Oxford: Blackwell. Pp. 397–418.

Owens, Mackubin Thomas (2017). Civil-Military Relations. *Oxford Research Encyclopedias, International Studies*. Retrieved at: https://doi.org/10.1093/acrefore/9780190846626.013.123, on 15 February, 2022.

Padfield, Stefan J. (2014). Rehabilitating Concession Theory. *Oklahoma Law Review* 66(2): 327–361.

(2015). Corporate Social Responsibility and Concession Theory. *William and Mary Business Law Review* 6(1): 1–34.

Palfreyman, David, and Paul Temple (2017). *Universities and Colleges: A Short Introduction*. Oxford: Oxford University Press.

Palmer, R. R. (1959). *The Age of Democratic Revolutions: A Political History of Europe and America, 1760–1800, Volume 1: The Challenge*. Princeton: Princeton University Press.

Pansardi, Pamela (2011). Power To and Power Over. In K. Dowding (ed.), *Encyclopedia of Power*. Los Angeles: Sage. Pp. 521–524.

Parker, Geoffrey (1996). *The Military Revolution: Military Innovation and the Rise of the West, 1500–1800*. 2nd ed. Cambridge: Cambridge University Press.

Parrott, David (2012). *The Business of War: Military Enterprise and Military Revolution in Early Modern Europe*. Cambridge: Cambridge University Press.

Parsons, Lynn Hudson (2009). *The Birth of Modern Politics: Andrew Jackson, John Quincy Adams, and the Election of 1828*. Oxford: Oxford University Press.

Parsons, Talcott (1951). *The Social System*. New York: Free Press.

Paterson, Orlando, Alan Tomlinson, and Christopher Young (2011). The Culture of Sports. *Journal of Historical Sociology* 24(4): 549–563.

Pedersen, Olaf (2009). *The First Universities: Studium Generale and the Origins of University Education in Europe*. Cambridge: Cambridge University Press.

Perrow, Charles (1991). A Society of Organizations. *Theory and Society* 20 (6): 725–762.

(2002). *Organizing America: Wealth, Power, and the Origins of Corporate Capitalism*. Princeton: Princeton University Press.

Persily, Nathaniel, and Bruce E. Cain (2000). The Legal Status of Political Parties: A Reassessment of Competing Paradigms. *Columbia Law Review* 100(3): 775–812.

Philippon, Thomas (2019). *The Great Reversal: How America Gave Up on Free Markets*. Cambridge, MA, and London: Belknap Press of Harvard University Press.

Phillips, Andrew, and J. C. Sharman (2020). *Outsourcing Empire: How Company-States Made the Modern World*. Princeton and Oxford: Princeton University Press.

Phillipson, Nicholas (2011). *David Hume: Philosopher as Historian*. Revised ed. London: Penguin.

Piketty, Thomas (2014). *Capital in the Twenty-First Century*. Cambridge, MA, and London: Belknap Press of Harvard University Press.

Pinker, Steve (2002). *The Blank Slate*. London: Penguin.

Pipes, Richard (1999). *Property and Freedom*. New York: Alfred A. Knopf.

Plamenatz, John (1976). Two Types of Nationalism. In E. Kamenka (ed.), *Nationalism: The Nature and Evolution of an Idea*. London: Edward Arnold.

Plumb, J. H. (1967). *The Growth of Political Stability in England, 1675–1725*. London: Macmillan.

Poggi, Gianfranco (1978). *The Development of the Modern State: A Sociological Introduction*. Stanford: Stanford University Press.

(1983). *Calvinism and the Capitalist Spirit: Max Weber's Protestant Ethic*. Amherst: University of Massachusetts Press.

(2001). *Forms of Power*. Cambridge: Polity.

(2006). Political Power Un-manned: A Defence of the Holy Trinity from Mann's Military Attack. In J. A. Hall and R. Schroder (eds), *An Anatomy of Power: The Social Theory of Michael Mann*. Cambridge: Cambridge University Press. Pp. 135–149.

Polanyi, Karl (1957). *The Great Transformation: The Political and Economic Origins of Our Time*. Boston: Beacon Press.

Pollock, Frederick, and F. W. Maitland (1899). *The History of English Law, Before the Time of Edward I*. 2nd ed. Cambridge: Cambridge University Press, and Boston: Little, Brown, and Company.

Pomeranz, Kenneth (2000). *The Great Divergence: China, Europe, and the Making of the Modern World Economy*. Princeton and Oxford: Princeton University Press.

Popper, Karl (1945). *The Open Society and Its Enemies*. London: Routledge.

(1957). *The Poverty of Historicism*. London: Routledge.

Porter, Michael E. (1990). *The Competitive Advantage of Nations*. New York: Free Press.

Prak, Marteen (2015). Citizens, Soldiers and Civic Militias in Late Medieval and Early Modern Europe. *Past and Present* 228: 93–123.

Price, T. Douglas, and Ofer Bar-Yosef (2011). The Origins of Agriculture: New Data, New Ideas, an Introduction to Supplement 4. *Current Anthropology* 52(4): 163–174.

Pryor, John H. (1977). The Origins of the Commenda Contract. *Speculum* 52(1): 5–37.

Rabb, Theodore K. (1975). *The Struggle for Stability in Early Modern Europe*. Oxford: Oxford University Press.

Rahbek-Clemmensen, Jon, et al. (2012). Conceptualizing the Civil–Military Gap: A Research Note. *Armed Forces and Society* 38(4): 669–78.

Ramirez, Francisco O., and John W. Meyer (2013). Universalizing the University in a World Society. In J. C. Shin and B. M. Kehm (eds), *Institutionalization of World-Class University in Global Competition*. Dordrecht: Springer Netherlands. Pp. 257–273.

Rappaport, Roy A. (1968). *Pigs for the Ancestors: Ritual in the Ecology of a New Guinea People*. New Haven and London: Yale University Press.

(1999). *Ritual and Religion in the Making of Humanity*. Cambridge: Cambridge University Press.

Rauch, Jonathan (2013). *Kindly Inquisitors: The New Attacks on Free Thought*. Expanded ed. Chicago and London: University of Chicago Press.

Rawls, John (1971). *A Theory of Justice*. Cambridge, MA: Harvard University Press.

(1996). *Political Liberalism*. New York: Columbia University Press.

(2001). *Justice as Fairness: A Restatement*, E. Kelly (ed.). Cambridge, MA: Belknap Press of Harvard University Press.

Renda, Lex (1995). Review: Richard P. McCormick and the Second American Party System. *Reviews in American History* 23(2): 378–389.

Richerson, Peter J., and Robert Boyd (2005). *Not by Genes Alone: How Culture Transformed Human Evolution*. Chicago: University of Chicago Press.

Riddle, Phyllis (1993). Political Authority and University Formation in Europe, 1200–1800. *Sociological Perspectives* 36(1): 45–62.

Roberts, Michael (1967). The Military Revolution, 1560–1660. In M. Roberts (ed.), *Essays in Swedish History*. Minneapolis: University of Minnesota Press. Pp. 195–225.

Robertson, Ritchie (2020). *The Enlightenment: The Pursuit of Happiness, 1680–1790*. London and USA: Allen Lane.

Rochat, Jean (2018). Change for Continuity: The Making of the *Société Anonyme* in Nineteenth Century France. In H. Wells (ed.), *Research Handbook on the History of Corporate and Company Law*. Cheltenham: Edward Elgar. Pp. 244–268.

Rodgers, Clifford J. (ed.) (1995). *The Military Revolution Debate: Readings on the Military Transformation of Early Modern Europe*. Boulder, CO: Westview.

Roseberry, William (1988). Political Economy. *Annual Review of Anthropology* 17: 161–185.

Rosenberg, Nathan, and L. E. Birdzell, Jr (1986). *How the West Grew Rich: The Economic Transformation of the Industrial World*. New York: Basic Books.

Roser, Max (2020). Democracy. Published online at OurWorldInData.org. Retrieved from: https://ourworldindata.org/democracy, on 3 November, 2020.

Roy, William G. (1997). *Socializing Capital: The Rise of the Large Industrial Corporation in America*. Princeton: Princeton University Press.

Rubenstein, Dustin R. and Patrick Abbot (eds) (2017). *Comparative Social Evolution*. Cambridge: Cambridge University Press.

Rubin, Jared (2018). Islamic Law and Economic Development. In H. Wells (ed.), *Research Handbook on the History of Corporate and Company Law*. Cheltenham: Edward Elgar. Pp. 17–32.

Rüegg, Walter (2004). Chapter 1: Themes. In W. Rüegg (ed.), *A History of the University in Europe, Volume III: Universities in the Nineteenth and*

Early Twentieth Centuries (1800–1945). Cambridge: Cambridge University Press. Pp. 3–31.

(ed) (2004). *A History of the University in Europe, Volume III: Universities in the Nineteenth and Early Twentieth Centuries (1800–1945)*. Cambridge: Cambridge University Press.

Runciman, David (1997). *Pluralism and the Personality of the State*. Cambridge: Cambridge University Press.

Runciman, David, and Magnus Ryan (2003). Editors Introduction. In D. Runciman and M. Ryan (eds), *Maitland: State Trust and Corporation*. Cambridge: Cambridge University Press. Pp. ix–xxix.

Runciman, W. G. (2005). Rejoinder to Fracchia and Lewontin. *History and Theory* 44(1): 30–41.

(2009). *The Theory of Cultural and Social Selection*. Cambridge: Cambridge University Press.

Ruskola, Teemu (2018). Corporation Law in Late Imperial China. In H. Wells (ed.), *Research Handbook on the History of Corporate and Company Law*. Cheltenham: Edward Elgar. Pp. 355–380.

Russell, Paul (2008). *The Riddle of Hume's Treatise, Skepticism, Naturalism, and Irreligion*. Oxford: Oxford University Press.

Sabaté, Oriol (2016). Does Military Pressure Boost Fiscal Capacity? Evidence from Late-Modern Military Revolutions in Europe and North America. *European Review of Economic History* 20: 275–298.

Sage, George H. (2011). *Globalizing Sports: How Organizations, Corporations, Media and Politics are Changing Sports*. London: Routledge.

Sahlins, Marshal (1963). Poor Man, Rich Man, Big Man, Chief: Political Types in Melanesia and Polynesia. *Comparative Studies in Society and History* 5:285–303.

Sandel, Michael J. (2020). *The Tyranny of Merit: What Becomes of the Common Good?* London: Allen Lane.

Sartori, Giovanni (1976). *Parties and Party Systems: A Framework for Analysis*. Cambridge and New York: Cambridge University Press.

Sayer, Andrew (2016). *Why We Can't Afford the Rich*. Bristol: Policy Press.

Scarborough, Vernon L. and David R. Wilcox (eds) (1993). *The Mesoamerican Ballgame*. Tucson: University of Arizona Press.

Scarrow, Susan E. (2006). The Nineteenth-Century Origins of Modern Political Parties: The Unwanted Emergence of Party-Based Politics. In R. S. Katz and W. Crotty (eds), *Handbook of Party Politics*. London: Sage. Pp. 16–24.

Schachner, Nathan (1962). *The Medieval Universities*. New York: A. S. Barnes and Company, Inc.

Schattschneider, E. E. (1975). *The Semisovereign People: A Realist's View of Democracy in America*. Reissued with an Introduction by D. Adamany. Boston: Wadsworth Cengage Learning.

Scheidel, Walter (2019). *Escape from Rome: The Failure of Empire and the Road to Prosperity*. Princeton and Oxford: Princeton University Press.

Schluter, Dolph (2000). *The Ecology of Adaptive Radiation*. Oxford and New York: Oxford University Press.

Schmidt, James (2000). What Enlightenment Project? *Political Theory* 28(6): 734–757.

Schofer, Evan, and John W. Meyer (2005). The Worldwide Expansion of Higher Education in the Twentieth Century. *American Sociological Review* 70: 898–920.

Seidentop, Larry (2014). *Inventing the Individual: The Origins of Western Liberalism*. London and USA: Penguin Books.

Seligman, Adam, Robert P. Weller, Michael J. Puett, and Bennett Simon (2008). *Ritual and Its Consequences: An Essay on the Limits of Sincerity*. Oxford: Oxford University Press.

Sewell, William H. Jr (1992). A Theory of Structure: Duality, Agency, and Transformation. *American Journal of Sociology* 98(1): 1–29.

Shapiro, Susan P. (2005). Agency Theory. *Annual Review of Sociology* 31 (1): 263–284.

Sharma, Vivek S. (2015). Kinship, Property, and Authority: European Territorial Consolidation Reconsidered. *Politics and Society* 43(2): 151–180.

(2017). War, Conflict and the State Reconsidered. In L. B. Kaspersen and J. Strandsbjerg (eds), *Does War Make States?* Cambridge: Cambridge University Press. Pp. 181–218.

Shearmur, Jeremy, and Geoffrey Stokes (2016). Popper and His Philosophy: An Overview. In J. Shearmur and G. Stokes (eds), *The Cambridge Companion to Popper*. Cambridge: Cambridge University Press. Pp. 1–29.

Simmel, Georg (1964). *Conflict and the Web of Group-Affiliations*. New York: Free Press.

Smith, Adam (1981[1776]). *An Inquiry into the Nature and Causes of the Wealth of Nations*, 2 Vols. Indianapolis: Liberty Fund.

Smith, Anthony D. (1986). *The Ethnic Origins of Nations*. Cambridge: Cambridge University Press.

Smith, Anthony D., and Ernest Gellner (1995). The Warwick Debate. *Nations and Nationalism* 2(3): 358–388.

Smith, Bryant (1928). Legal Personality. *Yale Law Journal* 37(3): 283–299.

Spade, Paul Vincent, and Claude Panaccio (2019). William of Ockham. E. N. Zalta (ed.), *The Stanford Encyclopedia of Philosophy* (Spring 2019

Edition). Retrieved at: https://plato.stanford.edu/archives/spr2019/entries/ockham/, on 15 February 2022.

Speer, Albert (1971). *Inside the Third Reich*. New York: Avon.

Spruyt, Hendrik (1994). *The Sovereign State and Its Competitors*. Princeton, NJ: Princeton University Press.

Stahl, Titus (2013). What Is Immanent Critique? SSRN Working Paper. Retrieved at: http://ssrn.com/abstract=2357957, doi: 10.2139/ssrn.2357957, on 15 February 2022.

Stark, David (ed.) (2020). *Competition and Competitions in Social Life*. Oxford: Oxford University Press.

Staum, Martin S. (1985). The Enlightenment Transformed: The Institute Prize Contests. *Eighteenth-Century Studies* 19(2): 153–179.

Stern, Philip J. (2008). 'A Politie of Civill and Military Power': Political Thought and the Late Seventeenth-Century Foundations of the East India Company-State. *Journal of British Studies* 47(2): 253–283.

Steward, Julian H. (1972). *Theory of Culture Change: The Methodology of Multilinear Evolution*. Urbana and Chicago: University of Illinois Press.

Stiglitz, Joseph E. (2013). *The Price of Inequality*. London: Penguin.

Stokes, Geoffrey (2016). Popper and Habermas: Convergent Arguments for a Postmetaphysical Universalism. In J. Shearmur and G. Stokes (eds), *The Cambridge Companion to Popper*. Cambridge: Cambridge University Press. Pp. 318–351.

Stone, Lawrence (1965). *The Crisis of the Aristocracy, 1558–1641*. Abridged ed. Oxford and New York: Oxford University Press.

Storrs, Christopher (ed.) (2008). *The Fiscal-Military State in Eighteenth-Century Europe: Essays in Honour of P. G. M. Dickson*. Farnham: Ashgate.

Storrs, Christopher, and H. M. Scott (1996). The Military and the European Nobility, c. 1600–1800. *War in History* 3(1): 1–41.

Swartz, David L. (2013). *Symbolic Power, Politics, and Intellectuals. The Political Sociology of Pierre Bourdieu*. Chicago and London: University of Chicago Press.

Swidler, Ann (1973). The Concept of Rationality in the Work of Max Weber. *Sociological Inquiry* 43(1): 35–41.

Sylla, Richard, and Robert E. Wright (2013). Corporation Formation in the Antebellum United States in Comparative Context. *Business History* 55(4): 653–669.

Taleb, Nassim Nicholas (2012). *Antifragile: Things that Gain from Disorder*. London: Penguin Books.

Tamanaha, Brian Z. (2017). *A Realistic Theory of Law*. Cambridge: Cambridge University Press.

Tamir, Yael (1993). *Liberal Nationalism*. Princeton: Princeton University Press.

Taylor, Charles (1999). Nationalism and Modernity. In R. Beiner (ed.), *Theorizing Nationalism*. Albany, NY: SUNY Press.

Teece, David J. (2010). Alfred Chandler and 'Capabilities' Theories of Strategy and Management. *Industrial and Corporate Change* 19(2): 297–316.

Thomas, Keith (1971). *Religion and the Decline of Magic*. Harmondsworth: Penguin Books.

Thorndike, Lynn (ed.) (1944). *University Records and Life in the Middle Ages*. New York: Columbia University Press.

Tilly, Charles (1975). Reflections on the History of European State-Making. In C. Tilly (ed.), *The Formation of National States in Europe*. Princeton: Princeton University Press.

(1992). *Coercion, Capital, and European States, AD 990–1992*. Cambridge, MA and Oxford: Basil Blackwell.

Tocqueville, Alexis de (2000). *Democracy in America*, H. C. Mansfield and D. Winthrop (eds). Chicago and London: University of Chicago Press.

(2011). *The Ancien Régime and the French Revolution*, J. Elster (ed.). Cambridge: Cambridge University Press.

Tomasello, Michael (1999). The Human Adaptation for Culture. *Annual Review of Anthropology* 28: 509–529.

(2014). *A Natural History of Human Thinking*. Cambridge, MA: Harvard University Press.

(2016). *A Natural History of Human Morality*. Cambridge, MA: Harvard University Press.

Tönnies, Ferdinand (2001). *Community and Civil Society*, J. Harris (ed.). Cambridge: Cambridge University Press.

Tooby, John, and Leda Cosmides (1992). The Psychological Foundations of Culture. In J. Barkow, L. Cosmides and J. Tooby (eds), *The Adapted Mind: Evolutionary Psychology and the Generation of Culture*. New York: Oxford University Press. Pp. 19–136.

Tsang, Rachel and Eric T. Woods (eds) (2014). *The Cultural Politics of Nationalism and Nation Building: Ritual and Performance in the Forging of Nations*. London: Routledge.

Turner, John D. (2018). The Development of English Company Law before 1900. In H. Wells (ed.), *Research Handbook on the History of Corporate and Company Law*. Cheltenham: Edward Elgar. Pp. 121–141.

Turner, Victor (1967). *The Forrest of Symbols: Aspects of Ndembu Ritual*. Ithica, NY: Cornell University Press.

Udehn, Lars (2002). The Changing Face of Methodological Individualism. *Annual Review of Sociology* 28: 479–507.

Udovitch, Abraham L. (1962). At the Origins of the Western Commenda: Islam, Israel, Byzantium? *Speculum* 37(2): 198–207.

Van Gennep, Arnold (1960). *The Rites of Passage*. Chicago: University of Chicago Press.

Vattel, Emer de (2008). *The Law of Nations*, B. Kapossy and R. Whatmore (eds). Indianapolis: Liberty Fund.

Verger, Jacques (1992). Chapter 2: Patterns. In H. De Ridder-Symoens (ed.), *A History of the University in Europe: Volume I, Universities in the Middle Ages*. Cambridge: Cambridge University Press. Pp. 35–74.

Vermeij, Geerat J. (1987). *Evolution and Escalation: An Ecological History of Life*. Princeton, NJ: Princeton University Press.

Vico, Giambattista (1988[1710]). *On the Most Ancient Wisdom of the Italians: Unearthed from the Origins of the Latin Language: Including the Disputation with the Giornale De' Letterati D'italia*. Ithica and London: Cornell University Press.

Vinogradoff, Paul (1924). Juridical Persons. *Columbia Law Review* 24(6): 594–604.

Wallerstein, Immanuel (1974). *The Modern World-System, Vol. 1*. New York: Academic Press.

(2007). *World-Systems Analysis: An Introduction*. Durham, NC: Duke University Press.

Wallerstein, Immanuel, Randall Collins, Michael Mann, Georgi Derlugian, and Craig Calhoun (2013). *Does Capitalism Have a Future?* Oxford: Oxford University Press.

Walzer, Michael (1983). *Spheres of Justice: A Defense of Pluralism and Equality*. New York: Basic Books.

(1984). Liberalism and the Art of Separation. *Political Theory* 12(3): 315–330.

(1993). *Interpretation and Social Criticism*. Revised ed. Cambridge, MA: Harvard University Press.

Washington, Robert E., and David Karen (2001). Sport and Society. *Annual Review of Sociology* 27: 187–212.

Watson, James L. (1982). Chinese Kinship Reconsidered: Anthropological Perspectives on Historical Research. *China Quarterly* 92: 589–622.

Weber, Max (1978). *Economy and Society, 2 Vols*. Berkeley: University of California Press.

(2002). *The Protestant Ethic and the Spirit of Capitalism*. Los Angeles: Roxbury Publishing.

(2003). *The History of Commercial Partnerships in the Middle Ages*. Lanham, MD: Rowman and Littlefield.

(2005). *Max Weber: Readings and Commentary on Modernity*, S. Kalberg (ed.). London: Blackwell.

(2019). *Economy and Society: A New Translation*, K. Tribe (ed. and trans.). Cambridge, MA and London: Harvard University Press.

Weintraub, Jeff (1997). The Theory and Politics of the Public/Private Distinction. In J. Weintraub and K. Kumar (eds), *Public and Private in Thought and Practice: Perspectives on a Grand Dichotomy*. Chicago: University of Chicago Press. Pp. 1–42.

Wenke, Robert J., and Deborah I. Olszewski (2007). *Patterns in Prehistory: Humankind's First Three Million Years*. 5th ed. New York and Oxford: Oxford University Press.

Werron, Tobias (2015). Why Do We Believe in Competition? A Historical-Sociological View of Competition as an Institutionalized Modern Imaginary. *Journal of Social Theory* 16(2): 186–210.

Wilentz, Sean (2005). *The Rise of American Democracy: Jefferson to Lincoln*. New York and London: W. W. Norton and Company.

Williamson, Oliver E. (1975). *Markets and Hierarchies: Analysis and Anti-Trust Implications: A Study in the Economics of Internal Organization*. New York: Free Press.

Wilson, David Sloan, and John M. Gowdy (2013). Evolution as a General Theoretical Framework for Economics and Public Policy. *Journal of Economic Behavior and Organization* 90: S3–S10.

Wimmer, Andreas (2018). *Nation Building: Why Some Countries Come Together While Other Fall Apart*. Princeton: Princeton University Press.

Winkler, Adam (2018). *We The Corporations: How American Business Won Their Civil Rights*. New York: W. W. Norton and Co.

Wokler, Robert (1998). The Enlightenment Project as Betrayed by Modernity. *History of European Ideas* 24(4–5): 301–313.

Wolf, Eric R. (1982). *Europe and the People Without History*. Berkeley: University of California Press.

(1984). Culture: Panacea or Problem? *American Antiquity* 49(2): 393–400.

Wolinetz, Steven B. (2006). Party Systems and Party System Types. In R. S. Katz and W. Crotty (eds), *Handbook of Party Politics*. London: Sage. Pp. 51–62.

Wood, Gordon S. (1991). *The Radicalism of the American Revolution*. New York: Vintage.

(2009). *Empire of Liberty: A History of the Early Republic, 1789–1815*. Oxford: Oxford University Press.

Wooldridge, Adrian (2021). *The Aristocracy of Talent: How Meritocracy Made the Modern World*. London and USA: Allen Lane.

Wootton, David (2016). *The Invention of Science: A New History of the Scientific Revolution*. London: Penguin.

Wright, Robert E. (2011). Rise of the Corporation Nation. In D. A. Irwin and R. Sylla (eds), *Founding Choices: American Economic Policy in the 1790s*. Chicago Scholarship Online. Pp. 217–258.

(2014). *Corporation Nation*. Philadelphia: University of Pennsylvania Press.

(2018). For- and Non-Profit Special Corporations in America, 1608–1860. In H. Wells (ed.), *Research Handbook on the History of Corporate and Company Law*. Cheltenham: Edward Elgar. Pp. 480–509.

Wrong, Dennis H. (2002). *Power: Its Forms, Bases and Uses*. 3rd ed. London: Transaction.

Wuthnow, Robert (1987). *Meaning and Moral Order: Explorations in Cultural Analysis*. Berkeley: University of California Press.

Yack, Bernard (1992). *The Longing for Total Revolution: Philosophical Sources of Social Discontent from Rousseau to Marx and Nietzsche*. Berkeley: University of California Press.

(1999). The Myth of the Civic Nation. In R. Beiner (ed.), *Theorizing Nationalism*. Albany, NY: SUNY Press.

Young, Michael D. (1958). *The Rise of the Meritocracy, 1870–2033*. London: Penguin.

Zamora, Daniel and Michael C. Behrent (eds) (2016). *Foucault and Neoliberalism*. Cambridge: Polity.

Zelin, Madeleine (2009). The Firm in Early Modern China. *Journal of Economic Behavior and Organization* 71: 623–637.

Zhao, Dingxin (2009). The Mandate of Heaven and Performance Legitimation in Historical and Contemporary China. *American Behavioral Scientist* 53(3): 416–433.

(2015). *The Confucian-Legalist State: A New Theory of Chinese History*. Oxford: Oxford University Press.

Zhenman, Zheng (2001). *Family Lineage Organization and Social Change in Ming and Qing Fujian*. Honolulu: University of Hawaii Press.

Zinnes, Dina A. (1967). An Analytic Study of the Balance of Power Theories. *Journal of Peace Research* 4(3): 270–288.

Index